Texts and Monographs in Computer Science

Editor
David Gries

Advisory Board
F. L. Bauer
K. S. Fu
J. J. Horning
R. Reddy
D. C. Tsichritzis
W. M. Waite

Texts and Monographs in Computer Science

Suad Alagić and Michael A. Arbib
The Design of Well-Structured and Correct Programs
1978. x, 292pp. 14 illus. cloth

Michael A. Arbib, A.J. Kfoury, and Robert N. Moll
A Basis for Theoretical Computer Science
1981. vii, 220pp. 49 illus. cloth

F.L. Bauer and H. Wössner
Algorithmic Language and Program Development
1982. xvi, 497pp. 109 illus. cloth

Edsger W. Dijkstra
Selected Writings on Computing: A Personal Perspective
1982. xvii, 362pp. 1 illus. cloth

Peter W. Frey, Ed.
Chess Skill in Man and Machine, 2nd Edition
1983. xiv, 329pp. 104 illus. cloth

David Gries, Ed.
Programming Methodology: A Collection of Articles by Members of IFIP WG2.3
1978. xiv, 437pp. 68 illus. cloth

David Gries
The Science of Programming
1981. xvi, 366pp. cloth

A.J. Kfoury, Robert N. Moll, and Michael A. Arbib
A Programming Approach to Computability
1982. viii, 251pp. 36 illus. cloth

Brian Randell, Ed.
The Origins of Digital Computers: Selected Papers
3rd Edition. 1982. xvi, 580pp. 126 illus. cloth

Arto Salomaa and Matti Soittola
Automata-Theoretic Aspects of Formal Power Series
1978. x, 171pp. cloth

Jeffrey R. Sampson
Adaptive Information Processing: An Introductory Survey
1976. x, 214pp. 83 illus. cloth

William M. Waite and Gerhard Goos
Compiler Construction
1984, xiv, 446pp. 196 illus. cloth

Niklaus Wirth
Programming in Modula-2
2nd Corr. Edition. 1983. iv, 176pp. cloth

R.T. Gregory and E.V. Krishnamurthy
Methods and Applications of Error-Free Computation
1984. xii, 189pp. 1 illus. cloth

Foreword

This is the textbook I hoped someone like Professor David Gries would write —and, since the latter has no rivals, that means I just hoped he would write it. The topic deserves no lesser author.

During the last decade, the potential meaning of the word "program" has changed profoundly. While the "program" we wrote ten years ago and the "program" we can write today can both be executed by a computer, that is about all they have in common. Apart from that superficial similarity, they are so fundamentally different that it is confusing to denote both with the same term. The difference between the "old program" and the "new program" is as profound as the difference between a conjecture and a proven theorem, between pre-scientific knowledge of mathematical facts and consequences rigorously deduced from a body of postulates.

Remembering how many centuries it has taken Mankind to appreciate fully the profundity of this latter distinction, we get a glimpse of the educational challenge we are facing: besides teaching technicalities, we have to overcome the mental resistance always evoked when it is shown how the techniques of scientific thought can be fruitfully applied to a next area of human endeavour. (We have already heard all the objections, which are so traditional they could have been predicted: "old programs" are good enough, "new programs" are no better and are too difficult to design in realistic situations, correctness of programs is much less important than correctness of specifications, the "real world" does not care about proofs, etc. Typically, these objections come from people that don't master the techniques they object to.)

It does not suffice just to explain the formal machinery that enables us to design "new programs". New formalisms are always frightening, and it takes much careful teaching to convince the novice that the formalism is

not only helpful but even indispensable. Choice and order of examples
are as important as the good taste with which the formalism is applied.
To get the message across requires a scientist that combines his scientific
involvement in the subject with the precious gifts of a devoted teacher.
We should consider ourselves fortunate that Professor David Gries has
met the challenge.

Edsger W. Dijkstra

Preface

The *Oxford English Dictionary* contains the following sentence concerning the term *science*:

> Sometimes, however, the term *science* is extended to denote a department of practical work which depends on the knowledge and conscious application of principles; an art, on the other hand, being understood to require merely knowledge of traditional rules and skill acquired by habit.

It is in this context that the title of this book was chosen. Programming began as an art, and even today most people learn only by watching others perform (e.g. a lecturer, a friend) and through habit, with little direction as to the principles involved. In the past 10 years, however, research has uncovered some useful theory and principles, and we are reaching the point where we can begin to teach the principles so that they can be consciously applied. This text is an attempt to convey my understanding of and excitement for this just-emerging science of programming.

The approach does require some mathematical maturity and the will to try something new. A programmer with two years experience, or a junior or senior computer science major in college, can master the material —at least, this is the level I have aimed at.

A common criticism of the approach used in this book is that it has been used only for small (one or two pages of program text), albeit complex, problems. While this may be true so far, it is not an argument for ignoring the approach. In my opinion it is the best approach to reasoning about programs, and I believe the next ten years will see it extended to and practiced on large programs. Moreover, since every large program consists of many small programs, it is safe to say the following:

> One cannot learn to write large programs effectively until
> one has learned to write small ones effectively.

While success cannot be guaranteed, my experience is that the approach often leads to shorter, clearer, *correct* programs in the same amount of time. It also leads to a different frame of mind, in that one becomes more careful about definitions of variables, about style, about clarity. Since most programmers currently have difficulty developing even small programs, and the small programs they develop are not very readable, studying the approach should prove useful.

The book contains little or no discussion of checking for errors, of making programs robust, of testing programs and the like. This is not because these aspects are unimportant or because the approach does not allow for them. It is simply that, in order to convey the material as simply as possible, it is necessary to concentrate on the one aspect of developing correct programs. The teacher using this book may want to discuss these other issues as well.

The Organization of the Book

Part I is an introduction to the propositional and predicate calculi. Mastery of this material is important, for the predicate calculus should be used as a *tool* for doing practical reasoning about programs. Any discipline in which severe complexity arises usually turns to mathematics to help control that complexity. Programming is no different.

Rest assured that I have attempted to convey this material from the programmer's viewpoint. Completeness, soundness, etc., are not mentioned, because the programmer has no need to study these issues. He needs to be able to manipulate and simplify propositions and predicates when developing programs.

Chapter 3, which is quite long, discusses reasoning using a "natural deduction system". I wrote this chapter to learn about such systems and to see how effective they were for reasoning about programs, because a number of mechanical verifier systems are based on them. My conclusion is that the more traditional approach of chapter 2 is far more useful, but I have left chapter 3 in for those whose tastes run to the natural deduction systems. Chapter 3 may be skipped entirely, although it may prove useful in a course that covers some formal logic and theory.

If one is familiar with a few concepts of logic, it is certainly possible to begin reading this book with Part II and to refer to Part I only for conventions and notation. The teacher using this text in a course may also want to present the material in a different order, presenting, for example, the material on quantification later in the course when it is first needed.

Part II defines a small language in terms of weakest preconditions. The important parts —the ones needed for later understanding of the development of programs— are chapters 7 and 8, sections 9.1 and 9.2, and chapters 10 and 11. Further, it is possible to skip some of the material, for example the formal definition of the iterative construct and the proof of theorem 11.6 concerning the use of a loop invariant, although I believe that mastering this material will be beneficial.

Part III is the heart of the book. Within it, in order to get the reader more actively involved, I have tried the following technique. At a point, a question will be raised, which the reader is expected to answer. The question is followed by white space, a horizontal¹ line, and more white space. After answering the question, the reader can then continue and discover my answer. Such active involvement will be more difficult than simply reading the text, but it will be far more beneficial.

Chapter 21 is fun. It concerns inverting programs, something that Edsger W. Dijkstra and his colleague Wim Feijen dreamed up. Whether it is really useful has not been decided, but it is fun. Chapter 22 presents a few simple rules on documenting programs; the material can be read before the rest of the book. Chapter 23 contains a brief, personal history of this science of programming and an anecdotal history of the programming problems in the book.

Answers to some exercises are included —all answers are not given so the exercises can be used as homework. A complete set of answers can be obtained at nominal cost by requesting it, on appropriate letterhead.

Notation. The notation *iff* is used for "if and only if". A few years ago, while lecturing in Denmark, I used *fif* instead, reasoning that since "if and only if" was a symmetric concept its notation should be symmetric also. Without knowing it, I had punned in Danish and the audience laughed, for *fif* in Danish means "a little trick". I resolved thereafter to use *fif* so I could tell my joke, but my colleagues talked me out of it.

The symbol □ is used to mark the end of theorems, definitions, examples, and so forth. When beginning to produce this book on the phototypesetter, it was discovered that the mathematical quantifiers "forall" and "exists" could not be built easily, so A and E have been used for them.

Throughout the book, in the few places they occur, the words *he, him* and *his* denote a person of either sex.

Acknowledgements

Those familiar with Edsger W. Dijkstra's monograph *A Discipline of Programming* will find his influence throughout this book. The calculus for the derivation of programs, the style of developing programs, and many of the examples are his. In addition, his criticisms of drafts of this book have been invaluable.

Just as important to me has been the work of Tony Hoare. His paper on an axiomatic basis for programming was the start of a new era, not only in its technical contribution but in its taste and style, and his work since then has continued to influence me. Tony's excellent, detailed criticisms of a draft of Part I caused me to reorganize and rewrite major parts of it.

I am grateful to Fred Schneider, who read the first drafts of all chapters and gave technical and stylistic suggestions on almost every paragraph.

A number of people have given me substantial constructive criticisms on all or parts of the manuscript. For their help I would like to thank Greg Andrews, Michael Gordon, Eric Hehner, Gary Levin, Doug McIlroy, Bob Melville, Jay Misra, Hal Perkins, John Williams, Michael Woodger and David Wright.

My appreciation goes also to the Cornell Computer Science Community. The students of course CS600 have been my guinea pigs for the past five years, and the faculty and students have tolerated my preachings about programming in a very amiable way. Cornell has been an excellent place to perform my research.

This book was typed and edited by myself, using the departmental PDP11/60-VAX system running under UNIX[+] and a screen editor written for the Terak. (The files for the book contain 844,592 characters.) The final copy was produced using *troff* and a Comp Edit phototypesetter at the Graphics Lab at Cornell. Doug McIlroy introduced me to many of the intricacies of *troff*; Alan Demers, Dean Krafft and Mike Hammond provided much help with the PDP11/60-VAX system; and Alan Demers, Barbara Gingras and Sándor Halász spent many hours helping me connect the output of *troff* to the phototypesetter. To them I am grateful.

The National Science Foundation has given me continual support for my research, which led to this book.

Meetings of the IFIP Working Group on programming methodology, WG2.3, have had a strong influence on my work in programming methodology over the past 8 years.

+UNIX is a trademark of Bell Laboratories.

Finally, I thank my wife, Elaine, and children, Paul and Susan, for their love and patience while I was writing this book.

In preparing the second printing of this book, over 150 changes were made without significantly changing the page numbering. Thanks go to the following people for notifying me of errors: Roland Backhouse, Alfs T. Berztiss, Ed Cohen, Cui Jing, Cui Yan-Nong, Pavel Curtis, Alan Demers, David Gries, Robert Harper, Cliff Jones, Donald E. Knuth, Liu Shau-Chung, Michael Marcotty, Alain Martin, James Mildrew, Ken Perry, Hal Perkins, Paul Pritchard, Willem de Roever, J.L.A. van de Snepsheut, R.C. Shaw, Jorgan Steensgaard-Madsen, Rodney Topor, Solveig Torgerson, Wlad Turski, V. Vitek, David Wright, Zhou Bing-Sheng.

Table of Contents

Part 0
Why Use Logic?
Why Prove Programs Correct?

A story

We have just finished writing a large program (3000 lines). Among other things, the program computes as intermediate results the quotient q and remainder r arising from dividing a non-negative integer x by a positive integer y. For example, with $x = 7$ and $y = 2$, the program calculates $q = 3$ (since $7 \div 2 = 3$) and $r = 1$ (since the remainder when 7 is divided by 2 is 1).

Our program appears below, with dots "..." representing the parts of the program that precede and follow the remainder-quotient calculation. The calculation is performed as given because the program will sometimes be executed on a micro-computer that has no integer division, and portability must be maintained at all costs! The remainder-quotient calculation actually seems quite simple; since $\div$ cannot be used, we have elected to subtract divisor y from a copy of x repeatedly, keeping track of how many subtractions are made, until another subtraction would yield a negative integer.

```
   . . .
r := x;  q := 0;
while r > y do
   begin r := r − y;  q := q + 1 end;
   . . .
```

We're ready to debug the program. With respect to the remainder-quotient calculation, we're smart enough to realize that the divisor should initially be greater than 0 and that upon its termination the variables should satisfy the formula

$$x = y*q + r,$$

so we add some output statements to check the calculations:

```
    . . .
write ('dividend x =', x, 'divisor y =', y);
r := x;  q := 0;
while r > y do
    begin r := r −y;  q := q +1 end;
write ('y *q +r =', y *q +r);
    . . .
```

Unfortunately, we get voluminous output because the program segment occurs in a loop, so our first test run is wasted. We try to be more selective about what we print. Actually, we need to know values only when an error is detected. Having heard of a new feature just inserted into the compiler, we decide to try it. If a Boolean expression appears within braces { and } at a point in the program, then, whenever "flow of control" reaches that point during execution, it is checked: if false, a message and a dump of the program variables are printed; if true, execution continues normally. These Boolean expressions are called *assertions*, since in effect we are asserting that they should be true when flow of control reaches them. The systems people encourage leaving assertions in the program, because they help document it.

Protests about inefficiency during production runs are swept aside by the statement that there is a switch in the compiler to turn off assertion checking. Also, after some thought, we decide it may be better always to check assertions —detection of an error during production would be well worth the extra cost.

So we add assertions to the program:

```
       . . .
    {y > 0}
    r := x;  q := 0;
(1) while r > y do
        begin r := r −y;  q := q +1 end;
    {x = y *q +r}
       . . .
```

Testing now results in far less output, and we make progress. Assertion checking detects an error during a test run because y is 0 just before a remainder-quotient calculation, and it takes only four hours to find the error in the calculation of y and fix it.

But then we spend a day tracking down an error for which we received no nice false-assertion message. We finally determine that the remainder-quotient calculation resulted in

$$x = 6, y = 3, q = 1, r = 3.$$

Sure enough, both assertions in (1) are true with these values; the problem is that the remainder should be less than the divisor, and it isn't. We determine that the loop condition should be $r \geqslant y$ instead of $r > y$. If only the result assertion were strong enough —if only we had used the assertion $x = y*q + r$ **and** $r < y$— we would have saved a day of work! Why didn't we think of it?

We fix the error and insert the stronger assertion:

```
    . . .
{y > 0}
r := x;  q := 0;
while r ⩾ y do
    begin r := r − y;  q := q + 1 end;
{x = y*q + r and r < y}
    . . .
```

Things go fine for a while, but one day we get incomprehensible output. It turns out that the quotient-remainder algorithm resulted in a negative remainder $r = -2$. But the remainder shouldn't be negative! And we find out that r was negative because initially x was -2. Ahhh, another error in calculating the input to the quotient-remainder algorithm —x isn't *supposed* to be negative! But we could have caught the error earlier and saved two days searching, in fact we *should* have caught it earlier; all we had to do was make the initial and final assertions for the program segment strong enough. Once more we fix an error and strengthen an assertion:

```
    . . .
{0 ⩽ x and 0 < y}
r := x;  q := 0;
while r ⩾ y do
    begin r := r − y;  q := q + 1 end;
{x = y*q + r and 0 ⩽ r < y}
    . . .
```

It sure would be nice to be able to invent the right assertions to use in a less *ad hoc* fashion. Why can't we think of them? Does it have to be a trial-and-error process? Part of our problem here was carelessness in specifying what the program segment was to do —we should have written the initial assertion ($0 \leqslant x$ **and** $0 < y$) and the final assertion ($x = y*q + r$ **and** $0 \leqslant r < y$) *before* writing the program segment, for they form the definition of quotient and remainder.

But what about the error we made in the condition of the while loop? Could we have prevented that from the beginning? Is there is a way to prove, just from the program and assertions, that the assertions are true when flow of control reaches them? Let's see what we can do.

Just before the loop it seems that part of our result,

(2) $x = y*q + r$

holds, since $x = r$ and $q = 0$. And from the assignments in the loop body we conclude that if (2) is true before execution of the loop body then it is true after its execution, so it will be true just before and after *every* iteration of the loop. Let's insert it as an assertion in the obvious places, and let's also make all assertions as *strong* as possible:

```
    . . .
    {0 ≤ x and 0 < y}
    r := x;  q := 0;
    {0 ≤ r and 0 < y and x = y*q + r}
    while r ≥ y do
       begin {0 ≤ r and 0 < y ≤ r and x = y*q + r}
          r := r - y;  q := q + 1
          {0 ≤ r and 0 < y and x = y*q + r}
    end;
    {0 ≤ r < y and x = y*q + r}
    . . .
```

Now, how can we easily determine a correct loop condition, or, given the condition, how can we prove it is correct? When the loop terminates the condition is false. Upon termination we want $r < y$, so that the complement, $r \geqslant y$ must be the correct loop condition. How easy that was!

It seems that if we knew how to make all assertions as strong as possible and if we learned how to reason carefully about assertions and programs, then we wouldn't make so many mistakes, we would *know* our program was correct, and we wouldn't need to debug programs at all! Hence, the days spent running test cases, looking through output and searching for errors could be spent in other ways.

Discussion

The story suggests that assertions, or simply Boolean expressions, are really needed in programming. But it is not enough to know how to write Boolean expressions; one needs to know how to *reason* with them: to simplify them, to prove that one follows from another, to prove that one is not true in some state, and so forth. And, later on, we will see that it is necessary to use a kind of assertion that is not part of the usual Boolean expression language of Pascal, PL/I or FORTRAN, the "quantified" assertion.

Knowing how to reason about assertions is one thing; knowing how to reason about *programs* is another. In the past 10 years, computer science has come a long way in the study of proving programs correct. We are reaching the point where the subject can be taught to undergraduates, or to anyone with some training in programming and the will to become more proficient. More importantly, the study of program correctness proofs has led to the discovery and elucidation of methods for *developing* programs. Basically, one attempts to develop a program and its proof hand-in-hand, with the proof ideas leading the way! If the methods are practiced with care, they can lead to programs that are free of errors, that take much less time to develop and debug, and that are much more easily understood (by those who have studied the subject).

Above, I mentioned that programs could be free of errors and, in a way, I implied that debugging would be unnecessary. This point needs some clarification. Even though we can become more proficient in programming, we will still make errors, even if only of a syntactic nature (typos). We are only human. Hence, some testing will always be necessary. But it should not be called debugging, for the word debugging implies the existence of bugs, which are terribly difficult to eliminate. No matter how many flies we swat, there will always be more. A disciplined method of programming should give more confidence than that! We should run test cases not to look for bugs, but to increase our confidence in a program we are quite sure is correct; finding an error should be the exception rather than the rule.

With this motivation, let us turn to our first subject, the study of logic.

Part I
Propositions
and Predicates

Chapter 1 defines the syntax of propositions —Boolean expressions using only Boolean variables— and shows how to evaluate them. Chapter 2 gives rules for manipulating propositions, which is often done in order to find simpler but equivalent ones. This chapter is important for further work on programming, and should be studied carefully.

Chapter 3 introduces a *natural deduction system* for proving theorems about propositions, which is supposed to mimic in some sense the way we "naturally" argue. Such systems are used in research on mechanical verification of proofs of program correctness, and one should become familiar with them. But the material is not needed to understand the rest of the book and may be skipped entirely.

Chapter 4 extends propositions to include variables of types besides Boolean and introduces quantification. A *predicate calculus* is given, in which one can express and manipulate the assertions we make about program variables. "Bound" and "free" variables are introduced and the notion of textual substitution is studied. This material is necessary for further reading.

Chapter 5 concerns arrays. Thinking of an array as a function from subscript values to array element values, instead of as a collection of independent variables, leads to some neat notation and rules for dealing with arrays. The first two sections of this chapter should be read, but the third may be skipped on first reading.

Finally, chapter 6 discusses briefly the use of assertions in programs, thus motivating the next two parts of the book.

Chapter 1
Propositions

We want to be able to describe sets of states of program variables and to write and manipulate clear, unambiguous assertions about program variables. We begin by considering only variables (and expressions) of type *Boolean*: from the operational point of view, each variable contains one of the values T and F, which represent our notions of "truth" and "falsity", respectively. The word *Boolean* comes from the name of a 19th century English mathematician, George Boole, who initiated the algebraic study of truth values.

Like many logicians, we will use the word *proposition* for the kind of Boolean or logical expression to be defined and discussed in this chapter.

Propositions are similar to arithmetic expressions. There are operands, which represent the values T or F (instead of integers), and operators (e.g. **and**, **or** instead of *, +), and parentheses are used to aid in determining order of evaluation. The problem will not be in defining and evaluating propositions, but in learning how to express assertions written in English as propositions and to reason with those propositions.

1.1 Fully Parenthesized Propositions

Propositions are formed according to the following rules (the operators will be defined subsequently). As can be seen, parentheses are required around each proposition that includes an operation. This restriction, which will be weakened later on, allows us to dispense momentarily with problems of precedence of operators.

1. T and F are propositions.

2. An identifier is a proposition. (An identifier is a sequence of one or more digits and letters, the first of which is a letter.)

3. If b is a proposition, then so is $(\neg b)$.

4. If b and c are propositions, then so are $(b \wedge c)$, $(b \vee c)$, $(b \Rightarrow c)$, and $(b = c)$.

This syntax may be easier to understand in the form of a BNF grammar (Appendix 1 gives a short introduction to BNF):

(1.1.1) <proposition> ::= T | F | <identifier>
         | ($\neg$ <proposition>)
         | (<proposition> $\wedge$ <proposition>)
         | (<proposition> $\vee$ <proposition>)
         | (<proposition> $\Rightarrow$ <proposition>)
         | (<proposition> = <proposition>)

Example. The following are propositions (separated by commas):

F, $(\neg T)$, $(b \vee xyz)$, $((\neg b) \wedge (c \Rightarrow d))$,
$((abc1 = id) \wedge (\neg d))$ □

Example. The following are not propositions:

$F\ F$, $(b \vee (c)$, $(b) \wedge)$, $a+b$ □

As seen in the above syntax, five operators are defined over values of type *Boolean*:

negation: (**not** b), or $(\neg b)$
conjunction: (b **and** c), or $(b \wedge c)$
disjunction: (b **or** c), or $(b \vee c)$
implication: (b **imp** c), or $(b \Rightarrow c)$
equality: (b **equals** c), or $(b = c)$

Two different notations have been given for each operator, a name and a mathematical symbol. The name indicates how to pronounce it, and its use also makes typing easier when a typewriter does not have the corresponding mathematical symbol.

The following terminology is used. $(b \wedge c)$ is called a *conjunction*; its operands b and c called *conjuncts*. $(b \vee c)$ is called a *disjunction*; its operands b and c are called *disjuncts*. $(b \Rightarrow c)$ is called an *implication*; its *antecedent* is b and its *consequent* is c.

1.2 Evaluation of Constant Propositions

Thus far we have given a *syntax* for propositions; we have defined the set of well-formed propositions. We now give a semantics (meaning) by showing how to evaluate them.

We begin by defining evaluation of *constant propositions* —propositions that contain only constants as operands— and we do this in three cases based on the structure of a proposition e: for e with no operators, for e with one operator, and for e with more than one operator.

(1.2.1)   **Case 1.** The value of proposition T is T; the value of F is F.

(1.2.2)   **Case 2.** The values of $(\neg b)$, $(b \wedge c)$, $(b \vee c)$, $(b \Rightarrow c)$ and $(b = c)$, where b and c are each one of the constants T and F, are given by the following table (called a *truth table*). Each row of the table contains possible values for the operands b and c and, for these values, shows the value of each of the five operations. For example, from the last row we see that the value of $(\neg T)$ is F and that the values of $(T \wedge T)$, $(T \vee T)$, $(T \Rightarrow T)$ and $(T = T)$ are all T.

	b	c	$(\neg b)$	$(b \wedge c)$	$(b \vee c)$	$(b \Rightarrow c)$	$(b = c)$
	F	F	T	F	F	T	T
(1.2.3)	F	T	T	F	T	T	F
	T	F	F	F	T	F	F
	T	T	F	T	T	T	T

(1.2.4)   **Case 3.** The value of a constant proposition with more than one operator is found by repeatedly applying (1.2.2) to a subproposition of the constant proposition and replacing the subproposition by its value, until the proposition is reduced to T or F.

We give an example of evaluation of a proposition:

$$((T \wedge T) \Rightarrow F)$$
$$= (T \Rightarrow F)$$
$$= F$$

Remark: The description of the operations in terms of a truth table, which lists *all* possible operand combinations and their values, can be given only because the set of possible values is finite. For example, no such table could be given for operations on integers. $\square$

The names of the operations correspond fairly closely to their meanings in English. For example, "not true" usually means "false", and "not false" "true". But note that operation **or** denotes "inclusive or" and not "exclusive or". That is, $(T \vee T)$ is T, while the "exclusive or" of T and T is false.

Also, there is no causality implied by operation **imp**. The sentence "If it rains, the picnic is cancelled" can be written in propositional form as $(rain \Rightarrow no \ picnic)$. From the English sentence we infer that the lack of rain means there will be a picnic, but *no* such inference can be made from the proposition $(rain \Rightarrow no \ picnic)$.

1.3 Evaluation of Propositions in a State

A proposition like $((\neg c) \vee d)$ can appear in a program in several places, for example in an assignment statement $b := ((\neg c) \vee d)$ and in an **if**-statement **if** $((\neg c) \vee d)$ **then** $\cdots$. When the statement in which the proposition appears is to be executed, the proposition is evaluated in the current machine "state" to produce either T or F. To define this evaluation requires a careful explanation of the notion of "state".

A state associates identifiers with values. For example, in state s (say), identifier c could be associated with value F and identifier d with T. In terms of a computer memory, when the computer is in state s, locations named c and d contain the values F and T, respectively. In another state, the associations could be (c, T) and (d, F). The crucial point here is that a state consists of a set of pairs (identifier, value) in which all the identifiers are distinct, i.e. the state is a function:

(1.3.1)   **Definition.** A *state* s is a function from a set of identifiers to the set of values T and F. □

Example. Let state s be the function defined by the set $\{(a, T), (bc, F), (y1, T)\}$. Then $s(a)$ denotes the value determined by applying state (function) s to identifier a: $s(a) = T$. Similarly, $s(bc) = F$ and $s(y1) = T$. □

(1.3.2)   **Definition.** Proposition e is *well-defined in state* s if each identifier in e is associated with either T or F in state s. □

In state $s = \{(b, T), (c, F)\}$, proposition $(b \vee c)$ is well-defined while proposition $(b \vee d)$ is not.

Let us now extend the notation $s(identifier)$ to define the value of a proposition in a state. For any state s and proposition e, $s(e)$ will denote the value resulting from evaluating e in state s. Since an identifier b is also a proposition, we will be careful to make sure that $s(b)$ will still denote the value of b in state s.

(1.3.3) **Definition**. Let proposition e be well-defined in state s. Then $s(e)$, the value of e in state s, is the value obtained by replacing all occurrences of identifiers b in e by their values $s(b)$ and evaluating the resulting constant proposition according to the rules given in the previous section 1.2. □

Example. $s(((\neg b)\lor c))$ is evaluated in state $s = \{(b, T), (c, F)\}$:

$$s(((\neg b)\lor c))$$
$$= ((\neg T)\lor F) \quad (b \text{ has been replaced by } T, c \text{ by } F)$$
$$= (F \lor F)$$
$$= F \qquad \square$$

1.4 Precedence Rules for Operators

The previous sections dealt with a restricted form of propositions, so that evaluation of propositions could be explained without having to deal with the precedence of operators. We now relax this restriction.

Parentheses can be omitted or included at will around any proposition. For example, the proposition $((b \lor c)\Rightarrow d)$ can be written as $b \lor c \Rightarrow d$. In this case, additional rules define the order of evaluation of subpropositions. These rules, which are similar to those for arithmetic expressions are:

1. Sequences of the same operator are evaluated from left to right, e.g. $b \land c \land d$ is equivalent to $((b \land c)\land d)$.

2. The order of evaluation of different, adjacent operators is given by the list: **not** (has highest precedence and binds tightest), **and, or, imp, equals**.

It is usually better to make liberal use of parentheses in order to make the order of evaluation clear, and we will usually do so.

Examples $\neg b = b \land c$ is equivalent to $(\neg b) = (b \land c)$
                   $b \lor \neg c \Rightarrow d$ is equivalent to $(b \lor (\neg c))\Rightarrow d$
                   $b \Rightarrow c \Rightarrow d \land e$ is equivalent to $(b \Rightarrow c)\Rightarrow(d \land e)$ □

The following BNF grammar defines the syntax of propositions, giving enough structure so that precedences can be deduced from it. (The non-terminal <identifier> has been left undefined and has its usual meaning).

1. <proposition> ::= <imp-expr>
2. | <proposition> = <imp-expr>
3. <imp-expr> ::= <expr>
4. | <imp-expr> ⇒ <expr>
5. <expr>   ::= <term>
6. | <expr> ∨ <term>
7. <term>   ::= <factor>
8. | <term> ∧ <factor>
9. <factor>   ::= ￢ <factor>
10. | (<proposition>)
11. | T
12. | F
13. | <identifier>

We now define $s(e)$, the value of proposition e in state s, recursively, based on the structure of e given by the grammar. That is, for each rule of the grammar, we show how to evaluate e if it has the form given by that rule. For example, rule 6 indicates that for an <expr> of the form <expr> ∨ <term>, its value is the value found by applying operation **or** to the values $s(<expr>)$ and $s(<term>)$ of its operands <expr> and <term>. The values of the five operations =, ⇒, ∨, ∧ and ￢ used in rules 2, 4, 6, 8 and 9 are given by truth table (1.2.3).

1. $s(<proposition>) = s(<imp-expr>)$
2. $s(<proposition>) = s(<proposition>) = s(<imp-expr>)$
3. $s(<imp-expr>)   = s(<expr>)$
4. $s(<imp-expr>)   = s(<imp-expr>) ⇒ s(\hat{}<expr>)$
5. $s(<expr>)   = s(<term>)$
6. $s(<expr>)   = s(<expr>) ∨ s(<term>)$
7. $s(<term>)   = s(<factor>)$
8. $s(<term>)   = s(<term>) ∧ s(<factor>)$
9. $s(<factor>)   = ￢ s(<factor>)$
10. $s(<factor>)   = s(<proposition>)$
11. $s(<factor>)   = T$
12. $s(<factor>)   = F$
13. $s(<factor>)   = s(<identifier>)$ (the value of <identifier> in s)

An example of evaluation using a truth table

Let us compute values of the proposition $(b ⇒ c) = (￢b ∨ c)$ for all possible operand values using a truth table. In the table below, each row gives possible values for b and c and the corresponding values of $￢b$, $￢b ∨ c$, $b ⇒ c$ and the final proposition. This truth table shows how one builds a truth table for a proposition, by beginning with the values of the

identifiers, then showing the values of the smallest subpropositions, then
the next smallest, and building up to the complete proposition.

As can be seen, the values of $\neg b \vee c$ and $b \Rightarrow c$ are the same in each
state, and hence the propositions are equivalent and can be used inter-
changeably. In fact, one often finds $b \Rightarrow c$ *defined* as $\neg b \vee c$. Similarly,
$b = c$ is often defined as an abbreviation for $(b \Rightarrow c) \wedge (c \Rightarrow b)$ (see exercise 2i).

b	c	$\neg b$	$\neg b \vee c$	$b \Rightarrow c$	$(b \Rightarrow c) = (\neg b \vee c)$
F	F	T	T	T	T
F	T	T	T	T	T
T	F	F	F	F	T
T	T	F	T	T	T

1.5 Tautologies

A *Tautology* is a proposition that is true in every state in which it is
well-defined. For example, proposition T is a tautology and F is not.
The proposition $b \vee \neg b$ is a tautology, as can be seen by evaluating it with
$b = T$ and $b = F$:

$$T \vee \neg T = T \vee F = T$$
$$F \vee \neg F = F \vee T = T$$

or, in truth-table form:

b	$\neg b$	$b \vee \neg b$
T	F	T
F	T	T

The basic way to show that a proposition is a tautology is to show that its
evaluation yields T in every possible state. Unfortunately, each extra
identifier in a proposition doubles the number of combinations of values
for identifiers —for a proposition with i distinct identifiers there are 2^i
cases! Hence, the work involved can become tedious and time consum-
ing. To illustrate this, (1.5.1) contains the truth table for proposition
$(b \wedge c \wedge d) \Rightarrow (d \Rightarrow b)$, which has three distinct identifiers. By taking some
shortcuts, the work can be reduced. For example, a glance at truth table
(1.2.3) indicates that operation **imp** is true whenever its antecedent is false,
so that its consequent need only be evaluated if its antecedent is true. In
example (1.5.1) there is only one state in which the antecedent $b \wedge c \wedge d$ is
true —the state in which b, c and d are true— and hence we need only
the top line of truth table (1.5.1).

	b c d	$b \wedge c \wedge d$	$d \Rightarrow b$	$(b \wedge c \wedge d) \Rightarrow (d \Rightarrow b)$
	T T T	T	T	T
	T T F	F	T	T
	T F T	F	T	T
(1.5.1)	T F F	F	T	T
	F T T	F	F	T
	F T F	F	T	T
	F F T	F	F	T
	F F F	F	T	T

Using such informal reasoning helps reduce the number of states in which the proposition must be evaluated. Nevertheless, the more distinct identifiers a proposition has the more states to inspect, and evaluation soon becomes infeasible. Later chapters investigate other methods for proving that a proposition is a tautology.

Disproving a conjecture

Sometimes we conjecture that a proposition e is a tautology, but are unable to develop a proof of it, so we decide to try to disprove it. What does it take to disprove such a conjecture?

It may be possible to prove the converse —i.e. that $\neg e$ is a tautology— but the chances are slim. If we had reason to believe a conjecture, it is unlikely that its converse is true. Much more likely is that it is true in most states but false in one or two, and to disprove it we need only find one such state:

> To prove a conjecture, it is necessary to prove that it is true in all cases; to disprove a conjecture, it is sufficient to find a single case where it is false.

1.6 Propositions as Sets of States

A proposition *represents*, or describes, the set of states in which it is true. Conversely, for any set of states containing only identifiers associated with T or F we can derive a proposition that represents that state set. Thus, the empty set, the set containing no states, is represented by proposition F because F is true in no state. The set of all states is represented by proposition T because T is true in all states. The following example illustrates how one can derive a proposition that represents a given set of states. The resulting proposition contains only the operators **and, or** and **not**.

Example. The set of two states $\{(b,T),(c,T),(d,T)\}$ and $\{(b,F),$ $(c,T),(d,F)\}$, is represented by the proposition

$$(b \wedge c \wedge d) \vee (\neg b \wedge c \wedge \neg d) \quad \square$$

The connection between a proposition and the set of states it represents is so strong that we often *identify* the two concepts. Thus, instead of writing "the set of states in which $b \vee \neg c$ is true" we may write "the states in $b \vee \neg c$". Though it is a sloppy use of English, it is at times convenient.

In connection with this discussion, the following terminology is introduced. Proposition b is *weaker* than c if $c \Rightarrow b$. Correspondingly, c is said to be *stronger* than b. A stronger proposition makes more restrictions on the combinations of values its identifiers can be associated with, a weaker proposition makes fewer. In terms of sets of states, b is as weak as c if it is "less restrictive": if b's set of states includes at least c's states, and possibly more. The weakest proposition is T (or any tautology), because it represents the set of all states; the strongest is F, because it represents the set of no states.

1.7 Transforming English to Propositional Form

At this point, we translate a few sentences into propositional form. Consider the sentence "If it rains, the picnic is cancelled." Let identifier r stand for the proposition "it rains" and let identifier pc represent "the picnic is cancelled". Then the sentence can be written as $r \Rightarrow pc$.

As shown by this example, the technique is to represent "atomic parts" of a sentence —how these are chosen is up to the translator— by identifiers and to describe their relationship using Boolean operators. Here are some more examples, using identifiers r, pc, wet, and s defined as follows:

it rains: r
picnic is cancelled: pc
be wet: wet
stay at home: s

1. If it rains but I stay at home, I won't be wet: $(r \wedge s) \Rightarrow \neg wet$

2. I'll be wet if it rains: $r \Rightarrow wet$

3. If it rains and the picnic is not cancelled or I don't stay home, I'll be wet: Either $((r \wedge \neg pc) \vee \neg s) \Rightarrow wet$ or $(r \wedge (\neg pc \vee \neg s)) \Rightarrow wet$. The English is ambiguous; the latter proposition is probably the desired one.

4. Whether or not the picnic is cancelled, I'm staying home if it rains: $(pc \lor \neg pc) \land r \Rightarrow s$. This reduces to $r \Rightarrow s$.

5. Either it doesn't rain or I'm staying home: $\neg r \lor s$.

Exercises for Chapter 1

1. Each line contains a proposition and two states $s1$ and $s2$. Evaluate the proposition in both states.

proposition		state $s1$				state $s2$			
		m	n	p	q	m	n	p	q
(a)	$\neg(m \lor n)$	T	F	T	T	F	T	T	T
(b)	$\neg m \lor n$	T	F	T	T	F	T	T	T
(c)	$\neg(m \land n)$	T	F	T	T	F	T	T	T
(d)	$\neg m \land n$	T	F	T	T	F		T	
(e)	$(m \lor n) \Rightarrow p$	T	F	T	T	T	T	F	T
(f)	$m \lor (n \Rightarrow p)$	T	F	T	T	T	T	F	T
(g)	$(m = n) \land (p = q)$	F	F	T	F	T	F	T	F
(h)	$m = (n \land (p = q))$	F	F	T	F	T	F	T	F
(i)	$m = (n \land p = q)$	F	F	T	F	T	F	T	F
(j)	$(m = n) \land (p \Rightarrow q)$	F	T	F	T	T	T	F	F
(k)	$(m = n \land p) \Rightarrow q$	F	T	F	T	T	T	F	F
(l)	$(m \Rightarrow n) \Rightarrow (p \Rightarrow q)$	F	F	F	F	T	T	T	T
(m)	$(m \Rightarrow (n \Rightarrow p)) \Rightarrow q$	F	F	F	F	T	T	T	T

2. Write truth tables to show the values of the following propositions in all states:

(a) $b \lor c \lor d$ (e) $\neg b \Rightarrow (b \lor c)$

(b) $b \land c \land d$ (f) $\neg b = (b \lor c)$

(c) $b \land (c \lor d)$ (g) $(\neg b = c) \lor b$

(d) $b \lor (c \land d)$ (h) $(b \lor c) \land (b \Rightarrow c) \land (c \Rightarrow b)$

                      (i) $(b = c) = (b \Rightarrow c) \land (c \Rightarrow b)$

3. Translate the following sentences into propositional form.

(a) $x < y$ or $x = y$.

(b) Either $x < y$, $x = y$, or $x > y$.

(c) If $x > y$ and $y > z$, then $v = w$.

(d) The following are all true: $x < y$, $y < z$ and $v = w$.

(e) At most one of the following is true: $x < y$, $y < z$ and $v = w$.

(f) None of the following are true: $x < y$, $y < z$ and $v = w$.

(g) The following are not all true at the same time: $x < y$, $y < z$ and $v = w$.

(h) When $x < y$, then $y < z$; when $x \geq y$, then $v = w$.

(i) When $x < y$ then $y < z$ means that $v = w$, but if $x \geq y$ then $y < z$ doesn't hold; however, if $v = w$ then $x < y$.

(j) If execution of program P is begun with $x < y$, then execution terminates with $y = 2^x$.

(k) Execution of program P begun with $x < 0$ will not terminate.

4. Below are some English sentences. Introduce identifiers to represent the simple ones (e.g. "it's raining cats and dogs.") and then translate the sentences into propositions.

(a) Whether or not it's raining, I'm going swimming.
(b) If it's raining I'm not going swimming.
(c) It's raining cats and dogs.
(d) It's raining cats or dogs.
(e) If it rains cats and dogs I'll eat my hat, but I won't go swimming.
(f) If it rains cats and dogs while I am swimming I'll eat my hat

Chapter 2
Reasoning using Equivalence Transformations

Evaluating propositions is rarely our main task. More often we wish to manipulate them in some manner in order to derive "equivalent" but simpler ones (easier to read and understand). Two propositions (or, in general, expressions) are equivalent if they have the same value in every state. For example, since $a+(c-a)=c$ is always true for integer variables a and c, the two integer expressions $a+(c-a)$ and c are equivalent, and $a+(c-a)=c$ is called an equivalence.

This chapter defines equivalence of propositions in terms of the evaluation model of chapter 1. A list of useful equivalences is given, together with two rules for generating others. The idea of a "calculus" is discussed, and the rules are put in the form of a formal calculus for "reasoning" about propositions.

These rules form the basis for much of the manipulations we do with propositions and are very important for later work on developing programs. The chapter should be studied carefully.

2.1 The Laws of Equivalence

For propositions, we define equivalence in terms of operation **equals** and the notion of a tautology as follows:

(2.1.1) **Definition.** Propositions *E1* and *E2* are *equivalent iff E1 = E2* is a tautology. In this case, *E1 = E2* is an *equivalence.* □

Thus, an equivalence is an equality that is a tautology.

Below, we give a list of equivalences; these are the basic equivalences from which all others will be derived, so we call them the *laws of equivalence*. Actually, they are "schemas": the identifiers *E1*, *E2* and *E3* within them are parameters, and one arrives at a particular equivalence by substituting particular propositions for them. For example, substituting $x \lor y$ for $E1$ and z for $E2$ in the first law of Commutativity, $(E1 \land E2) = (E2 \land E1)$, yields the equivalence

$$((x \lor y) \land z) = (z \land (x \lor y))$$

Remark: Parentheses are inserted where necessary when performing a substitution so that the order of evaluation remains consistent with the original proposition. For example, the result of substituting $x \lor y$ for b in $b \land z$ is $(x \lor y) \land z$, and not $x \lor y \land z$, which is equivalent to $x \lor (y \land z)$. □

1. **Commutative Laws** (These allow us to reorder the operands of **and**, **or** and **equality**):
$(E1 \land E2) = (E2 \land E1)$
$(E1 \lor E2) = (E2 \lor E1)$
$(E1 = E2) = (E2 = E1)$

2. **Associative Laws** (These allow us to dispense with parentheses when dealing with sequences of **and** and sequences of **or**):
$E1 \land (E2 \land E3) = (E1 \land E2) \land E3$ (so write both as $E1 \land E2 \land E3$)
$E1 \lor (E2 \lor E3) = (E1 \lor E2) \lor E3$

3. **Distributive Laws** (These are useful in factoring a proposition, in the same way that we rewrite $2*(3+4)$ as $(2*3)+(2*4)$):
$E1 \lor (E2 \land E3) = (E1 \lor E2) \land (E1 \lor E3)$
$E1 \land (E2 \lor E3) = (E1 \land E2) \lor (E1 \land E3)$

4. **De Morgan's Laws** (After Augustus De Morgan, a 19th century English mathematician who, along with Boole, laid much of the foundations for mathematical logic):
$\lnot(E1 \land E2) = \lnot E1 \lor \lnot E2$
$\lnot(E1 \lor E2) = \lnot E1 \land \lnot E2$

5. **Law of Negation**: $\lnot(\lnot E1) = E1$

6. **Law of the Excluded Middle**: $E1 \lor \lnot E1 = T$

7. **Law of Contradiction**: $E1 \land \lnot E1 = F$

8. **Law of Implication**: $E1 \Rightarrow E2 = \lnot E1 \lor E2$

9. **Law of Equality**: $(E1 = E2) = (E1 \Rightarrow E2) \land (E2 \Rightarrow E1)$

10. **Laws of or-simplification**:
$$E1 \lor E1 = E1$$
$$E1 \lor T = T$$
$$E1 \lor F = E1$$
$$E1 \lor (E1 \land E2) = E1$$

11. **Laws of and-simplification**:
$$E1 \land E1 = E1$$
$$E1 \land T = E1$$
$$E1 \land F = F$$
$$E1 \land (E1 \lor E2) = E1$$

12. **Law of Identity**: $E1 = E1$

Don't be alarmed at the number of laws. Most of them you have used many times, perhaps unknowingly, and this list will only serve to make you more aware of them. Study the laws carefully, for they are used over and over again in manipulating propositions. Do some of the exercises at the end of this section until the use of these laws becomes second nature. Knowing the laws by name makes discussions of their use easier.

The law of the Excluded Middle deserves some comment. It means that at least one of b and $\neg b$ must be true in any state; there can be no middle ground. Some don't believe this law, at least in all its generality. In fact, here is a counterexample to it, in English. Consider the sentence

This sentence is false.

which we might consider as the meaning of an identifier b. Is it true or false? It can't be true, because it says it is false; it can't be false, because then it would be true! The sentence is neither true nor false, and hence violates the law of the Excluded Middle. The paradox arises because of the self-referential aspect of the sentence —it indicates something about itself, as do all paradoxes. [Here is another paradox to ponder: a barber in a small town cuts the hair of every person in town except for those who cut their own. Who cuts the barber's hair?] In our formal system, there will be no way to introduce such self-referential treatment, and the law of the Excluded Middle holds. But this means we cannot express *all* our thoughts and arguments in the formal system.

Finally, the laws of Equality and Implication deserve special mention. Together, they define **equality** and **imp** in terms of other operators: $b = c$ can always be replaced by $(b \Rightarrow c) \land (c \Rightarrow b)$ and $\neg b \Rightarrow c$ by $b \lor c$. This reinforces what we said about the two operations in chapter 1.

Proving that the logical laws are equivalences

We have stated, without proof, that laws 1-12 are equivalences. One way to prove this is to build truth tables and note that the laws are true in all states. For example, the first of De Morgan's laws, $\neg(E1 \wedge E2) = \neg E1 \vee \neg E2$, has the following truth table:

E1	E2	$E1 \wedge E2$	$\neg(E1 \wedge E2)$	$\neg E1$	$\neg E2$	$\neg E1 \vee \neg E2$	$\neg(E1 \wedge E2) = \neg E1 \vee \neg E2$
F	F	F	T	T	T	T	T
F	T	F	T	T	F	T	T
T	F	F	T	F	T	T	T
T	T	T	F	F	F	F	T

Clearly, the law is true in all states (in which it is well-defined), so that it is a tautology.

Exercise 1 concerns proving all the laws to be equivalences.

2.2 The Rules of Substitution and Transitivity

Thus far, we have just discussed some basic equivalences. We now turn to ways of generating other equivalences, without having to check their truth tables. One rule we all use in transforming expressions, usually without explicit mention, is the rule of "substitution of equals for equals". Here is an example of the use of this rule. Since $a + (c - a) = c$, we can substitute for expression $a + (c - a)$ in $(a + (c - a))*d$ to conclude that $(a + (c - a))*d = c*d$; we simply replace $a + (c - a)$ in $(a + (c - a))*d$ by the simpler, but equivalent, expression c.

The rule of substitution is:

(2.2.1)   **Rule of Substitution**. Let $e1 = e2$ be an equivalence and $E(p)$ be a proposition, written as a function of one of its identifiers p. Then $E(e1) = E(e2)$ and $E(e2) = E(e1)$ are also equivalences.   □

Here is an example of the use of the rule of Substitution. The law of Implication indicates that $(b \Rightarrow c) = (\neg b \vee c)$ is an equivalence. Consider the proposition $E(p) = d \vee p$. With

$$e1 = b \Rightarrow c \text{ and}$$
$$e2 = \neg b \vee c$$

we have

$$E(e1) = d \vee (b \Rightarrow c)$$
$$E(e2) = d \vee (\neg b \vee c)$$

so that $d \vee (b \Rightarrow c) = d \vee (\neg b \vee c)$ is an equivalence.

In using the rule of Substitution, we often use the following form. The proposition that we conclude is an equivalence is written on one line. The initial proposition appears to the left of the equality sign and the one that results from the substitution appears to the right, followed by the name of the law $e1 = e2$ used in the application:

$$d \vee (b \Rightarrow c) = d \vee (\neg b \vee c) \quad \text{(Implication)}$$

We need one more rule for generating equivalences:

(2.2.2)   **Rule of Transitivity.**   If $e1 = e2$ and $e2 = e3$ are equivalences, then so is $e1 = e3$ (and hence $e1$ is equivalent to $e3$).   □

Example.   We show that $(b \Rightarrow c) = (\neg c \Rightarrow \neg b)$ is an equivalence (an explanation of the format follows):

$$
\begin{aligned}
& b \Rightarrow c \\
&= \neg b \vee c \quad && \text{(Implication)} \\
&= c \vee \neg b \quad && \text{(Commutativity)} \\
&= \neg \neg c \vee \neg b \quad && \text{(Negation)} \\
&= \neg c \Rightarrow \neg b \quad && \text{(Implication)}
\end{aligned}
$$

This is read as follows. First, lines 1 and 2 indicate that $b \Rightarrow c$ is equivalent to $\neg b \vee c$, by virtue of the rule of Substitution and the law of Implication. Secondly, lines 2 and 3 indicate that $(\neg b \vee c)$ is equivalent to $c \vee \neg b$, by virtue of the rule of Substitution and the law of Commutativity. We also conclude, using the rule of Transitivity, that the first proposition, $b \Rightarrow c$, is equivalent to the third, $c \vee \neg b$. Continuing in this fashion, each pair of lines gives an equivalence and the reasons why the equivalence holds. We finally conclude that the first proposition, $b \Rightarrow c$, is equivalent to the last, $\neg c \Rightarrow \neg b$.   □

Example.   We show that the law of Contradiction can be proved from the others. The portion of each proposition to be replaced in each step is underlined in order to make it easier to identify the substitution.

$$
\begin{aligned}
\underline{\neg(b \wedge \neg b)} &= \neg b \vee \underline{\neg \neg b} \quad && \text{(De Morgan's Law)} \\
&= \underline{\neg b \vee b} \quad && \text{(Negation)} \\
&= \underline{b \vee \neg b} \quad && \text{(Commutativity)} \\
&= T \quad && \text{(Excluded Middle)}   □
\end{aligned}
$$

Generally speaking, such fine detail is unnecessary. The laws of Commutativity and Associativity are often used without explanation, and the application of several steps can appear on one line. For example:

$$(b \wedge (b \Rightarrow c)) \Rightarrow c$$
$$= \neg (b \wedge (\neg b \vee c)) \vee c \qquad \text{(Implication, 2 times)}$$
$$= \neg b \vee \neg (\neg b \vee c) \vee c \qquad \text{(De Morgan)}$$
$$= T \qquad\qquad\qquad\qquad \text{(Excluded Middle)}$$

Transforming an implication

Suppose we want to prove that

(2.2.3) $E1 \wedge E2 \wedge E3 \Rightarrow E$

is a tautology. The proposition is transformed as follows:

$$(E1 \wedge E2 \wedge E3) \Rightarrow E$$
$$= \neg (E1 \wedge E2 \wedge E3) \vee E \qquad \text{(Implication)}$$
$$= \neg E1 \vee \neg E2 \vee \neg E3 \vee E \qquad \text{(De Morgan)}$$

The final proposition is true in any state in which at least one of $\neg E1$, $\neg E2$, $\neg E3$ and E is true. Hence, to prove that (2.2.3) is a tautology we need only prove that in any state in which three of them are false the fourth is true. And we can choose which three to assume false, based on their form, in order to develop the simplest proof.

With an argument similar to the one just given, we can see that the five statements

$$E1 \wedge E2 \wedge E3 \Rightarrow E$$
$$E1 \wedge E2 \wedge \neg E \Rightarrow \neg E3$$
$$E1 \wedge \neg E \wedge E3 \Rightarrow \neg E2$$
$$\neg E \wedge E2 \wedge E3 \Rightarrow \neg E1$$
$$(2.2.4) \quad \neg E1 \vee \neg E2 \vee \neg E3 \vee E$$

are equivalent and we can choose which to work with. When given a proposition like (2.2.3), eliminating implication completely in favor of disjunctions like (2.2.4) can be helpful. Likewise, when formulating a problem, put it in the form of a disjunction right from the beginning.

Example. Prove that

$$(\neg (b \Rightarrow c) \wedge \neg (\neg b \Rightarrow (c \vee d))) \Rightarrow (\neg c \Rightarrow d)$$

is a tautology. Eliminate the main implication and use De Morgan's law:

$$\neg \neg (b \Rightarrow c) \vee \neg \neg (\neg b \Rightarrow (c \vee d)) \vee (\neg c \Rightarrow d)$$

Now simplify using Negation and eliminate the other implications:

$$(\neg b \vee c) \vee (b \vee c \vee d) \vee (c \vee d)$$

Use the laws of Associativity, Commutativity and **or**-simplification to arrive at

$$b \vee \neg b \vee c \vee d$$

which is true because of the laws of the Excluded Middle, $b \vee \neg b = T$, and **or**-simplification. This problem, which at first looked quite difficult, became simple when the implications were eliminated.

2.3 A Formal System of Axioms and Inference Rules

A *calculus*, according to Webster's Third International Dictionary, is a method or process of reasoning by computation of symbols. In section 2.2 we presented a calculus, for by performing some symbol manipulation according to rules of Substitution and Transitivity we can reason with propositions. For obvious reasons, the system presented here is called a *propositional calculus.*

We are careful to say *a* propositional calculus, and not *the* propositional calculus. With slight changes in the rules we can have a different calculus. Or we can invent a completely different set of rules and a completely different calculus, which is better suited for other purposes.

We want to emphasize the nature of this calculus as a formal system for manipulating propositions. To do this, let us put aside momentarily the notions of state and evaluation and see whether equivalences, which we will call *theorems*, can be discussed without them. First, define the propositions that arise directly from laws 1-12 to be *theorems*. They are also called *axioms* (and the laws 1-12 are *axiom schemas*), because their *theorem*hood is taken at face value, without proof.

(2.3.1)   **Axioms.** Any proposition that arises by substituting propositions for *E1*, *E2* and *E3* in one of the Laws 1-12 is called a *theorem.* □

Next, define the propositions that arise by using the rules of Substitution and Transitivity and an already-derived *theorem* to be a *theorem*. In this context, the rules are often called *inference rules*, for they can be used to *infer* that a proposition is a *theorem*. An inference rule is often written in the form

$$\frac{E_1, \; \cdots \; , E_n}{E} \quad \text{and} \quad \frac{E_1, E_2, \; \cdots \; , E_n}{E, E_0}$$

where the E_i and E stand for arbitrary propositions. The inference rule has the following meaning. If propositions $E_1, \cdots, E_n$ are *theorems*, then so is proposition E (and E_0 in the second case). Written in this form, the rules of Substitution and Transitivity are

(2.3.2)   **Rule of Substitution:** $$\frac{e1 = e2}{E(e1) = E(e2),\ E(e2) = E(e1)}$$

(2.3.3)   **Rule of Transitivity:** $$\frac{e1 = e2,\ e2 = e3}{e1 = e3}$$

A *theorem* of the formal system, then, is either an axiom (according to (2.3.1)) or a proposition that is derived from one of the inference rules (2.3.2) and (2.3.3).

Note carefully that this is a totally different system for dealing with propositions, which has been defined without regard to the notions of states and evaluation. The syntax of propositions is the same, but what we do with propositions is entirely different. Of course, there is a relation between the formal system and the system of evaluation given in the previous chapter. Exercises 9 and 10 call for proof of the following relationship: for any tautology e in the sense of chapter 1, $e = T$ is a *theorem*, and vice versa.

Exercises for Chapter 2

1. Verify that laws 1-12 are equivalences by building truth tables for them.

2. Prove the law of Identity, $e = e$, using the rules of Substitution and Transitivity and the laws 1-11.

3. Prove that $\neg T = F$ is an equivalence, using the rules of Substitution and Transitivity and the laws 1-12.

4. Prove that $\neg F = T$ is an equivalence, using the rules of Substitution and Transitivity and the laws 1-12.

5. Each column below consists of a sequence of propositions, each of which (except the first) is equivalent to its predecessor. The equivalence can be shown by one application of the rule of Substitution and one of the laws 1-12 or the results of exercises 3-4. Identify the law (as is done for the first two cases).

(a) $(x \wedge y) \vee (z \wedge \neg z)$
(b) $(x \wedge y) \vee F$ Contradiction
(c) $x \wedge y$ **or-simplification**
(d) $(x \wedge y) \vee F$
(e) $(x \wedge y) \vee (F \wedge z)$
(f) $(x \wedge y) \vee (F \wedge z)$
(g) $(x \wedge y) \vee ((x \wedge \neg x) \wedge z)$

(a) $\neg(\neg b \wedge (\neg b \Rightarrow z)) \vee z$
(b) $(\neg b \wedge (\neg b \Rightarrow z)) \Rightarrow z$
(c) $(\neg b \wedge (\neg \neg b \vee z)) \Rightarrow z$
(d) $(\neg b \wedge (\neg \neg b \vee \neg \neg z)) \Rightarrow z$
(e) $(\neg b \wedge \neg(\neg b \wedge \neg z)) \Rightarrow z$
(f) $(\neg b \wedge \neg(\neg b \wedge \neg z)) \Rightarrow z$
(g) $\neg(b \vee (\neg b \wedge \neg z)) \Rightarrow z$

(h) $(x \wedge y) \vee (x \wedge (\neg x \wedge z))$
(i) $x \wedge (y \vee (\neg x \wedge z))$
(j) $x \wedge (y \vee \neg x) \wedge (y \vee z)$
(k) $x \wedge (\neg x \vee y) \wedge (z \vee y)$
(l) $x \wedge (\neg x \vee \neg \neg y) \wedge (z \vee y)$
(m) $x \wedge \neg (x \wedge \neg y) \wedge (z \vee y)$

(h) $\neg ((b \vee \neg b) \wedge (b \vee \neg z)) \Rrightarrow z$
(i) $\neg (T \wedge (b \vee \neg z)) \Rrightarrow z$
(j) $\neg (b \vee \neg z) \Rrightarrow z$
(k) $\neg \neg (b \vee \neg z) \vee z$
(l) $(b \vee \neg z) \vee z$
(m) $b \vee (\neg z \vee z)$

6. Each proposition below can be simplified to one of the six propositions F, T, x, y, $x \wedge y$, and $x \vee y$. Simplify them, using the rules of Substitution and Transitivity and the laws 1-12.

(a) $x \vee (y \vee x) \vee \neg y$
(b) $(x \vee y) \wedge (x \vee \neg y)$
(c) $x \vee y \vee \neg x$
(d) $(x \vee y) \wedge (x \vee \neg y) \wedge (\neg x \vee y) \wedge (\neg x \vee \neg y)$
(e) $(x \wedge y) \vee (x \wedge \neg y) \vee (\neg x \wedge y) \vee (\neg x \wedge \neg y)$
(f) $(\neg x \wedge y) \vee x$

(g) $\neg x \Rrightarrow (x \wedge y)$
(h) $T \Rrightarrow (\neg x \Rrightarrow x)$
(i) $x \Rrightarrow (y \Rrightarrow (x \wedge y))$
(j) $\neg x \Rrightarrow (\neg x \Rrightarrow (\neg x \wedge y))$
(k) $\neg y \Rrightarrow y$
(l) $\neg y \Rrightarrow \neg y$

7. Show that any proposition e can be transformed into an equivalent proposition in *disjunctive normal form* —i.e. one that has the form

$$e_0 \vee \cdots \vee e_n \text{ where each } e_i \text{ has the form } g_0 \wedge \cdots \wedge g_m$$

Each g_j is an identifier id, a unary operator $\neg id$, T or F. Furthermore, the identifiers in each e_i are distinct.

8. Show that any proposition e can be transformed into an equivalent proposition in *conjunctive normal form* —i.e. one that has the form

$$e_0 \wedge \cdots \wedge e_n \text{ where each } e_i \text{ has the form } g_0 \vee \cdots \vee g_m$$

Each g_j is an identifier id, a unary operator $\neg id$, T or F. Furthermore, the identifiers in each e_i are distinct.

9. Prove that any *theorem* generated using laws 1-12 and the rules of Substitution and Transitivity is a tautology, by proving that laws 1-12 are tautologies (see exercise 1) and showing that the two rules can generate only tautologies.

10. Prove that if e is a tautology, then $e = T$ can be proved to be an equivalence using only the laws 1-12 and the rules of Substitution and Transitivity. Hint: use exercise 8.

Chapter 3
A Natural Deduction System

This chapter introduces another formal system of axioms and inference rules for deducing proofs that propositions are tautologies. It is called a "natural-deduction system" because it is meant to mimic the patterns of reasoning that we "naturally" use in making arguments in English.

This material is not used later and can be skipped. The equivalence-transformation system discussed in chapter 2 serves more than adequately in developing correct programs later on. One could go further and say that the equivalence-transformation system is more suited to our needs. The fact that the natural-deduction system was developed in order to mimic our natural patterns of reasoning may be the best reason for *not* using it, for our "natural" patterns of reasoning are far from adequate.

Nevertheless, study of this chapter is worthwhile for several reasons. The formal system presented here is minimal: there are *no* axioms and a minimal number of inference rules. Thus, one can see what it takes to start with a bare-bones system and build up enough theorems to the point where further theorems are not cumbersome to prove. The equivalence-transformation system, on the other hand, provided as axioms all the useful basic equivalences. Secondly, such systems are being used more and more in mechanical verification systems, and the computer science student should be familiar with them. (A natural-deduction system is also used in the popular game WFF'N PROOF.) Finally, it is useful to see and compare two totally different formal systems for dealing with propositions.

3.1 Introduction to Deductive Proofs

Consider the problem of proving that a conclusion follows from certain premises. For example, we might want to prove that $p \wedge (r \vee q)$ follows from $p \wedge q$ —i.e. $p \wedge (r \vee q)$ is true in every state in which $p \wedge q$ is. This problem can be written in the following form:

(3.1.1)   premise: $p \wedge q$
          conclusion:$p \wedge (r \vee q)$

In English, we might argue as follows.

(3.1.2)   *Proof of (3.1.1)*: Since $p \wedge q$ is true (in state s), so is p, and so is q. One property of **or** is that, for any r, $r \vee q$ is true if q is, so $r \vee q$ is true. Finally, since p and $r \vee q$ are both true, the properties of **and** allow us to conclude that $p \wedge (r \vee q)$ is true in s also.

In order to get at the essence of such proofs, in order to determine just what is involved in such arguments, we are going to strip away the verbiage from the proof and present simply the bare details. Admittedly, the proofs will look (at first) complicated and detailed. But once we have worked with the proof method for a while, we will be able to return to informal proofs in English with much better facility. We will also be able to give some guidelines for developing proofs (section 3.5).

The bare details of proof (3.1.2) are, in order: a statement of the theorem, the sequence of propositions initially assumed to be true, and the sequence of propositions that are true based on previous propositions and various rules of inference.

These bare details are presented in (3.1.3). The first line states the theorem to be proved: "**From** $p \wedge q$ **infer** $p \wedge (r \vee q)$". The second line gives the premise (if there were more premises, they would be given on successive lines). Each of the succeeding lines gives a proposition that one can infer, based on the truth of the propositions in the previous lines and an inference rule. The last line contains the conclusion.

From $p \wedge q$ infer $p \wedge (r \vee q)$

	1	$p \wedge q$	premise
(3.1.3)	2	p	property of **and**, 1
	3	q	property of **and**, 1
	4	$r \vee q$	property of **or**, 3
	5	$p \wedge (r \vee q)$	property of **and**, 2, 4

To the right of each proposition appears an explanation of how the proposition's "truth" is derived. For example, line 4 of the proof indicates that $r \vee q$ is true because of a property of **or** —that $r \vee q$ is true if q is— and because q appears on the preceding line 3. Note that parentheses are introduced freely in order to maintain priority of operators. We shall continue to do this without formal description.

In this formal system, a theorem to be proved has the form

From $e_1,$ $\cdots$, e_n **infer** e.

In terms of evaluation of propositions, such a theorem is interpreted as: if e_1, ..., e_n are true in a state, then e is true in that state also. If n is 0, meaning that there are no premises, then it can be interpreted as: e is true in all states, i.e. e is a tautology. In this case we write it as

Infer e.

Finally, a proposition on a line of a proof can be interpreted to mean that it is true in any state in which the propositions on previous lines are true.

As mentioned earlier, our natural deduction system has no axioms. The properties of operators used above are captured in the inference rules, which we begin to introduce and explain in the next section. (Inference rules were first introduced in section 2.3; review that material if necessary.) The inference rules for the natural deduction system are collected in Figure 3.3.1 at the end of section 3.3.

3.2 Inference Rules

There are ten inference rules in the natural deduction system. Ten is a rather large number, and we can work with that many only if they are organized so that they are easy to remember. In this system, there are two inference rules for each of the five operators **not**, **and**, **or**, **imp** and **equals**. One of the rules allows the introduction of the operator in a new proposition; the other allows its elimination. Hence there are five rules of introduction and five rules of elimination. The rules for introducing and eliminating **and** are called ∧-I and ∧-E, respectively, and similarly for the other operators.

Inference rules ∧-I, ∧-E and ∨-I

Let us begin by giving three rules: ∧-I, ∧-E and ∨-I.

(3.2.1)   ∧-I: $\dfrac{E_1,\ \cdots,\ E_n}{E_1 \wedge\ \cdots\ \wedge E_n}$

(3.2.2) ∧-E: $\dfrac{E_1 \wedge \cdots \wedge E_n}{E_i}$

(3.2.3) ∨-I: $\dfrac{E_i}{E_1 \vee \cdots \vee E_n}$

Rule ∧-I indicates that if E_1 and E_2 occur on previous lines of a proof (i.e. are assumed to be true or have been proved to be true), then their conjunction may be written on a line. If we assert "it is raining", and we assert "the sun is shining", then we can conclude "it is raining and the sun is shining". The rule is called "∧-Introduction", or "∧-I" for short, because it shows how a conjunction can be introduced.

Rule ∧-E shows how **and** can be eliminated to yield one of its conjuncts. If $E_1 \wedge E_2$ appears on a previous line of a proof (i.e. is assumed to be true or has been proved to be true), then either E_1 or E_2 may be written on the next line. Based on the assumption "it is raining and the sun is shining", we can conclude "it is raining", and we can conclude "the sun is shining".

Remark: There *are* places where it frequently rains while the sun is shining. Ithaca, the home of Cornell University, is one of them. In fact, it sometimes rains when perfectly blue sky seems to be overhead. The weather can also change from a furious blizzard to bright, calm sunshine and then back again, within minutes. When the weather acts so strangely, as it often does, one says that it is *Ithacating*. □

Rule ∨-I indicates that if E_1 is on a previous line, then we may write $E_1 \vee E_2$ on a line. If we assert "it is raining", then we can conclude "it is raining or the sun is shining".

Remember, these rules hold for *all* propositions E_1 and E_2. They are really "schemas", and we get an instance of the rule by replacing E_1 and E_2 by particular propositions. For example, since $p \vee q$ and r are propositions, the following is an instance of ∧-I.

$$\frac{p \vee q, \, \neg r}{(p \vee q) \wedge \neg r}$$

Let us redo proof (3.1.3) in (3.2.4) below and indicate the exact inference rule used at each step. The top line states what is to be proved. The line numbered 1 contains the first (and only) premise (pr 1). Each other line has the following property. Let the line have the form

line #| E "name of rule", line #, ..., line #

Then one can form an instance of the named inference rule by writing the propositions on lines line #, ..., line # above a line and proposition E below. That is, the truth of E is inferred by one inference rule from the truth of previous propositions. For example, from line 4 of the proof we see that $q \, / \, r \vee q$ is an instance of rule $\vee$-I: $(r \vee q)$ is being inferred from q.

(3.2.4)

1	$p \wedge q$	pr 1
2	p	$\wedge$-E, 1
3	q	$\wedge$-E, 1
4	$r \vee q$	$\vee$-I, 3
5	$p \wedge (r \vee q)$	$\wedge$-I, 2, 4

From $p \wedge q$ infer $p \wedge (r \vee q)$

Note how rule $\wedge$-E is used to break a proposition into its constituent parts, while $\wedge$-I and $\vee$-I are used to build new ones. This is typical of the use of introduction and elimination rules.

Proofs (3.2.5) and (3.2.6) below illustrate that **and** is a commutative operation; if $p \wedge q$ is true then so is $q \wedge p$, and vice versa. This is obvious after our previous study of propositions, but it must be proved in this formal system before it can be used. Note that both proofs are necessary; one cannot derive the second as an instance of the first by replacing p and q in the first by q and p, respectively. In this formal system, a proof holds only for the particular propositions involved. It is not a schema, the way an inference rule is.

(3.2.5)

1	$p \wedge q$	pr 1
2	p	$\wedge$-E, 1
3	q	$\wedge$-E, 1
4	$q \wedge p$	$\wedge$-I, 3, 2

From $p \wedge q$ infer $q \wedge p$

To illustrate the relation between the proof system and English, we give an argument in English for lemma (3.2.5): Suppose $p \wedge q$ is true [line 1]. Then so is p, and so is q [lines 2 and 3]. Therefore, by the definition of **and**, $q \wedge p$ is true [line 4].

(3.2.6)

1	$q \wedge p$	pr 1
2	q	$\wedge$-E, 1
3	p	$\wedge$-E, 1
4	$p \wedge q$	$\wedge$-I, 3, 2

From $q \wedge p$ infer $p \wedge q$

Proof (3.2.6) can be abbreviated by omitting lines containing premises and using "pr i" to refer to the ith premise later on, as shown in (3.2.7). This abbreviation will occur often. But note that this is only an abbreviation, and we will continue to use the phrase "occurs on a previous line" to include the premises, even though the abbreviation is used.

(3.2.7)

From $q \wedge p$ infer $p \wedge q$

1	q	$\wedge$-E, pr 1
2	p	$\wedge$-E, pr 1
3	$p \wedge q$	$\wedge$-I, 2, 1

Inference rule $\vee$-E

The inference rule for elimination of **or** is

(3.2.8) $\vee$-E: $$\dfrac{E_1 \vee \cdots \vee E_n, E_1 \Rightarrow E, \cdots, E_n \Rightarrow E}{E}$$

Rule $\vee$-E indicates that if a disjunction appears a previous line, and if $E_i \Rightarrow E$ appears on a previous line for each disjunct E_i, then E may be written on a line of the proof. If we assert "it will rain tomorrow or it will snow tomorrow", and if we assert "rain implies no sun", and if we also assert "snow implies no sun", then we can conclude "there will be no sun tomorrow". From

$$(rain \vee snow), (rain \Rightarrow no\ sun), (snow \Rightarrow no\ sun)$$

we conclude *no sun*.

Here is a simple example.

From $p \vee (q \wedge r), p \Rightarrow s, (q \wedge r) \Rightarrow s$ infer $s \vee p$

1	$p \vee (q \wedge r)$	pr 1
2	$p \Rightarrow s$	pr 2
3	$(q \wedge r) \Rightarrow s$	pr 3
4	s	$\vee$-E, 1, 2, 3
5	$s \vee p$	$\vee$-I (rule (3.2.3)), 4

Inference rule $\Rightarrow$-E

(3.2.9) $\Rightarrow$-E: $$\dfrac{E1 \Rightarrow E2, E1}{E2}$$

Rule $\Rightarrow$-E is called *modus ponens*. It allows us to write the consequent of an implication on a line of the proof if its antecedent appears on a previous line. If we assert that $x > 0$ implies that y is even, and if we determine that $x > 0$, then we can conclude that y is even.

We show an example of its use in proof (3.2.10). To show the relation between the formal proof and an English one, we give the proof in English: Suppose $p \wedge q$ and $p \Rightarrow r$ are both true. From $p \wedge q$ we conclude that p is true. Because $p \Rightarrow r$, the truth of p implies the truth of r, and r is true. But if r is true, so is r "ored" with anything; hence $r \vee (q \Rightarrow r)$ is true.

$$\text{From } p \wedge q, p \Rightarrow r \text{ infer } r \vee (q \Rightarrow r)$$

1	$p \wedge q$	pr 1
2	$p \Rightarrow r$	pr 2
3	p	$\wedge$-E (rule (3.2.2)), 1
4	r	$\Rightarrow$-E, 2, 3
5	$r \vee (q \Rightarrow r)$	$\vee$-I (rule (3.2.3)), 4

(3.2.10)

To emphasize the use of the abbreviation to refer to premises, we show (3.2.10) in its abbreviated form in (3.2.11).

$$\text{From } p \wedge q, p \Rightarrow r \text{ infer } r \vee (q \Rightarrow r)$$

1	p	$\wedge$-E, pr 1
2	r	$\Rightarrow$-E, pr 2, 1
3	$r \vee (q \Rightarrow r)$	$\vee$-I, 2

(3.2.11)

Inference rules =-I and =-E

(3.2.12) =-I: $\dfrac{E1 \Rightarrow E2,\ E2 \Rightarrow E1}{E1 = E2}$

(3.2.13) =-E: $\dfrac{E1 = E2}{E1 \Rightarrow E2,\ E2 \Rightarrow E1}$

Rules $=$-I and $=$-E together define equality in terms of implication. The premises of one rule are the conclusions of the other, and vice versa. This is quite similar to how equality is defined in the system of chapter 2. Rule $=$-I is used, then, to introduce an equality $e1 = e2$ based on the previous proof of $e1 \Rightarrow e2$ and $e2 \Rightarrow e1$.

Here is an example of the use of these rules.

From p, $p = (q \Rrightarrow r)$, $r \Rrightarrow q$ **infer** $r = q$

1	$p \Rrightarrow (q \Rrightarrow r)$	=-E, pr 2
2	$q \Rrightarrow r$	$\Rrightarrow$-E, 1, pr 1
3	$r = q$	=-I, pr 3, 2

Exercises for Section 3.2

1. Each of the following theorems can be proven using exactly one basic inference rule (using the abbreviation that premises need not be written on lines; see the text preceding (3.2.7)). Name that inference rule.

(a) **From** a, b **infer** $a \wedge b$
(b) **From** $a \wedge b \wedge (q \vee r)$, a **infer** $q \vee r$
(c) **From** $\neg a$ **infer** $\neg a \vee a$
(d) **From** $c = d$, $d \vee c$ **infer** $d \Rrightarrow c$
(e) **From** $b \Rrightarrow c$, b **infer** $b \vee \neg b$
(f) **From** $\neg a$, $\neg b$, c **infer** $\neg a \vee c$
(g) **From** $(a \Rrightarrow b) \wedge b$, a **infer** $a \Rrightarrow b$
(h) **From** $a \vee b \Rrightarrow c$, $c \Rrightarrow a \vee b$ **infer** $a \vee b = c$
(i) **From** $a \wedge b$, $q \vee r$ **infer** $(a \wedge b) \wedge (q \vee r)$
(j) **From** $p \Rrightarrow (q \Rrightarrow r)$, p, $q \vee r$ **infer** $q \Rrightarrow r$
(k) **From** $c \Rrightarrow d$, $d \Rrightarrow e$, $d \Rrightarrow c$ **infer** $c = d$
(l) **From** $a \vee b$, $a \vee c$, $(a \vee b) \Rrightarrow c$ **infer** c
(m) **From** $a \Rrightarrow (d \vee c)$, $(d \vee c) \Rrightarrow a$ **infer** $a = (d \vee c)$
(n) **From** $(a \vee b) \Rrightarrow c$, $(a \vee d) \Rrightarrow c$, $(a \vee b) \vee (a \vee d)$ **infer** c
(o) **From** $a \Rrightarrow (b \vee c)$, $b \Rrightarrow (b \vee c)$, $a \vee b$ **infer** $b \vee c$

2. Here is one proof that p follows from p. Write another proof that uses only one reference to the premise.

From p **infer** p

1	p	pr 1
2	p	pr 1

3. Prove the following theorems using the inference rules.

(a) **From** $p \wedge q$, $p \Rrightarrow r$ **infer** r
(b) **From** $p = q$, q **infer** p
(c) **From** p, $q \Rrightarrow r$, $p \Rrightarrow r$ **infer** $p \wedge r$
(d) **From** $b \wedge \neg c$ **infer** $\neg c$
(e) **From** b **infer** $b \vee \neg c$

(f) **From** $b \Rrightarrow c \wedge d$, b **infer** d
(g) **From** $p \wedge q$, $p \Rrightarrow r$ **infer** r
(h) **From** p, $q \wedge (p \Rrightarrow s)$ **infer** $q \wedge s$
(i) **From** $p = q$ **infer** $q = p$
(j) **From** $b \Rrightarrow (c \wedge d)$, b **infer** d

4. For each of your proofs of exercise 3, give an English version. (The English versions need not mimic the formal proofs exactly.)

3.3 Proofs and Subproofs

Inference rule ⇒-I

A theorem of the form "**From** $e_1 \cdots, e_n$ **infer** e" is interpreted as: if $e_1, ..., e_n$ are true in a state, then so is e. If $e_1, ..., e_n$ appear on lines of a proof, which is interpreted to mean that they are assumed or proven true, then we should be able to write e on a line also. Rule ⇒-I, (3.3.1), gives us permission to do so. Its premise need not appear on a previous line of the proof; it can appear elsewhere as a separate proof, which we refer to in substantiating the use of the rule. Unique names should be given to proofs to avoid ambiguous references.

$$(3.3.1) \quad \text{⇒-I:} \quad \frac{\textbf{From } E_1, \cdots, E_n \textbf{ infer } E}{(E_1 \wedge \cdots \wedge E_n) \Rightarrow E}$$

Proof (3.3.2) uses ⇒-I twice in order to prove that $p \wedge q$ and $q \wedge p$ are equivalent, using lemmas proved in the previous section.

$$(3.3.2)$$

	Infer $(p \wedge q) = (q \wedge p)$	
1	$(p \wedge q) \Rightarrow (q \wedge p)$	⇒-I, (3.2.5)
2	$(q \wedge p) \Rightarrow (p \wedge q)$	⇒-I, (3.2.6)
3	$(p \wedge q) = (q \wedge p)$	=-I, 1, 2

Rule ⇒-I allows us to conclude $p \Rightarrow q$ if we have a proof of q given premise p. On the other hand, if we take $p \Rightarrow q$ as a premise, then rule ⇒-E allows us to conclude that q holds when p is given. We see that the following relationship holds:

> **Deduction Theorem.** "**Infer** $p \Rightarrow q$" is a theorem of the natural deduction system, which can be interpreted to mean that $p \Rightarrow q$ is a tautology, *iff* "**From** p **infer** q" is a theorem. □

Another example of the use of ⇒-I shows that p implies itself:

$$(3.3.3)$$

	Infer $p \Rightarrow p$	
1	$p \Rightarrow p$	⇒-I, exercise 2 of section 3.2

Subproofs

A proof can be included within a proof, much the way a procedure can be included within a program. This allows the premise of ⇒-I to appear as a line of a proof. To illustrate this, (3.3.2) is rewritten in (3.3.4) to include proof (3.2.5) as a subproof. The subproof happens to be on line 1 here, but it could be on any line. If the subtheorem appears on line j

(say) of the main proof, then its proof appears indented underneath, with its lines numbered $j.1$, $j.2$, etc. We could have replaced the reference to (3.2.6) by a subproof in a similar manner.

Infer $(p \wedge q) = (q \wedge p)$

	1	**From** $p \wedge q$ **infer** $q \wedge p$		
		1.1	p	$\wedge$-E, pr 1
		1.2	q	$\wedge$-E, pr 1
(3.3.4)		1.3	$q \wedge p$	$\wedge$-I, 1.2, 1.1
	2	$(p \wedge q) \Rightarrow (q \wedge p)$		$\Rightarrow$-I, 1
	3	$(q \wedge p) \Rightarrow (p \wedge q)$		$\Rightarrow$-I, (3.2.6)
	4	$(p \wedge q) = (q \wedge p)$		=-I, 2, 3

Another example of a proof with a subproof is given in (3.3.5). Again, it may be instructive to compare the proof to an English version:

> Suppose $(q \vee s) \Rightarrow (p \wedge q)$. To prove equivalence, we must show also that $(p \wedge q) \Rightarrow (q \vee s)$. [Note how this uses rule $=$-I, that $a \Rightarrow b$ and $b \Rightarrow a$ means $a = b$. These sentences correspond to lines 1, 3 and 4 of the formal proof.] To prove $(p \wedge q) \Rightarrow (q \vee s)$, argue as follows. Assume $p \wedge q$ is true. Then so is q. By the definition of **or**, so is $q \vee s$. [Note the correspondence to lines 2.1-2.2.] □

From $(q \vee s) \Rightarrow (p \wedge q)$ **infer** $(q \vee s) = (p \wedge q)$

	1	$(q \vee s) \Rightarrow (p \wedge q)$		pr 1
	2	**From** $p \wedge q$ **infer** $q \vee s$		
(3.3.5)		2.1	q	$\wedge$-E, pr 1
		2.2	$q \vee s$	$\vee$-I, 2.1
	3	$(p \wedge q) \Rightarrow (q \vee s)$		$\Rightarrow$-I, 2
	4	$(q \vee s) = (p \wedge q)$		=-I, 1, 3

As mentioned earlier, the relationship between proofs and sub-proofs in logic is similar to the relationship between procedures and sub-procedures (modules and sub-modules) in programs. A theorem and its proof can be used in two ways: first, use the theorem to prove something else; secondly, study the proof of the theorem. A procedure and its description can be used in two ways: first, understand the description so that calls of the procedure can be written; secondly, study the procedure body to understand how the procedure works. This similarity should make the idea of subproofs easy to understand.

Scope rules

A subproof can contain references not only to previous lines in its proof, but also to previous lines that occur in surrounding proofs. We call these *global* line references. However, "recursion" is not allowed; a line j (say) may not contain a reference to a theorem whose proof is not finished by line j.

The reader skilled in the use of block structure in languages like PL/I, ALGOL 60 and Pascal will have no difficulty in understanding this scope rule, for essentially the same scope mechanism is employed here (except for the restriction against recursion). Let us state the rule more precisely.

(3.3.6)   **Scope rule.** Line i of a proof, where i is an integer, may contain references to lines $1, ..., i-1$. Line $j.i$, where i is an integer, may contain references to lines $j.1, ..., j.(i-1)$ and to any lines referenceable from line j (this excludes references to line j itself).   □

Example (3.3.7) illustrates the use of this scope rule; line 2.2 refers to line 1, which is outside the proof of line 2.

	From $p \Rightarrow (q \Rightarrow r)$ infer $(p \wedge q) \Rightarrow r$		
1	$p \Rightarrow (q \Rightarrow r)$		pr 1
2	**From $p \wedge q$ infer r**		
(3.3.7)	2.1	p	$\wedge$-E, pr 1
	2.2	$q \Rightarrow r$	$\Rightarrow$-E, 1, 2.1
	2.3	q	$\wedge$-E, pr 1
	2.4	r	$\Rightarrow$-E, 2.2, 2.3
3	$(p \wedge q) \Rightarrow r$		$\Rightarrow$-I, 2

Below we illustrate an invalid use of the scope rule.

	From p infer $p \Rightarrow \neg p$ (Proof INVALID)		
1	p		pr 1
2	**From p infer $\neg p$**		
	2.1	p	pr 1
	2.2	$p \Rightarrow \neg p$	$\Rightarrow$-I, 2 (invalid reference to line 2)
3	$p \Rightarrow \neg p$		$\Rightarrow$-I, 2 (valid reference to line 2)

We illustrate another common mistake below; the use of a line that is not in a surrounding proof. Below, on line 6.1 an attempt is made to reference s on line 4.1. Since line 4.1 is not in a *surrounding* proof, this is not allowed.

A subproof using global references is being proved *in a particular context*. Taken out of context, the subproof may not be true because it relies

From $p \lor q, p \Rightarrow s, s \Rightarrow r$ **infer** r (proof INVALID)

1	$p \lor q$		pr 1
2	$p \Rightarrow s$		pr 2
3	$s \Rightarrow r$		pr 3
4	**From** p **infer** r		
	4.1	s	$\Rightarrow$-E, 2, pr 1 (valid reference to 2)
	4.2	r	$\Rightarrow$-E, 3, 4.1 (valid reference to 3)
5	$p \Rightarrow r$		$\Rightarrow$-I, 4
6	**From** q **infer** r		
	6.1	r	$\Rightarrow$-E, 3, 4.1 (invalid reference to 4.1)
7	$q \Rightarrow r$		$\Rightarrow$-I, 6
8	r		$\lor$-E, 1, 5, 7

on assumptions about the context. This again points up the similarity between ALGOL-like procedures and subproofs. Facts assumed outside a subproof can be used within the proof, just as variables declared outside a procedure can be used within a procedure, using the same scope mechanism.

To end this discussion of scope, we give a proof with two levels of subproof. It can be understood most easily as follows. First read lines 1, 2 and 3 (don't read the the proof of the lemma on line 2) and satisfy yourself that *if* the proof of the lemma on line 2 is correct, then the whole proof is correct. Next, study the proof of the lemma on line 2 (only lines 2.1, 2.2 and 2.3). Finally, study the proof of the lemma on line 2.2, which refers to a line two levels out in the proof.

From $(p \land q) \Rightarrow r$ **infer** $p \Rightarrow (q \Rightarrow r)$

	1	$(p \land q) \Rightarrow r$		pr 1
	2	**From** p **infer** $q \Rightarrow r$		
(3.3.8)		2.1	p	pr 1
		2.2	**From** q **infer** r	
			2.2.1	$p \land q$ $\land$-I, 2.1, pr 1
			2.2.2	r $\Rightarrow$-E, 1, 2.2.1
		2.3	$q \Rightarrow r$	$\Rightarrow$-I, 2.2
	3	$p \Rightarrow (q \Rightarrow r)$		$\Rightarrow$-I, 2

Proof by contradiction

A proof by contradiction typically proceeds as follows. One makes an assumption. From this assumption one proceeds to prove a contradiction, say, by showing that something is both true and false. Since such a contradiction cannot possibly happen, and since the proof from assumption to contradiction is valid, the assumption must be false.

Proof by contradiction is embodied in the proof rules ¬-I and ¬-E:

$$(3.3.9) \quad \text{¬-I:} \quad \frac{\textbf{From } E \textbf{ infer } E1 \wedge \text{¬} E1}{\text{¬} E}$$

$$(3.3.10) \quad \text{¬-E:} \quad \frac{\textbf{From } \text{¬} E \textbf{ infer } E1 \wedge \text{¬} E1}{E}$$

Rule ¬-I indicates that if "**From** E **infer** $E1 \wedge \text{¬} E1$" has been proved for some proposition $E1$, then one can write $\text{¬} E$ on a line of the proof.

Rule ¬-I similarly allows us to conclude that E holds if a proof of "**From** $\text{¬} E$ **infer** $E1 \wedge \text{¬} E1$" exists, for some proposition $E1$.

We show in (3.3.11) an example of the use of rule ¬-I, that from p we can conclude $\text{¬¬} p$.

		From p infer $\text{¬¬} p$	
	1	p	pr 1
(3.3.11)	2	**From $\text{¬} p$ infer $p \wedge \text{¬} p$**	
		2.1 $\quad p \wedge \text{¬} p$	∧-I, 1, pr 1
	3	$\text{¬¬} p$	¬-I, 2

Rule ¬-I is used to prove that $\text{¬¬} p$ follows from p; similarly, rule ¬-E is used in (3.3.12) to prove that p follows from $\text{¬¬} p$.

		From $\text{¬¬} p$ infer p	
	1	$\text{¬¬} p$	pr 1
(3.3.12)	2	**From $\text{¬} p$ infer $\text{¬} p \wedge \text{¬¬} p$**	
		2.1 $\quad \text{¬} p \wedge \text{¬¬} p$	∧-I, pr 1, 1
	3	p	¬-E, 2

Theorems (3.3.11) and (3.3.12) look quite similar, and yet both proofs are needed; one cannot simply get one from the other more easily than they are proven here. More importantly, both of the *rules* ¬-I and ¬-E are needed; if one is omitted from the proof system, we will be unable to deduce some propositions that are tautologies in the sense described in section 1.5. This may seem strange, since the rules look so similar.

Let us give two more proofs. The first one indicates that from p and $\text{¬} p$ one can prove *any* proposition q, even one that is equivalent to false. This is because both p and $\text{¬} p$ cannot both be true at the same time, and hence the premises form an absurdity.

From p, $\neg p$ **infer** q

1	p	pr 1
2	$\neg p$	pr 2

(3.3.13) 3 **From** $\neg q$ **infer** $p \wedge \neg p$

3.1	$p \wedge \neg p$	$\wedge$-I, 1, 2
4	q	$\neg$-E, 3

From $p \wedge q$ **infer** $\neg(p \Rightarrow \neg q)$

1	$p \wedge q$	pr 1
2	**From** $p \Rightarrow \neg q$ **infer** $q \wedge \neg q$	

(3.3.14)

2.1	p	$\wedge$-E, 1
2.2	q	$\wedge$-E, 1
2.3	$\neg q$	$\Rightarrow$-E, pr 1, 2.1
2.4	$q \wedge \neg q$	$\wedge$-I, 2.2, 2.3
3	$\neg(p \Rightarrow \neg q)$	$\neg$-I, 2

For comparison, we give an English version of proof (3.3.14). Let $p \wedge q$ be true. Then both p and q are true. Assume that $p \Rightarrow \neg q$ is true. Because p is true this implication allows us to conclude that $\neg q$ is true, but this is absurd because q is true. Hence the assumption that $p \Rightarrow \neg q$ is true is wrong, and $\neg(p \Rightarrow \neg q)$ holds.

Summary

The reader may have noticed a difference between the natural deduction system and the previous systems of evaluation and equivalence transformation: the natural deduction system does not allow the use of constants T and F! The connection between the systems can be stated as follows. If "**Infer** e" is a theorem of the natural deduction system, then e is a tautology and $e = T$ is an equivalence. On the other hand, if $e = T$ is a tautology and e does not contain T and F, then "**Infer** e" is a theorem of the natural deduction system. The omission of T and F is no problem because, by the rule of Substitution, in any proposition T can be replaced by a tautology (e.g. $b \vee \neg b$) and F by the complement of a tautology (e.g. $b \wedge \neg b$) to yield an equivalent proposition.

We summarize what a proof is as follows. A proof of a theorem "**From** $e_1, \cdots, e_n$ **infer** e" or of a theorem "**Infer** e" consists of a sequence of lines. The first line contains the theorem. If the first line is unnumbered, the rest are indented and numbered 1, 2, etc. If the first line has the number i, the rest are indented and numbered $i.1$, $i.2$, etc. The last line must contain proposition e. Each line i must have one of the following four forms:

Form 1: $(i)\ e_j$ pr j

where $1 \leqslant j \leqslant n$. The line contains premise j.

Form 2: $(i)\ p$ *Name, ref* $_1$, ..., *ref* $_q$

Each *ref* $_k$ either (1) is a line number (which is valid according to scope rule (3.3.6)), or (2) has the form "pr j", in which case it refers to premise e_j of the theorem, or (3) is the name of a previously proven theorem. Let r_k denote the proposition or theorem referred to by *ref* $_k$. Then the following must be an instance of inference rule *Name*:

$$\frac{r_1, \ \cdots \ , r_q}{p}$$

Form 3: $(i)\ p$ *Theorem name, ref* $_1$, ..., *ref* $_q$

Theorem name is the name of a previously proved theorem; *ref* $_k$ is as in Form 2. Let r_k denote the proposition referred to be *ref* $_k$. Then "**From** $r_1, \ \cdots \ , r_q$ **infer** p" must be the named theorem.

Form 4: (i) [Proof of another theorem]

That is, the line contains a complete subproof, whose format follows these rules.

Figure 3.3.1 contains a list of the inference rules.

Historical Notes

The style of the logical system defined in this chapter was conceived principally to capture our "natural" patterns of reasoning. Gerhard Gentzen, a German mathematician who died in an Allied prisoner of war camp just after World War II, developed such a system for mathematical arguments in his 1935 paper *Untersuchungen ueber das logische Schliessen* [20], which is included in [43].

Several textbooks on logic are based on natural deduction, for example W.V.O. Quine's book *Methods of Logic* [41].

The particular block-structured system given here was developed using two sources: *WFF'N PROOF: The Game of Modern Logic*, by Layman E. Allen [1], and the monograph *A Programming Logic*, by Robert Constable and Michael O'Donnell [7]. The former introduces the deduction system through a series of games; it uses prefix notation, partly to avoid problems with parentheses, which we have sidestepped through informality. *A Programming Logic* describes a mechanical program verifier for

PL/CS (a subset of PL/C, which is a subset of PL/I), developed at Cornell University. Its inference rules were developed with ease of presentation and mechanical verification in mind. Actually, the verifier can be used to verify proofs of programs, and includes not only the propositional calculus but also a predicate calculus, including a theory of integers and a theory of strings.

$$\wedge\text{-I:} \quad \frac{E_1, \ldots, E_n}{E_1 \wedge \ldots \wedge E_n} \qquad\qquad \wedge\text{-E:} \quad \frac{E_1 \wedge \ldots \wedge E_n}{E_i}$$

$$\vee\text{-I:} \quad \frac{E_i}{E_1 \vee \ldots \vee E_n} \qquad\qquad \vee\text{-E:} \quad \frac{E_1 \vee \ldots \vee E_n, \; E_1 \Rightarrow E, \; \ldots, \; E_n \Rightarrow E}{E}$$

$$\neg\text{-I:} \quad \frac{\textbf{From } E \textbf{ infer } E1 \wedge \neg E1}{\neg E} \qquad \neg\text{-E:} \quad \frac{\textbf{From } \neg E \textbf{ infer } E1 \wedge \neg E1}{E}$$

$$=\text{-I:} \quad \frac{E1 \Rightarrow E2, \; E2 \Rightarrow E1}{E1 = E2} \qquad\qquad =\text{-E:} \quad \frac{E1 = E2}{E1 \Rightarrow E2, \; E2 \Rightarrow E1}$$

$$\Rightarrow\text{-I:} \quad \frac{\textbf{From } E_1, \ldots, E_n \textbf{ infer } E}{(E_1 \wedge \ldots \wedge E_n) \Rightarrow E} \qquad \Rightarrow\text{-E:} \quad \frac{E1 \Rightarrow E2, \; E1}{E2}$$

Figure 3.3.1 The Set of Basic Inference Rules

Exercises for Section 3.3

1. Use lemma (3.2.11) and inference rule $\Rightarrow$-I to give a 1-line proof that $(p \wedge q \wedge (p \Rightarrow r)) \Rightarrow (r \vee (q \Rightarrow r))$.

2. Prove that $(p \wedge q) \Rightarrow (p \vee q)$, using rule $\Rightarrow$-I.

3. Prove that $q \Rightarrow (q \wedge q)$. Prove that $(q \wedge q) \Rightarrow q$. Use the first two results to prove that $q = (q \wedge q)$. Then rewrite the last proof so that it does not refer to outside proofs.

4. Prove that $p = (p \vee p)$.

5. Prove that $p \Rightarrow ((r \vee s) \Rightarrow p)$.

6. Prove that $q \Rightarrow (r \Rightarrow (q \wedge r))$.

7. Prove that from $p \Rightarrow (r \Rightarrow s)$ follows $r \Rightarrow (p \Rightarrow s)$.

8. What is wrong with the following proof?

Infer $a \Rightarrow b$ (Proof INVALID)

1	a	pr 1
2	**From** $\lnot b$ **infer** $b \land \lnot b$	
	2.1	$\lnot b$	pr 1
	2.2	$\lnot b \Rightarrow b \land \lnot b$	$\Rightarrow$-I, 2
	2.3	$b \land \lnot b$	$\Rightarrow$-E, 2.2, 2.1
2	b	$\lnot$-E, 2

9. Prove that from $\lnot p$ and $(\lnot p \Rightarrow q) \lor (p \land (r \Rightarrow q))$ follows $r \Rightarrow q$.

10. Prove that $q \Rightarrow (p \land r)$ follows from $q \Rightarrow p$ and $q \Rightarrow r$.

11. Prove that from $\lnot q$ follows $q \Rightarrow p$.

12. Prove that from $\lnot q$ follows $q \Rightarrow \lnot p$.

13. Prove that from $\lnot q$ follows $q \Rightarrow (p \land \lnot p)$.

14. Prove that from $p \lor q$, $\lnot q$ follows p.

15. Prove $p \land (p \Rightarrow q) \Rightarrow q$.

16. Prove $((p \Rightarrow q) \land (q \Rightarrow r)) \Rightarrow (p \Rightarrow r)$.

17. Prove $(p \Rightarrow q) \Rightarrow ((p \land \lnot q) \Rightarrow q)$.

18. Prove $((p \land \lnot q) \Rightarrow q) \Rightarrow (p \Rightarrow q)$. [This, together with exercise 17, allows us to prove $(p \Rightarrow q) = ((p \land \lnot q) \Rightarrow q)$.]

19. Prove $(p \Rightarrow q) \Rightarrow ((p \land \lnot q) \Rightarrow \lnot p)$.

20. Prove $((p \land \lnot q) \Rightarrow \lnot p) \Rightarrow (p \Rightarrow q)$. [This, together with exercise 19, allows us to prove $(p \Rightarrow q) = ((p \land \lnot q) \Rightarrow \lnot p)$.]

21. Prove that $(p = q) \Rightarrow (\lnot p = \lnot q)$.

22. Prove that $(\lnot p = \lnot q) \Rightarrow (p = q)$. [This, together with exercise 21, allows us to prove $(p = q) = (\lnot p = \lnot q)$.]

23. Prove $\lnot(p = q) \Rightarrow (\lnot p = q)$

24. Prove $(\lnot p = q) \Rightarrow \lnot(p = q)$. [This, together with exercise 21, allows us to prove the law of Inequality, $\lnot(p = q) = (\lnot p = q)$.]

25. Prove $(p = q) \Rightarrow (q = p)$.

26. Use a rule of Contradiction to prove **From** p **infer** p.

27. For each of the proofs of exercise 1-7, 9-25, give a version in English. (It need not follow the formal proof exactly.)

3.4 Adding Flexibility to the Natural Deduction System

We first introduce some flexibility by showing how theorems can be viewed as schemas —i.e. how identifiers in a theorem can be viewed as standing for any arbitrary proposition. Next, we introduce a rule of substitution of equals for equals, incorporating into the natural deduction system the method of proving equivalences of chapter 2. We prove a number of theorems, including the laws of equivalence of chapter 2.

Using theorems as schemas

The inference rules given in Figure 3.3.1 hold for any propositions E, $E_1, ..., E_n$. They are really "schemas", and one gets a particular inference rule by substituting particular propositions for the "placeholders" E, E_1, ..., E_n. On the other hand, theorems of the form "**From** *premises* **infer** *conclusion*" are proved only for particular propositions. For example, proof (3.3.2) used the following two theorems (3.2.5) and (3.2.6):

> **From** $p \land q$ **infer** $q \land p$
>
> **From** $q \land p$ **infer** $p \land q$

Even though it looks like the second should follow directly from the first, in the formal system both must be proved.

But we can prove something *about* the formal system: systematic substitution of propositions for identifiers in a theorem and its proof yields another theorem and proof. So we can consider any theorem to be a schema also. For example, from proof (3.2.5) of "**From** $p \land q$ **infer** $q \land p$ " we can generate a proof of "**From** $(a \lor b) \land c$ **infer** $c \land (a \lor b)$" simply by substituting $a \lor b$ for p and c for q everywhere in proof (3.2.5):

From $(a \lor b) \land c$ **infer** $c \land (a \lor b)$

1	$(a \lor b) \land c$	pr 1
2	$a \lor b$	$\land$-E, 1
3	c	$\land$-E, 1
4	$c \land (a \lor b)$	$\land$-I, 3, 2

Let us state more precisely this idea of textual substitution in theorem and proof.

(3.4.1)   **Theorem**. Write a theorem as a function of one of its identifiers, p: "**From** $E_1(p), ..., E_n(p)$ **infer** $E(p)$". Let G be any proposition. Then "**From** $E_1(G), ..., E_n(G)$ **infer** $E(G)$" can also be proved.

Informal proof. Without loss of generality, assume the proof of the theorem contains no references to other theorems outside the proof. (If it does, first change the proof to include them as subproofs, as was done in generating proof (3.3.4) from proof (3.3.2), repeating the process until no references to outside theorems exist.) Then we can obtain a proof of the new theorem simply by substituting G for p everywhere in the proof of the original theorem. □

Theorems like (3.4.1) are often called *meta*-theorems, because they are not theorems in the proof system, like "**From** ... **infer** ...", but are proofs *about* the proof system. The use of meta-theorems takes us outside the formal system just a bit, but it is worthwhile to relax formality in this way.

We can put meta-theorem (3.4.1) in the form of a *derived rule of inference* as follows:

$$(3.4.2) \quad \frac{\textbf{From } E_1(p), \cdots, E_n(p) \textbf{ infer } E(p)}{\textbf{From } E_1(G), \cdots, E_n(G) \textbf{ infer } E(G)} \quad (p \text{ an identifier})$$

We use this derived rule of inference to rewrite theorem (3.3.2) using only theorem (3.2.5) (and not (3.2.6)). Note how line 2 refers to theorem (3.2.5) and indicates what propositions are being replaced. We often leave out this indication if it is obvious enough.

Infer $(p \wedge q) = (q \wedge p)$

1	$(p \wedge q) \Rightarrow (q \wedge p)$	(3.2.5)
2	$(q \wedge p) \Rightarrow (p \wedge q)$	(3.2.5) (with p for q, q for p)
3	$(p \wedge q) = (q \wedge p)$	=-I, 1, 2

Earlier, we discussed the relation between procedures of a program and subproofs of a proof. We can now extend this relation to procedures with parameters and subproofs with parameters. Consider rule (3.4.2). The proof of the premise corresponds to the definition of a procedure with a parameter p. The use of the conclusion in another proof corresponds to a call of the procedure with an argument G.

The Rule of Substitution of equals for equals

The rule of Substitution, introduced in section 2.2, will be used in this section in the following form.

(3.4.3)   **Theorem.** Let proposition E be thought of as a function of one of its identifiers, p, so that we write it as $E(p)$. Then if $e1 = e2$ and $E(e1)$ appear on previous lines, then we may write $E(e2)$ on a line.   □

For example, given that $c \Rightarrow a \lor b$ is true, to show that $c \Rightarrow b \lor a$ is true we take $E(p)$ to be $c \Rightarrow p$, $e1 = e2$ to be $a \lor b = b \lor a$ (the law of Commutativity, which will be proved later) and apply the theorem.

    The rule of Substitution was an inference rule in the equivalence system of chapter 2. However, it is a meta-theorem of the natural deduction system and must be proved. Its proof, which would be performed by induction on the structure of proposition $E(p)$, is left to the interested reader in exercise 10, so let us suppose it has been done. We put the rule of Substitution in the form of a derived inference rule:

(3.4.4)   subs: $\dfrac{e1 = e2,\; E(e1)}{E(e2)}$ ($E(p)$ is a function of p)

To show the use of (3.4.4), we give a schematic proof to show that the rule of substitution as given in section 2.2 holds here also.

	From $e1 = e2$ infer $E(e1) = E(e2)$	
1	$e1 = e2$	pr 1
2	**From $E(e1)$ infer $E(e2)$**	
	2.1 | $E(e2)$	subs, pr 1, 1
3	$E(e1) \Rightarrow E(e2)$	$\Rightarrow$-I, 2
4	**From $E(e2)$ infer $E(e1)$**	
	4.1 | $e2 = e1$	=-I, (3.3.3) $(p \Rightarrow p)$
	4.2 | $E(e1)$	subs, 4.1, pr 1
5	$E(e2) \Rightarrow E(e1)$	$\Rightarrow$-I, 4
6	$E(e1) = E(e2)$	=-I, 3, 5

(3.4.5)

With this derived rule of inference, we have the flexibility of both the equivalence and the natural deduction systems. But we must make sure that the laws of section 2.1 actually hold! We do this next.

Some basic theorems

    A number of theorems are used often, including the laws of section 2.1. We want to state them here and prove some of them; the rest of the proofs are left as exercises. The first to be proved is quite useful. It states that if at least one of two propositions is true, and if the first is false, then the second is true.

From $p \vee q$, $\neg p$ **infer** q

	1	$\neg p$		pr 2
(3.4.6)	2	**From** p **infer** q		
		2.1	p	pr 1
		2.2	**From** $\neg q$ **infer** $p \wedge \neg p$	
			2.2.1 $\quad p \wedge \neg p$	$\wedge$-I, 2.1, 1
		2.3	q	$\neg$-E, 2.2
	3	$p \Rightarrow q$		$\Rightarrow$-I, 2
	4	q		$\vee$-E, pr 1, 3, (3.3.3)

We now turn to the laws of section 2.1. Some of their proofs are given here; the others are left as exercises to the reader.

1. *Commutative laws.* $(p \wedge q) = (q \wedge p)$ was proven in theorem (3.3.4); the other two commutative laws are left to the reader to prove.

2. *Associative laws.* These we don't need to prove since the inference rules for **and** and **or** were written using any number of operands and no parentheses.

3. *Distributive laws.* Here is a proof of the first; the second is left to the reader. The proof is broken into three parts. The first part proves an implication $\Rightarrow$ and the second part proves it in the other direction, so that the third can prove the equivalence. The second part uses a case analysis (rule $\vee$-E) on $b \vee \neg b$ —the law of the Excluded Middle— which is not proved until later. The use of $b \vee \neg b$ in this fashion occurs often

From $b \vee (c \wedge d)$ **infer** $(b \vee c) \wedge (b \vee d)$

	1	**From** b **infer** $(b \vee c) \wedge (b \vee d)$		
		1.1	$b \vee c$	$\vee$-I, pr 1
		1.2	$b \vee d$	$\vee$-I, pr 1
(3.4.7)		1.3	$(b \vee c) \wedge (b \vee d)$	$\wedge$-I, 1.1, 1.2
	2	$b \Rightarrow (b \vee c) \wedge (b \vee d)$		$\Rightarrow$-I, 1
	3	**From** $c \wedge d$ **infer** $(b \vee c) \wedge (b \vee d)$		
		3.1	c	$\wedge$-E, pr 1
		3.2	d	$\wedge$-E, pr 1
		3.3	$b \vee c$	$\vee$-I, 3.1
		3.4	$b \vee d$	$\vee$-I, 3.2
		3.5	$(b \vee c) \wedge (b \vee d)$	$\wedge$-I, 3.3, 3.4
	4	$(c \wedge d) \Rightarrow (b \vee c) \wedge (b \vee d)$		$\Rightarrow$-I, 3
	5	$(b \vee c) \wedge (b \vee d)$		$\vee$-E, pr 1, 2, 4

From $(b \lor c) \land (b \lor d)$ **infer** $b \lor (c \land d)$

1	$b \lor c$	$\land$-E, pr 1
2	$b \lor d$	$\land$-E, pr 1
3	$b \lor \neg b$	(3.4.14)
4	**From** b **infer** $b \lor (c \land d)$	

	4.1	$b \lor (c \land d)$	$\lor$-I, pr 1

5	$b \Rightarrow b \lor (c \land d)$	$\Rightarrow$-I, 4

(3.4.8) 6 **From** $\neg b$ **infer** $b \lor (c \land d)$

	6.1	c	(3.4.6), 1, pr 1
	6.2	d	(3.4.6), 2, pr 1
	6.3	$c \land d$	$\land$-I, 6.1, 6.2
	6.4	$b \lor (c \land d)$	$\lor$-I, 6.3

7	$\neg b \Rightarrow b \lor (c \land d)$	$\Rightarrow$-I, 6
8	$b \lor (c \land d)$	$\lor$-E, 3, 5, 7

(3.4.9) **Infer** $b \lor (c \land d) = (b \lor c) \land (b \lor d)$

1	$b \lor (c \land d) \Rightarrow (b \lor c) \land (b \lor d)$	$\Rightarrow$-I, (3.4.7)
2	$(b \lor c) \land (b \lor d) \Rightarrow b \lor (c \land d)$	$\Rightarrow$-I, (3.4.8)
3	$b \lor (c \land d) = (b \lor c) \land (b \lor d)$	=-I, 1, 2

4. *De Morgans's laws.* We prove only the first one here.

From $\neg(b \land c)$ **infer** $\neg b \lor \neg c$

1	$\neg(b \land c)$	pr 1
2	**From** $\neg(\neg b \lor \neg c)$ **infer** $(b \land c) \land \neg(b \land c)$	

	2.1	$\neg(\neg b \lor \neg c)$	pr 1
	2.2	**From** $\neg b$ **infer** $(\neg b \lor \neg c) \land \neg(\neg b \lor \neg c)$	

(3.4.10)

		2.2.1	$\neg b \lor \neg c$	$\lor$-I, pr 1
		2.2.2	$(\neg b \lor \neg c) \land \neg(\neg b \lor \neg c)$	$\land$-I, 2.2.1, 2.1

	2.3	b	$\neg$-E, 2.2
	2.4	**From** $\neg c$ **infer** $(\neg b \lor \neg c) \land \neg(\neg b \lor \neg c)$	

		2.4.1	$\neg b \lor \neg c$	$\lor$-I, pr 1
		2.4.2	$(\neg b \lor \neg c) \land \neg(\neg b \lor \neg c)$	$\land$-I, 2.4.1, 2.1

	2.5	c	$\neg$-E, 2.4
	2.6	$b \land c$	$\land$-I, 2.3, 2.5
	2.7	$(b \land c) \land \neg(b \land c)$	$\land$-I, 2.6, 1

3	$\neg b \lor \neg c$	$\neg$-E, 2

From $\neg b \vee \neg c$ **infer** $\neg(b \wedge c)$

1	**From** $\neg b$ **infer** $\neg(b \wedge c)$		
	1.1	$\neg b$	pr 1
	1.2	**From** $b \wedge c$ **infer** $b \wedge \neg b$	
		1.2.1	b	$\wedge$-E, pr 1
		1.2.2	$b \wedge \neg b$	$\wedge$-I, 1.2.1, 1.1
	1.3	$\neg(b \wedge c)$	$\neg$-I, 1.2
2	$\neg b \Rightarrow \neg(b \wedge c)$		$\Rightarrow$-I, 1
3	**From** $\neg c$ **infer** $\neg(b \wedge c)$		
	3.1	$\neg c$	pr 1
	3.2	**From** $b \wedge c$ **infer** $c \wedge \neg c$	
		3.2.1	c	$\wedge$-E, pr 1
		3.2.2	$c \wedge \neg c$	$\wedge$-I, 3.2.1, 3.1
	3.3	$\neg(b \wedge c)$	$\neg$-I, 3.2
4	$\neg c \Rightarrow \neg(b \wedge c)$		$\Rightarrow$-I, 3
5	$\neg(b \wedge c)$		$\vee$-E, pr 1, 2, 4

(3.4.11) appears to the left of this proof.

(3.4.12) **Infer** $\neg(b \wedge c) = \neg b \vee \neg c$

1	$\neg(b \wedge c) \Rightarrow \neg b \vee \neg c$	$\Rightarrow$-I, (3.4.10)
2	$\neg b \vee \neg c \Rightarrow \neg(b \wedge c)$	$\Rightarrow$-I, (3.4.11)
3	$\neg(b \wedge c) = \neg b \vee \neg c$	=-I, 1, 2

5. *Law of Negation.* This one is extremely simple because we have already done the necessary groundwork in previous theorems:

(3.4.13) **Infer** $\neg \neg b = b$

1	$b \Rightarrow \neg \neg b$	$\Rightarrow$-I, (3.3.11)
2	$\neg \neg b \Rightarrow b$	$\Rightarrow$-I, (3.3.12)
3	$\neg \neg b = b$	=-I, 1, 2

6. *Law of the Excluded Middle.* This proof proceeds by assuming the converse and proving a contradiction in a straightforward manner.

Infer $b \vee \neg b$

1	**From** $\neg(b \vee \neg b)$ **infer** $(b \vee \neg b) \wedge \neg(b \vee \neg b)$	
	1.1 $\quad \neg(b \vee \neg b)$	pr 1
	1.2 $\quad$ **From** $\neg b$ **infer** $(b \vee \neg b) \wedge \neg(b \vee \neg b)$	
(3.4.14)	$\qquad$ 1.2.1 $\quad b \vee \neg b$	$\vee$-I, pr 1
	$\qquad$ 1.2.2 $\quad (b \vee \neg b) \wedge \neg(b \vee \neg b)$	$\wedge$-I, 1.2.1, 1.1
	1.3 $\quad b$	$\neg$-E, 1.2
	1.4 $\quad b \vee \neg b$	$\vee$-I, 1.3
	1.5 $\quad (b \vee \neg b) \wedge \neg(b \vee \neg b)$	$\wedge$-I, 1.4, pr 1
2	$b \vee \neg b$	$\neg$-E, 1

7. *Law of Contradiction.* Left to the reader.

8. *Law of Implication.* Left to the reader.

9. *Law of Equality.* Left to the reader.

10–11. *Laws of* **or-** *and* **and-***Simplification.* These laws use the constants T and F, which don't appear in the inference system.

Exercises for Section 3.4

1. Use the idea in theorem (3.4.1) to derive from (3.3.7) a proof that $(p \wedge q) \Rightarrow (p \vee q)$ follows from $p \Rightarrow (q \Rightarrow p \vee q)$.

2. Use the idea in theorem (3.4.1) to derive from (3.3.8) a proof that from $(q \wedge r \wedge q) \Rightarrow r$ follows $(q \wedge r) \Rightarrow (q \Rightarrow r)$.

3. Use the idea in theorem (3.4.1) to derive from (3.3.4) a proof that $(a \wedge b \wedge c) = (c \wedge a \wedge b)$.

4. Prove the second and third Commutative laws, $(b \vee c) = (c \vee b)$ and $(b = c) = (c = b)$.

5. Prove the second Distributive law, $b \wedge (c \vee d) = (b \wedge c) \vee (b \wedge d)$.

6. Prove the second of De Morgan's laws, $\neg(b \vee c) = \neg b \wedge \neg c$.

7. Prove the law of Contradiction, $\neg(b \wedge \neg b)$.

8. Prove the law of Implication, $b \vee c = (\neg b \Rightarrow c)$.

9. Prove the law of Equality, $(b = c) = (b \Rightarrow c) \wedge (c \Rightarrow b)$.

10. Prove theorem (3.4.3).

11. Prove the rule of Transitivity: from $a = b$ and $b = c$ follows $a = c$.

12. Prove that from $p \vee q$ and $\neg q$ follows p (see (3.4.6)).

3.5 Developing Natural Deduction System Proofs

The reader has no doubt struggled to prove some theorems in the natural deduction system, and has wondered whether such proofs could be developed in a systematic manner. This section should provide some help.

We will begin to be less formal, stating facts without formal proof and taking larger steps in a proof when doing so does not hamper understanding. This is not only convenient; it is necessary. While the formal methods are indispensable for learning about propositions, one must begin to use the insight they supply instead of the complete formality they require in order to keep from being buried under mounds of detail.

To help the reader take a more active role in the development of the proofs, they will be presented as follows. At each step, a question will be posed, which must be answered in order to invent the next step in the proof. The answer will be separated from the question by white space and an underline, so that the reader can try to answer the question before proceeding. In this way, the reader can actually develop each step of the proof and check it with the one presented.

Some general hints on developing proofs

Suppose a theorem of the form "**From** *e1*, *e2* **infer** *e3*" is to be proved. The proof must have the form

From *e1*, *e2* infer *e3*

1	*e1*	pr 1
2	*e2*	pr 2
3	*e3*	Why?

and we need only substantiate line 3 —i.e. give a reason why *e3* can be written on it. We can look to three things for insight. First, we may be able to combine the premises or derive sub-propositions from them in some fashion, if not to produce *e3* at least to get something that looks similar to it.

Secondly, we can investigate *e3* itself. Since an inference rule must be used to substantiate line 3, the form of *e3* should help us decide which inference rule to use. And this leads us to the third piece of information we can use, the inference rules themselves. There are ten inference rules, which yields a lot of possibilities. Fortunately, few of them will apply to any particular proposition *e3*, because *e3* must have the form of the conclusion of the inference rule used to substantiate it. And, with the additional information of the premises, the number of actual possibilities can be reduced even more.

For example, if $e3$ has the form $e4 \Rightarrow e5$, the two most likely inference rules to use are =-E and $\Rightarrow$-I, and if a suitable equivalence does not seem possible to derive from the premises, then =-E can be eliminated from consideration.

Let us suppose we try to substantiate line 3 using rule $\Rightarrow$-I, because it has the form $e4 \Rightarrow e5$. Then we would expand the proof as follows.

From $e1$, $e2$ infer $e4 \Rightarrow e5$

1	$e1$	pr 1
2	$e2$	pr 2
3	**From $e4$ infer $e5$**	
	3.1 $e4$	pr 1
	3.2 $e5$	Why?
4	$e4 \Rightarrow e5$	$\Rightarrow$-I, 3

Thus, we have reduced the problem of proving $e4 \Rightarrow e5$ from $e1$ and $e2$ to the problem of proving $e5$ from $e4$, and the new problem promises to be simpler because propositions $e4$ and $e5$ each contain fewer operations than $e3$ did —they are in some sense smaller and simpler.

The above discussion shows basically how to go about developing a proof. At each step, investigate the inference rules to determine which are most likely to be applicable, based mainly on the proposition to be proved and secondly on previous assumptions and already-proved theorems, and attempt to apply one of them in order to reduce the problem to a simpler one.

As the proof expands and more assumptions are made, try to invent and substantiate new propositions (from the already proved ones) that may be helpful for proving the desired result. But remember that, while the premises are certainly useful, proof development is a *goal-oriented* activity, and it is mainly the goal, the proposition that must be substantiated; we should look to the goal and possible inference rules for the most insight.

Successful proof development requires some experience with the inference rules, so the reader should spend some time studying them and deciding when they might be employed. We can give some hints here.

Rules =-I and =-E together define operation **equals**. They are used only to derive an equivalence or to turn one into implications. If equivalence is not a part of the premises or goal, they can be eliminated from consideration.

The other rules of introduction are used to introduce longer propositions from shorter ones. Hence, they are useful when the desired goal, or parts of it, can be built from shorter propositions that occur on previous lines. Note that, except for $=$-I, the forms of the conclusions of the rules of introduction are all different, so that at most one of these rules can be used to substantiate a proposition.

The rules of elimination are generally used to "break apart" a proposition so that one of its sub-propositions can be derived. All the rules of elimination (except for $=$-E) have a general proposition as their conclusion. This means that they may possibly be used to substantiate *any* proposition. Whether an elimination rule can be used depends on whether its premises have appeared on previous lines, so to decide whether these rules should be used requires a look at previous lines.

The Development of a proof

Problem. Prove that if $p \Rightarrow q$ is true then so is $(p \wedge \neg q) \Rightarrow \neg p$. The first step in developing a proof is to draw the outline for the proof and fill in the first line with the theorem, the next lines with the premises and the last line with the goal —i.e the proposition to be inferred. Perform this step.

The problem description yields the following start of a proof:

From $p \Rightarrow q$ infer $(p \wedge \neg q) \Rightarrow \neg p$

1	$p \Rightarrow q$	pr 1
2	$(p \wedge \neg q) \Rightarrow \neg p$	Why?

At this point, it is wise to study the premises to see whether propositions can be derived from them. Do this.

Little can be derived from $p \Rightarrow q$, except the disjunction $\neg p \vee q$ (using the rule of Substitution). We will keep this proposition in mind. Which rules of inference could be used to substantiate line 2? That is, which rules of inference could have $(p \wedge \neg q) \Rightarrow \neg p$ as their conclusion?

Possible inference rules are: $\Rightarrow$-I, $\wedge$-E, $\vee$-E, $\neg$-E, $=$-E and $\Rightarrow$-E. Which seems most applicable, and why? Expand the proof accordingly.

There is little to suppose that the elimination rules could be useful, for their premises are different from the propositions on previous lines. This leaves only $\Rightarrow$-I.

From $p \Rightarrow q$ infer $(p \wedge \neg q) \Rightarrow \neg p$

1	$p \Rightarrow q$	pr 1
2	**From $p \wedge \neg q$ infer $\neg p$**	
	2.1 | $p \wedge \neg q$	pr 1
	2.2 | $\neg p$	Why?
3	$(p \wedge \neg q) \Rightarrow \neg p$	$\Rightarrow$-I, 2

What can be derived from the propositions appearing on lines previous to 2.2?

_____

Using $\wedge$-E, we can derive p and $\neg q$ from premise $p \wedge \neg q$. We then see that q can be derived from $p \Rightarrow q$ and p. (Is it strange that both q and $\neg q$ can be derived?) Keeping these in mind, list the inference rules that could be used to substantiate line 2.2.

_____

Possible inference rules are $\neg$-I, $\wedge$-E, $\vee$-E, $\neg$-E and $\Rightarrow$-E. Choose the rule that is most applicable and expand the proof accordingly.

_____

The elimination rules don't seem useful here; elimination of **imp** on line 1 results in q, and we already know that $\wedge$-E can be used to derive only p and $\neg q$ from $p \wedge \neg q$. Only $\neg$-I seems helpful:

From $p \Rightarrow q$ infer $(p \wedge \neg q) \Rightarrow \neg p$

1	$p \Rightarrow q$	pr 1
2	**From $p \wedge \neg q$ infer $\neg p$**	
	2.1 | $p \wedge \neg q$	pr 1
	2.2 | **From p infer $e \wedge \neg e$**	(which e?)
	2.2.1 | p	pr 1
	2.2.2 | $e \wedge \neg e$	Why?
	2.3 | $\neg p$	$\neg$-I, 2.2
3	$(p \wedge \neg q) \Rightarrow \neg p$	$\Rightarrow$-I, 2

What proposition e should be used on lines 2.2 and 2.2.2? To make the choice, look at the propositions that occur on lines previous to 2.2 and

the propositions we know we can derive from them. Expand the proof
accordingly.

We reasoned above that we could derive both q and $\neg q$, so the obvious
choice is $e = q$. We complete the proof as follows:

From $p \Rightarrow q$ infer $(p \wedge \neg q) \Rightarrow \neg p$			
1	$p \Rightarrow q$		pr 1
2	**From $p \wedge \neg q$ infer $\neg p$**		
	2.1	$p \wedge \neg q$	pr 1
	2.2	p	$\wedge$-E, 2.1
	2.3	$\neg q$	$\wedge$-E, 2.1
	2.4	**From p infer $q \wedge \neg q$**	
		2.4.1	q	$\Rightarrow$-E, 1, 2.2
		2.4.2	$q \wedge \neg q$	$\wedge$-I, 2.4.1, 2.3
	2.5	$\neg p$	$\neg$-I, 2.4
3	$(p \wedge \neg q) \Rightarrow \neg p$		$\Rightarrow$-I, 2

The Development of a second proof

Problem. Prove that from $\neg p = q$ follows $\neg(p = q)$. Draw the outline of
the proof and fill in the obvious details.

From $\neg p = q$ infer $\neg(p = q)$		
1	$\neg p = q$	pr 1
2	$\neg(p = q)$	Why?

What information can be gleaned from the premises?

Rule $=$-E can be used to derive two implications. This seems useful here,
since implications will be needed to derive the goal, and we derive both.

From $\neg p = q$ **infer** $\neg(p = q)$

1	$\neg p \Rightarrow q$	=-E, pr 1
2	$q \Rightarrow \neg p$	=-E, pr 1
3	$\neg(p = q)$	Why?

The following rules could be used to substantiate line 3: $\neg$-I, $\wedge$-E, $\vee$-E, $\neg$-E and $\Rightarrow$-E. Choose the most likely one and expand the proof accordingly.

The elimination rules don't seem helpful at all, because the premises that would be needed in order to use them are not available and don't seem easy to derive. The *only* rule to try at this point is $\neg$-I —we have little choice!

From $\neg p = q$ **infer** $\neg(p = q)$

1	$\neg p \Rightarrow q$		=-E, pr 1
2	$q \Rightarrow \neg p$		=-E, pr 1
3	**From** $p = q$ **infer** $e \wedge \neg e$ (which e?)		
	3.1	$p = q$	pr 1
	3.2	$e \wedge \neg e$	Why?
4	$\neg(p = q)$		$\neg$-I, 3

What proposition e should be used on lines 3 and 3.2, and how should it be proved? Expand the proof accordingly.

The propositions $\neg p \Rightarrow q$ and $q \Rightarrow \neg p$ are available. In addition, from line 3.1 $p \Rightarrow q$ and $q \Rightarrow p$ can be derived. Let's rearrange these as follows:

$$p \Rightarrow q, q \Rightarrow \neg p, q \Rightarrow p, \quad \text{and}$$
$$\neg p \Rightarrow q, q \Rightarrow \neg p, q \Rightarrow p.$$

If we assume p we can prove both p and $\neg p$; if we assume $\neg p$ we can also prove p and $\neg p$. Hence we should be able to prove the contradiction $p \wedge \neg p$. So try $e = p$ and write the following proof.

From $\neg p = q$ infer $\neg(p = q)$

1	$\neg p \ggg q$	=-E, pr 1
2	$q \ggg \neg p$	=-E, pr 1
3	**From $p = q$ infer $p \wedge \neg p$**	

		3.1	$p \ggg q$	=-E, pr 1
		3.2	$q \ggg p$	=-E, pr 1
		3.3	p	Why?
		3.4	$\neg p$	Why?
		3.5	$p \wedge \neg p$	$\wedge$-I, 3.3, 3.4

4	$\neg(p = q)$	$\neg$-I, 3

So we are left with concluding the two propositions p and $\neg p$. These are quite simple, using the above reasoning, so let us just show the final proof.

From $\neg p = q$ infer $\neg(p = q)$

1	$\neg p \ggg q$	=-E, pr 1
2	$q \ggg \neg p$	=-E, pr 1
3	**From $p = q$ infer $p \wedge \neg p$**	
	3.1	$p \ggg q$	=-E, pr 1
	3.2	$q \ggg p$	=-E, pr 1
	3.3	**From $\neg p$ infer $p \wedge \neg p$**	
		3.3.1	q	$\ggg$-E, 1, pr 1
		3.3.2	p	$\ggg$-E, 3.2, 3.3.1
		3.3.3	$p \wedge \neg p$	$\wedge$-I, 3.3.2, pr 1
	3.4	p	$\neg$-E, 3.3
	3.5	**From p infer $p \wedge \neg p$**	
		3.5.1	q	$\ggg$-E, 3.1, pr 1
		3.5.2	$\neg p$	$\ggg$-E, 2, 3.5.1
		3.5.3	$p \wedge \neg p$	$\wedge$-I, pr 1, 3.5.2
	3.6	$\neg p$	$\neg$-I, 3.5
	3.7	$p \wedge \neg p$	$\wedge$-I, 3.4, 3.6
5	$\neg(p = q)$	$\neg$-I, 2

At each step of the development of the proof there was little choice. The crucial —and most difficult— point of the development was the choice of inference rule $\neg$-I to substantiate the last line of the proof, but careful study of the inference rules led to it as the *only* likely candidate. Thus, directed study of the available information can lead quite simply to the proof.

The Tardy Bus Problem

The Tardy Bus Problem is taken from *WFF'N PROOF: The Game of Modern Logic* [1].

THE TARDY BUS PROBLEM. Given are the following premises:

1. If Bill takes the bus, then Bill misses his appointment, if the bus is late.

2. Bill shouldn't go home, if (a) Bill misses his appointment, and (b) Bill feels downcast.

3. If Bill doesn't get the job, then (a) Bill feels downcast, and (b) Bill shouldn't go home.

Which of the following conjectures are true? That is, which can be validly proved from the premises? Give proofs of the true conjectures and counterexamples for the others.

1. If Bill takes the bus, then Bill does get the job, if the bus is late.

2. Bill gets the job, if (a) Bill misses his appointment, and (b) Bill should go home.

3. If the bus is late, then (a) Bill doesn't take the bus, or Bill doesn't miss his appointment, if (b) Bill doesn't get the job.

4. Bill doesn't take the bus if, (a) the bus is late, and (b) Bill doesn't get the job.

5. If Bill doesn't miss his appointment, then (a) Bill shouldn't go home, and (b) Bill doesn't get the job.

6. Bill feels downcast, if (a) the bus is late, or (b) Bill misses his appointment.

7. If Bill does get the job, then (a) Bill doesn't feel downcast, or (b) Bill shouldn't go home.

8. If (a) Bill should go home, and Bill takes the bus, then (b) Bill doesn't feel downcast, if the bus is late.

This problem is typical of the puzzles one comes across from time to time. Most people are confused by them —they just don't know how to deal with them effectively and are amazed at those that do. It turns out, however, that knowledge of propositional calculus makes the problem fairly easy.

The first step in solving the problem is to translate the premises into propositional form. Let the identifiers and their interpretations be:

> tb :   Bill *t*akes the *b*us
> ma : Bill *m*isses his *a*ppointment
> bl :   The *b*us is *l*ate
> gh : Bill should *g*o *h*ome
> fd :   Bill *f*eels *d*owncast
> gj :   Bill *g*ets the *j*ob.

The premises are given below. Each has been put in the form of an implication and in the form of a disjunction, knowing that the disjunctive form
is often helpful.

> Premise 1. $tb \Rightarrow (bl \Rightarrow ma)$ or $\neg tb \lor \neg bl \lor ma$
> Premise 2. $(ma \land fd) \Rightarrow \neg gh$ or $\neg ma \lor \neg fd \lor \neg gh$
> Premise 3. $\neg gj \Rightarrow (fd \land \neg gh)$ or $gj \lor (fd \land \neg gh)$

Now let's solve the first few problems. In order to save space, Premises 1,
2 and 3 are not written in every proof, but are simply referred to as Premises 1, 2 and 3. Included, however, are propositions derived from them in
order to get more true propositions from which to conclude the result.

Conjecture 1: If Bill takes the bus, then Bill does get the job, if the bus is
late. Translate the conjecture into propositional form.

In propositional form, the conjecture is $tb \Rightarrow (bl \Rightarrow gj)$. We try to prove
"**From** tb **infer** $bl \Rightarrow gj$", which would prove that the conjecture is true.
Write the outline for the proof and fill in the obvious details.

From tb **infer** $bl \Rightarrow gj$

1	tb	pr 1
2	$bl \Rightarrow gj$	Why?

What propositions can be derived from line 1 and Premises 1, 2 and 3?
Expand the proof accordingly.

Proposition $bl \Rightarrow ma$ can be derived from Premise 1 and line 1:

From *tb* **infer** *bl* $\Rightarrow$ *gj*

1	*tb*	pr 1
2	*bl* $\Rightarrow$ *ma*	$\Rightarrow$-E, Premise 1, 1
3	*bl* $\Rightarrow$ *gj*	Why?

Which rules could be used to substantiate line 3?

Proposition *bl* $\Rightarrow$ *gj* could be an instance of the conclusion of rules $\Rightarrow$-I, $\wedge$-E, $\vee$-E, $\neg$-E, =-E and $\Rightarrow$-E. Which seems most useful here? Expand the proof accordingly.

The necessary propositions for the use of the elimination rules are not available, so try $\Rightarrow$-I:

From *tb* **infer** *bl* $\Rightarrow$ *gj*

1	*tb*		pr 1
2	*bl* $\Rightarrow$ *ma*		$\Rightarrow$-E, Premise 1, 1
3	**From** *bl* **infer** *gj*		
	3.1	*bl*	pr 1
	3.2	*gj*	Why?
4	*bl* $\Rightarrow$ *gj*		$\Rightarrow$-I, 3

Can any propositions be inferred at line 3.2 from the propositions on previous lines and Premises 1, 2 and 3? Expand the proof accordingly.

Proposition *ma* can be derived from lines 2 and 3.1:

From *tb* **infer** *bl* $\Rightarrow$ *gj*

1	*tb*		pr 1
2	*bl* $\Rightarrow$ *ma*		$\Rightarrow$-E, Premise 1, 1
3	**From** *bl* **infer** *gj*		
	3.1	*bl*	pr 1
	3.2	*ma*	$\Rightarrow$-E, 2, 3.1
	3.3	*gj*	Why?
4	*bl* $\Rightarrow$ *gj*		$\Rightarrow$-I, 3

What rules could be used to substantiate line 3.3?

Proposition gj could be an instance of the conclusion of rules ∧-E, ∨-E, ¬-E and ⇒-E. Which ones seem helpful here?

None of the the rules seem helpful. The only proposition available that contains gj is Premise 3, and its disjunctive form indicates that gj must necessarily be true only in states in which $(fd \land \neg gh)$ is false (according to theorem (3.4.6)). But there is nothing in Premise 2, the only other place fd and gh appear, to make us believe that $fd \land \neg gh$ must be false. Perhaps the conjecture is false. What counterexample —i.e. state in which the conjecture is false— does the structure of the proof and this argument lead to?

Up to line 3.2 of the proof we have assumed or proved $tb = T$, $bl = T$ and $ma = T$. To contradict the conjecture, we need $gj = F$. Finally, the above argument indicates we should try to let $fd \land \neg gh$ be true, so we try $fd = T$ and $gh = F$. Indeed, in this state Premises 1, 2 and 3 are true and the conjecture is false.

Conjecture 2: Bill gets the job, if (a) Bill misses his appointment and (b) Bill should go home. Translate the conjecture into propositional form.

This conjecture can be translated as $(ma \land gh) \Rightarrow gj$. To prove it we need to prove "**From** $ma \land gh$ **infer** gj". Draw the outline of a proof and fill in the obvious details.

From $ma \land gh$ **infer** gj

| 1 | $ma \land gh$ | pr 1 |
| 2 | gj | Why? |

What can we derive from line 1 and Premises 1, 2 and 3? Expand the proof accordingly.

Both line 1 and Premise 2 contain *ma* and *gh*. Premise 2 can be put in the form $¬(ma \wedge gh) \vee ¬fd$. Since $ma \wedge gh$ is on line 1, theorem (3.4.6) together with the law of Negation allows us to conclude that $¬fd$ is true, or that *fd* is false. Putting this argument into the proof yields

From $ma \wedge gh$ **infer** *gj*

1	$ma \wedge gh$	pr 1
2	$¬(ma \wedge gh) \vee ¬fd$	subs, De Morgan, Premise 2
3	$¬¬(ma \wedge gh)$	subs, Negation, 1
4	$¬fd$	(3.4.6), 2, 3
5	*gj*	Why?

What inference rule should be used to substantiate line 5? Expand the proof accordingly.

The applicable rules are $\wedge$-E, $\vee$-E, $¬$-E and $\Rightarrow$-E. This means that an earlier proposition must be broken apart to derive *gj*. The one that contains *gj* is Premise 3, and in its disjunctive form it looks promising. To show that *gj* is true, we need only show that $fd \wedge ¬gh$ is false. But we already know that *fd* is false, so that we can complete the proof as follows.

From $ma \wedge gh$ **infer** *gj*

1	$ma \wedge gh$	pr 1
2	$¬(ma \wedge gh) \vee ¬fd$	subs, De Morgan, Premise 2
3	$¬¬(ma \wedge gh)$	subs, Negation, 1
4	$¬fd$	(3.4.6), 2, 3
5	$¬fd \vee ¬¬gh$	$\vee$-I, 4
6	$¬(fd \wedge ¬gh)$	subs, De Morgan, 5
7	*gj*	(3.4.6), Premise 3, 6

Conjecture 3: If the bus is late, then (a) Bill doesn't take the bus, or Bill doesn't miss his appointment, if (b) Bill doesn't get the job. Translate the conjecture into propositional form.

Is this conjecture ambiguous? Two possible translations are

$$bl \Rightarrow (¬gj \Rightarrow (¬tb \vee ¬ma)), \text{ and}$$
$$bl \Rightarrow (¬tb \vee (¬gj \Rightarrow ¬ma))$$

Let us assume the first proposition is intended. It is true if we can prove "**From** *bl* **infer** $¬gj \Rightarrow (¬tb \vee ¬ma)$". Draw the outline of the proof and fill in the obvious details.

From bl **infer** $\neg gj \Rightarrow (\neg tb \vee \neg ma)$

1	bl	pr 1
2	$\neg gj \Rightarrow (\neg tb \vee \neg ma)$	Why?

What propositions can be derived from line 1 and the Premises?

No propositions can be derived, at least easily, so let's proceed to the next step. What rule should be used to substantiate line 2? Expand the proof accordingly.

Quite obviously, rule $\Rightarrow$-I should be tried:

From $b1$ **infer** $\neg gj \Rightarrow (\neg tb \vee \neg ma)$

1	bl		pr 1
2	**From** $\neg gj$ **infer** $\neg tb \vee \neg ma$		
	2.1	$\neg gj$	pr 1
	2.2	$\neg tb \vee \neg ma$	Why?
3	$\neg gj \Rightarrow (\neg tb \vee \neg ma)$		

Just before line 2.2, what propositions can be inferred from earlier propositions and Premises 1, 2 and 3? Expand the proof accordingly.

The antecedent of Premise 3 is true, so we can conclude that the consequent is also true:

From *bl* **infer** ⌐*gj* ⇒(⌐*tb* ∨ ⌐*ma*)

1	*bl*	pr 1
2	**From** ⌐*gj* **infer** ⌐*tb* ∨ ⌐*ma*	
	2.1 ⌐*gj*	pr 1
	2.2 *fd* ∧ ⌐*gh*	⇒-E, Premise 3, 2.1
	2.3 *fd*	∧-E, 2.2
	2.4 ⌐*gh*	∧-E, 2.2
	2.5 ⌐*tb* ∨ ⌐*ma*	Why?
3	⌐*gj* ⇒(⌐*tb* ∨ ⌐*ma*)	

What inference rule should be used to substantiate line 2.5? Expand the proof accordingly.

The proposition on line 2.5 could have the form of the conclusion of rules ∨-I, ∧-E, ∨-E, ⌐-E and ⇒-E. The first rule to try is ∨-I. Its use would require proving that one of ⌐*tb* and ⌐*ma* is true. But, looking at the Premises, this seems difficult. For from Premise 1 we see that both *tb* and *ma* could be true, while the other premises are true also because both their conclusions are true. Perhaps there is a contradiction. What is it?

In a state with *tb* = T, *ma* = T, *bl* = T, *gh* = F, *fd* = T and *gj* = F Premises 1, 2 and 3 are true, but the conjecture is false.

Exercises for Section 3.5

1. Prove or disprove conjectures 4-8 of the Tardy Bus problem.

2. For comparison, prove the valid conjectures of the Tardy Bus problem using a mixture of the equivalence-transformation system of chapter 2 and English.

Chapter 4
Predicates

In section 1.3, a state was defined as a function from identifiers to the set of values $\{T, F\}$. The notion of a state is now extended to allow identifiers to be associated with other values, e.g. integers, sequences of characters, and sets. The notion of a proposition will then be generalized in two ways:

1. In a proposition, an identifier may be replaced by any expression (e.g. $x \leqslant y$) that has the value T or F.

2. The quantifiers E, meaning "there exists"; A, meaning "for all"; and N, meaning "number of", are introduced. This requires an explanation of the notions of free identifier and bound identifier and a careful discussion of scope of identifiers in expressions.

Expressions resulting from these generalizations are called *predicates*, and the addition to a formal system (like the system of chapter 2 or 3) of inference rules to deal with them yields a *predicate calculus*.

4.1 Extending the Range of a State

We now consider a state to be a function from identifiers to values, where these values may be other than T and F. In any given context, an identifier has a type, such as *Boolean*, which defines the set of values with which it may be associated. The notations used to indicate the standard types required later are:

Boolean(i): identifier i can be associated (only) with T or F.

natural number(i): i can be associated with a member of $\{0, 1, 2, \cdots\}$.

integer(i): i can be associated with an integer —a member of $\{\cdots, -2, -1, 0, 1, 2, \cdots\}$.

integerset(i): i can be associated with a set of integers.

Other types will be introduced where necessary.

Let P be the expression $x < y$, where x and y have type *integer*. When evaluated, P yields either T or F, so it may replace any identifier in a proposition. For example, replacing b in $(b \wedge c) \vee d$ by P yields

$$((x < y) \wedge c) \vee d.$$

The new assertions like P are called *atomic expressions*, while an expression that results from replacing an identifier by an atomic expression is called a *predicate*. We will not go into detail about the syntax of atomic expressions; instead we will use conventional mathematical notation and rely on the reader's knowledge of mathematics and programming. For example, any expression of a programming language that yields a Boolean result is an acceptable atomic expression. Thus, the following are valid predicates:

$$((x \leqslant y) \wedge (y < z)) \vee (x + y < z)$$
$$(x \leqslant y \wedge y < z) \vee x + y < z$$

The second example illustrates that parentheses are not always needed to isolate the atomic expressions from the rest of a predicate. The precedences of operators in a predicate follow conventional mathematics. For example, the Boolean operators $\wedge$, $\vee$, and $\Rightarrow$ have lower precedence than the arithmetic and relational operators. We will use parentheses to make the precedence of operations explicit where necessary.

Evaluating predicates

Evaluating a predicate in a state is similar to evaluating a proposition. All identifiers are replaced by their values in the state, the atomic expressions are evaluated and replaced by their values (T or F), and the resulting constant proposition is evaluated. For example, the predicate $x < y \vee b$ in the state $\{(x, 2), (y, 3), (b, F)\}$ has the value of $2 < 3 \vee F$, which is equivalent to $T \vee F$, which is T.

Using our earlier notation $s(e)$ to represent the value of expression e in state s, and writing a state as the set of pairs it contains, we show the evaluation of three predicates:

$s((x \leqslant y \wedge y < z) \vee (x+y < z))$ where $s = \{(x, 1), (y, 3), (z, 5)\}$
$\quad = (1 \leqslant 3 \wedge 3 < 5) \vee (1+3 < 5)$
$\quad = (T \wedge T) \vee T$
$\quad = T.$
$s((x \leqslant y \wedge y < z) \vee (x+y < z))$ where $s = \{(x, 3), (y, 1), (z, 5)\}$
$\quad = (3 \leqslant 1 \wedge 1 < 5) \vee (3+1 < 5)$
$\quad = (F \wedge T) \vee T$
$\quad = T.$
$s((x \leqslant y \wedge y < z) \vee (x+y < z))$ where $s = \{(x, 5), (y, 1), (z, 3)\}$
$\quad = (5 \leqslant 1 \wedge 1 < 3) \vee (5+1 < 3)$
$\quad = (F \wedge T) \vee F$
$\quad = F.$

Reasoning about atomic expressions

Just as inference rules were developed for reasoning with propositions, so they should be developed to deal with atomic expressions. For example, we should be able to prove formally that $i < k$ follows from $(i < j \wedge j < k)$. We shall not do this here; as they say, "it is beyond the scope of this book." Instead, we rely on the reader's knowledge of mathematics and programming to reason, as he always has done, about the atomic expressions within predicates.

As mentioned earlier, we will be using expressions dealing with integer arithmetic, real arithmetic (though rarely) and sets. The operators we will be using in these expressions are described in Appendix 2.

The operators **cand** and **cor**

Every proposition is well-defined in any state in which all its identifiers have one of the values T and F. When we introduce other types of values and expressions, however, the possibility of undefined expressions (in some states) arises. For example, the expression x/y is undefined if y is 0. We should, of course, be sure that an expression in a program is well-defined in each state in which it will be evaluated, but at times it is useful to allow *part* of an expression to be undefined.

Consider, for example, the expression

$$y = 0 \vee (x/y = 5) .$$

Formally, this expression is undefined if $y = 0$, because x/y is undefined if $y = 0$ and **or** is itself defined only when its operands are T or F. And yet some would argue that the expression should have a meaning in any state where $y = 0$. Since in such states the first operand of **or** is true, and since **or** is defined to be true if either of its operands is true, the expression should be true. Furthermore, such an interpretation would be quite useful in programming, for it would allow us to say many things more clearly and compactly. For example, consider being able to write

if $y = 0 \lor (x/y = 5)$ **then** $s1$ **else** $s2$

as opposed to

if $y = 0$ **then** $s1$
      else if $x/y = 5$ **then** $s1$
            else $s2$

Rather than change the definition of **and** and **or**, which would require us to change our formal logic completely, we introduce two new operators: **cand** (for conditional **and**) and **cor** (for conditional **or**). The operands of these new operators can be any of *three* values: F, T and U (for Undefined). The new operators are defined by the following truth table.

b	c	b **cand** c	b **cor** c	b	c	b **cand** c	b **cor** c
T	T	T	T	F	U	F	U
T	F	F	T	U	T	U	U
T	U	U	T	U	F	U	U
F	T	F	T	U	U	U	U
F	F	F	F				

This definition says nothing about the *order* in which the operands should be evaluated. But the intelligent way to evaluate these operations, at least on current computers, is in terms of the following equivalent conditional expressions:

      b **cand** c: **if** b **then** c **else** F
      b **cor** c: **if** b **then** T **else** c

Operators **cand** and **cor** are not commutative. For example, b **cand** c is not equivalent to c **cand** b. Hence, care must be exercised in manipulating expressions containing them. The following laws of equivalence *do* hold for **cand** and **cor** (see exercise 5). These laws are numbered to correspond to the numbering of the laws in chapter 2.

2. **Associativity**: $E1$ **cand** $(E2$ **cand** $E3) = (E1$ **cand** $E2)$ **cand** $E3$
                $E1$ **cor** $(E2$ **cor** $E3) = (E1$ **cor** $E2)$ **cor** $E3$

3. **Distributivity**:
      $E1$ **cand** $(E2$ **cor** $E3) = (E1$ **cand** $E2)$ **cor** $(E1$ **cand** $E3)$
      $E1$ **cor** $(E2$ **cand** $E3) = (E1$ **cor** $E2)$ **cand** $(E1$ **cor** $E3)$

4. **De Morgan**: $\neg(E1 \textbf{ cand } E2) = \neg E1 \textbf{ cor } \neg E2)$
$\neg(E1 \textbf{ cor } E2) = \neg E1 \textbf{ cand } \neg E2)$

6. **Excluded Middle**: $E1 \textbf{ cor } \neg E1 = T$ (provided $E1$ is well-defined)

7. **Contradiction**: $E1 \textbf{ cand } \neg E1 = F$ (provided $E1$ is well-defined)

10. **cor-simplification**
$E1 \textbf{ cor } E1 = E1$
$E1 \textbf{ cor } T = T$ (provided $E1$ is well-defined)
$E1 \textbf{ cor } F = E1$
$E1 \textbf{ cor } (E1 \textbf{ cand } E2) = E1$

11. **cand-simplification**
$E1 \textbf{ cand } E1 = E1$
$E1 \textbf{ cand } T = E1$
$E1 \textbf{ cand } F = F$ (provided $E1$ is well-defined)
$E1 \textbf{ cand } (E1 \textbf{ cor } E2) = E1$

In addition, one can derive various laws that combine **cand** and **cor** with the other operations, for example,

$$E1 \textbf{ cand } (E2 \vee E3) = (E1 \textbf{ cand } E2) \vee (E1 \textbf{ cand } E3)$$

Further development of such laws are left to the reader.

Exercises for Section 4.1

1. The first two exercises consist of evaluating predicates and other expressions involving integers and sets. Appendix 2 gives more information on the operations used. The state s in which the expressions should be evaluated consists of two integer identifiers x, y, a Boolean identifier b, two set identifiers m, n and an integer array $c[1:3]$. Their values are:

$$x = 7, \ y = 2, \ b = T, \ m = \{1,2,3,4\}, \ n = \{2,4,6\}, \ c = (2,4,6)$$

(a) $x \div y = 3$
(b) $(x-1) \div y = 3$
(c) $(x+1) \div y = 3$
(d) $ceil(x/y) = x \div y + 1$
(e) $floor((x+1)/y) = (x+1) \div y$
(f) $floor(-x/y) = -3$
(g) $ceil(x/y) = x \div y$

(h) $-ceil(-x/y) = x \div y$
(i) $7 \textbf{ mod } 2$
(j) $floor(x/y) = x \div y$
(k) $min(floor(x/2), ceil(x/2)) < ceil(x/2)$
(l) $(abs(-x) = -abs(x)) = b$
(m) $b \vee x < y$
(n) $19 \textbf{ mod } 3$

2. Evaluate the following expressions in the state given in exercise 1.

(a) $m \cup n$
(b) $m \cap n$

(g) $|m| \in m$
(h) $|n| \in n$

    (c) $x \in m \wedge b$ (i) $(\{\mid m \mid\} \cup \{6, 7\}) \subset n$

    (d) $m \subset n \wedge b$ (j) $\mid m \mid + \mid n \mid = \mid m \cup n \mid$

    (e) $\varnothing \subset m$ (k) $min(m)$

    (f) $\{i \mid i \in m \wedge even(i)\} \subset n$ (l) $\{i \mid i \in m \wedge i \in n\}$

3. Evaluate the following predicates in the state given in exercise 1. Use U for the value of an undefined expression.

    (a) $b \vee x / (y-2) = 0$ (f) $x = 0$ **cand** $x / (y-2) = 0$

    (b) b **cor** $x / (y-2) = 0$ (g) $1 \leqslant y \leqslant 3$ **cand** $c[y] \in m$

    (c) $b \wedge x / (y-2) = 0$ (h) $1 \leqslant y \leqslant 3$ **cor** $c[x] \in m$

    (d) b **cand** $x / (y-2) = 0$ (i) $1 \leqslant y \leqslant 3$ **cand** $c[y+1] \in m$

    (e) $x = 0 \wedge x / (y-2) = 0$ (j) $1 \leqslant x \leqslant 3$ **cor** $c[y] \in m$

4. Consider propositions a, b and c as having the values F, T or U (for undefined). Describe all states where the commutative laws a **cor** $b = b$ **cor** a and a **cand** $b = b$ **cand** a do not hold.

5. Prove that the laws of Associativity, Distributivity, De Morgan, Excluded Middle, Contradiction, **cor**-simplification and **cand**-simplification, given just before these exercises, hold. Do this by building a truth table for each one.

4.2 Quantification

Existential quantification

    Let m and n be two integer expressions satisfying $m \leqslant n$. Consider the predicate

(4.2.1) $E_m \vee E_{m+1} \vee \cdots \vee E_{n-1}$,

where each E_i is a predicate. (4.2.1) is true in any state in which at least one of the E_i is true. It can be expressed using the *existential quantifier* E (read "there exists") as

(4.2.2) $(Ei: m \leqslant i < n: E_i)$.

The set of values that satisfy $m \leqslant i < n$ is called the *range* of the *quantified identifier* i. Predicate (4.2.2) is read in English as follows.

$(Ei$	there exists at least one (integer) i
$:$	such that
$m \leqslant i < n$	i is between m and $n-1$ (inclusive)
$:$	for which the following holds:
$E_i)$	E_i.

The reader is no doubt already familiar with some forms of quantification in mathematics. For example,

$$\sum_{i=m}^{n-1} s_i = s_m + s_{m+1} + \cdots + s_{n-1}$$

$$\prod_{i=m}^{n-1} s_i = s_m * s_{m+1} * \cdots * s_{n-1}.$$

stand for the sum and product of the values s_m, s_{m+1}, ..., s_{n-1}, respectively. These can be written in a more linear fashion, similar to (4.2.1), as follows, and we shall continue to use this new form:

$$(\Sigma\, i\colon m \leqslant i < n\colon s_i)$$

$$(\Pi\, i\colon m \leqslant i < n\colon s_i)$$

At this point, (4.2.2) is simply an abbreviation for (4.2.1). It can be recursively defined as follows:

(4.2.3)   **Definition of E**:
$(E\, i\colon m \leqslant i < m\colon E_i) = F,$ and, for $k \geqslant m$,
$(E\, i\colon m \leqslant i < k+1\colon E_i) = (E\, i\colon m \leqslant i < k\colon E_i) \vee E_k$ $\square$

Remark: The base case of this recursive definition, which concerns an empty range $m \leqslant i < m$ for i, brings out an interesting point. The disjunction of zero predicates, $(E\, i\colon m \leqslant i < m\colon E_i)$, has the value F: "oring" 0 predicates together yields a predicate that is always false. For example, the following predicates are equivalent to F:

$(E\, i\colon 0 \leqslant i < 0\colon i = i)$
$(E\, i\colon -3 \leqslant i < -3\colon T)$

The disjunction of zero disjuncts is F. The conjunction of zero conjuncts turns out to be T. Similarly, the sum of zero values is 0 and the product of zero values is 1. These four facts are expressed as

$(\Sigma\, i\colon 0 \leqslant i < 0\colon x_i) = 0,$
$(\Pi\, i\colon 0 \leqslant i < 0\colon x_i) = 1,$
$(E\, i\colon 0 \leqslant i < 0\colon E_i) = F,$
$(A\, i\colon 0 \leqslant i < 0\colon E_i) = T.$ (Notation explained subsequently)

The value 0 is called the *identity element* of addition, because any number added to 0 yields that number. Similarly, 1, F and T are the identity elements of the operators *, **or** and **and**, respectively. $\square$

The following examples use quantification over two identifiers. They are equivalent; they assert the existence of i and j between 1 and 99 such that i is prime and their product is 1079 (is this true?). The third one uses the convention that successive quantifications with the same range, $(E\,i : m \leqslant i < n: \ (E\,j : m \leqslant j < n: \ (E\,k : m \leqslant k < n: \ \cdots\ )))$ can be written as $(E\,i, j, k : m \leqslant i, j, k < n: \ \cdots\ )$.

$$(1)\ (E\,i : 0 \leqslant i < 100 : (E\,j : 0 \leqslant j < 100 : prime\,(i) \wedge i*j = 1079))$$
$$(2)\ (E\,i : 0 \leqslant i < 100 : prime\,(i) \wedge (E\,j : 0 \leqslant j < 100 : i*j = 1079))$$
$$(3)\ (E\,i, j : 0 \leqslant i, j < 100 : prime\,(i) \wedge i*j = 1079))$$

Universal quantification

The *universal quantifier*, A, is read as "for all". The predicate

$$(4.2.4)\quad (A\,i : m \leqslant i < n : E_i)$$

is true in a state *iff*, for all values i in the range $m \leqslant i < n$, E_i is true in that state.

We now define A in terms of E, so that, formally, we need deal only with one of them as a new concept. Predicate (4.2.4) is true *iff* all the E_i are true, so we see that it is equivalent to

$$
\begin{aligned}
& E_m \wedge E_{m+1} \wedge \ \cdots \ \wedge E_{n-1} \\
=\ & \neg\,\neg(E_m \wedge E_{m+1} \wedge \ \cdots \ \wedge E_{n-1}) && \text{(Negation)} \\
=\ & \neg(\neg E_m \vee \neg E_{m+1} \vee \ \cdots \ \vee \neg E_{n-1}) && \text{(De Morgan)} \\
=\ & \neg(E\,i : m \leqslant i < n : \neg E_i)
\end{aligned}
$$

This leads us to define (4.2.4) as

$(4.2.5)$ **Definition.** $(A\,i : m \leqslant i < n : E_i) = \neg(E\,i : m \leqslant i < n : \neg E_i)$.   □

Now we can prove that (4.2.4) is true if its range is empty:

$$
\begin{aligned}
& (A\,i : m \leqslant i < m : E_i) \\
=\ & \neg(E\,i : m \leqslant i < m : \neg E_i) \\
=\ & \neg F && \text{(because the range of } E \text{ is empty)} \\
=\ & T
\end{aligned}
$$

Numerical quantification

Consider predicates E_0, E_1, ... It is quite easy to assert formally that k is the smallest integer such that E_k holds. We need only indicate that E_0 through E_{k-1} are false and that E_k is true:

$$0 \leqslant k \ \wedge \ (A \ i : 0 \leqslant i < k : \neg E_i) \ \wedge \ E_k$$

It is more difficult to assert that k is the *second* smallest integer such that E_k holds, because we also have to describe the first such predicate E_j:

$$0 \leqslant j < k \ \wedge \ (A \ i : 0 \leqslant i < j : \neg E_i) \ \wedge \ E_j \ \wedge$$
$$(A \ i : j+1 \leqslant i < k : \neg E_i) \ \wedge \ E_k$$

Obviously, describing the *third* smallest value k such that E_k holds will be clumsier, and to write a function that yields the *number* of true E_i will be even harder. Let us introduce some notation:

(4.2.6)   **Definition.** $(N \ i : m \leqslant i < n : E_i)$ denotes the number of different values i in range $m \leqslant i < n$ for which E_i' is true. N is called the *counting* quantifier.   □

This means that

$$(E \ i : m \leqslant i < n : E_i) = ((N \ i : m \leqslant i < n : E_i) \geqslant 1)$$
$$(A \ i : m \leqslant i < n : E_i) = ((N \ i : m \leqslant i < n : E_i) = n - m)$$

Now it is easy to assert that k is the third smallest integer such that E_k holds:

$$((N \ i : 0 \leqslant i < k : E_i) = 2) \ \wedge \ E_k$$

A Note on ranges

Thus far, the ranges of quantifiers have been given in the form $m \leqslant i < n$, for integer expressions m and n. The lower bound m is included in the range, the upper bound n is not. Later, the form of ranges will be generalized, but this is a useful convention, and we will use it where it is suitable.

Note that the number of values in the range is $n - m$. Note also that quantifications with adjacent ranges can be combined as follows:

$$(E \ i : m \leqslant i < n : E_i) \vee (E \ i : n \leqslant i < p : E_i) = (E \ i : m \leqslant i < p : E_i)$$
$$(A \ i : m \leqslant i < n : E_i) \wedge (A \ i : n \leqslant i < p : E_i) = (A \ i : m \leqslant i < p : E_i)$$
$$(N \ i : m \leqslant i < n : E_i) + (N \ i : n \leqslant i < p : E_i) = (N \ i : m \leqslant i < p : E_i)$$

Exercises for Section 4.2

1. Consider character strings in PL/I or Pascal. Let $|$ denote catenation of strings. For example, the value of the expression 'ab:'$|$ 'x1' is the character string 'ab:x1'. What is the identity element of operation catenation?

2. Define the notation $(A\ i: m \leqslant i < n: E_i)$ recursively.

3. Define the notation $(N\ i: m \leqslant i < n: E_i)$ recursively.

4. Write a predicate that asserts that the value x occurs the same number of times in arrays $b[0:n-1]$ and $c[0:m-1]$.

5. Write a predicate $perm(b, c)$ that asserts that array $b[0:n-1]$ is a permutation of array $c[0:n-1]$. Array b is a permutation of c if it is just a rearrangement of it: each value occurs the same number of times in b and c. (See exercise 4.)

6. Consider array $b[0:n-1]$, where $n > 0$. Let j, k be two integers satisfying $0 \leqslant j \leqslant k+1 \leqslant n$. By $b[j:k]$ we mean the set of array elements $b[j]$, ..., $b[k]$, where the list is empty if $j = k+1$.

Translate the following sentences into predicates. For example, the first one can be written as $(A\ i: j \leqslant i < k+1: b[i]=0)$. Some of the statements may be ambiguous, in which case you should try to translate both possibilities.

(a) All elements of $b[j:k]$ are zero.

(b) No values of $b[j:k]$ are zero.

(c) Some values of $b[j:k]$ are zero. (What does "some" mean?)

(d) All zeroes of $b[0:n-1]$ are in $b[j:k]$.

(e) Some zeroes of $b[0:n-1]$ are in $b[j:k]$.

(f) Those values in $b[0:n-1]$ that are not in $b[j:k]$ are in $b[j:k]$.

(g) It is not the case that all zeroes of $b[0:n-1]$ are in $b[j:k]$.

(h) If $b[0:n-1]$ contains a zero then so does $b[j:k]$.

(i) If $b[j:k]$ contains two zeroes then $j = 1$.

(j) Either $b[1:j]$ or $b[j:k]$ contains a zero (or both).

(k) The values of $b[j:k]$ are in ascending order.

(l) If x is in $b[j:k]$, then $x+1$ is in $b[k+1:n-1]$.

(m) $b[j:k]$ contains at least two zeroes.

(n) Every value in $b[j:k]$ is also in $b[k+1:n-1]$.

(o) j is a power of 2 if j is in $b[j:k]$.

(p) Every element of $b[0:j]$ is less than x, and every element of $b[j+1:n-1]$ exceeds x.

(q) If $b[1]$ is 3 or $b[2]$ is 4 and $b[3]$ is 5 then $j = 3$.

4.3 Free and Bound Identifiers

The predicate

(4.3.1) $(A\ i: m \leqslant i < n: x*i > 0)$

asserts that x multiplied by any integer between m and $n-1$ (inclusive) exceeds 0. This is true if both x and m exceed 0 or if x is less than 0 and n is at most 0. Hence, (4.3.1) is equivalent to the predicate

$$(x > 0 \wedge m > 0) \vee (x < 0 \wedge n \leqslant 0)$$

Thus, the truth of (4.3.1) in a state s depends on the values of m, n and x in s, but *not* on the value of i —in fact, i need not even occur in state s. And it should also be clear that the meaning of the predicate does not change if all occurrences of i are replaced by j:

$$(A\ j: m \leqslant j < n: x*j > 0)$$

Obviously, identifier i in (4.3.1) plays a different role than identifiers m, n and x. So we introduce terminology to help make the different roles clear. Identifiers m, n and x are *free* identifiers of the predicate. Identifier i is *bound in* (4.3.1), and it is *bound to the quantifier A* in that predicate.

Now consider the predicate

(4.3.2) $i > 0 \wedge (A\ i: m \leqslant i < n: x*i > 0)$.

This is confusing, because the leftmost occurrence of i is free (and during an evaluation will be replaced by the value of i in the state), while the other occurrences of i are bound to the quantifier A. Clearly, it would be better to use a different identifier j (say) for the bound i and to rewrite (4.3.2) as

$$i > 0 \wedge (A\ j: m \leqslant j < n: x*j > 0).$$

While it is possible to allow predicates like (4.3.2), and most logical systems do, it is advisable to enforce the use of each identifier in only one way:

(4.3.3)   **Restriction on identifiers**: In an expression, an identifier may not be both bound and free, and an identifier may not be bound to two different quantifiers.   □

Note that the predicate

$$(A\ i:m \leqslant i < n : x * i > 0) \wedge (A\ i:m \leqslant i < n : y * i < 0)$$

does not comply with the restriction. An equivalent predicate that does is

$$(A\ i:m \leqslant i < n : x * i > 0) \wedge (A\ k:m \leqslant k < n : y * k < 0)$$

At times, for convenience a predicate will be written that does not follow restriction (4.3.3). In this case, be sure to view each quantified identifier as being used nowhere else in the world. *Think* of the two different uses of the same identifier as different identifiers.

Let us now formally define the terms *free* and *bound*, based on the structure of expressions.

(4.3.4)   **Definition** (of a free identifier i in an expression).
1. i is *free in the expression* consisting simply of i.
2. i is *free in expression* $(\,E\,)$ if it is free in E.
3. i is *free in expression op* E, where op is a unary operator (e.g. $\neg, -$), if it is free in E.
4. i is *free in expression E1 op E2*, where op is a binary operator (e.g. $\vee, +$) if it is free in *E1* or *E2* (or both).
5. i is *free in expression* $(A\ j:m \leqslant j < n : E)$, $(E\ j:m \leqslant j < n : E)$ and $(N\ j:m \leqslant j < n : E))$ if it is not the same identifier as j and if it is free in m, n or E.   □

(4.3.5)   **Definition** (of a bound identifier i in an expression).
1. i is *bound in expression* $(\,E\,)$ if it is bound in E.
2. i is *bound in expression op* E, where op is a unary operator, if it is bound in E.
3. i is *bound in expression E1 op E2*, where op is a binary operator, if it is bound in *E1* or *E2*.
4. i is *bound to the quantifier in expression* $(E\ i:m \leqslant i < n : E)$ (and similarly for A and N). The *scope* of the bound identifier i is the complete predicate $(E\ i:m \leqslant i < n : E)$.
5. i is *bound* (but not to the shown quantifier) *in expression* $(E\ j:m \leqslant j < n : E)$ if it is bound in m, n or E. Similar statements hold for quantifiers A and N.   □

Note that both x and y are free in the predicate $x \leqslant y$, while x remains free and y becomes bound when the predicate is embedded in the expression $(N\ y:0 \leqslant y < 10: x \leqslant y) = 4$.

Examples. In the predicates given below, bound occurrences of identifiers are denoted by arrows leading to the quantifier to which they are bound, while all other occurrences are free. Invalid predicates are marked as invalid.

$$2 \leqslant m < n \; \wedge \; (A\, i : 2 \leqslant i < m : m \div i \neq 0)$$

$$2 \leqslant m < n \; \wedge \; (A\, n : 2 \leqslant n < m : m \div n \neq 0) \text{ INVALID (why?)}$$

$$(E\, i : 1 \leqslant i < 25 : 25 \div i = 0) \; \wedge \; (E\, i : 1 \leqslant i < 25 : 26 \div i = 0) \text{ INVALID}$$

$$(E\, t : 1 \leqslant t < 25 : 25 \div t = 0) \; \wedge \; (E\, i : 1 \leqslant i < 25 : 26 \div i = 0)$$

$$(E\, i : 1 \leqslant i < 25 : 25 \div i = 0 \wedge 26 \div i = 0)$$

$$(A\, m : n < m < n + 6 : (E\, i : 2 \leqslant i < m : m \div i = 0))$$

$$(A\, m : n < m < n + 6 : (E\, n : 2 \leqslant n < m : m \div n = 0)) \text{ INVALID}$$

$$(A\, m : n < m < n + 6 : (E\, k : 2 \leqslant k < m : m \div k = 0)) \quad \square$$

The scope mechanism being employed here is similar to the ALGOL 60 scope mechanism (which is also used in Pascal and PL/I). Actually, its use in the predicate calculus came first. A phrase $(A\, i : R : E)$ introduces a new level of nomenclature, much like a procedure declaration "**proc** $p(i)$; **begin** ... **end**" does. Inside the phrase, one can refer to all variables used outside, *except* for i; these are *global* identifiers of the phrase. The part $A\, i$ is a "declaration" of a new local identifier i.

As in ALGOL 60, the name of a local identifier has no significance and can be changed systematically without destroying the meaning. But care must be taken to "declare" bound identifiers in the right place to get the intended meaning.

Exercises for Section 4.3

1. In the following predicates, draw an arrow from each bound identifier to the quantifier to which it is bound. Indicate the invalid predicates.

(a) $(E\ k: 0 \leqslant k < n: P \wedge H_k(T)) \wedge k > 0$

(b) $(A\ j: 0 \leqslant j < n: B_j \Rightarrow wp(SL_j, R))$

(c) $(E\ j: 0 \leqslant j < n: (A\ i: 0 \leqslant i < j+1: f(i) < f(j+1)))$

(d) $(A\ j: 0 \leqslant j < n: B_j \vee c_j) \wedge (A\ k: 0 \leqslant k < n: B_k \Rightarrow (E\ s: 0 \leqslant s < n: C_s))$

(e) $(A\ j: 0 \leqslant j < n: (E\ t: j+1 \leqslant t < m: (A\ k: 0 \leqslant k < n: F(k, t))))$

4.4 Textual Substitution

Textual substitution will be used in Part II to provide an elegant and useful definition of assignment to variables.

Let E and e be expressions and x an identifier. The notation

$$E_e^x$$

denotes the expression obtained by simultaneously substituting e for all free occurrences of x in E (with suitable use of parentheses around e to maintain precedence of operators).

A simple example is: $(x+y)_z^x = (z+y)$.

Some more examples of textual substitution are given using the following predicate E, which asserts that x and all elements of array $b[0:n-1]$ are less than y:

(4.4.1) $\quad E = x < y \wedge (A\ i: 0 \leqslant i < n: b[i] < y)$.

We have

(4.4.2) $\quad E_z^x = z < y \wedge (A\ i: 0 \leqslant i < n: b[i] < y)$.

(4.4.3) $\quad E_{x+y}^y = x < x+y \wedge (A\ i: 0 \leqslant i < n: b[i] < x+y)$.

(4.4.4) $\quad E_k^i = E$ (only free occurrences of i are replaced, and i is not free in E)

(4.4.5) $\quad (E_w *z^y)_{a+u}^z = (x < w*z \wedge (A\ i: 0 \leqslant i < n: b[i] < w*z))_{a+u}^z$
$$= x < w*(a+u) \wedge (A\ i: 0 \leqslant i < n: b[i] < w*(a+u))$$

Example (4.4.2) shows the replacement of free identifier x by identifier z; (4.4.3) the replacement of a free identifier by an expression. Example (4.4.4) illustrates that only free occurrences of an identifier are replaced. Example (4.4.5) shows two successive substitutions and the introduction of parentheses around the expression being inserted. In the second substitution of (4.4.5), z is being replaced by $a+u$, so that $w*z$ should be changed to $w*(a+u)$ and not $w*a+u$, which, because of our precedence conventions, would be viewed as $(w*a)+u$. (If we always fully parenthesized expressions or used prefix notation, the need for this extra parenthesization would not arise.)

Substitution has already been used, but with a different notation. If we consider E of (4.4.1) to be a function of identifier x, $E(x)$, then E_z^x is equivalent to $E(z)$. The new notation describes both the identifier being replaced and its replacement. Therefore, an English description is not needed to indicate the identifier being replaced.

There are some problems with textual substitution as just defined, which we illustrate with some examples. First, E_{c+1}^b would not make sense because it would result in $\cdots c+1[i]\cdots$, which is syntactically incorrect. Textual replacement must result in a well-formed expression.

Secondly, suppose we want to indicate that identifier x and the array elements of b are all less than $y-i$, where i is a program variable. Noting the similarity between this assertion and E, (4.4.1), we try to write this by replacing y in E by $y-i$:

$$E \ \ \ = x<y \qquad \wedge (A\,i:0\leqslant i<n:b[i]<y)$$
$$E_{y-i}^y = x<y-i \ \ \wedge (A\,i:0\leqslant i<n:b[i]<y-i).$$

But this is not the desired predicate, because the i in $y-i$ has become bound to the quantifier A, since it now occurs within the scope of A. Care must be taken to avoid such "capturing" of an identifier in the expression being substituted. To avoid this conflict we can call for first (automatically) replacing identifier i of E by a fresh identifier k (say), so that we arrive at

$$E_{y-i}^y = x<y-i \wedge (A\,k:0\leqslant k<n:b[k]<y-i).$$

Let us now define textual substitution more carefully:

(4.4.6) **Definition.** The notation E_e^x, where x is an identifier and E and e expressions, denotes the predicate created by simultaneously replacing every free occurrence of x in E by e. To be valid, the substitution must yield a syntactically correct predicate. If the substitution would cause an identifier in e to become bound, then a suitable replacement of bound identifiers in E must take place before the substitution in order to avoid the conflict. □

The following two lemmas are stated without proof, for they are fairly obvious:

(4.4.7)   *Lemma.* $(E_u^x)_v^x = E_{u_v^x}^x$ $\square$

(4.4.8)   *Lemma.* If y is not free in E, then $(E_u^x)_v^y = E_{u_v^y}^x$ $\square$

Simultaneous substitution

Let $\bar{x}$ denote a list (vector) of *distinct* identifiers:

$$\bar{x} = x_1, x_2, \cdots, x_n$$

Let $\bar{e}$ be a list (of the same length as $\bar{x}$) of expressions. Then *simultaneous substitution* of all occurrences of the x_i by the corresponding e_i in an expression E is denoted by

(4.4.9) $E_{\bar{e}}^{\bar{x}}$,   or $E_{e_1, \cdots, e_n}^{x_1, \cdots, x_n}$

The caveats placed on simple substitution in definition 4.4.6 apply here also. Here are some examples.

$$(x+x+y)_{a+b,c}^{x,y} = a+b+a+b+c$$

$$(x+x+y)_{x+y,z}^{x,y} = x+y+x+y+z$$

$$(A\ i:0 \leqslant i < n: b(i) \vee c(i+1))_{n+i,d}^{n,b}$$
$$= (A\ k:0 \leqslant k < n+i: d(k) \vee c(k+1))$$

The second example illustrates the fact that the substitutions must be simultaneous; if one first replaces all occurrences of x and *then* replaces all occurrences of y, the result is $x+z+x+z+z$, which is not the same.

In general, $E_{u,v}^{x,y}$ can be *different from* $(E_u^x)_v^y$.

Exercises for Section 4.4

1. Consider the predicate $E: (A\ i:0 \leqslant i < n: b[i] < b[i+1])$. Indicate which of the following textual substitutions are invalid and perform the valid ones.

$$E_j^i, E_{n+1}^n, E_c^b, E_{n+i}^n, E_{b+1}^b, E_{m,k}^{n,b}$$

2. Consider the predicate $E: n>i \wedge (N\ j:1 \leqslant j < n: n \div j = 0) > 1$. Indicate which of the following textual substitutions are invalid and perform the valid ones.

$$E_j^i, E_{m+i}^n, E_{j+1}^j, E_k^i, (E_{n+i}^n)_t^i, E_{n+i,t}^{n,i}$$

3. Consider the predicate $E = (A\ i:1 \leqslant i < n:(E\ j: b[j] = i))$. Indicate which of the following textual substitutions are invalid and perform the valid ones.

E_j^i, E_k^n, E_{n*i}^n

4. Consider the assignment statement $x := x + 1$. Suppose that after its execution we want $R: x > 0$ to be true. What condition, or "precondition", must be true before execution in order to have R true after? Can you put your answer in terms of a textual substitution in R?

5. Consider the assignment statement $a := a*b$. Suppose that after its execution we want $R: a*b = c$ to be true. What condition, or "precondition", must be true before execution in order to have R true after? Can you put your answer in terms of a textual substitution in R?

6. Define textual substitution recursively, based on the structure of an expression.

4.5 Quantification Over Other Ranges

Until now, we have viewed the predicate $(E\, i: m \leqslant i < n: E_i)$ as an abbreviation for $E_m \lor \cdots \lor E_{n-1}$. The notion of quantification is now generalized to allow quantification over other ranges, including infinite ones. This results in a system with more "power"; we will be able to make assertions that were previously not possible. But predicates with infinite ranges cannot always be computed by a general method in a finite amount of time. Hence, although such predicates may be used heavily in discussing programs, they won't appear *in* programs.

A predicate can have the form

(4.5.1) $(E\, i: R: E)$ or

(4.5.2) $(A\, i: R: E)$,

where i is an identifier and R and E are predicates (usually, but not necessarily, containing i). The first has the interpretation "there exists a value of i in range R (for which R is true) for which E is true". The second has the interpretation "for all values of i in range R, E is true".

The notions of free and bound identifiers and the restrictions on their occurrence in predicates, as given in section 4.3, hold here in the same manner and will not be discussed further.

Example 1. Let *Person*(p) represent the sentence "p is a person". Let *Mortal*(x) represent the sentence "x is mortal". Then the sentence "All men are mortal", or, less poetically but more in keeping with the times, "All persons are mortal", can be expressed by $(A\, p:\ Person(p):\ Mortal(p))$. □

Example 2. It has been proved that arbitrarily large primes exist. This theorem can be stated as follows:

$$(A\ n:0<n:(E\ i:n<i:prime\,(i))),\quad \text{where}$$
$$prime\,(i) = (1<i \wedge (A\ j:1<j<i:i \textbf{ mod } j \neq 0))$$

In fact, Chebyshev proved in 1850 that there is a prime between every integer and its double, which we state as

$$(A\ n:1<n:(E\ i:n\leqslant i<2n:prime\,(i)))\quad \square$$

Example 3. The predicate below asserts that the maximum of an integer and its negation is the absolute value of that integer:

$$(A\ n:integer\,(n):max\,(n,-n)=abs\,(n))\quad \square$$

The type of a quantified identifier

Implicit in our use of $(E\ i:n<i:prime\,(i))$ above is that i has type *integer*. However, when dealing with more general ranges this is not always the case. Consider, for example, the predicate $(A\ p:\ Person\,(p):\ Mortal\,(p))$, where the range of p is the set of all objects (see example 1 above). Hence, the type of a quantified identifier must be made clear in some fashion so that the set of values that the identifier ranges over is unambiguously identified. The formal way to do this is to include the type as part of the range predicate. This has been done in example 3 above, where the range is *integer*(n).

Often, however, the text surrounding a predicate and the form of the predicate itself will identify the type of the quantified identifier, making it unnecessary to give it explicitly in the predicate.

The range can even be omitted completely when it can be determined from the context; this is just the usual attempt to suppress unnecessary details. For example, the predicate in example 3 could have been written as

$$(A\ n:max\,(n,-n)=abs\,(n))$$

since the context indicated that only integers were under consideration.

Tautologies and implicit quantification

Suppose a predicate like $max\,(n,-n)=abs\,(n)$, where n has type integer, has been proved to hold in all states: it is a tautology. Then it is true for all (integer) values of n, so that the following is also true:

$$(A\ n:integer\,(n):max\,(n,-n)=abs\,(n))$$

or, as an abbreviation,

$$(A \; n: max(n, \; -n) = abs(n))$$

Thus we see that

(4.5.3) any tautology E is equivalent to the same predicate E but with all its identifiers $i_1, \; \cdots, i_m$ universally quantified, i.e. it is equivalent to $(A \; i_1, \; \cdots, i_m: E)$.

This simple fact will be useful in chapter 6 in determining how to describe initial and final values of variables of a program.

Inference rules for A and E

The rest of this section 4.5, which requires knowledge of chapter 3, need not be read to understand later material. It gives introduction and elimination rules for A and E, thus extending the natural deduction system given in chapter 3. The purpose is to show as briefly as possible how this can be done.

First, consider a rule for introducing A. For it, we need conditions under which $(A \; i: R: E)$ holds in a state s. It will be true in s if $R \Rightarrow E$ is true in s, and if the proof of $R \Rightarrow E$ does not depend on i, so that it is true for all i. The simplest way to require this condition is to require that i not even be mentioned in anything that the proof of $R \Rightarrow E$ depends upon. Thus, we require that i be a fresh identifier, which occurs nowhere in proofs that the proof of $R \Rightarrow E$ depends upon. Thus, the inference rule is

(4.5.4) A-I: $\dfrac{R \Rightarrow E}{(A \; i: R: E)}$ where i is a fresh identifier.

Now assume that $(A \; i: R: E)$ is true in state s. Then it is true for any value of i, so that $R \Rightarrow E_e^i$ holds in state s for any predicate e. Thus we have the elimination rule

(4.5.5) A-E: $\dfrac{(A \; i: R: E)}{R_e^i \Rightarrow E_e^i}$ for any predicate e

Let us now turn to the inference rules for E. Using the techniques of earlier sections, E can be defined in terms of A:

(4.5.6) E-I: $\dfrac{(A \; i: R: E)}{\neg(E \; i: R: \neg E)}$

(4.5.7)   **E**-E: $\dfrac{(\mathbf{E}\,i : R : E)}{\neg(\mathbf{A}\,i : R : \neg E)}$

A final inference rule allows substitution of one bound variable for another without changing the value of the predicate:

(4.5.8)   **bound-variable substitution**: $\dfrac{(\mathbf{E}\,i : R : E)}{(\mathbf{E}\,k : R_k^i : E_k^i)}$

(provided k does not appear free in R and E)

Exercises for Section 4.5

1. Let $fool(p, t)$ stand for "you can fool person p at time t". Translate the following sentences into the predicate calculus.

(a) You can fool some of the people some of the time.

(b) You can fool all the people some of the time.

(c) You can't fool all the people all the time.

2. Write the following statements as predicates.

(a) The square of an integer is nonnegative.

(b) Three integers are the lengths of the sides of a triangle if and only if the sum of any two is at least the third (use $sides(a, b, c)$ to mean that a, b and c are the lengths of the sides of a triangle).

(c) For any positive integer n a solution to the equation $w^n + x^n + y^n = z^n$ exists, where w, x, y and z are positive integers.

(d) The sum of the divisors of integer n, but not including n itself, is n. (An integer with this property is called a *perfect number*. The smallest perfect number is 6, since $1+2+3 = 6$.)

4.6 Some Theorems About Textual Substitution and States

In general, the two expressions E and E_e^x are not the same; evaluated in the same state they can yield different results. But they are related. We now investigate this relation.

Let us first review terminology. If e is an expression and s a state, then $s(e)$ denotes the *value* of expression e in state s, found by substituting the values in s for the identifiers in e and then evaluating the resulting constant expression. If an identifier is undefined in s, the symbol U is used for its value.

We need to be able to talk about a state s' that is the same as state s except for the value of identifier x (say), which is v in s'. We describe state s' by the notation

$(s; \ x:v)$

For example, execution of the assignment $x := 2$ in state s terminates in the state $s' = (s; \ x:2)$. In general, execution of the assignment $x := e$ beginning in state s terminates in the state $(s; \ x:s(e))$, since the value of expression e in state s is being assigned to x. Note that

$$s = (s; \ x:s(x))$$

holds because the value of x in state s is $s(x)$.

We now give three simple lemmas dealing with textual substitution. Formal proofs would rely heavily on the caveats given on textual substitution in definition (4.4.6), and would be based on the structure of the expressions involved. We give informal proofs.

(4.6.1) **Lemma.** $s(E_e^x) = s(E_{s(e)}^x)$.

That is, substituting an expression e for x in E and then evaluating in s yields the same result as substituting the *value* of e in s for x and then evaluating.

Proof. Consider evaluating the lefthand side (LHS). Wherever x occurs in the original expression E, instead of replacing it by its value in s we must evaluate e in s and use this value, since x has been replaced by e. This value is $s(e)$. Hence, to evaluate the LHS we can evaluate E in s, but wherever x occurs use the value $s(e)$. But this is the way the RHS is evaluated, so the two are the same. $\Box$

The following lemma will be extremely helpful in understanding the definition of the assignment statement in Part II.

(4.6.2) **Lemma.** Consider a state s. Let $s' = (s; \ x:s(e))$. Then

$$s'(E) = s(E_e^x).$$

In other words, evaluating E_e^x in state s yields the same value as evaluating E in $(s; \ x:s(e))$.

Proof. $s'(E) = (s; \ x:s(e))(E)$ (Definition of state s')

$\qquad = (s; \ x:s(e))(E_{s(e)}^x)$ (In evaluating E in $(s; \ x:s(e))$, the value $s(e)$ is used for x)

$\qquad = (s; \ x:s(x))(E_{s(e)}^x)$ (x does not occur in $E_{s(e)}^x$, so the value of $E_{s(e)}^x$ is independent of the value of x)

$$= s(E^x_{s(e)}) \qquad \text{(Since state } s = (s; \; x{:}s(x)))$$

$$= s(E^x_e) \qquad \text{(Lemma 4.6.1)} \quad \square$$

The above lemmas generalize easily to the case of simultaneous substitution, and we will not discuss the matter further. The final lemma, a trivial but important fact, is stated without proof.

(4.6.3) **Lemma.** For a list of distinct identifiers $\bar{x}$, expression E and a list $\bar{u}$ (of the same length as $\bar{x}$) of fresh, distinct identifiers, we have

$$(E^{\bar{x}}_{\bar{u}})^{\bar{u}}_{\bar{x}} = E \quad \square$$

Exercises for Section 4.6

1. Let state s contain: $x = 5, y = 6, b = T$. What are the contents of the following states? $(s; \; x{:}6)$, $(s; \; y{:}s(x))$, $(s; \; y{:}s(x+y))$, $(s; \; b{:}F)$, $(s; \; b{:}T)$, $((s; \; x{:}6); \; y{:}4)$, $((s; \; x{:}y); \; y{:}x)$.

Chapter 5
Notations and Conventions for Arrays

The array is a major feature of our programming languages. It is important to have the right viewpoint and notation for dealing with arrays, so that making assertions and reasoning about programs using them can be done effectively. Traditionally, an array has been considered to be a collection of subscripted independent variables, which share a common name. This chapter presents a different view, introduces suitable notation, and gives examples of its use.

This material is presented here because it discusses notations and concepts needed for reasoning about arrays, rather than with the notations used in the programming language itself. The first two sections will be needed for defining assignment to array elements in Part II.

5.1 One-dimensional Arrays as Functions

Consider an array defined in Pascal-like notation by

var a: **array** [1:3] **of** *integer*

In PL/I and FORTRAN, this would be written as

DECLARE a(1:3) FIXED;   and
INTEGER a(3)

respectively. Except in older versions of FORTRAN, the lower bound need not be one; it can be any integer —negative, zero or positive. Zero is often a more suitable lower bound than one, especially if the range of a quantified identifier i (say) is written in the form $m \leqslant i < n$. For example, suppose an array b is to have n values in it, each being $\geqslant 2$. Giving b the lower bound 0 and putting these values in $b[0]$, $b[1]$, ..., $b[n-1]$

allows us to express this as

$$(A \; i: 0 \leqslant i < n : b[i] \geqslant 2)$$

Throughout this section we will use as an example an array b declared as

(5.1.1)   **var** b: **array** [0:2] **of** *integer*

Let us introduce some notation. First, sequence notation (see Appendix 2) is used to describe the value of an array. For example, $b = (4, -2, 7)$ means that $b[0]=4$, $b[1]=-2$ and $b[2]=7$. Secondly, for any array b, *b.lower* denotes its lower subscript bound and *b.upper* its upper bound. For example, for b declared in (5.1.1), *b.lower* $= 0$ and *b.upper* $= 2$. Then we define *domain*(b), the subscript range of an array, as

$$domain(b) = \{i \mid b.lower \leqslant i \leqslant b.upper\}$$

As mentioned earlier, the conventional view is that b declared in (5.1.1) is a collection of three independent *subscripted variables*, $b[0]$, $b[1]$ and $b[2]$, each of type *integer*. One can refer to a subscripted variable using $b[i]$, where the value of integer expression i is in *domain*(b). One can assign value e to subscripted variable $b[2]$ (say) by using an assignment $b[i]:= e$ where expression i currently has the value 2.

It is advantageous to introduce a second view. Array b is considered to be a (*partial*) *function*: b is a simple variable that contains a function from subscript values to integers. With this view, $b[i]$ denotes *function application*: the function currently in simple variable b is applied to argument i to yield an integer value, in the same way that *abs*(i) does.

Remark: On my first encounter with it, this functional view of arrays bewildered me. It seemed useless and difficult to work with. Only after gaining experience with it did I come to appreciate its simplicity, elegance and usefulness. I hope the reader ends up with the same appreciation.   □

When considering an array as a function, what does the assignment $b[i]:= e$ mean? Well, it assigns a new function to b, a function that is the same as the old one except that at argument i its value is e. For example, execution of $b[1]:= 8$ beginning with

$$b[0]=2, b[1]=4, b[2]=6$$

terminates with b the same as before, except at position 1:

$$b[0] = 2, b[1] = 8, b[2] = 6.$$

It is convenient to introduce a notation to describe such altered arrays.

(5.1.2) **Definition**. Let b be an array (function), i an expression and e an expression of the type of the array elements. Then $(b; i\!:\!e)$ denotes the array (function) that is the same as b except that when applied to the value of i it yields e:

$$(b; i\!:\!e)[j] = \begin{cases} i = j \;\rightarrow\; e \\ i \neq j \;\rightarrow\; b[j] \end{cases} \quad \square$$

Notice the similarity between the notation $(s; x\!:\!v)$ used in section 4.6 to denote a modified state s and the notation $(b; i\!:\!e)$ to denote a modified array b.

Example 1. Let $b[0\!:\!2] = (2, 4, 6)$. Then

$(b; 0\!:\!8)[0] = 8$ (i.e. function $(b; 0\!:\!8)$ applied to 0 yields 8)
$(b; 0\!:\!8)[1] = b[1] = 4$ (i.e. $(b; 0\!:\!8)$ applied to 1 yields $b[1]$)
$(b; 0\!:\!8)[2] = b[2] = 6$ (i.e. $(b; 0\!:\!8)$ applied to 2 yields $b[2]$)

so that $(b; 0\!:\!8) = (8, 4, 6)$. $\square$

Example 2. Let $b[0\!:\!2] = (2, 4, 6)$. Then

$(b; 1\!:\!8) = (2, 8, 6)$
$(b; 2\!:\!8) = (2, 4, 8)$
$((b; 0\!:\!8); 2\!:\!9) = (8, 4, 9)$
$(((b; 0\!:\!8); 2\!:\!9); 0\!:\!7) = (7, 4, 9)$ $\square$

Example 2 illustrates nested use of the notation. Since $(b; 0\!:\!8)$ is the array (function) $(8, 4, 6)$, it can be used in the first position of the notation. Nested parentheses do become burdensome, so we drop them and rely instead on the convention that rightmost pairs "$i\!:\!e$" are dominant and have precedence. Thus the last line of example 2 is equivalent to $(b; 0\!:\!8; 2\!:\!9; 0\!:\!7)$.

Example 3. Let $b[0\!:\!2] = (2, 4, 6)$. Then

$(b; 0\!:\!8; 2\!:\!9; 0\!:\!7)[0] = 7$
$(b; 0\!:\!8; 2\!:\!9; 0\!:\!7)[1] = (b; 0\!:\!8; 2\!:\!9)[1] = (b; 0\!:\!8)[1] = b[1] = 4$
$(b; 0\!:\!8; 2\!:\!9; 0\!:\!7)[2] = (b; 0\!:\!8; 2\!:\!9)[2] = 9$ $\square$

The assignment statement $b[i] := e$ can now be explained in terms of the functional view of arrays; it is simply an abbreviation for the following assignment to simple variable b!

$$b := (b;\ i{:}e)$$

We now have two conflicting views of arrays: an array is a collection of independent variables and an array is a partial function. Each view has its advantages, and, as with the particle and wave theories of light, we switch back and forth between them, always using the most convenient one for the problem at hand.

One advantage of the functional view is that it simplifies the programming language, because there is now only *one* kind of variable, the simple variable. It may contain a function, which can be applied to arguments, but function application already exists in most programming languages. On the other hand, with the collection-of-independent-variables view the notion of state becomes confused, because a state must map not only identifiers but also entities like $b[1]$ into values.

In describing $b[i] := e$ as an abbreviation of $b := (b;\ i{:}e)$ the functional view is being used to describe the *effect* of execution, but not how the assignment is to be implemented. Execution can still be performed using the collection-of-independent-variables view —by evaluating i and e, selecting the subscripted variable to assign to, and assigning e to it. It is not necessary to create a whole new array $(b;\ i{:}e)$ and then assign it.

The functional view has other uses besides describing assignment. For example, for an array $c[0{:}n-1]$ the assertion

$$perm((c;\ 0{:}x), C)$$

asserts that c, but with the value x in position 0, is a permutation of array C. It is clumsy to formally assert this in another fashion.

Simplifying expressions

It is sometimes necessary to simplify expressions (including predicates) containing the new notation. This can often be done using a two-case analysis as shown below, which is motivated by definition (5.1.2). The first step is the hardest, so let us briefly explain it. First, note that either $i = j$ or $i \neq j$. In the former case $(b;\ i{:}5)[j] = 5$ reduces to $5 = 5$; in the second case it reduces to $b[j] = 5$.

$$
\begin{aligned}
&(b;\ i{:}5)[j] = 5 \\
&= (i = j \wedge 5 = 5) \vee (i \neq j \wedge b[j] = 5) \quad &&\text{(Def. of } (b;\ i{:}5)) \\
&= (i = j) \vee (i \neq j \wedge b[j] = 5) \quad &&((5 = 5) = T, \textbf{ and}\text{-simpl.}) \\
&= (i = j \vee i \neq j) \wedge (i = j \vee b[j] = 5) \quad &&\text{(Distributivity)} \\
&= T \wedge (i = j \vee b[j] = 5) \quad &&\text{(Excluded middle)} \\
&= i = j \vee b[j] = 5 \quad &&(\textbf{and}\text{-simpl.})
\end{aligned}
$$

Exercises for Section 5.1

1. Let $b[1:4] = (2, 4, 6, 8)$. What are the contents of the following arrays?

(a) $(b; \ 1:3)$ (d) $(b; \ 1:b(4); \ 2:b(3); \ 3:b(2); \ 4:b(1))$

(b) $(b; \ 1:b(1))$ (e) $(b; \ 4:b(4); \ 3:b(3); \ 2:b(2); \ 1:b(1))$

(c) $(b; \ 1:b(4))$ (f) $(b; \ 1:b(1); \ 1:b(2); \ 1:b(3); \ 1:b(4))$

2. Let a state contain $i = 2$, $j = 3$ and $b(0:5) = (-3, -2, -1, 0, 1, 2)$. Evaluate the following:

(a) $(b; \ i:2)[j]$ (e) $(b; \ i+j:6)[4]$

(b) $(b; \ i+1:2)[j]$ (f) $(b; \ i:2; \ j:3)[j+i-2]$

(c) $(b; \ i+2:2)[j]$ (g) $(b; \ i:2; \ j:3)[j+i-1]$

(d) $(b; \ i+j:6)[5]$ (h) $(b; \ i:2; \ j-1:3)[i]$

3. Simplify the following predicates by eliminating the notation $(b; \ ...)$.

(a) $(b; \ i:5)[i] = (b; \ i:5)[j]$

(b) $(b; \ i:b[i])[i] = i$

(c) $(b; \ i:b[i]; \ j:b[j])[i] = (b; \ j:b[j]; \ i:b[i])[j]$

(d) $(b; \ i:b[j]; \ j:b[i])[i] = (b; \ j:b[i]; \ i:b[j])[j]$

(e) $(b; \ i:b[j]; \ j:b[j])[i] = (b; \ i:b[i]; \ j:b[j])[j]$

(f) $(b; \ i:b[i])[j] = (b; \ j:b[j])[j]$

4. The programming language Pascal contains the type **record**, which allows one to build a new type consisting of a fixed number of components (fields) with other types. For example, the Pascal-like declarations

> **type** t: **record** n: **array** $[0:10]$ **of** *char*; *age*: *integer* **end**;
> **var** $p, q : t$

define a type t and two variables p and q with type t. Each variable contains two fields; the first is named n and can contain a string of 0 to 10 characters —e.g. a person's name— and the second is named *age* and can contain an integer. The following assignments indicate how the components of p and q can be assigned and referenced. After their execution, both p and q contain 'Hehner' in the first component and 32 in the second. Note how *q.age* refers to field *age* of record variable q.

> $p.n := \ 'Hehner'; \quad p.age := 32; \quad q.n := p.n; \quad q.age := q.age + 1 - 1$

An array consists of a set of individual values, all of the same type (the old view). A record consists of a set of individual values, which can be of different types. In order to allow components to have different types we have sacrificed some flexibility: components must be referenced using their name (instead of an expression). Nevertheless, arrays and records are similar.

Develop a functional view for records, similar to the functional view for arrays just presented.

5.2 Array Sections and Pictures

Given integer expressions $e1$ and $e2$ satisfying $e1 \leqslant e2+1$, the notation $b[e1:e2]$ denotes array b restricted to the range $e1:e2$. Thus, for an array declared as

var b: **array** $[0:n-1]$ **of** *integer*

$b[0:n-1]$ denotes the whole array, while if $0 \leqslant i \leqslant j < n$, $b[i:j]$ refers to the array section composed of $b[i]$, $b[i+1]$, ..., $b[j]$. If $i=j+1$, $b[i:j]$ refers to an *empty section* of b.

Quite often, we have to assert something like "all elements of array b are less than x", or "array b contains only zeroes". These might be written as follows.

$$(A\ i:0 \leqslant i < n: b[i] < x)$$
$$(A\ i:0 \leqslant i < n: b[i]=0)$$

Because such assertions occur so frequently, we abbreviate them; these two assertions would be written as $b < x$ and $b = 0$, respectively. That is, the relational operators denote element-wise comparison when applied to arrays. Here are some more examples, using arrays $b[0:n-1]$ and $c[0:n-1]$ and simple variable x.

Abbreviation	Equivalent predicate
$b[1:5]=x$	$(A\ i:1 \leqslant i \leqslant 5: b[i]=x)$
$b[6:10] \neq x$	$(A\ j:6 \leqslant j \leqslant 10: b[j] \neq x)$
$b[0:k-1] < x < b[k:n-1]$	$(A\ i:0 \leqslant i < k: b[i] < x) \wedge$
	$(A\ i:k \leqslant i < n: x < b[i])$
$b[i:j] \leqslant b[j:k]$	$(A\ p,q:i \leqslant p \leqslant j \leqslant q \leqslant k: b[p] \leqslant b[q])$
$\neg (b[6:10] \neq x)$	$\neg (A\ j:6 \leqslant j \leqslant 10: b[j] \neq x)$
	$= (E\ j:6 \leqslant j \leqslant 10: \neg (b[j] \neq x))$
	$= (E\ j:6 \leqslant j \leqslant 10: b[j]=x)$

Be very careful with $=$ and $\neq$, for the last example shows that $b=y$ can be different from $\neg (b \neq y)$! Similarly, $b \leqslant y$ can be different from $\neg (b > y)$.

We also use the notation $x \in b$ to assert that the value of x is equal to (at least) one of the values $b[i]$. Thus, using $domain(b)$ to represent the set of subscript values for b, $x \in b$ is equivalent to

$$(E\ i: i \in domain(b): x=b[i])$$

Such abbreviations can make program specification —and understanding the specification later— easier. However, when developing a program to meet the specification it is often advantageous to expand the abbreviations into their full form, because the full form can give more insight into program development. In a sense, the abbreviations are a form of abstraction; they let us concentrate on what is meant, while how that meaning is formally expressed is put aside for the moment. This is similar to procedural abstraction; when writing a call of a procedure we concentrate on what the procedure does, and how it is implemented does not concern us at the moment.

Array pictures

Let us now turn to a slightly different subject, using pictures for some predicates that describe arrays. Suppose we are writing a program to sort an array $b[0:n-1]$, with initial values $B[0:n-1]$ —i.e. initially, $b = B$. We want to describe the following conditions:

(1) $b[0:k-1]$ is sorted and all its elements are at most x,

(2) the value that belongs in $b[k]$ is in simple variable x,

(3) every value in $b[k+1:n-1]$ is at least x.

To express this formally, we write

(5.2.1) $0 \leqslant k < n \wedge ordered(b[0:k-1]) \wedge perm((b; k:x), B) \wedge$
         $b[0:k-1] \leqslant x \leqslant b[k+1:n-1]$

where

$$ordered(b[0:k-1]) = (Ai : 0 \leqslant i < k-1 : b[i] \leqslant b[i+1])$$

and the notation $perm(X, Y)$ means "array X is a permutation of array Y".

Looks complicated, doesn't it? Because such assertions occur frequently when dealing with arrays, we introduce a "picture" notation to present them in a manner that allows easier understanding. We replace assertion (5.2.1) by

$$0 \leqslant k < n \wedge b \begin{array}{|c|c|c|} \hline \overset{0}{ordered, \leqslant x} & \overset{k-1 \quad k}{} & \overset{k+1 \quad n-1}{\geqslant x} \\ \hline \end{array} \wedge perm(B, (b; k:x))$$

The second term describes the current partitioning of b in a straightforward manner. The array name b appears to the left of the picture. The properties of each partition of the array are written inside the box for that partition. The lower and upper bounds are given at the top for a partition whose size is $\geqslant 0$, while just the subscript value is given for a partition known to be of size 1 (like $b[k:k]$). Bounds may be omitted if the picture is unambiguous; the above picture can be written in at least two other ways:

$$\begin{array}{ccc} & 0 & k & n-1 \\ b & \boxed{ordered, \;\leqslant x \quad | \quad \geqslant x} \end{array} \quad \text{and} \quad \begin{array}{ccc} & 0 & k-1 \;\; k+1 \;\; n-1 \\ b & \boxed{ordered, \;\leqslant x \quad | \quad \geqslant x} \end{array}$$

Note that some of the partitions may be empty. For example, if $k = 0$, $b[0:k-1]$ is empty and the picture reduces to

$$\begin{array}{c} k \;\; k+1 \quad n-1 \\ b \;\; \boxed{\quad | \quad \leqslant x \quad} \end{array}$$

while if $k = n$ the section $b[k+1:n]$ is empty. One disadvantage of such pictures is that they often cause us to forget about singular cases. We unconsciously think that, since section $b[0:k-1]$ is in the picture, it must contain something. So use such pictures with care.

An essential property of such pictures is that the formal definition of assignment (given later in Part II) is useable on pictures when they appear in predicates. This will be discussed in detail in Part II.

Exercises for Section 5.2

1. Redo exercise 6 of section 4.2, using the abbreviations introduced in this section.

2. Translate the following predicates into the picture notation.
(a) $0 \leqslant p \leqslant q+1 \leqslant n \;\wedge\; b[0:p-1] \leqslant x < b[q+1:n]$
(b) $0 \leqslant k-1 \leqslant f \leqslant h-1 < n \;\wedge$
  $1 = b[1:k-1] \;\wedge\; 2 = b[k:f-1] \;\wedge\; 3 = b[h+1:n]$

3. Change the following predicates into equivalent ones that don't use pictures.

$$\text{(a)} \quad 0 \leqslant k \leqslant h \leqslant n \;\wedge\; b \begin{array}{cccc} 0 & k & h & n \\ \boxed{\leqslant x \;\; | \;\; =x \quad | \quad =x \;\; | \;\; \geqslant x} \end{array}$$

$$\text{(b)} \quad 0 \leqslant i < n \;\wedge\; b \begin{array}{ccc} 0 & i & n \\ \boxed{ordered \quad | \quad} \end{array}$$

5.3 Handling Arrays of Arrays of ...

This section may be skipped on first reading.

The Pascal declaration

(5.3.1) **var** b: **array** [0:1] **of array** [1:3] **of** *integer*

defines an array of arrays. That is, $b[0]$ (and similarly $b[1]$) is an array consisting of three elements named $b[0][1]$, $b[0][2]$ and $b[0][3]$. One can also have an "array of arrays of arrays", in which case three subscripts could be used —e.g. $d[i][j][k]$— and so forth.

Array of arrays take the place of two-dimensional arrays in FORTRAN and PL/I. For example, (5.3.1) could be thought of as equivalent to the PL/I declaration

$$DECLARE\ b(0{:}1,\ 1{:}3)\ FIXED;$$

because both declarations define an array that can be thought of as two-dimensional:

$b[0][1]$	$b[0][2]$	$b[0][3]$		$b[0,1]$	$b[0,2]$	$b[0,3]$
			or			
$b[1][1]$	$b[1][2]$	$b[1][3]$		$b[1,1]$	$b[1,2]$	$b[1,3]$

We now extend the notation $(b; i{:}e)$ to allow a sequence of subscripts in the position where i appears, for the following reason. If the assignment $c[i]{:=}\ 2$ is equivalent to $c := (c; i{:}2)$, then the assignment $b[i][j]{:=}3$ should be equivalent to $b := (b; [i][j]{:}3)$, where brackets are placed around each of the subscripts i and j in order to have an easy-to-read notation.

We need to be able to refer to sequences of subscript expressions (enclosed in brackets), like $[i], [i+1][j]$ and $[i][j][k]$. We introduce some terminology to make it easier. The term *selector* denotes a finite sequence of subscript expressions, each enclosed in brackets. The null selector —the sequence containing 0 subscripts— is written as ε. The null selector enjoys a nice property; it is the identity element of the operation catenation on sequences (see the remark following definition (4.2.3)). That is, using $\circ$ to denote catenation, for any identifier or selector s we have $s \circ \varepsilon = s$. Any reference to a variable —simple or subscripted— now consists of an identifier catenated with a selector; the reference x to a simple variable is really $x \circ \varepsilon$.

Example 1. $b \circ \varepsilon$ is identifier b followed by the null selector. It refers to the complete array b.

$b[0]$ consists of identifier b catenated with the selector $[0]$. For b declared in (5.3.1), it refers to the array $(b[0][1], b[0][2], b[0][3])$.

$b[i][j]$ consists of identifier b followed by the selector $[i][j]$. For b declared in (5.3.1), it refers to a single integer. □

We want to define the notation $(b; s:e)$ for any selector s. We do this recursively on the length of s. The first step is to determine the base case, $(b; \varepsilon:e)$.

Let x be a simple variable (which contains a scalar or function). Since x and $x \circ \varepsilon$ are equivalent, the assignments $x := e$ and $x \circ \varepsilon := e$ are also equivalent. But, by our earlier notation the latter should be equivalent to $x := (x; \varepsilon:e)$. Therefore, the two expressions e and $(x; \varepsilon:e)$ must yield the same value, and we have

$$e = (x; \varepsilon:e)$$

With this insight, we define the notation $(b; s:e)$.

(5.3.2)   **Definition.** Let b and g be functions or variables of the same type. Let s be a suitable selector for b. The notation $(b; s:e)$ for a suitable expression e is defined by

$$(b; \varepsilon:g) \quad\quad = g$$

$$(b; [i] \circ s:e)[j] = \begin{cases} i \neq j \;\rightarrow\; b[j] \\ i = j \;\rightarrow\; (b[j]; s:e) \end{cases} \quad □$$

Example 2. In this and the following examples, let $c[1:3] = (6, 7, 8)$ and $b[0:1][1:3] = ((0, 1, 2), (3, 4, 5))$. Then

$$(c; \varepsilon:b[1]) = b[1], \text{ so that}$$
$$(c; \varepsilon:b[1])[2] = b[1][2] = 4. \quad □$$

Example 3. $(c; 1:3)[1] = (c; [1] \circ \varepsilon:3)[1]$
$$\quad\quad\quad\quad\quad = (c[1]; \varepsilon:3) = 3.$$
$$(c; 1:3)[2] = (c; [1] \circ \varepsilon:3)[2] = c[2] = 7.$$
$$(c; 1:3)[3] = (c; [1] \circ \varepsilon:3)[3] = c[3] = 8. \quad □$$

Example 4. $(b; [1][3]:9)[0] = b[0] = (0, 1, 2)$.
$$(b; [1][3]:9)[1] = (b[1]; [3]:9) = (3, 4, 9). \quad □$$

Again, all but the outer parentheses can be omitted. For example, the following two expressions are equivalent. They define an array (function) that is the same as b except in three positions —$[i][j]$, $[j]$ and $[k][i]$.

$(((b; [i][j]:e); [j]:f); [k][i]:g)$ and
$(b; [i][j]:e; [j]:f; [k][i]:g)$.

Exercises for Section 5.3

1. Exercise 4 of section 5.1 was to develop a functional view of records. One can also have arrays of records and records of arrays. For example, the following Pascal-like declarations are valid.

> **type** t: **record** x: *integer*; y: **array** $[0:10]$ **of** *integer* **end**;
> **var** b: **array** $[0:n-1]$ **of** t

Modify the notation of this section to allow references to subrecords of arrays and subarrays of records, etc.

Chapter 6
Using Assertions To Document Programs

This chapter introduces the use of predicates as assertions for documenting programs in an informal manner, thus paving the way for the more formal treatment given in Parts II and III.

6.1 Program Specifications

A program specification must describe exactly *what* execution of a program is to accomplish. Another part of a specification might also deal with speed, size, and so forth, but for now we will concentrate on the part that describes only the *what*.

One way to specify a program is to give a high-level, English command for it. For example, the following specifies a program to multiply two non-negative integer variables.

(6.1.1)   Store in z the product $a*b$, assuming a and b are initially ≥ 0.

When written as a comment for a program segment within a program, (6.1.1) is called a *command-comment*; it is a comment that is a statement or command to perform some action.

A naive programmer might think that a program that sets a, b and z to 0 satisfies (6.1.1), because (6.1.1) does not indicate that a and b should not be changed. The wise programmer, however, remembers that a program should do nothing more than is *explicitly* required, and also nothing less. Since the specification does not mention changing a and b, they should not be changed. A command-comment like (6.1.1) should define precisely *all* input and output variables; nothing is more useless than a partial specification that cannot be understood without reading the program itself. For example, the specification

    Multiply *a* and *b* together

does not indicate where the result of the multiplication should be stored, and hence it cannot be understood in isolation, as it should be.

    English can be ambiguous, so we often rely on more formal specification techniques. The notation

(6.1.2) $\{Q\}\ S\ \{R\}$

where Q and R are predicates and S is a program (sequence of commands), has the following interpretation:

(6.1.3)   If execution of S is begun in a state satisfying Q, then it is guaranteed to terminate in a finite amount of time in a state satisfying R. □

Q is called the *precondition* or *input assertion* of S; R the *postcondition*, *output assertion* or *result assertion*. The braces { and } around the assertions are used to separate the assertions from the program itself.

    Note that nothing is said about execution beginning in a state that does not satisfy Q; the specification deals only with some initial states. If the program is to deal with all possible initial states, for example by printing error messages for erroneous input, then these cases form part of the specification and must be covered by the predicates Q and R.

    Note also that termination is *guaranteed* to happen in a finite amount of time —provided, of course, that execution continues.

    Finally, we stress the fact that (6.1.2) is itself a predicate —a statement that is either true or false— which we usually want to be true. When writing a program S to satisfy (6.1.2), it is our business to prove in some fashion that $\{Q\}\ S\ \{R\}$ does indeed hold. Part II will describe how to write such a predicate in the predicate calculus introduced in earlier sections and to formally prove that it is a tautology.

    As an example of the use of notation (6.1.2), we write specification (6.1.1) in it —note the use of the label R in the postcondition to give the postcondition a name:

(6.1.4) $\{0 \leqslant a \wedge 0 \leqslant b\}\ S\ \{R: z = a*b\}$

    Unfortunately, (6.1.4) does not indicate which variables should be changed, and in fact the program segment $z := 0;\ a := 0;\ b := 0$ satisfies it. Typically, we use common sense and English to rectify the problem (but see also section 6.2). And we often use a mixture of the command-comment and the formal notation (6.1.2) in the following standardized form:

(6.1.5)   Given fixed a, $b \geq 0$, establish (the truth of) $R: z = a*b$.

The precondition of the program is *given*, the *fixed* variables, which must not be changed, are listed and the postcondition is to be *established*.

Here are some more examples of specifications (all variables are integer valued).

Example 1 (array summation). Given are fixed $n \geq 0$ and fixed array $b[0:n-1]$. Establish

$$R: s = (\Sigma i: 0 \leq i < n: b[i]). \quad \square$$

Example 2 (square root approximation). Given fixed integer $n \geq 0$, store in s an approximation to the square root of n; i.e. establish

$$R: s^2 \leq n < (s+1)^2. \quad \square$$

Example 3 (sorting). Given fixed $n \geq 0$ and array $b[0:n-1]$, sort b, i.e. establish

$$R: (A i: 0 \leq i < n-1: b[i] \leq b[i+1]). \quad \square$$

Again, there is a problem with this specification; the result can be established simply by setting all elements of b to zeroes. This problem can be overcome by including a comment to the effect that the only way to alter b is to swap two of its elements.

Naturally, with large, complex problems there may be difficulty in specifying programs in this simple manner, and new notation may have to be introduced to cope with the complexity. But for the most part, the simple specification forms given above will suffice. Even a compiler can be specified in such a notation, by judicious use of abstraction:

> {*Pascal program* (p)}
> *compiler*
> {*IBM* 370 *program* $(q) \wedge$ *equivalent* (p, q)}

where the predicates *Pascal program*, *IBM* 370 *program* and *equivalent* must be defined elsewhere.

6.2 Representing Initial and Final Values of Variables

The program

$$swap: t := x; \; x := y; \; y := t$$

swaps or exchanges the values of integer variables x and y, using a "local" variable t. In order to state formally what *swap* does, we need a way to describe the initial and final values of x and y. To do this, we use identifiers X and Y:

(6.2.1) $\{x = X \wedge y = Y\} \; swap \; \{x = Y \wedge y = X\}$

Now, we are asserting that (6.2.1) is always true; it is a tautology. Recall from section 4.5 that a tautology with free identifiers is equivalent to the same predicate but with all previously free identifiers universally bound. That is, (6.2.1) is equivalent to

(6.2.2) $(A \; X, Y : \{x = X \wedge y = Y\} \; swap \; \{x = Y \wedge y = X\})$

and actually to

$$(A \; X, Y, x, y : \{x = X \wedge y = Y\} \; swap \; \{x = Y \wedge y = X\})$$

(6.2.2) can be read in English as follows: for all (integer) values of X and Y, if initially $x = X$ and $y = Y$, then execution of *swap* establishes $x = Y$ and $y = X$.

X and Y denote the *initial* values of variables x and y, but they also denote the *final* values of y and x. An identifier can denote either an initial or a final value, or even a value upon which the initial or final value depends. For example, the following is also a specification of *swap*, although it is not as easy to understand:

$$\{x = X+1 \wedge y = Y-1\} \; swap \; \{x = Y-1 \wedge y = X+1\}.$$

Generally, we will use capital letters in identifiers that represent initial and final values of program variables, and small letters for identifiers that name variables in a program.

As a final example, we specify a sort program again, this time using an extra identifier to alleviate the problem mentioned in example 3 of section 6.1. The predicate $perm(c, C)$ has the meaning "array c is a permutation of array C, i.e. a rearrangement of C". See exercise 5 of section 4.2.

Example 1 (sorting). Given fixed $n \geqslant 0$ and array $c[0:n-1]$ with $c = C$, establish

$$R: perm(c, C) \land (A\ i: 0 \leqslant i < n-1: c[i] \leqslant c[i+1]).$$

Exercises for Section 6.2

1. Write specifications for the following problems. Put them in the form used in example 1 above (sorting) and also in the form $\{Q\}\,S\,\{R\}$. The problems may be vaguely stated, so you may have to use common sense and your experience to derive a precise specification.

(a) Set x to the maximum value in array $b[0:n-1]$.

(b) Set x to the absolute value of x.

(c) Find the position of a maximum value in array $b[0:n-1]$.

(d) Find the position of the first maximum value in $b[0:n-1]$.

(e) Tell whether a given integer that is greater than 1 is prime. (An integer >1 is prime if it is divisible only by 1 and itself.)

(f) Find the nth Fibonacci number f_n. The Fibonacci numbers are defined by $f_0 = 0$, $f_1 = 1$ and, for $n > 1$, $f_n = f_{n-1} + f_{n-2}$. Thus, the Fibonacci number sequence begins with (0, 1, 1, 2, 3, 5, 8).

(g) Tell whether integer array $b[0:n-1]$ is sorted (is in ascending order).

(h) Set each value of array $b[0:n-1]$ to the sum of the values in b.

(i) Let $c[0:n-1]$ be the list of people teaching at Cornell and $w[0:m-1]$ be the list of people on welfare in Ithaca. Both lists are alphabetically ordered. It is known that at least one person is on both lists. Find the first such person!

(j) The same problem as (i), except that there are three lists: c, the Cornellians; w, those on welfare; and m, those making money consulting for the federal government.

(k) Consider a two-dimensional array $g[0:n-1, 0:3]$. $g[i, 0]$, $g[i, 1]$, $g[i, 2]$ and $g[i, 3]$ are the grades for student i in his courses this semester, with $A = 4.0$, $B = 3.0$, $C = 2.0$, etc. Let $name[0:n-1]$ contain the names of the students. Find the student with the highest average. You may use "real variables", which can contain floating point numbers.

6.3 Proof Outlines

We have shown how to write a predicate (within braces) before and after a program in order to assert what is to be true before and after execution. In the same manner, a predicate may appear *between* two statements in order to show what must be true at that point of execution. For example, here is a complete formulation of program *swap*, which swaps (exchanges) the values of two variables x and y, using a local variable t.

$$\{X = x \wedge y = Y\}$$
$$t := x;$$
$$\{t = X \wedge x = X \wedge y = Y\}$$
$$x := y;$$
$$\{t = X \wedge x = Y \wedge y = Y\}$$
$$y := t$$
$$\{y = X \wedge x = Y\}$$

The reader can informally verify that, for each statement of the program, if its precondition —the predicate in braces preceding it— is true, then execution of the statement terminates with its postcondition —the predicate in braces following it— true.

A predicate placed in a program is called an *assertion*; we assert it is true at that point of execution. A program together with an assertion between each pair of statements is called a *proof outline*, because it is just that; it is an outline of a formal proof, and one can understand that the program satisfies its specification simply by showing that each triple (precondition, statement, postcondition) satisfies {precondition} statement {postcondition}. The formal proof method is described in Part II.

Placing assertions in a program for purposes of documentation is often called *annotating* the program, and the final program is also called an *annotated* program.

Below is a proof outline for

$$\{i \geqslant 0 \wedge s = 1+2+ \cdots +i\}$$
$$i := i+1; \quad s := s+i$$
$$\{i > 0 \wedge s = 1+2+ \cdots +i\}$$

The proof outline illustrates two new conventions. First, an assertion can be named so that it can be discussed more easily, by placing the name at its beginning followed by a colon. Secondly, adjacent assertions —e.g. {P} {P1}— mean that the first implies the second —e.g. $P \Rightarrow P1$. The lines have been numbered solely for reference in a later discussion.

(1) $\{P : i \geqslant 0 \wedge s = 1+2+ \cdots +i\}$
(2) $\{P1 : i+1 > 0 \wedge s = 1+2+ \cdots +(i+1-1)\}$
(3) $i := i+1;$
(4) $\{P2 : i > 0 \wedge s = 1+2+ \cdots +(i-1)\}$
(5) $\{P3 : i > 0 \wedge s+i = 1+2+ \cdots +i\}$
(6) $s := s+i$
(7) $\{R : i > 0 \wedge s = 1+2+ \cdots +i\}$

The above proof outline indicates the following facts, in order:

1. $P \Rightarrow P1$ (lines 1, 2)
2. $\{P1\}\ i := i+1\ \{P2\}$ (lines 2, 3, 4)
3. $P2 \Rightarrow P3$ (lines 4, 5)
4. $\{P3\}\ s := s+i\ \{R\}$ (lines 5, 6, 7)

Together, these give the desired result: execution of $i := i+1;\ s := s+i$ begun in a state satisfying P terminates in a state satisfying R.

The next example illustrates the use of a conditional statement. Note how the assertion following **then** is the conjunction of the precondition of the conditional statement and the test, since this is what is true at that point of execution. Since both the **then**-part and the **else**-part end with the assertion $x = abs(X)$, this is what we may conclude about execution of the conditional statement.

$$\{x = X\}$$
if $x < 0$ **then** $\{x = X \wedge x < 0\}$
  $x := -x$
  $\{x = -X \wedge x > 0\}\ \{x = abs(X)\}$
    else $\{x = X \wedge x \geqslant 0\}$
  $skip$
  $\{x = X \wedge x \geqslant 0\}\ \{x = abs(X)\}$
$\{x = abs(X)\}$

More details on annotating a program will be forthcoming when we study loops in Part II. However, one point should be made here. It is not always necessary to give a complete proof outline. Enough assertions should be inserted to make the program understandable, but not so many that the program is hidden from view. In general, a good practice is to insert those assertions that are not so easily determined by the reader, and to omit those that are.

Part II
The Semantics of
a Small Language

This Part introduces a programming notation and defines it in terms of the notion of a "weakest precondition". The main concern is the statements, or *commands*, of the notation and how they can be understood. The syntax of declarations and expressions is a secondary concern, and instead of formally defining them we appeal to the reader's knowledge of mathematics and programming. In general, a Pascal-like notation for declarations is used, which the reader should have no trouble understanding. It is understood that each simple variable and expression has a *type*, usually *integer* or *Boolean*, and that variables are considered to be of type *integer* unless otherwise specified or obvious from the context.

Chapter 7
The Predicate Transformer wp

Our task is to define the commands (statements) of a small language. This will be done as follows. For any command S and predicate R, which describes the desired result of executing S, we will define another predicate, denoted by $wp(S, R)$, that represents

(7.1) the set of *all* states such that execution of S begun in any one of them is guaranteed to terminate in a finite amount of time in a state satisfying R. □

Let's give some examples for some ALGOL-like commands, based on our knowledge of how these commands are executed.

Example 1. Let S be the assignment command $i := i+1$ and let R be $i \leqslant 1$. Then

$$wp(\text{``}i := i+1\text{''}, \ i \leqslant 1) = (i \leqslant 0)$$

for if $i \leqslant 0$, then execution of $i := i+1$ terminates with $i \leqslant 1$, while if $i > 0$, execution cannot make $i \leqslant 1$. □

Example 2. Let S be **if** $x \geqslant y$ **then** $z := x$ **else** $z := y$ and R be $z = max(x, y)$. Execution of S *always* sets z to $max(x, y)$, so that $wp(S, R) = T$. □

Example 3. Let S be as in Example 2 and let R be $z = y$. Then $wp(S, R) = (y \geqslant x)$, for execution of S beginning with $y \geqslant x$ sets z to y and execution of S beginning with $y < x$ sets z to x, which is $\neq y$. □

Example 4. Let S be as in Example 2 and let R be $z = y-1$. Then $wp(S, R) = F$ (the set of no states), for execution of S can never set z less than y. □

Example 5. Let S be as in Example 2 and R be $z = y + 1$. Then $wp(S, R) = (x = y + 1)$, for only then will execution of S set z to $y + 1$.   □

Example 6. For a command S, $wp(S, T)$ represents the set of all states such that execution of S begun in any one of them is guaranteed to terminate.   □

In section 6.1, we used the notation $\{Q\}\ S\ \{R\}$ to mean that execution of S begun in any state satisfying predicate Q would terminate in a state satisfying predicate R. In this context, Q is called the *precondition* and R the *postcondition* of S. Similarly, we call $wp(S, R)$ the **weakest precondition** of S with respect to R, since it represents the set of *all* states such that execution begun in any one of them will terminate with R true. (See section 1.6 for a definition of *weaker* and *weakest* in this context.) We see, then, that the notation $\{Q\}\ S\ \{R\}$ is simply another notation for

(7.2) $Q \Rightarrow wp(S, R)$.

Note carefully that $\{Q\}\ S\ \{R\}$ is really a statement in the predicate calculus, since it is equivalent to $Q \Rightarrow wp(S, R)$. Thus, it is either true or false in any state. When we write it, we usually mean it to be a tautology —we expect it to be universally true.

A command S is usually designed for a specific purpose —to establish the truth of one particular postcondition R. So we are not always interested in the general properties of S, but only in those pertaining to R. Moreover, even for this R we may not be interested in the weakest precondition $wp(S, R)$, but usually in some stronger precondition Q (say) that represents a subset of the set represented by $wp(S, R)$. Thus, if we can show that $Q \Rightarrow wp(S, R)$ without actually forming $wp(S, R)$, then we are content to use Q as a precondition.

The ability to work with a precondition that is not the weakest is useful, because the derivation of $wp(S, R)$ itself can be impractical, as we shall see when we consider loops.

Note that wp is a function of two arguments: a command S and a predicate R. Consider for the moment an arbitrary but fixed command S. We can then write $wp(S, R)$ as a function of one argument: $wp_S(R)$. The function wp_S transforms any predicate R into another predicate $wp_S(R)$. This is the origin of the term "predicate transformer" for wp_S.

Remark: The notation $Q\ \{S\}\ R$ was first used in 1969 (see chapter 23) to denote *partial correctness*. It has the interpretation: if execution of S begins in a state satisfying Q, and *if* execution terminates, then the final state will satisfy R. We use braces around the predicates (instead of around the command) to denote *total correctness*: execution is guaranteed to terminate. As an example, note that

$$T \ \{\textbf{while } T \textbf{ do } skip\} \ T$$

where *skip* is a null command, is a tautology, because execution of the loop never halts. But

$$\{T\} \ \textbf{while } T \textbf{ do } skip \ \{T\}$$

which is equivalent to $T \ \Rightarrow \ wp\,(\text{"}\textbf{while } T \textbf{ do } skip\text{"}, T)$, is everywhere false. ☐

Some properties of wp

If we are to define a programming notation using the concept of wp, then we had better be sure that wp is well-behaved. By this we mean that we should be able to define reasonable, implementable commands using wp. Furthermore, it would be nice if unimplementable commands would be rejected from consideration. Let us therefore analyze our interpretation (7.1) of $wp(S, R)$, and see whether any properties can be derived from it.

First, consider the predicate $wp(S, F)$ (for any command S). This describes the set of states such that execution of S begun in any one of them is guaranteed to terminate in a state satisfying F. But no state ever satisfies F, because F represents the empty set. Hence there could not possibly be a state in $wp(S, F)$, and we have our first property:

(7.3) **Law of the Excluded Miracle**: $wp(S, F) = F$.

The name of this property is appropriate, for it would indeed be a miracle if execution could terminate in no state.

The second law is as follows. For any command S and predicates Q and R the following holds:

(7.4) **Distributivity of Conjunction**:

$$wp(S, Q) \wedge wp(S, R) = wp(S, Q \wedge R)$$

Let us see why (7.4) is a tautology. First, consider any state s that satisfies the lefthand side (LHS) of (7.4). Execution of S begun in s will terminate with both Q and R true. Hence $Q \wedge R$ will also be true, and s is in $wp(S, Q \wedge R)$. This shows that LHS $\Rightarrow$ RHS. Next, suppose s is in $wp(S, Q \wedge R)$. Then execution of S begun in s is guaranteed to terminate in some state s' of $Q \wedge R$. Any such s' must be in Q and in R, so that s is in $wp(S,Q)$ and in $wp(S,R)$. This shows that RHS $\Rightarrow$ LHS. Together with LHS $\Rightarrow$ RHS, this yields RHS = LHS.

We have thus shown that (7.3) and (7.4) hold. The arguments were based solely on the informal interpretation (7.1) that we wanted to give to the notation $wp(S,R)$. We now take them as basic axioms, and use them as we do other axioms and laws of the predicate calculus. Using them, we can prove two other useful laws; their proofs are left as exercises.

(7.5)   **Law of Monotonicity**: if $Q \Rightarrow R$ then $wp(S,Q) \Rightarrow wp(S,R)$

(7.6)   **Distributivity of Disjunction**:

$$wp(S,Q) \vee wp(S,R) \Rightarrow wp(S,Q \vee R)$$

It is interesting to compare (7.4) and (7.6). One is an equivalence, the other an implication. Why? The reason is that execution of commands may be *nondeterministic*. Execution of a command is nondeterministic if it need not always be exactly the same each time it is begun in the same state. It may produce different answers, or it may simply take different "paths" en route to the same answer. Most sequential programming notations, like Algol and FORTRAN, are implemented in a *deterministic* fashion —execution begun in the same state is always the same— so this idea of nondeterminism may be new to you.

As an example of a nondeterministic action for which the LHS and RHS of (7.6) are not equivalent, consider the act of flipping a coin that is, theoretically, so thin that it cannot land on its side. There is no guarantee that flipping the coin will yield a head, so that $wp(flip, head) = F$. Similarly, $wp(flip, tail) = F$. Hence,

$$wp(flip, head) \vee wp(flip, tail) = F$$

But the coin *is* guaranteed to land with either a head or a tail up, so that

$$wp(flip, head \vee tail) = T$$

If we know that a command is deterministic, we can show (see exercise 6) that

(7.7) $wp(S,Q) \vee wp(S,R) = wp(S,Q \vee R)$ (for deterministic S)

Note carefully that nondeterminism is a property of the implementation of a command, and not a property of the command itself. If a command satisfies (7.7), then it should be possible to implement it in a deterministic fashion without restricting its generality. If a command does *not* satisfy (7.7), then if it is implemented in a deterministic fashion, the implementation is likely to restrict the command somewhat —for example, by requiring so much skill in flipping a coin that landing head up is guaranteed.

In the next chapter we will begin defining a programming notation in terms of wp. In doing so, we must be extremely careful. For any command S, the function $wp_S(R)$ yields a predicate, and at first glance it might seem that any function with domain and range the set of predicates will do. But remember that such functions must represent implementable commands. At the least, it is our duty to certify that such functions satisfy (7.3) and (7.4), because these properties were developed based on our notion of command execution. We shall not always perform this duty in later chapters (because it has been done before); rather, we will leave this task to the reader as exercises.

Exercises for Chapter 7

1. Determine $wp(S, R)$ for the following S and R, based on your own knowledge of how S is executed. Assume that all variables are of type *integer* and that all subscripts are in range.

	S	R
(a)	$i := i+1$	$i > 0$
(b)	$i := i+2;\ j := j-2$	$i+j = 0$
(c)	$i := i+1;\ j := j-1$	$i*j = 0$
(d)	$z := z*j;\ i := i-1$	$z*j^i = c$
(e)	$a[i] := 1$	$a[i] = a[j]$
(f)	$a[a[i]] := i$	$a[i] = i$

2. Examples 1-5 of this section each gave a predicate in the form $wp(S, R) = Q$. Rewrite each of these in the form $\{Q\}\ S\ \{R\}$, just to get used to the two different notations. For example, example 2 would be written as

$$\{T\}\ \textbf{if}\ x \geqslant y\ \textbf{then}\ z := x\ \textbf{else}\ z := y\ \{z = max(x, y)\}.$$

3. Prove (7.5) and (7.6). Don't rely on the notion of execution and interpretation (7.1); prove them only from (7.4) and the laws of predicate calculus.

4. Prove using (7.4) that $(wp(S, R) \wedge wp(S, \neg R)) = F$.

5. Give an example to show that the following is *not* true for all states: $(wp(S, R) \vee wp(S, \neg R)) = T$.

6. Show that (7.7) holds for deterministic S. (It cannot be proved from axioms (7.3)-(7.4); it must be argued based on the definitions of determinism and wp, as was done for (7.3) and (7.4).)

7. Suppose $Q \Rightarrow wp(S, R)$ has been proven for particular Q, R and S. Analyze fully the statement

(7.8) $\{(A\,x:Q)\}\ \ S\ \ \{(A\,x:R)\}$

(Is it true in general; if not, what restrictions must be made so that it holds for "reasonable" classes of predicates Q, R and commands S, etc.) Hint: be careful to consider the case where x appears in S. You may want to answer the question under the ground rule that the appearance of x in S means that (7.8) is invalid, and that the quantified identifier x should be changed before proceeding. It is also instructive, however, to answer this question without using this ground rule. See section 4.3.

8. Suppose $Q \Rightarrow wp(S, R)$ has been proven for particular Q, R and S. Analyze fully the statement

$$\{(E\,x:Q)\}\ \ S\ \ \{(E\,x:R)\}$$

(Is it true in general; if not, what restrictions must be made so that it holds for "reasonable" classes of predicates Q, R and commands S, etc.) See the hint on exercise 7.

Chapter 8
The Commands skip, abort and Composition

We now define a programming notation in terms of *wp*. We will also indicate how each command of the programming notation is to be executed, so that the reader can relate it to statements of other conventional languages. Also, by showing how the command can be executed we establish that it really is useful. But the definition in terms of *wp* should be viewed as *the* definition of the command.

We begin with the command *skip*. Execution of *skip* does nothing (and, we assume, very quickly). It is equivalent to the "empty" command of ALGOL 60 and Pascal and to the PL/I command consisting solely of a semicolon ";". It is included in the notation for two reasons. First, it is often useful to be able to explicitly say that "nothing" should be done. But just as importantly its predicate transformer is mathematically very simple —it is the identity transformation:

(8.1) **Definition**. $wp(skip, R) = R$. □

The second command is *abort*, which is introduced not because of its usefulness in programming but because it, too, has a definition that is mathematically simple. It is the only possible command whose predicate transformer is a "constant" function (see exercise 3).

(8.2) **Definition**. $wp(abort, R) = F$. □

How is *abort* executed? Well, it should never *be* executed, because it can only be executed in a state satisfying F and no state satisfies F! If execution ever reaches a point at which *abort* is to be executed, then obviously the program (and its proof) is in error, and abortion is called for.

Sequential composition is one way of composing larger program segments from smaller segments. Let *S1* and *S2* be two commands. Then

S1; S2 is a new command. It is executed by first executing *S1* and then executing *S2*. Its formal definition is:

(8.3)   **Definition.** $wp(\text{``}S1; \ S2\text{''}, R) = wp(S1, wp(S2, R))$. □

As a (trivial) example, we have

$$wp(\text{``}skip;\ skip\text{''}, R) = wp(skip, wp(skip, R))$$
$$= wp(skip, R) \quad (\text{since } wp(skip, R) = R)$$
$$= R.$$

Now consider a sequence of three commands: *S1; S2; S3*. Executing it should involve first executing *S1*, then *S2*, and finally *S3*, but we must make sure that the sequence also makes sense in terms of *wp*. Is it to be interpreted as *(S1; S2); S3* or as *S1; (S2; S3)*? Fortunately, the operation of function composition, which is used in defining sequential composition, is associative (see Appendix 3). Therefore

$$wp(\text{``}S1;\ (S2;\ S3)\text{''}, R) = wp(\text{``}(S1;\ S2);\ S3\text{''}, R).$$

That is, it doesn't matter whether one thinks of *S1; S2; S3* as *S1* composed with *S2; S3* or as *S1; S2* composed with *S3*, and it is all right to leave the parentheses out. (Similarly, because addition is associative, $a+b+c$ is well-defined because $a+(b+c)$ yields the same result as $(a+b)+c$.)

Be aware of the role of the semicolon; it is used to *combine* adjacent, independent commands into a single command, much the way it is used in English to combine independent clauses. (For an example of its use in English, see the previous sentence.) It can be thought of as an operator that combines, just as catenation is used in Pascal and PL/I to combine two strings of characters. Once this is understood, there should be no confusion about where to put a semicolon.

Our use of the semicolon conforms not only to English usage, but also to its original use in the first programming notation that contained it, ALGOL 60. It is a pity that the designers of PL/I and Ada saw fit to go against convention and use the semicolon as a statement terminator, for it has caused great confusion.

Thus far, we don't have much of a programming notation —about all we can write is a sequence of *skip*s and *abort*s. In the next chapter we define the assignment command. Before reading ahead, though, perform some of the exercises in order to get a firm grasp of this (still simple) material.

Exercises for Chapter 8

1. Prove that definition (8.1) satisfies laws (7.3), (7.4) and (7.7).

2. Prove that definition (8.2) satisfies laws (7.3), (7.4) and (7.7).

3. Consider introducing a command *make —true* with a constant predicate transformer:

$$wp(make-true, R) = T \qquad \text{for all predicates } R.$$

Why isn't *make —true* a valid command?

4. Prove that definition (8.3) satisfies laws (7.3) and (7.4), provided *S1* and *S2* do.

5. Prove that definition (8.3) satisfies (7.7) provided *S1* and *S2* do. This shows that sequential composition does not introduce nondeterminism.

6. Prove that $wp(\text{``}x := e; \ abort\text{''}, R) = F$, for any predicate $R$, regardless of the definition of $wp(\text{``}x := e\text{''}, R)$.

Chapter 9
The Assignment Command

9.1 Assignment to Simple Variables

For the moment, we consider assignment to a simple variable, where a "simple" variable is a variable of type *integer*, *Boolean* and the like. We treat assignment to array elements in section 9.3.

The assignment command has the form

$$x := e$$

where x is a simple variable, e is an expression, and the types of x and e are the same. This command is read as "x becomes e". As a convention, it is written with a blank separating the assignment symbol $:=$ from e but no blank separating x from $:=$.

The command $x := e$ can be executed properly only in a state in which e can be evaluated (e.g. there is no division by zero). Execution consists of evaluating e and storing the resulting value in the location named x. In effect, (the value of) x is replaced by (the value of) e, and a similar, but textual, replacement forms the heart of the definition:

(9.1.1) **Definition.** $wp(\text{"}x := e\text{"}, R) = domain(e)$ **cand** R_e^x

where

(9.1.2) $domain(e)$ is a predicate that describes the set of all states in which e may be evaluated —i.e. is well-defined. $\square$

Predicate $domain(e)$ will not be formally defined, since expressions e are not. However, it must exclude all states in which evaluation of e would be undefined —e.g. because of division by zero or subscript out of range.

It can be defined recursively on the structure of expressions (see exercise 6).

Often, we tend to omit $domain(e)$ entirely, writing

(9.1.3) $wp(\text{``}x := e\text{''}, R) = R_e^x$

because assignments should always be written in contexts in which the expressions can be properly evaluated.

Definition (9.1.3) can be bewildering at first, for it seems to require "thinking backwards". Our operational habits make us feel that the precondition should be R and the postcondition R_e^x! Here is an informal explanation of (9.1.1): Since x will contain the value of e after execution, then R will be true after execution *iff* R, with the value of x replaced by e, is true before execution. A more formal explanation is left to exercise 3. The following examples should lend some confidence in the definition. In particular, examples 7 and 8 should convince the reader that this definition is consistent with our conventional model of execution.

Example 1. $wp(\text{``}x := 5\text{''}, x = 5) = (5 = 5) = T$.   Hence execution of $x := 5$ always establishes $x = 5$.   □

Example 2. $wp(\text{``}x := 5\text{''}, x \neq 5) = (5 \neq 5) = F$.   Hence execution of $x := 5$ never establishes $x \neq 5$.   □

Example 3. $wp(\text{``}x := x+1\text{''}, x < 0) = (x+1 < 0) = (x < -1)$.   □

Example 4. $wp(\text{``}x := x*x\text{''}, x^4 = 10) = ((x*x)^4 = 10) = (x^8 = 10)$.   □

Example 5. For any predicate p of one argument,

$$wp(\text{``}x := a \div b\text{''}, p(x)) = (b \neq 0 \textbf{ cand } p(a \div b)).$$

This example required explicit use of the term $domain(e)$ of definition (9.1.1).   □

Example 6. Suppose array b is declared with subscript range $0:100$. Then

$$wp(\text{``}x := b[i]\text{''}, x = b[i])) = (0 \leqslant i \leqslant 100 \textbf{ cand } b[i] = b[i])$$
$$= (0 \leqslant i \leqslant 100).$$

Thus, x will contain the value $b[i]$ upon termination *iff* i is a valid subscript for array b.   □

Example 7. Assume c is a constant. Then $wp(\text{``}x := e\text{''}, x = c) = (e = c)$. This means that execution of $x := e$ is guaranteed to terminate with c in x *iff* the value of expression e *before* execution is c. □

Example 8. Assume c is a constant and x and y are distinct identifiers. Then

$$wp(\text{``}x := e\text{''}, y = c) = (y = c). \quad \square$$

Example 8 is particularly illuminating. Since y must retain its original value c, execution of the assignment $x := e$ cannot change y. Since the above must hold for *all* variables y and values c, execution of $x := e$ may change *only* x, and no other variable. Hence, no so-called "side effects" are allowed. This restriction holds universally: execution of an assignment may change only the variable indicated and evaluation of an expression may change no variable. This prohibits functions with side effects.

The ban on side effects is extremely important, for it allows us to consider expressions as conventional mathematical entities. This means that we can use all the conventional properties with which we are used to working when dealing with them —such as associativity and commutativity of addition and the logical laws of chapter 2.

Swapping the values of two variables

The sequence $t := x;\ x := y;\ y := t$ can be used to "swap" or exchange the values of variables x and y, as the following shows.

$$
\begin{aligned}
wp(\text{``}t := x;\ x := y;\ y := t\text{''}, x = X \wedge y = Y) \\
= \ & wp(\text{``}t := x;\ x := y\text{''}, wp(\text{``}y := t\text{''}, x = X \wedge y = Y)) \\
= \ & wp(\text{``}t := x;\ x := y\text{''}, x = X \wedge t = Y) \\
= \ & wp(\text{``}t := x\text{''}, wp(\text{``}x := y\text{''}, x = X \wedge t = Y)) \\
= \ & wp(\text{``}t := x\text{''}, y = X \wedge t = Y) \\
= \ & (y = X \wedge x = Y)
\end{aligned}
$$

The above is comparatively difficult to read and write. Instead, we use a proof outline, as illustrated to the left in (9.1.4).

(9.1.4)
$$
\begin{array}{ll}
\{y = X \wedge x = Y\} & \{y = X \wedge x = Y\} \\
t := x; & t := x; \\
\{y = X \wedge t = Y\} & x := y; \\
x := y; & y := t \\
\{x = X \wedge t = Y\} & \{x = X \wedge y = Y\} \\
y := t & \\
\{x = X \wedge y = Y\} &
\end{array}
$$

Recall from section 6.3 that, in a proof outline, an assertion appears between each pair of commands. The assertion is a postcondition for the first command and a precondition for the second: The proof outline is often read backwards, since a precondition is determined from a postcondition and a command. We could also abbreviate this proof outline as shown to the right in (9.1.4), since determining the intermediate assertions is a simple, almost mechanical, chore.

Exercises for Section 9.1

1. Determine and simplify $wp(S, R)$ for the pairs (S, R). Variable *all5* has type *Boolean*; all other variables have type *integer*.

	S	R
(a)	$x := 2*y + 3$	$x = 13$
(b)	$x := x + y$	$x < 2*y$
(c)	$j := j + 1$	$0 < j \wedge (A\ i : 0 \leqslant i \leqslant j : b[i] = 5)$
(d)	$all5 := (b[j] = 5)$	$all5 = (A\ i : 0 \leqslant i \leqslant j : b[i] = 5)$
(e)	$all5 := all5 \wedge (b[j] = 5)$	$all5 = (A\ i : 0 \leqslant i \leqslant j : b[i] = 5)$
(f)	$x := x*y$	$x*y = c$
(g)	$x := (x - y)*(x + y)$	$x + y^2 \neq 0$

2. Prove that definition (9.1.3) satisfies laws (7.3), (7.4) and (7.7). The latter shows that assignment is deterministic.

3. Review section 4.6 (*Some theorems about textual substitution*). Let s be the machine state before execution of $x := e$ and let s' be the final state. Describe s and s' in terms of how $x := e$ is executed. (What, for example, should be the value in x upon termination?) Then show that for any predicate R, $s'(R)$ is true *iff* $s(R_e^x)$ is true. Finally, argue that this last fact shows that the definition of assignment is consistent with our operational view of assignment.

4. One can write a "forward rule" for assignment, which from a precondition derives the strongest postcondition $sp(Q, \text{"}x := e\text{"})$ such that execution of $x := e$ with Q true leaves $sp(Q, \text{"}x := e\text{"})$ true (in the definition below, v represents the initial value of x):

$$sp(Q, \text{"}x := e\text{"}) = (E\,v : Q_v^x \wedge x = e_v^x)$$

Show that this definition is also consistent with our model of execution. One way to do this is to show that execution of $x := e$ with Q true is guaranteed to terminate with $sp(Q, \text{"}x := e\text{"})$ true:

$$\{Q\}\ x := e\ \{sp(Q, \text{"}x := e\text{"})\}$$

5. See exercise 4. Give an example to show that Q is not equivalent to $wp(\text{"}x := e\text{"}, sp(Q, \text{"}x := e\text{"}))$.

6. Consider integer expressions defined using the syntax (see Appendix 1)

$$\begin{aligned}
\text{<expr>} &::= \text{<term>} \mid \text{<expr>} + \text{<term>}\\
\text{<term>} &::= \text{<factor>} \mid \text{<term>} * \text{<factor>}\\
&\mid \text{<term>} \div \text{<factor>}\\
\text{<factor>} &::= \text{<integer constant>} \mid \text{<identifier>}\\
&\mid \text{<array identifier>} [\,\text{<expr>}\,]
\end{aligned}$$

Let *domain*(*b*) denote the set of subscript values for any array *b*. Define *domain*(<expr>) for any expression <expr> recursively, on the structure of expressions. Assume the errors that can occur are subscript out of range and division by zero.

9.2 Multiple Assignment to Simple Variables

A multiple assignment to simple variables has the form

(9.2.1) $x_1, x_2, ..., x_n := e_1, e_2, ..., e_n$

where the x_i are *distinct* simple variables and the e_i are expressions. For purposes of explanation the assignment is abbreviated as $\bar{x} := \bar{e}$. That is, any identifier with a bar over it represents a vector (of appropriate length).

The multiple assignment command can be executed as follows. First evaluate the expressions, in any order, to yield values $v_1, \cdots, v_n$. Then assign v_1 to x_1, v_2 to x_2, ..., v_n to x_n, *in that order*. (Because the x_i are distinct, the order of assignment doesn't matter. However, a later generalization will require left-to-right assignment.)

The multiple assignment is useful because it easily describes a state change involving more than one variable. Its formal definition is a simple extension of assignment to one variable:

(9.2.2)   **Definition.** $wp(\text{``}\bar{x} := \bar{e}\text{''}, R) = domain(\bar{e}) \textbf{ cand } R^{\bar{x}}_{\bar{e}}$. □

where domain($\bar{e}$) describes the set of states in which all the expressions in the vector $\bar{e}$ can be evaluated:

$$domain(\bar{e}) = (A\, i: domain(e_i)).$$

Example 1. $x, y := y, x$ can be used to "swap" the values of x and y. □

Example 2. $x, y, z := y, z, x$ "rotates" the values of x, y and z. □

Example 3. $wp(\text{``}z, y := z*x, y-1\text{''}, y \geqslant 0 \wedge z*x^y = c)$
$= (y-1 \geqslant 0 \wedge (z*x)*x^{y-1} = c)$
$= (y \geqslant 1 \wedge z*x^y = c).$ □

Example 4. $wp(\text{``}s, i := s + b[i], i+1\text{''}, i > 0 \wedge s = (\Sigma j : 0 \leqslant j < i : b[j]))$
$= \;\; i+1 > 0 \wedge s + b[i] = (\Sigma j : 0 \leqslant j < i+1 : b[j])$
$= \;\; i \geqslant 0 \wedge s = (\Sigma j : 0 \leqslant j < i : b[j])$

Note that execution leaves $s = (\Sigma j : 0 \leqslant j < i : b[j])$ unchanged. □

Example 4. $wp(\text{``}x, y := x-y, y-x\text{''}, x+y = c)$
$= \;\; (x-y+y-x = c)$
$= \;\; (0 = c).$ □

Example 5. $wp(\text{``}x, y := x-y, x+y\text{''}, x+y = c)$
$= \;\; (x-y+x+y = c)$
$= \;\; (2*x = c).$ □

It is difficult at first to use the assignment command definition, for our old habits of reasoning about assignments in terms of execution get in the way. We have to consciously force ourselves to use it. Surprisingly enough, with practice it *does* help. Here is an example to illustrate this.

Suppose we have an array b and variables i, m, and p, with $i \leqslant m < i+p$. Values i and $i+p-1$ define the boundaries of a partition $b[i:i+p-1]$ of b, while m is an index in that partition, as shown in the first predicate below. It is desired to make the middle partition smaller by setting i to $m+1$, but at the same time p should be changed so that $i+p-1$ still describes the rightmost boundary of the partition, which does not change, as shown by the second predicate below.

$\wedge \; i < m < i+p$

$\wedge \; i = m+1 \leqslant i+p$

Now, what value should be assigned to p? Instead of determining it through *ad hocery*, let us use the definition of wp. Letting c be the initial value of $i+p$, we want to find the expression x that makes the following true:

$$\{i+p = c\} \;\; i, p := m+1, x \;\; \{i+p = c\}$$

We have:

$$wp(\text{“}i, p := m+1, x\text{”}, \ i+p = c)$$
$$= (i+p = c)_{m+1,x}^{i,p}$$
$$= (m+1+x) = c$$

Since initially $i+p = c$, we substitute for c to get

$$m+1+x = i+p$$

Solving for variable x yields $x = p+i-m-1$, so the desired assignment is $i,p := m+1, p+i-m-1$.

The definition of wp was used to *derive* the assignment, and not only to show that the assignment was correct. This is a hint as to the usefulness of wp in deriving programs.

Remark: Consider finding a solution for x in the assertion

(9.2.3) $\{T\} \ a := a+1; \ b := x \ \{a = b\}$

Blind analysis leads to

$$wp(\text{“}a := a+1; \ b := x\text{”}, \ a = b)$$
$$= wp(\text{“}a := a+1\text{”}, \ a = x)$$
$$= a+1 = x$$

which clearly is wrong; we cannot substitute $a+1$ for x in (9.2.3) and achieve a tautology. The problem is that x must be considered a function of a and b. If we write x as $x(a, b)$, then we get

$$wp(\text{“}a := a+1; \ b := x(a, b)\text{”}, \ a = b)$$
$$= wp(\text{“}a := a+1\text{”}, \ a = x(a, b))$$
$$= a+1 = x(a+1, b)$$

Thus, we see that x is not dependent on b, and we can take x as the expression a, which is the obvious answer. $\square$

Exercises for Section 9.2

1. Prove that $x, y := e1, e2$ is semantically equivalent to $x := e1; \ y := e2$, and also to $y := e2; \ x := e1$, provided that x does not occur in $e2$ and y does not occur in $e1$.

2. Show by counterexample that $x, y := e1, e2$ and $x := e1; \ y := e2$ and $y := e2; \ x := e1$ are generally not equivalent if x occurs in $e2$ or y in $e1$.

3. Determine and simplify $wp(S, R)$ for the pairs (S, R) given below.

	S	R
(a)	$z, x, y := 1, c, d$	$z * x^y = c^d$
(b)	$i, s := 1, b[0]$	$1 \leqslant i < n \wedge s = b[0] + ... + b[i-1]$
(c)	$a, n := 0, 1$	$a^2 < n \wedge (a+1)^2 \geqslant n$
(d)	$i, s := i+1, s+b[i]$	$0 < i < n \wedge s = b[0] + ... + b[i-1]$
(e)	$i := i+1; \ j := j+i$	$i = j$
(f)	$j := j+i; \ i := i+1$	$i = j$
(g)	$i, j := i+1, j+i$	$i = j$

4. In each of the following predicates, x represents an unknown expression that is to be determined. That is, an expression for x involving the other variables is to be determined so that the assertion is a tautology. Do so, as was done in the example preceding the exercises. The first few exercises are simple, so that you can easily become familiar with the technique.

(a) $\{T\} \ a, b := a+1, x \ \{b = a+1\}$
(b) $\{T\} \ a := a+1; \ b := x \ \{b = a+1\}$
(c) $\{T\} \ b := x; \ a := a+1 \ \{b = a+1\}$
(d) $\{i = j\} \ i, j := i+1, x \ \{i = j\}$
(e) $\{i = j\} \ i := i+1; \ j := x \ \{i = j\}$
(f) $\{i = j\} \ j := x; \ i := i+1 \ \{i = j\}$
(g) $\{z + a*b = c\} \ z, a := z+b, x \ \{z + a*b = c\}$
(h) $\{even(a) \wedge z + a*b = c\} \ a, b := a/2, x \ \{z + a*b = c\}$
(i) $\{even(a) \wedge z + a*b = c\} \ a := a/2; \ b := x \ \{z + a*b = c\}$
(j) $\{T\} \ i, s := 0, x \ \{s = (\Sigma j: 0 \leqslant j \leqslant i: b[j])\}$
(k) $\{T\} \ i, s := 0, x \ \{s = (\Sigma j: 0 \leqslant j < i: b[j])\}$
(l) $\{i > 0 \wedge s = (\Sigma j: 0 \leqslant j < i: b[j])\} \ i, s := i+1, x \ \{s = (\Sigma j: 0 \leqslant j < i: b[j])\}$

9.3 Assignment to an Array Element

Recall (section 5.1) that in the functional view of arrays an array b is a simple variable that contains a function, and that conventional "array subscripting", $b[i]$, is simply application of the function currently in b to the argument i. Recall also that $(b; i:e)$ denotes a function that is the same as b, except that at the argument i it yields the value e.

We can therefore view a subscripted variable assignment $b[i] := e$ as equivalent to the assignment

$$(9.3.1) \quad b := (b; \ i:e)$$

since both change b to represent the function $(b; i:e)$. But (9.3.1) is an assignment to a simple variable. Since assignment to a simple variable is already defined in (9.1.1), so is assignment to a subscripted variable! We have, using definition (9.1.1),

$$wp(``b[i]:= e\text{''}, \ R) = wp(``b := (b; \ i:e)\text{''}, \ R)$$
$$= domain((b; \ i:e)) \ \textbf{cand} \ R^b_{(b; \ i:e)}$$

Using $inrange(b, i)$ to mean that the value of i is a valid subscript, we can rewrite the definition of $b[i]:= e$ as

(9.3.2)   **Definition.** $wp(``b[i]:= e\text{''}, \ R)$
$$= inrange(b, i) \ \textbf{cand} \ domain(e) \ \textbf{cand} \ R^b_{(b; \ i:e)} \quad \square$$

Typically, we tend to leave off $inrange$ and $domain$, writing simply

(9.3.3) $wp(``b[i]:= e\text{''}, \ R) = R^b_{(b; \ i:e)}$

Remark: The notation $(b; \ i:e)$ is used in defining assignment to array elements and in reasoning about programs, but not *in* programs. For traditional reasons, the assignment command is still written as $b[i]:= e$. $\quad \square$

We have managed to make the definition of assignment to an array element look quite simple and, in fact, determining $wp(``b[i]:= e\text{''}, \ R)$ is a mechanical chore. In making the definition simple, however, we have pushed the complications into the predicate calculus; it is not always easy to manipulate a precondition into an understandable form. The following examples are designed to illustrate how this can be done. In the examples, assume that all subscripts are in range.

Example 1. $wp(``b[i]:= 5\text{''}, \ b[i]=5)$

$$\begin{aligned} &= (b[i]=5)^b_{(b; \ i:5)} &&\text{(Definition)} \\ &= (b; \ i:5)[i]=5 &&\text{(Textual substitution)} \\ &= 5=5 \\ &= T \end{aligned}$$

Hence, execution of $b[i]:= 5$ always sets $b[i]$ to 5. $\quad \square$

Example 2. $wp(``b[i]:= 5\text{''}, \ b[i]=b[j])$

$$\begin{aligned} &= (b[i]=b[j])^b_{(b; \ i:5)} &&\text{(Definition)} \\ &= (b; \ i:5)[i]=(b; \ i:5)[j] &&\text{(Textual subs.)} \\ &= (i \neq j \wedge 5=b[j]) \vee (i=j \wedge 5=5) &&\text{(Case anal.: } i \neq j \vee i=j) \\ &= (i \neq j \wedge 5=b[j]) \vee (i=j) \\ &= (i \neq j \vee i=j) \wedge (5=b[j] \vee i=j) &&\text{(Distributivity)} \\ &= T \wedge (i=j \vee b[j]=5) \\ &= i=j \vee b[j]=5 \end{aligned}$$

Often, the case $i=j$ is omitted carelessly when basing arguments on intuition only; the formal definition really helps here. The case analysis performed here was explained at the end of section 5.1, so reread that part if you are having trouble with it. □

Example 3. $wp\,(\text{``}b[b[i]]:=i\text{''},\ b[i]=i)$

$$
\begin{aligned}
&= (b[i]=i)_{(b;\,b[i]:i)}^{b} & \text{(Definition)}\\
&= (b;\ b[i]:i)[i]=i & \text{(Textual subs.)}\\
&= (b[i]\neq i \wedge b[i]=i) \vee (b[i]=i \wedge i=i) & \text{(Case analysis)}\\
&= F \vee (b[i]=i \wedge T)\\
&= b[i]=i
\end{aligned}
$$

Hence, execution of $b[b[i]]:=i$ has no effect on the predicate $b[i]=i$. This exercise is quite difficult to perform using only operational reasoning. □

Example 4. Assume $n>1$. Let $ordered(b[1{:}n])$ mean that the elements of b are in ascending order. Then

$$
\begin{aligned}
wp(\text{``}b[n]&:= x\text{''},\ ordered(b[1{:}n]))\\
&= (ordered(b[1{:}n]))_{(b;\,n:x)}^{b} & \text{(Definition)}\\
&= ordered((b;\ n:x)[1{:}n]) & \text{(Textual substitution)}\\
&= ordered(b[1{:}n-1]) \wedge b[n-1]\leqslant x & \text{(Definition of } ordered)
\end{aligned}
$$

By replacing $ordered(b[1{:}n])$ by its definition, we get a more formal derivation:

$$
\begin{aligned}
wp(\text{``}b[n]&:= x\text{''},\ (A\,i{:}\,1\leqslant i<n{:}\,b[i]\leqslant b[i+1]))\\
&= (A\,i{:}\,1\leqslant i<n{:}\,(b;\ n:x)[i]\leqslant(b;\ n:x)[i+1])\\
&= (b;\ n:x)[n-1]\leqslant(b;\ n:x)[n]\ \wedge\\
&\quad\ (A\,i{:}\,1\leqslant i<n-1{:}\,(b;\ n:x)[i]\leqslant(b;\ n:x)[i+1])\\
&= b[n-1]\leqslant x \wedge (A\,i{:}\,1\leqslant i<n-1{:}\,b[i]\leqslant b[i+1]) \quad \square
\end{aligned}
$$

Exercises for Section 9.3

1. Determine and simplify the following weakest preconditions, where array b is declared as $b[0{:}n-1]$ and it is known that all subscripts are in range.

(a) $wp\,(\text{``}b[i]:= i\text{''},\ b[b[i]]=i)$
(b) $wp\,(\text{``}b[i]:= 5\text{''},\ (E\,j{:}\,i\leqslant j<n{:}\,b[i]\leqslant b[j]))$
(c) $wp\,(\text{``}b[i]:= 5\text{''},\ (E\,j{:}\,i\leqslant j<n{:}\,b[i]<b[j]))$
(d) $wp\,(\text{``}b[i]:= 5\text{''},\ b[0{:}n-1]=B[0{:}n-1])$
(e) $wp\,(\text{``}b[i]:= b[i-1]+b[i]\text{''},\ b[i]=(\Sigma\,j{:}\,1\leqslant j<i{:}\,b[j]))$
(f) $wp\,(\text{``}t:= b[i];\ b[i]:= b[j];\ b[j]:= t\text{''},\ b[i]=x \wedge b[j]=y)$
(g) $wp\,(\text{``}t:= b[i];\ b[i]:= b[j];\ b[j]:= t\text{''},\ k\neq i \wedge k\neq j \wedge b[k]=C)$

2. Derive a definition for an assignment $r.s:=e$ for a Pascal-like record r with field name s (see exercise 4 of section 5.1).

9.4 The General Multiple Assignment Command

This section may be skipped, since it is not needed to understand program development described in Part III. The material is used heavily in defining procedure calls in chapter 12.

Thus far, we have defined the assignment $x := e$ for a simple variable x, the assignment $\bar{x} := \bar{e}$ for distinct simple variables x_j, and the assignment $b[i] := e$ to an array element $b[i]$. We now want to define the general multiple assignment command. For example, it allows us to swap the values of two array elements:

$$b[i], b[j] := b[j], b[i].$$

In addition, it allows us to deal with assignments to elements of sub-arrays. For example, for array c declared as,

var c : **array** $[0:10]$ **of array** $[0:10]$ **of** *integer*,

the assignment $c[i][j] := e$ has not yet been defined.

Recall (from section 5.3) that a selector is a sequence of bracketed expressions (subscripts). The null selector is denoted by ε. For any identifier x (say), we have $x = x \circ \varepsilon$, where $\circ$ denotes catenation of identifiers and selectors.

The multiple assignment command has the form

(9.4.1) $x_1 \circ s_1, \; \cdots, \; x_n \circ s_n := e_1, \; \cdots, \; e_n$

where each x_i is an identifier, each s_i is a selector and each expression e_i has the same type as $x_i \circ s_i$. Using $\overline{x \circ s}$ for $x_1 \circ s_1, \; \cdots, \; x_n \circ s_n$ and $\bar{e}$ for $e_1, \; \cdots, \; e_n$, we abbreviate the multiple assignment by

(9.4.2) $\overline{x \circ s} := \bar{e}$.

Note that a simple assignment $x := e$ has form (9.4.1) —with $n = 1$ and $s_1 = \varepsilon$— since it is the same as $x \circ \varepsilon := e$. Also, the assignment $b[i] := e$ has this form, with $n = 1$, $x_1 = b$, $s_1 = [i]$ and $e_1 = e$.

The multiple assignment can be executed in a manner consistent with the formal definition given below as follows:

(9.4.3)   **Execution of a multiple assignment**. First, determine the variables specified by the $x_i \circ s_i$ and evaluate the expressions e_i to yield values v_i. Then assign v_1 to $x_1 \circ s_1$, v_2 to $x_2 \circ s_2$, ..., and v_n to $x_n \circ s_n$. The order of assignment *must* be from left to right. □

We define multiple assignment by giving a predicate transformer for it.

To get some idea for the predicate transformer, let's look at the definition of multiple assignment to simple variables:

$$wp(\text{``}\bar{x}:=\bar{e}\text{''}, R) = R_{\bar{e}}^{\bar{x}} .$$

We must be sure that the general multiple assignment definition includes this as a subcase. We therefore generalize the simpler definition to allow identifiers catenated with selectors instead of just identifiers x:

(9.4.4) **Definition.** $wp(\text{``}\overline{x \circ s}:=\bar{e}\text{''}, R) = R_{\bar{e}}^{\overline{x \circ s}} .$ $\square$

The difficulty with (9.4.4) is that textual substitution is defined only for identifiers, and so $R_{\bar{e}}^{\overline{x \circ s}}$ is as yet undefined. We now generalize the notion of textual substitution to include the new case by describing how to massage $R_{\bar{e}}^{\overline{x \circ s}}$ into the form of a conventional textual substitution. The generalization will be done so that the manner of execution given in (9.4.3), including the left-to-right order of assignment, will be consistent with definition (9.4.4).

To motivate the generalization, consider the assignment

(9.4.5) $b \circ s_1, \cdots, b \circ s_m := e_1, \cdots, e_m$

This assignment first assign e_1 to $b \circ s_1$, then e_2 to $b \circ s_2$, and so on. Thus, it should be equivalent to

(9.4.6) $b := (b; s_1:e_1; \cdots; s_m:e_m)$

Why? Suppose two of the selectors s_i and s_j (say), where $i < j$, are the same. Then, after execution of (9.4.5), the value of e_j (and not of e_i) will be in $b \circ s_j$, and thereafter a reference $b \circ s_j$ should yield e_j. But this is exactly the case with execution of (9.4.6); the left-to-right order of assignment during execution of (9.4.5) is reflected in the right-to-left precedence rule for applying function $(b; s_1:e_1; \cdots; s_m:e_m)$ to an argument.

Secondly, note that for distinct identifiers b and c and selectors s and t (which need not be distinct) the assignments $b \circ s, c \circ t := e, g$ and $c \circ t, b \circ s := g, e$ should have the same effect. This is because $b \circ s$ and $c \circ t$ refer to different parts of computer memory, and what is assigned to one cannot effect what is assigned to the other. (Remember, expressions e and g are evaluated before any assignments are made.)

This leads us to the following

(9.4.7) **Definition.** $P_{\bar{e}}^{\bar{x}}$, where each element of vector $\bar{x}$ is an identifier catenated with a selector, is given by the following three rules.

(a) Provided $\bar{x}$ is a list of distinct identifiers (thus, each of the selectors in $\bar{x}$ is the null selector ε), $P\frac{\bar{x}}{\bar{e}}$ denotes conventional textual substitution.

(b) $R_{\bar{e},\,f,\,h,\,\bar{g}}^{\bar{x},\,b\,\circ\,s,\,c\,\circ\,t,\,\bar{y}} = R_{\bar{e},\,h,\,f,\,\bar{g}}^{\bar{x},\,c\,\circ\,t,\,b\,\circ\,s,\,\bar{y}}$

provided that b and c are distinct identifiers. This rule indicates that adjacent reference-expression pairs may be permuted as long as they begin with different identifiers.

(c) $R_{e_1,\,\cdots,\,e_m,\,\bar{g}}^{b\,\circ\,s_1,\,\cdots,\,b\,\circ\,s_m,\,\bar{x}} = R_{(b;\,s_1:e_1;\,\cdots;\,s_m:e_m),\,\bar{g}}^{b,\,\bar{x}}$

provided that identifier b does not begin any of the x_i. This rule indicates how multiple assignments to subparts of an object b can be viewed as a single assignment to b.   □

Example 1. $wp(\text{``}x, x := 1, 2\text{''},\ R)$
$$= wp(\text{``}x \circ \varepsilon,\ x \circ \varepsilon := 1, 2\text{''},\ R)$$
$$= R_{(x;\ \varepsilon:1;\ \varepsilon:2)}^{x}$$
$$= R_2^x \qquad\qquad \text{(see definition (5.3.2))}$$

Execution of $x, x := 1, 2$ is equivalent to execution of $x := 2$; there is really no sense in using $x, x := 1, 2$.   □

Example 2. $wp(\text{``}b[i], b[j] := b[j], b[i]\text{''},\ b[i] = X \wedge b[j] = Y)$
$$= (b;\ i:b[j];\ j:b[i])[i] = X\ \wedge\ (b;\ i:b[j];\ j:b[i])[j] = Y$$
$$= (b;\ i:b[j];\ j:b[i])[i] = X\ \wedge\ b[i] = Y$$
$$= ((i = j \wedge b[i] = X) \vee (i \neq j \wedge b[j] = X))\ \wedge\ b[i] = Y$$
$$= b[j] = X\ \wedge\ b[i] = Y$$

Note that the swap performs correctly when $i = j$, since this case is automatically included in the above derivation. If this derivation seems too fast for you, reread section 5.1.   □

Example 3. $wp(\text{``}b[i], b[j] := b[j], b[i]\text{''},\ (A\ k : k \neq i \wedge k \neq j : b[k] = B[k]))$
$$= (A\ k : k \neq i \wedge k \neq j : (b;\ i:b[j];\ j:b[i])[k] = B[k]))$$
$$= (A\ k : k \neq i \wedge k \neq j : b[k] = B[k])$$

The last line follows because if $k \neq i$ and $k \neq j$ then $(b;\ i:b[j];\ j:b[i])[k] = b[k]$. The only array values changed by the swap are $b[i]$ and $b[j]$.   □

Exercises for Section 9.4

1. Transform the following using definition (9.4.7) so that they denote conventional textual substitution —i.e. the superscript in each is a list of distinct identifiers.

(a) $R_{e,f,g}^{b[i],b[j],x}$

(b) $R_{e,f,g}^{b[i],x,b[j]}$

(c) $R_{e,f,g}^{b[i],c[i],b[j]}$

(d) $R_{e,f,g,h}^{b[i],c[i],b[j],c[j]}$

2. Determine and simplify the following weakest preconditions, where b is an array of integers and it is assumed that all subscripts are in range.

(a) $wp(\text{``}b[i],b[2]:=3,4\text{''},\ b[i]=3)$

(b) $wp(\text{``}b[i],b[2]:=4,4\text{''},\ b[i]=3)$

(c) $wp(\text{``}p,b[p]:=b[p],p\text{''},\ p=b[p])$

(d) $wp(\text{``}i,b[i]:=i+1,0\text{''},\ 0<i \wedge (A\,j:0\leqslant j<i:b[j]=0))$

(e) $wp(\text{``}i,b[i]:=i+1,0\text{''},\ 0<i \wedge b[0:i-1]=0)$

(f) $wp(\text{``}p,b[p],b[q]:=b[p],b[q],p\text{''},\ p=b[q])$

(g) $wp(\text{``}p,b[p],b[b[p]]:=b[p],b[b[p]],p\text{''},\ p=b[b[p]])$

(h) $wp(\text{``}p,b[p],b[b[p]]:=b[p],b[b[p]],p\text{''},\ p\neq b[b[p]])$

3. Prove the following implication:

$$i=I \wedge b[i]=K \;\Rightarrow\; wp(\text{``}i,b[i]:=b[i],i\text{''},\ i=K \wedge b[I]=I)$$

4. Derive a definition for a general multiple assignment command that can include assignments to simple variables, array elements and Pascal record fields. (see exercise 1 of section 5.3.)

5. Prove that lemma 4.6.3 holds for the extended definition of textual substitution:

Lemma. Suppose each x_i of list $\bar{x}$ has the form *identifier* ∘ *selector* and suppose $\bar{u}$ is a list of fresh, distinct identifiers. Then

$$(E_{\bar{u}}^{\bar{x}})_{\bar{x}}^{\bar{u}} = E \quad \square$$

Chapter 10
The Alternative Command

Programming notations usually have a conditional command, or **if**-statement, which allows execution of a subcommand to be dependent on the current state of the program variables. An example of a conditional command, taken from ALGOL 60 and Pascal, is

if $x \geqslant 0$ **then** $z := x$ **else** $z := -x$

Execution of this command stores the absolute value of x in z: if $x \geqslant 0$ then the first alternative $z := x$ is executed; otherwise the second alternative $z := -x$ is executed. In our programming notation, this command can be written as

(10.1) **if** $x \geqslant 0 \rightarrow z := x$
    $[] \, x \leqslant 0 \rightarrow z := -x$
    fi

or, since it is short and simple enough, on one line as

if $x \geqslant 0 \rightarrow z := x \, [] \, x \leqslant 0 \rightarrow z := -x$ **fi**

Command (10.1) contains two entities of the form $B \rightarrow S$ (separated by the symbol $[]$) where B is a Boolean expression and S a command. $B \rightarrow S$ is called a *guarded command*, for B acts as a guard at the gate $\rightarrow$, making sure S is executed only under the right conditions. To execute (10.1), find one true guard and execute its corresponding command. Thus, with $x > 0$ execute $z := x$, with $x < 0$ execute $z := -x$, and with $x = 0$ execute *either* (but not both) of the assignments.

This brief introduction has glossed over a number of important points. Let us now be more precise in describing the syntax and execution of the alternative command.

The general form of the alternative command is

(10.2)   **if** $B_1 \rightarrow S_1$
    $[]\ B_2 \rightarrow S_2$
    $\cdots$
    $[]\ B_n \rightarrow S_n$
   fi

where $n \geqslant 0$ and each $B_i \rightarrow S_i$ is a guarded command. Each S_i can be *any* command —*skip*, *abort*, sequential composition, assignment, another alternative command, etc.

For purposes of abbreviation, we refer to the general command (10.2) as IF, while BB denotes the disjunction

$$B_1 \vee B_2 \vee \cdots \vee B_n .$$

Command IF can be executed as follows. First, if any guard B_i is not well-defined in the state in which execution begins, abortion may occur. This is because nothing is assumed about the order of evaluation of the guards. Secondly, at least one guard must be true; otherwise execution aborts. Finally, if at least one guard is true, then one guarded command $B_i \rightarrow S_i$ with true guard B_i is chosen and S_i is executed.

The definition of $wp(\text{IF}, R)$ is now quite obvious. The first conjunct indicates that the guards must be well-defined. The second conjunct indicates that at least one guard is true. The rest of the conjuncts indicate that execution of each command S_i with a true guard B_i terminates with R true:

(10.3a) **Definition.** $wp(\text{IF}, R) = domain(\text{BB}) \wedge \text{BB} \wedge$
               $(B_1 \Rightarrow wp(S_1, R)) \wedge \cdots \wedge (B_n \Rightarrow wp(S_n, R))$ $\square$

Typically, we assume that the guards are total functions —i.e. are well-defined in all states. This allows us to simplify the definition by deleting the first conjunct. Thus, with the aid of quantifiers we rewrite the definition in (10.3b) below. From now on, we will use (10.3b) as the definition, but be sure the guards are well-defined in the states in which the alternative command will be executed!

(10.3b) **Definition.** $wp(\text{IF}, R) = (E\, i : 1 \leqslant i \leqslant n : B_i) \wedge$
                $(A\, i : 1 \leqslant i \leqslant n : B_i \Rightarrow wp(S_i, R))$ $\square$

Example 1. Let us show that, under all initial conditions, execution of (10.1) stores the absolute value of x in z. That is, we want to show that $wp((10.1), z = abs(x)) = T$. We have:

$wp((10.1), z = abs(x))$
$= (x \geqslant 0 \vee x \leqslant 0) \wedge$
$\quad (x \geqslant 0 \Rightarrow wp(\text{``}z := x\text{''}, z = abs(x))) \wedge$
$\quad (x \leqslant 0 \Rightarrow wp(\text{``}z := -x\text{''}, z = abs(x)))$
$= T \wedge (x \geqslant 0 \Rightarrow x = abs(x)) \wedge$
$\quad (x \leqslant 0 \Rightarrow -x = abs(x))$
$= T \wedge T \wedge T$
$= T \quad \square$

$\begin{cases} BB \wedge \\ B_1 \Rightarrow wp(S_1, R) \wedge \\ B_2 \Rightarrow wp(S_2, R) \end{cases}$

Example 2. The following command is supposed to be the body of a loop that counts the number of positive values (p) in array $b[0:m-1]$.

(10.4)   **if** $b[i] > 0 \rightarrow p, i := p+1, i+1$
$\quad [] \ b[i] < 0 \rightarrow i := i+1$
fi

After execution of this command we expect to have $i \leqslant m$ and p equal to the number of values in $b[0:i-1]$ that are greater than zero. Letting R be the assertion

$$i \leqslant m \ \wedge \ p = (N j : 0 \leqslant j < i : b[j] > 0)$$

we calculate:

$wp((10.4), R) = (b[i] > 0 \vee b[i] < 0) \wedge$
$\quad (b[i] > 0 \Rightarrow wp(\text{``}p, i := p+1, i+1\text{''}, R)) \wedge$
$\quad (b[i] < 0 \Rightarrow wp(\text{``}i := i+1\text{''}, R)$
$= b[i] \neq 0 \wedge$
$\quad (b[i] > 0 \Rightarrow i+1 \leqslant m \ \wedge \ p+1 = (N j : 0 \leqslant j < i+1 : b[j] > 0)) \wedge$
$\quad (b[i] < 0 \Rightarrow i+1 \leqslant m \ \wedge \ p = (N j : 0 \leqslant j < i+1 : b[j] > 0))$
$= b[i] \neq 0 \wedge i < m \ \wedge$
$\quad p = (N j : 0 \leqslant j < i : b[j] > 0) \wedge$
$\quad p = (N j : 0 \leqslant j < i : b[j] > 0)$
$= b[i] \neq 0 \wedge i < m \ \wedge p = (N j : 0 \leqslant j < i : b[j] > 0)$

Hence we see that array b should not contain the value 0, and that the definition of p as the number of values greater than zero in $b[0:i-1]$ will be true after execution of the alternative command if it is true before. $\square$

The reader may feel that there was too much work in proving what we did in example 2. After all, the result can be obtained in an intuitive manner, and perhaps fairly easily (although one is likely to overlook the problem with zero elements in array b). At this point, it is important to practice such formal manipulations. It results in better understanding of the theory and better understanding of the alternative command itself.

Moreover, the kind of manipulations performed in example 2 will indeed be necessary in developing some programs, and the facility needed for this can only come through practice. Even the act of performing a few exercises will begin to change the way you "naturally" think about programs and thus what you call your intuition about programming.

Later on, when attacking a problem that is similar to one worked on earlier, it may not be necessary to be so formal, but the formality will be at your fingertips when you need it on the more difficult problems.

Some comments about the alternative command

The alternative command differs from the conventional **if**-statement in several respects. We now discuss the reasons for these differences.

First, the alternative command allows any number of alternatives, not just two. Thus, it serves also as a "case statement" (Pascal) or "SELECT statement" (PL/I). There is no need to have two different notations, one for two alternatives and one for more. One notation for one concept —in this case alternation or choice— is a well-known, reasonable principle.

There are no defaults: each alternative command must be preceded by a guard that describes the conditions under which it may be executed. For example, the command to set x to the absolute value of x must be written with two guarded commands:

$$\textbf{if } x \geqslant 0 \rightarrow skip \; [] \; x \leqslant 0 \rightarrow x := -x \textbf{ fi}$$

Its counterpart in ALGOL, **if** $x < 0$ **then** $z := -x$, has the default that if $x \geqslant 0$ execution is equivalent to execution of $skip$. Although a program may be a bit longer because of the lack of a default, there are advantages. The explicit appearance of each guard does aid the reader; each alternative is given in full detail, leaving less chance of overlooking something. More importantly, the lack of a default helps during program development. Upon deriving a possible alternative command, the programmer is *forced* to derive the conditions under which its execution will perform satisfactorily and, moreover, is *forced* to continue deriving alternatives until at least one is true in each possible initial state. This point will become clearer in Part III.

The absence of defaults introduces, in a reasonable manner, the possibility of nondeterminism. Suppose $x = 0$ when execution of command (10.1) begins. Then, since both guards $x \geqslant 0$ and $x \leqslant 0$ are true, *either* command may be executed (but only one of them). The choice is entirely up to the executor —for example it could be a random choice, or on days with odd dates it could be the first and on days with even dates it could be the second, or it could be chosen to minimize execution time. The point is that, since execution of either one leads to a correct result, the programmer should not have to worry about which one is executed. He is free to derive as many alternatives commands and corresponding guards as possible, without regard to overlap.

Of course, for purposes of efficiency the programmer could strengthen the guards to excise the nondeterminism. For example, changing the second guard in (10.1) from $x \leqslant 0$ to $x < 0$ would help if evaluation of unary minus is expensive, because in the case $x = 0$ only the first command $z := x$ could then be executed.

Finally, the lack of default allows the possibility of symmetry (see (10.1)), which is pleasing —if not necessary— to one with a mathematical eye.

A theorem about the alternative command

Quite often, we are not interested in the weakest precondition of an alternative command, but only in determining if a known precondition implies it. For example, if the alternative command appears in a program, we may already know that its precondition is the postcondition of the previous command, and we really don't need to calculate the weakest precondition. In such cases, the following theorem is useful.

(10.5)   **Theorem.** Consider command IF. Suppose a predicate Q satisfies

(1) $Q \Rightarrow BB$
(2) $Q \wedge B_i \Rightarrow wp(S_i, R)$, for all i, $1 \leqslant i \leqslant n$.

Then (and only then) $Q \Rightarrow wp(\text{IF}, R)$.   □

Proof. We first show how to take Q outside the scope of the quantification in assumption 2 of the theorem:

$$(A\ i: Q \wedge B_i \Rightarrow wp(S_i, R))$$
$$= (A\ i: \neg(Q \wedge B_i) \vee wp(S_i, R)) \quad \text{(Implication)}$$
$$= (A\ i: \neg Q \vee \neg B_i \vee wp(S_i, R)) \quad \text{(De Morgan)}$$
$$= \neg Q \vee (A\ i: \neg B_i \vee wp(S_i, R)) \quad (Q \text{ doesn't depend on } i)$$
$$= Q \Rightarrow (A\ i: B_i \Rightarrow wp(S_i, R)) \quad \text{(Implication, twice)}$$

Hence, we have

$$(Q \Rightarrow BB) \wedge (A\ i: Q \wedge B_i \Rightarrow wp(S_i, R)) \quad \text{(Assumptions (1), (2))}$$
$$= (Q \Rightarrow BB) \wedge (Q \Rightarrow (A\ i: B_i \Rightarrow wp(S_i, R))) \quad \text{(From above)}$$
$$= Q \Rightarrow (BB \wedge (A\ i: B_i \Rightarrow wp(S_i, R)))$$
$$= Q \Rightarrow wp(\text{IF}, R) \quad \text{(Definition (10.3b))}$$

Hence, the conjunction of the assumptions is equivalent to the conclusion, and the theorem is proved. □

Example 3. Suppose a binary search is being performed for a value x known to be in array $b[0:n-1]$. We are at the stage where the following predicate Q is true:

$$Q: ordered(b[0:n-1]) \land 0 \leqslant i < k < j < n \land x \in b[i:j].$$

That is, the search has been narrowed down to array section $b[i:j]$, and k is an index into this section. We want to prove that

(10.6) $\{Q\}$ **if** $b[k] \leqslant x \rightarrow i := k$ $[]$ $b[k] \geqslant x \rightarrow j := k$ **fi** $\{x \in b[i:j]\}$

holds. The first assumption $Q \Rightarrow BB$ of theorem (10.5) holds, because the disjunction of the guards in (10.6) is equivalent to T. The second assumption holds, because

$$Q \land b[k] \leqslant x \Rightarrow x \in b[k:j]$$
$$= wp(\text{``}i := k\text{''}, \ x \in b[i:j]) \ , \text{and}$$
$$Q \land b[k] \geqslant x \Rightarrow x \in b[i:k]$$
$$= wp(\text{``}j := k\text{''}, \ x \in b[i:j]) \ .$$

The two implications follow from the fact that Q indicates that the array is ordered and that x is in $b[i:j]$ and from the second conjunct of the antecedents. Hence the theorem allows us to conclude that (10.6) is true. □

Exercises for Chapter 10

1. Determine $wp(\text{``if fi''}, R)$, for any predicate R. Have you seen a command with this definition before?

2. Prove that command IF satisfies properties (7.3) and (7.4) of chapter 7, provided the sub-commands of IF do.

3. The following command $S3$ is used in an algorithm that finds the quotient and remainder when a value x is divided by a value y. Calculate and simplify $wp(S3, q*w+r = x \land r \geqslant 0)$.

$$S3: \textbf{if } w \leqslant r \rightarrow r, q := r-w, q+1 \ [] \ w > r \rightarrow skip \textbf{ fi}.$$

4. Calculate and simplify $wp(S4, a > 0 \land b > 0)$ for the command

$$S4: \textbf{if } a > b \rightarrow a := a-b \ [] \ b > a \rightarrow b := b-a \textbf{ fi}.$$

5. Calculate and simplify $wp(S5, x \leqslant y)$ for the command

$S5$: **if** $x > y \rightarrow x, y := y, x$ $[\!]$ $x \leqslant y \rightarrow skip$ **fi**.

6. Arrays $f[0:n]$ and $g[0:m]$ are alphabetically ordered lists of names of people. It is known that at least one name is on both lists. Let X represent the first (in alphabetic order) such name. Calculate and simplify the weakest precondition of the following alternative command with respect to predicate R given after it. Assume i and j are within the array bounds.

$S6$: **if** $f[i] < g[j] \rightarrow i := i+1$
$\quad\;\,[\!]$ $f[i] = g[j] \rightarrow skip$
$\quad\;\,[\!]$ $f[i] > g[j] \rightarrow j := j+1$
$\quad$ **fi**
$\{R: ordered(f[0:n]) \wedge ordered(g[0:m]) \wedge f[i] \leqslant X \wedge g[j] \leqslant X\}$

7. The command of the following proof outline could be used in an algorithm to store $a*b$ in variable z. Using theorem 10.5, prove that the proof outline is true.

$\{x > 0 \wedge z + y*x = a*b\}$
if $odd(x) \rightarrow z, x := z+y, x-1$ $[\!]$ $even(x) \rightarrow skip$ **fi**;
$y, x := 2*y, x \div 2$
$\{x \geqslant 0 \wedge z + y*x = a*b\}$

8. The command in the following proof outline could be used in an algorithm that determines the maximum value m of an array $b[0:n-1]$. Using theorem 10.5, prove that it is true.

$\{0 < i < n \wedge m = max(b[0:i-1])\}$
if $b[i] > m \rightarrow m := b[i]$ $[\!]$ $b[i] \leqslant m \rightarrow skip$ **fi**
$\{0 < i < n \wedge m = max(b[0:i])\}$

Chapter 11
The Iterative Command

The conventional while-loop and the iterative command

The *while*-loop in Pascal has the form "**while** B **do** S" and in PL/I the rather baroque form "DO WHILE (B) ; S END ;" for a Boolean expression B and command S. S is sometimes called the *body* of the loop. Execution of the *while*-loop can be expressed using a **goto** statement as

$loop$: **if** B **then begin** S ; **goto** $loop$ **end**

but it is often described by a flaw chart:

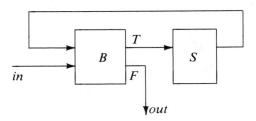

In our programming notation, the *while*-loop has the form

do $B \rightarrow S$ **od**

where $B \rightarrow S$ is a guarded command. This form allows us to generalize to the following, which we call the *iterative command* and refer to by the name DO.

$$(11.1) \quad \begin{aligned} &\textbf{do } B_1 \;\rightarrow\; S_1 \\ &\;\;\rlap{[}{]}\;\; B_2 \;\rightarrow\; S_2 \\ &\;\;\cdots \\ &\;\;\rlap{[}{]}\;\; B_n \;\rightarrow\; S_n \\ &\textbf{od} \end{aligned}$$

where $n \geqslant 0$ and each $B_i \rightarrow S_i$ is a guarded command. Note the syntactic similarity between DO and IF; one is a set of guarded commands enclosed in **do** and **od**, the other a set enclosed in **if** and **fi**.

In one sentence, here is how (11.1) can be executed. Repeat (or iterate) the following until no longer possible: choose a guard B_i that is true and execute the corresponding command S_i.

Upon termination all the guards are false. Choosing a true guard and executing its command is called performing an *iteration* of the loop.

Note that nondeterminism is allowed: if two or more guards are true, any one (but only one) is chosen and the corresponding command is executed at each iteration. Using IF to denote the alternative command with the same guarded commands and BB to denote the disjunction of the guards (see chapter 10), we see that (11.1) is equivalent to

$$\begin{aligned} &\textbf{do } BB \;\rightarrow\; \textbf{if } B_1 \;\rightarrow\; S_1 \\ &\qquad\qquad\;\; \rlap{[}{]}\;\; \cdots \\ &\qquad\qquad\;\; \rlap{[}{]}\;\; B_n \;\rightarrow\; S_n \\ &\qquad\qquad\; \textbf{fi} \\ &\textbf{od} \end{aligned}$$

or   **do** BB $\rightarrow$ IF **od**

That is, if all the guards are false, which means that BB is false, execution terminates; otherwise, the corresponding alternative command IF is executed and the process is repeated. One iteration of a loop, therefore, is equivalent to finding BB true and executing IF.

Thus, we can get by with only the simple *while*-loop. Nevertheless, we will continue to use the more general form because it is extremely useful in developing programs, as we will see in Part III.

The formal definition of DO

The following predicate $H_0(R)$ represents the set of states in which execution of DO terminates in 0 iterations with R true, because the guards are initially false:

$$H_0(R) = \neg BB \land R$$

Let us also write a predicate $H_k(R)$, for $k > 0$, to represent the set of all states in which execution of DO terminates in k *or fewer* iterations, with R true. The definition will be recursive —i.e. in terms of $H_{k-1}(R)$. One case is that DO terminates in 0 iterations, in which case $H_0(R)$ is true. The other case is that at least one iteration is performed. Thus, BB must initially be true and the iteration consists of executing a corresponding IF. This execution of IF must terminate in a state in which the loop will iterate $k-1$ or fewer times. This leads to

$$H_k(R) = H_0(R) \lor wp(\text{IF}, H_{k-1}(R)), \quad \text{for } k > 0.$$

Now, $wp(\text{DO}, R)$ is to represent the set of states in which execution of DO terminates in a bounded number of iterations with R true. That is, initially there must be some k such that at most k iterations will be performed. We therefore define

(11.2) **Definition.** $wp(\text{DO}, R) = (\mathbf{E}\, k : 0 \leqslant k : H_k(R))$ □

Two examples of reasoning about loops

The formal definition of DO is not easy to use, and it gives no insight into developing programs. Therefore, we want to develop a theorem that allows us to work with a useful precondition of a loop (with respect to a postcondition) that is not the weakest precondition. We first illustrate the idea with two examples.

Execution of the following algorithm is supposed to store in variable s the sum of the elements of array $b[0:10]$.

```
i, s := 1, b[0];
do i < 11 → i, s := i+1, s+b[i] od
{R: s = (Σk : 0 ≤ k < 11 : b[k])}
```

How can we argue that it works? Let's begin by giving a predicate P that shows the logical relationship between variables i, s and b —in effect, it serves as a definition of i and s:

$$P: 1 \leqslant i \leqslant 11 \land s = (\Sigma k : 0 \leqslant k < i : b[k])$$

We will show that P is true just before and after each iteration of the loop, so that it is also true upon termination. If P is true in all these places, then, with the additional help of the falsity of the guards, we can see that R is also true upon termination (since $P \land i \geqslant 11 \Rightarrow R$). We summarize what we need to show by annotating the algorithm:

$$\{T\}$$
$$i, s := 1, b[0];$$
$$\{P\}$$
(11.3)   **do** $i < 11 \rightarrow \{i < 11 \wedge P\}$ $i, s := i+1, s+b[i]$ $\{P\}$ **od**
$$\{i \geqslant 11 \wedge P\}$$
$$\{R\}$$

We repeat, because it is very important: if we can show that (1) P is true before execution of the loop and that (2) each iteration of the loop leaves P true, then P is true before and after each iteration and upon termination. Then, the truth of P and the falsity of the guard allow us to conclude that the desired result R has been established.

Now let's verify that P is true after the initialization $i,s := 1,b[0]$, no matter what the initial state is. We can see this informally, or we can prove it as follows:

$$
\begin{aligned}
wp\,(\text{``}i, s := 1, b[0]\text{''}, P) \\
&= \ 1 \leqslant 1 \leqslant 11 \ \wedge \ b[0] = (\Sigma k : 0 \leqslant k < 1 : b[k]) \\
&= \ T.
\end{aligned}
$$

Now let's show that an iteration of the loop terminates with P true —i.e. an execution of command $i, s := i+1, s+b[i]$ beginning with P and $i < 11$ true terminates with P still true. Again, we can see this informally or we can formally prove it:

$$
\begin{aligned}
wp\,(\text{``}i, s := i+1, s+b[i]\text{''}, P) \\
&= \ 1 \leqslant i+1 \leqslant 11 \ \wedge \ s+b[i] = (\Sigma k : 0 \leqslant k < i+1 : b[k]) \\
&= \ 0 \leqslant i < 11 \ \wedge \ s = (\Sigma k : 0 \leqslant k < i : b[k])
\end{aligned}
$$

and $(P \wedge i < 11)$ implies the last line.

Hence we know that if execution of the loop terminates, upon termination P and $i \geqslant 11$, and hence R, are true.

A predicate P that is true before and after each iteration of a loop is called an *invariant relation*, or simply an *invariant*, of the loop. (The adjective *invariant* means *constant*, or *unchanging*. In mathematics the term means *unaffected by the group of mathematical operations under consideration*, the single operation here being an iteration of the loop under the initial truth of P.)

To show that the loop terminates, we introduce an integer function, t, of the program variables that is an upper bound on the number of iterations still to be performed. Each iteration of the loop decreases t by at least 1 and, as long as execution of the loop has not terminated, t is bounded below by 0. Hence, the loop must terminate. Let t be:

$t: 11-i$.

Since each iteration increases i by 1, it obviously decreases t by 1. Also, as long as there is an iteration to perform, i.e. as long as $i < 11$, we know that t is greater than 0.

In this case, t indicates exactly how many iterations are still to be performed, but, in general, it may only provide an *upper bound* on the number of iterations still to be performed. Function t has been called a *variant* function, as opposed to the *invariant* relation P —the function changes at each iteration; the relation remains invariantly true. However, in order to emphasize its purpose, we will call t the *bound function*.

The previous example may seem to require too much of an explanation for such a simple algorithm. Let us now consider a second example, whose correctness is not so obvious. Indeed, it is only with the aid of the invariant that we will be able to understand it. Algorithm (11.4) is supposed to store in variable z the value $a*b$ for $b \geqslant 0$, but without the use of multiplication.

$$
\begin{array}{ll}
& \{b \geqslant 0\} \\
& x, y, z := a, b, 0; \\
(11.4) \quad & \textbf{do } y > 0 \wedge even(y) \rightarrow y, x := y \div 2, x + x \\
& \quad [\!] \; odd(y) \qquad\qquad \rightarrow y, z := y - 1, z + x \\
& \textbf{od} \\
& \{R: z = a*b\}
\end{array}
$$

One view of the loop is that it processes the binary representation of b, which has been stored in y. Testing for oddness and evenness is done by interrogating the rightmost bit, subtracting 1 when the rightmost bit is 1 means changing it to a zero, and dividing by 2 is done by shifting the binary representation 1 bit to the right, thus deleting the rightmost bit.

But, how do we know the algorithm works? We introduce —out of the old hat, so to speak— the invariant P (how to find invariants is a topic of Part III):

$$P: y \geqslant 0 \wedge z + x*y = a*b .$$

We determine that P is true just after the initialization:

$$wp(``x, y, z := a, b, 0", P) = b \geqslant 0 \wedge 0 + a*b = a*b ,$$

which is obviously implied by the precondition of algorithm (11.4). Next, we show that any iteration of the loop beginning with P true terminates with P true, so that P is an invariant of the loop. For the second guarded command, this can be observed by noting that the value of $z + x*y$ remains the same if y is decreased by 1 and x is added to z:

$z + x*y = z + x + x*(y-1)$. For the first guarded command, note that execution of $y, x := y \div 2, x + x$ with y even leaves the value of $z + x*y$ unchanged, because $x*y = (x+x)*(y \div 2)$ when y is even. We leave the more formal verification to the reader (exercise 7).

Since each iteration of the loop leaves P true, P must be true upon termination. We show that P together with the falsity of the guards implies the result R as follows:

$$
\begin{aligned}
P \wedge \neg(y > 0 \wedge even(y)) \wedge \neg odd(y) \\
= y \geqslant 0 \wedge z + x*y = a*b \wedge (y \leqslant 0 \wedge even(y)) \\
= y = 0 \wedge z + x*y = a*b \\
\Rightarrow z = a*b
\end{aligned}
$$

The work done thus far is conveyed by the following annotated program.

(11.5)
```
{b ⩾ 0}
x, y, z := a, b, 0;
{P}
do y > 0 ∧ even(y) → {P ∧ y > 0 ∧ even(y)} y, x := y÷2, x+x {P}
[] odd(y)         → {P ∧ odd(y)} y, z := y−1, z+x {P}
od
{P ∧ y ⩽ 0 ∧ ¬odd(y)}
{P ∧ y = 0}
{R: z = a*b}
```

To show that the loop terminates, use the bound function $t = y$: it is greater than 0 if there is another iteration to execute and is decreased by at least 1 on each iteration.

A theorem concerning a loop, an invariant and a bound function

In the two examples just given, the same kind of reasoning was used to argue that the loops performed as desired. This form of reasoning is embodied in theorem (11.6). By now, the theorem should be quite clear. Assumption 1 implies that P will be true upon termination of DO. Assumption 2 indicates that function t is bounded below by 0 as long as execution of DO has not terminated. Assumption 3 indicates that each iteration decreases t by at least one, so that termination is guaranteed to occur. An unbounded number of iterations would decrease t below any limit, which would lead to a contradiction. Finally, upon termination all the guards are false, so that $\neg$ BB is true.

(11.6)   **Theorem**. Consider loop DO. Suppose a predicate P satisfies

    1. $P \wedge B_i \Rrightarrow wp(S_i, P)$, for all i, $1 \leqslant i \leqslant n$.

Suppose, further, that an integer function t satisfies the following, where $t1$ is a fresh identifier:

    2. $P \wedge \mathrm{BB} \Rrightarrow (t > 0)$,
    3. $P \wedge B_i \Rrightarrow wp(\text{"}t1:= t;\ S_i\text{"}, t < t1)$, for $1 \leqslant i \leqslant n$.

Then $P \Rrightarrow wp(\mathrm{DO}, P \wedge \neg \mathrm{BB})$.   □

Proof. We leave to the reader (exercise 2) the proof that assumption 1 implies

    1'. $P \wedge \mathrm{BB} \Rrightarrow wp(\mathrm{IF}, P)$

We leave to the reader (exercise 3) the proof that assumption 3 implies

    3'. $P \wedge \mathrm{BB} \wedge t \leqslant t0 + 1 \Rrightarrow wp(\mathrm{IF}, t \leqslant t0)$, for all $t0$.

Finally, we leave to the reader (exercise 4) the proof that, for all $k \geqslant 0$,

(11.7) $P \wedge t \leqslant k \Rrightarrow H_k(P \wedge \neg \mathrm{BB})$.

Predicate (11.7) is interpreted to mean that in any state in which P is true, if $t \leqslant k$, then execution of the loop will terminate in k or fewer iterations with P true and BB false. Since t is a finite function, $(\boldsymbol{E}k: 0 \leqslant k: t \leqslant k)$ is true in any state. Therefore,

$$
\begin{aligned}
P &= P \wedge (\boldsymbol{E}k: 0 \leqslant k: t \leqslant k) \\
  &= (\boldsymbol{E}k: 0 \leqslant k: P \wedge t \leqslant k) \qquad \text{(Since } k \text{ is not free in } P) \\
  &\Rrightarrow (\boldsymbol{E}k: 0 \leqslant k: H_k(P \wedge \neg \mathrm{BB})) \qquad (11.7) \\
  &= wp(\mathrm{DO}, P \wedge \neg \mathrm{BB}) \qquad \text{(Definition (11.2))} \quad □
\end{aligned}
$$

Discussion

A loop has many invariants. For example, the predicate $x*0 = 0$ is an invariant of every loop since it is always true. But an invariant that satisfies the assumptions of theorem (11.6) is important because it provides understanding of the loop. Indeed, *every* loop, except the most trivial, should be annotated with an invariant that satisfies the theorem.

As we shall see in Part III, the invariant is not only useful to the reader, it is almost necessary for the programmer. We shall give heuristics for developing the invariant and bound function *before* developing the loop and argue that this is the more effective way to program. This makes sense if we view the invariant as simply the definition of the variables and remember the adage about precisely defining variables before

using them. At this point, of course, developing an invariant may seem
almost impossible, since even the idea of an invariant is new. Leave the
development process to Part III, and for now concentrate on understanding loops for which invariants are already provided.

Annotating a loop and understanding the annotation

Algorithms (11.3) and (11.5) are annotated to show when and where
the invariants are true. Rather than write the invariant in so many places,
it is often easier to give the invariant and bound function in the text
accompanying an algorithm. When it is necessary to include them in the
algorithm itself, it is advantageous to use an abbreviation, such as shown
in (11.8).

$$\{Q\}$$
$$\{inv\ P\text{: the invariant}\}$$
$$\{bound\ t\text{: the bound function}\}$$
(11.8)   **do** $B_1\ \rightarrow\ S_1$

     $[]\ \ \cdots$

     $[]\ B_n\ \rightarrow\ S_n$

     od
$$\{R\}$$

When faced with a loop with form (11.8), according to theorem (11.6)
the reader need only check the points given in (11.9) to understand that
the loop is correct. The existence of such a checklist is indeed an advantage, for it allows one to be sure that nothing has been forgotten. In fact,
the checklist is of use to the programmer himself, although after a while
(pun) its use becomes second-nature.

(11.9)   **Checklist for understanding a loop**:

1. Show that P is true before execution of the loop begins.

2. Show that $\{P \wedge B_i\}\ S_i\ \{P\}$, for $1 \leqslant i \leqslant n$. That is, execution of
each guarded command terminates with P true, so that P is
indeed an invariant of the loop.

3. Show that $P \wedge \neg BB \Rightarrow R$, i.e. upon termination the desired
result is true.

4. Show that $P \wedge BB \Rightarrow (t > 0)$, so that t is bounded from below
as long as the loop has not terminated.

5. Show that $\{P \wedge B_i\}\ t1 := t;\ S_i\ \{t < t1\}$, for $1 \leqslant i \leqslant n$, so that
each loop iteration is guaranteed to decrease the bound func-
tion. □

Often, only the invariant and bound function need be provided as documentation for a loop, because the algorithm is then almost trivial to verify. This is documentation at its best: just enough to provide the necessary understanding and not so much that the reader is lost in superfluous, obvious details.

In the same vein, the parts of an invariant that refer only to unchanged variables of a loop are often omitted, and the reader is expected to note this. For example, in algorithm (11.3) we did not indicate explicitly that array b remained unchanged (by including as a conjunct of the precondition, the invariant and the postcondition the predicate $b = B$ where B represents the initial value of b). Similarly, in algorithm (5.4) we did not indicate explicitly that a and b remained unchanged.

It is important to perform several of the exercises 7-13. In Part III we will be discussing the development of loops, but Part III will make sense and seem easy only if you are completely familiar with theorem 11.6 and the use of checklist 11.9 and if you have gained some facility in this way of thinking.

Exercises for Chapter 11

1. Determine $wp(\textbf{do od}, R)$, for any R. Have you seen a command with these characteristics before?

2. Prove that 1' follows from assumption 1 (see the proof of theorem (11.6)).

3. Prove that 3' follows from assumption 3 (see the proof of theorem (11.6)).

4. Prove by induction on k that (11.7) follows from 1', 2 and 3' (see the proof of theorem (11.6)).

5. Prove that properties (7.3) and (7.4) of chapter 7 hold for the definition of $wp(\text{DO}, R)$.

6. $H_k(R)$ represents the states in which execution of DO will terminate in k or fewer iterations with R true. Define $H'_k(R)$ to represent the set of states in which execution of DO will terminate in *exactly* k iterations. What set of states does the predicate $(E k: 0 \leqslant k: H'_k(R))$ represent? How does it differ from $wp(\text{DO}, R)$?

7. Formally prove the points of checklist 11.9 for algorithm 11.4.

8. Formally prove the points of checklist 11.9 for the following algorithm, which stores in s the sum of the elements of $b[1:10]$.

$$\{T\}$$
$$i, s := 10, 0;$$
$$\{inv\ P: 0 \leqslant i \leqslant 10 \wedge s = (\Sigma k: i+1 \leqslant k \leqslant 10: b[k])\}$$
$$\{bound\ t: i\}$$
$$\textbf{do } i \neq 0 \rightarrow i, s := i-1, s+b[i] \textbf{ od}$$
$$\{R: s = (\Sigma k: 1 \leqslant k \leqslant 10: b[k])\}$$

9. Formally prove the points of checklist 11.9 for the following algorithm. The algorithm finds the position i of x in array $b[0:n-1]$ if $x \in b[0:n-1]$ and sets i to n if it is not.

$\{0 \leqslant n\}$
$i := 0;$
$\{inv\ P: 0 \leqslant i \leqslant n \wedge x \notin b[0:i-1]\}$
$\{bound\ t: n-i\}$
$\textbf{do } i < n \textbf{ cand } x \neq b[i] \rightarrow i := i+1 \textbf{ od}$
$\{R: (0 \leqslant i < n \wedge x = b[i]) \vee (i = n \wedge x \notin b[0:n-1])\}$

10. Formally prove the points of checklist 11.9 for the following algorithm. The algorithm sets i to the highest power of 2 that is at most n.

$\{0 < n\}$
$i := 1;$
$\{inv\ P: 0 < i \leqslant n \wedge (E\,p: i = 2^p)\}$
$\{bound\ t: n-i\}$
$\textbf{do } 2*i \leqslant n \rightarrow i := 2*i \textbf{ od}$
$\{R: 0 < i \leqslant n < 2*i \wedge (E\,p: i = 2^p)\}$

11. Formally prove the points of checklist 11.9 for the following algorithm. The algorithm computes the nth Fibonacci number f_n for $n > 0$, which is defined by $f_0 = 0, f_1 = 1$, and $f_n = f_{n-1} + f_{n-2}$ for $n > 1$.

$\{n > 0\}$
$i, a, b := 1, 1, 0;$
$\{inv\ P: 1 \leqslant i \leqslant n \wedge a = f_i \wedge b = f_{i-1}\}$
$\{bound\ t: n-i\}$
$\textbf{do } i < n \rightarrow i, a, b := i+1, a+b, a \textbf{ od}$
$\{R: a = f_n\}$

12. Formally prove the points of checklist 11.9 for the following algorithm. The algorithm computes the quotient q and remainder r when x is divided by y.

$\{x \geqslant 0 \wedge 0 < y\}$
$q, r := 0, x;$
$\{inv\ P: 0 \leqslant r \wedge 0 < y \wedge q*y+r = x\}$
$\{bound\ t: r\}$
$\textbf{do } r \geqslant y \rightarrow r, q := r-y, q+1 \textbf{ od}$
$\{R: 0 \leqslant r < y \wedge q*y+r = x\}$

13. Formally prove the points of checklist 11.9 for the following algorithm. The algorithm finds an integer k such $b[k]$ is the maximum value of array $b[0:n-1]$ —note that if the maximum value occurs more than once the algorithm is non-deterministic.

$\{0 < n\}$
$i, k := 1, 0;$
$\{inv\ P: 0 < i \leqslant n \ \wedge\ b[k] \geqslant b[0:i-1]\}$
$\{bound\ t: n-i\}$
do $i < n\ \rightarrow$ **if** $b[i] \leqslant b[k]\ \rightarrow$ *skip*
$\qquad\qquad$ [] $b[i] \geqslant b[k]\ \rightarrow\ k := i$
$\qquad$ **fi**;
$\qquad$ $i := i+1$
od
$\{R:\ b[k] \geqslant b[0:n-1]\}$

Chapter 12
Procedure Call

This chapter develops the definition of the command *procedure call*, which invokes a procedure declared with value and result parameters. Two theorems are then proved in order to make proving procedure calls correct easier. Finally, the theorems are extended to include reference, or "var", parameters. This chapter relies heavily on the multiple assignment command, which was defined in section 9.4.

This material need not be read to understand Part III (program development), and this chapter may be skipped. The purpose of the chapter is to illustrate how the correctness issues extend to more complicated constructs, but the material will not be used formally. Because of the attempt to deal with a number of different parameter-passing mechanisms, the chapter contains quite a few theorems concerning procedure calls. When using any one programming notation, of course, the number of parameter-passing mechanisms and corresponding applicable theorems used is fewer.

In order to introduce this detailed material in as simple a manner as possible, it is assumed that procedures are not recursive.

The procedure, or subroutine as it called in FORTRAN, is a basic building-block in programming. (The word *routine* was used as early as 1949 on the EDSAC, generally accepted as the first practical stored program computer to be completed. It was built at Cambridge University by a team headed by Maurice Wilkes and executed its first program in May 1949.) The main use of the procedure is in *abstraction*. By abstraction we mean the act of singling out a few properties of an object for further use or study, omitting from consideration other properties that don't concern us for the moment. The main property that we single out, once a procedure is written, is *what* it does; the main property that we omit from consideration is *how* it does it.

In one sense, using a procedure is exactly like using any other operation (e.g. +) of the programming notation, and constructing a procedure is extending the language to include another operation. For example, when we use + in an expression, we never question how it is performed; we just assume that it works. Similarly, when writing a procedure call we rely only on what the procedure does, and not on how it does it. In another sense, a procedure (and its proof) is a lemma. A program can be considered a constructive proof that its specification is consistent and computable; a procedure is a lemma used in the constructive proof.

In the following sections, Pascal-like notations are used for procedure declaration and call, although the (possible) execution of a procedure call may not be exactly as in Pascal. The reason is that the main influence in developing the procedure call here was the need for a simple, understandable theorem about its use, and such an influence was beyond the state of the art when Pascal was developed.

12.1 Calls with Value and Result Parameters

Procedure declaration

A procedure declaration has the form

> **proc** <identifier>(<parameter specification>; $\cdots$;
> <parameter specification>);
> $\{P\}$ <body> $\{Q\}$

where each <parameter specification> has one of the three forms

> **value** <identifier list> : <type>
> **value result** <identifier list> : <type>
> **result** <identifier list> : <type>

As usual, an <identifier list> is a sequence of one or more identifiers, joined by commas. A parameter of a procedure has a type (e.g. *Boolean*, **array of** *integer*), which defines the type that a corresponding argument may have. We do not consider array bounds to be part of the type of an array; an array is simply a function of one integer argument.

Execution of a procedure call causes the procedure <body> to be executed. The <body> may be any command whatsoever —a sequence of commands, an assignment command, a loop, etc. It may contain suitably declared local variables. During execution of the <body>, the parameters are considered to be local variables of the <body>. The initial values of the parameters and the use of their final values are determined by the attributes **value** or **result** given to the parameters in the procedure heading. This will be explained later.

The precondition P and postcondition Q of the <body> are necessary for understanding, but not executing, a procedure call. It is assumed that $\{P\}$ <body> $\{Q\}$ has been proved, and that this information will be used in writing calls. A trend in documentation is to require both the pre- and postcondition to be written before the body, as shown below, because it is easier to find the information needed to write and understand procedure calls. To write a call, one need only understand the first three lines:

> $\{Pre: P\}$
> $\{Post: Q\}$
> **proc** <identifier>(<par.spec.>; $\cdots$; <par. spec.>);
>   <body>

The following restrictions are made on the use of identifiers in a procedure declaration. The only identifiers that can be used in the body are the parameters and the identifiers declared in the body itself —i.e. no "global variables" are allowed. The parameters must be distinct identifiers. Precondition P of the body may contain as free only the parameters with attribute **value** (and **value result**); postcondition Q only parameters with attribute **result** (and **value result**). This restriction is essential for a simple definition of procedure call, but it does not limit procedures or calls of them in any essential way. P and Q may, of course, contain as free other identifiers that are not used within the program (to denote initial values of variables, etc.). See section 12.4 for a way to eliminate this restriction.

Example. Given fixed x, fixed $n > 0$ and fixed array $b[0:n-1]$, where $x \in b$, the following procedure determines the position of x in b, thus establishing $x = b[i]$.

> $\{Pre: n = N \wedge x = X \wedge b = B \wedge X \in B[0:N-1]\}$
> $\{Post: 0 \leqslant i < N \wedge B[i] = X\}$
> **proc** $search($**value** $n, x:$ *integer*;
>   **value** $b:$ **array of** *integer*);
>   **result** $i:$ *integer*);
> $i := 0;$
> $\{invariant: 0 \leqslant i < N \wedge X \notin B[0:i-1]\}$
> $\{bound: N-i\}$
>   **do** $b[i] \neq x \rightarrow i := i+1$ **od**

Note that identifiers have been used to denote the initial values of the parameters that do not have attribute **result**, even though the parameters are not altered during execution of the procedure body. □

In the sequel, we assume the procedure has the following form:

(12.1.1)   **proc** p (**value** $\bar{x}$; **value result** $\bar{y}$; **result** $\bar{z}$);
$\quad\quad\quad \{P\}\ B\ \{Q\}$

Thus, the x_i are the value parameters of procedure p, the y_i the value-result parameters and the z_i the result parameters. We have left out the types of the parameters because they don't concern us at this point. (This is an example of the use of abstraction!)

The procedure call and its execution

We are interested in formally defining the command *procedure call*, which has the form

(12.1.2) $p(\bar{a},\ \bar{b},\ \bar{c})$

The name of the procedure is p. The a_i, b_i and c_i are the *arguments* of the procedure. The a_i are expressions; the b_i and c_i have the form *identifier ∘ selector* —in common parlance, they are "variables". The a_i are the value arguments corresponding to the x_i of (12.1.1), the b_i the value-result arguments and the c_i the result arguments. Each argument must have the same type as its corresponding parameter.

The identifiers accessible at the point of call must be different from the procedure parameters $\bar{x}$, $\bar{y}$ and $\bar{z}$. This restriction avoids extra notation needed to deal with the conflict of the same identifier being used for two different purposes and is not essential.

To illustrate, here is a call of procedure *search* of the previous example: *search*$(50, t, c, position[j])$. Its execution stores in *position*$[j]$ the position of the value of t in array $c[0:49]$.

A call $p(\bar{a}, \bar{b}, \bar{c})$ can be executed as follows:

> *All* parameters are considered to be local variables of the procedure. First, determine the values of the value arguments $\bar{a}$ and $\bar{b}$ and store them in the corresponding parameters $\bar{x}$ and $\bar{y}$. Second, determine the variables described by the result arguments $\bar{b}$, $\bar{c}$ —i.e. determine their addresses in memory. Note that all parameters with attribute **value** are initialized, and the others are not. Third, execute the procedure body. Fourth, store the values of the result parameters $\bar{y}$, $\bar{z}$ in the corresponding result arguments $\bar{b}$, $\bar{c}$ (using their previously determined addresses) *in left-to-right order.*

Formal definition of the procedure call

From the above description of execution, we see that execution of the call $p(\bar{a},\bar{b},\bar{c})$ is equivalent to execution of the sequence

$$\bar{x},\bar{y}:=\bar{a},\bar{b};\ B;\ \bar{b},\bar{c}:=\bar{y},\bar{z}$$

(The addresses of $\bar{b}$, $\bar{c}$ can be evaluated before or after execution of the procedure body B, since execution of B cannot change them.)   We define

(12.1.3) $wp(p(\bar{a},\bar{b},\bar{c}),R) = wp(\text{``}\bar{x},\bar{y}:=\bar{a},\bar{b};\ B;\ \bar{b},\bar{c}:=\bar{y},\bar{z}\text{''},R)$

12.2 Two Theorems Concerning Procedure Call

We now develop theorems that allow the use of procedural abstraction when writing procedure calls.   First, we state a theorem and argue about its validity based on our notion of procedure call execution.

(12.2.1)   **Theorem**.   Suppose procedure p is defined as in (12.1.1).   Then

$$\{PR:\ P^{\bar{x},\bar{y}}_{\bar{a},\bar{b}} \wedge (A\,\bar{u},\bar{v}:\ Q^{\bar{y},\bar{z}}_{\bar{u},\bar{v}} \Rightarrow R^{\bar{b},\bar{c}}_{\bar{u},\bar{v}})\}\ p(\bar{a},\bar{b},\bar{c})\ \{R\}$$

holds.   In other words, $PR \Rightarrow wp(p(\bar{a},\bar{b},\bar{c}),R)$.

Proof.   Suppose for the moment that we know the values $\bar{u}$, $\bar{v}$ that will be assigned to parameters with attribute **result**.   Then execution of the procedure body B, by itself, can be viewed as a multiple assignment $\bar{y},\bar{z}:=\bar{u},\bar{v}$.   From (12.1.3), we see that the procedure call can be viewed as the following sequence (12.2.2).   In (12.2.2), postcondition R has been placed at the end and assertions P and Q have been placed suitably because we expect to use that information subsequently.

(12.2.2) $\bar{x},\bar{y}:=\bar{a},\bar{b}\ \{P\};\ \bar{y},\bar{z}:=\bar{u},\bar{v}\ \{Q\};\ \bar{b},\bar{c}:=\bar{y},\bar{z}\ \{R\}$

Since this is a sequence of assignments, we can easily determine the weakest precondition such that its execution will establish each of the three predicates at the indicated places.   Note that these are necessary and sufficient conditions.   For example, R holds on termination *iff* (12.2.5) holds before execution:

(12.2.3)   Weakest precondition to establish P: $P^{\bar{x},\bar{y}}_{\bar{a},\bar{b}}$

(12.2.4)   Weakest precondition to establish Q: $(Q^{\bar{y},\bar{z}}_{\bar{u},\bar{v}})^{\bar{x},\bar{y}}_{\bar{a},\bar{b}}$

$$= Q^{\bar{y},\bar{z}}_{\bar{u},\bar{v}}\ \text{(since it contains no } x_i \text{ or } y_i!)$$

(12.2.5)   Weakest precondition to establish R: $((R_{y,\,z}^{\bar{b},\,\bar{c}})_{\bar{u},\,\bar{v}}^{\bar{y},\,\bar{z}})_{a,\,b}^{x,\,y}$

$$= R_{\bar{u},\,\bar{v}}^{\bar{b},\,\bar{c}} \quad \text{(since it contains no } x_i \text{ or } y_i!)$$

In order to be able to use the fact that $\{P\}\ B\ \{Q\}$ has been proved about the procedure body, we require that (12.2.3) be true before the call; this is the first conjunct in the precondition PR of the theorem. Therefore, no matter what values $\bar{u}$, $\bar{v}$ execution assigns to the result parameters, Q will be true in the indicated place in (12.2.2).

Now, we want to determine initial conditions that guarantee the truth of R upon termination, no matter what values $\bar{u}$, $\bar{v}$ are assigned to the result parameters and arguments. R holds after the call if, for all values $\bar{u}$, $\bar{v}$, the truth of Q in (12.2.2) implies the truth of R after the call. This can be written in terms of the initial conditions as

$$(A\ \bar{u},\bar{v}:\ (12.2.4) \Rightarrow (12.2.5))$$

This is the second conjunct of the precondition of the theorem.   □

Examples of the use of theorem 12.2.1

Each example illustrates an important point about the use of the theorem, so read the examples carefully. In each, the procedure body is omitted, since it is not needed to ascertain correctness of a call.

Example 1. Consider the procedure

proc *swap* (**value result** *y1, y2: integer*);
$$\{P:\ y1=X\ \wedge\ y2=Y\}\ B\ \{Q:\ y1=Y\ \wedge\ y2=X\}$$

We want to prove that

(12.2.6) $\{a=X\ \wedge\ b=Y\}\ swap\,(a,\,b)\ \{R:\ a=Y\ \wedge\ b=X\}$

holds, where a and b are integer variables and identifiers Y and X denote their final values, respectively. We apply theorem (12.2.1) to find a satisfactory precondition PR:

$$
\begin{aligned}
PR &= (a=X\ \wedge\ b=Y)\ \wedge \\
&\quad (A\ u1,u2:(y1=Y\ \wedge\ y2=X)_{u1,u2}^{y1,y2} \Rightarrow (a=Y\ \wedge\ b=X)_{u1,u2}^{a,b}) \\
&= (a=X\ \wedge\ b=Y)\ \wedge \\
&\quad (A\ u1,u2:(u1=Y\ \wedge\ u2=X) \Rightarrow (u1=Y\ \wedge\ u2=X)) \\
&= (a=X\ \wedge\ b=Y)\ \wedge\ T
\end{aligned}
$$

and this is implied by the precondition of (12.2.6). Hence, (12.2.6) is correct.   □

Example 2. Consider the procedure of Example 1. Suppose we want to prove that

(12.2.7) $\{a = A \wedge b = Y\}$ $swap\,(a, b)$ $\{a = Y \wedge b = A\}$

holds, where a and b are integer variables and identifiers A and Y denote their initial values, respectively. The difficulty here is that different identifiers are used in the declaration and in the call to denote the initial values X. We surmount this difficulty as follows. The following has been proved about the procedure body —i.e. it is a tautology:

$$\{P: y1 = X \wedge y2 = Y\}\ B\ \{Q: y1 = Y \wedge y2 = X\}$$

Therefore, it is equivalent to

$$(AX,Y: \{y1 = X \wedge y2 = Y\}\ B\ \{y1 = Y \wedge y2 = X\})$$

Now we can produce an *instance* of the above quantified predicate by replacing X by A and Y by Y, respectively, to yield

$$\{y1 = A \wedge y2 = Y\}\ B\ \{y1 = Y \wedge y2 = A\}$$

Thus, this last line is also true about the procedure body B. Now apply the theorem as in example 1 to yield the desired result. Hence, (12.2.7) holds.

This illustrates how initial and final values of parameters can be handled. The identifiers that denote initial and final values of parameters can be replaced by fresh identifiers —or any expressions— to yield another proof about the procedure body, which can then be used in theorem 12.2.1.   □

Example 3. We now prove correct a call that has array elements as arguments. Consider the procedure of example 1. We want to prove that $swap\,(i, b[i])$ interchanges i and $b[i]$ but leaves the rest of array b unchanged. It is assumed that the value of i is a valid subscript. Thus, we want to prove

(12.2.8) $\{i = I \wedge (A\,j: b[j] = B[j])\}$
          $swap\,(i, b[i])$
          $\{R: i = B[I] \wedge b[I] = I \wedge (A\,j: I \neq j: b[j] = B[j])\}$

Identifiers I and B denote the initial values of i and b, respectively. In the proof of the body of the procedure declaration, we can replace the expressions X and Y by I and $B[I]$, respectively, to yield

$$\{P: y1 = I \wedge y2 = B[I]\} \; B \; \{Q: y1 = B[I] \wedge y2 = I\}$$

Now apply theorem 12.2.1 to R of (12.2.8) to get the precondition PR

$$
\begin{aligned}
PR = \; & i = I \wedge b[i] = B[I] \wedge \\
& (A\, u1, u2: u1 = B[I] \wedge u2 = I \Rightarrow u1 = B[I] \wedge \\
& \qquad (b;\; i{:}u2)[I] = I \wedge (A\, j: I \neq j: (b;\; i{:}u2)[j] = B[j])) \\
= \; & i = I \wedge b[i] = B[I] \wedge B[I] = B[I] \wedge \\
& (b;\; i{:}I)[I] = I \wedge (A\, j: I \neq j: (b;\; i{:}I)[j] = B[j]) \\
= \; & i = I \wedge b[i] = B[I] \wedge T \wedge I = I \wedge (A\, j: I \neq j: b[j] = B[j])
\end{aligned}
$$

and this is implied by the precondition of (12.2.8). $\square$

Example 4. Consider the procedure

$$\textbf{proc } p \,(\textbf{value } x\,; \; \textbf{result } z1, z2)$$
$$\{P: x = X\} \; z1, z2 := x, x \; \{Q: z1 = z2 = X\}$$

which assigns the value parameter to both result parameters. Note that postcondition Q does not contain the value parameter. We want to execute the call $p\,(b[i], i, b[i+1])$, which assigns $b[i]$ to i and $b[i+1]$. Thus, it makes sense to try to prove

(12.2.9) $\{b[i] = C \wedge i = I\}\, p\,(b[i], i, b[i+1])\, \{R: i = b[I] = b[I+1] = C\}$

First, replace the free variable X in the proof of the procedure body by C:

$$\{P: x = C\} \; z1, z2 := x, x \; \{Q: z1 = z2 = C\}$$

Next, apply theorem 12.2.1 to yield the precondition

$$
\begin{aligned}
& b[i] = C \wedge \\
& (A\, v1, v2: v1 = v2 = C \Rightarrow \\
& \qquad v1 = (b;\; i+1{:}v2)[I] = (b;\; i+1{:}v2)[I+1] = C) \\
= \; & b[i] = C \wedge (b;\; i+1{:}C)[I] = (b;\; i+1{:}C)[I+1] = C
\end{aligned}
$$

Since the last line is implied by the precondition of (12.2.9), (12.2.9) holds. $\square$

A theorem that is easier to use

In the precondition of theorem 12.2.1, it would be nice not to have the complicated conjunct

$$(A\ \bar{u},\bar{v}:\ Q_{\bar{u},\bar{v}}^{\bar{y},\bar{z}} \Rightarrow R_{\bar{u},\bar{v}}^{\bar{b},\bar{c}})$$

If we restrict the postcondition R in some fashion, we may be able to eliminate this complicated conjunct. This may be the case, for example, if we allow only those R that satisfy

(12.2.10) $R_{\bar{u},\bar{v}}^{\bar{b},\bar{c}} = Q_{\bar{u},\bar{v}}^{\bar{y},\bar{z}} \wedge I$

where the free variables of I are disjoint from $\bar{b}$ and $\bar{c}$. For then the complicated conjunct may be simplified as follows:

$$(A\ \bar{u},\bar{v}:\ Q_{\bar{u},\bar{v}}^{\bar{y},\bar{z}} \Rightarrow R_{\bar{u},\bar{v}}^{\bar{b},\bar{c}})$$
$$= (A\ \bar{u},\bar{v}:\ Q_{\bar{u},\bar{v}}^{\bar{y},\bar{z}} \Rightarrow Q_{\bar{u},\bar{v}}^{\bar{y},\bar{z}} \wedge I)$$
$$= I \qquad \text{(since } \bar{u},\bar{v} \text{ are not free in } I)$$

Our task, then, is to determine predicates R that satisfy (12.2.10). To do this, we can textually replace $\bar{u}, \bar{v}$ by $\bar{b}, \bar{c}$ in (12.2.10) and use predicates R that satisfy

$$R = (R_{\bar{u},\bar{v}}^{\bar{b},\bar{c}})_{\bar{b},\bar{c}}^{\bar{u},\bar{v}} \qquad \text{(Lemma 4.6.3 and ex. 5 of 9.4)}$$
$$= (Q_{\bar{u},\bar{v}}^{\bar{y},\bar{z}} \wedge I)_{\bar{b},\bar{c}}^{\bar{u},\bar{v}} \qquad \text{(12.2.10)}$$
$$= Q_{\bar{b},\bar{c}}^{\bar{y},\bar{z}} \wedge I \qquad \text{(Lemma 4.6.3, def of } I)$$

Hence we restrict our attention to predicates R satisfying

(12.2.11) $R = Q_{\bar{b},\bar{c}}^{\bar{y},\bar{z}} \wedge I$

But this is not enough. From (12.2.11) we want to conclude that (12.2.10) holds, but this is not always the case, because

$$(Q_{\bar{b},\bar{c}}^{\bar{y},\bar{z}})_{\bar{u},\bar{v}}^{\bar{b},\bar{c}}$$

is not always equal to

$$Q_{\bar{u},\bar{v}}^{\bar{y},\bar{z}}$$

The two are equal, however, if $(\bar{b},\bar{c})$ consists of distinct identifiers, as we know from Lemma 4.6.3. Hence we have the following theorem, which is more restrictive but easier to use

(12.2.12) **Theorem.** Suppose procedure p is defined as in (12.1.1). Suppose $(\bar{b}, \bar{c})$ is a list of distinct identifiers. Suppose none of the free identifiers in predicate I appear in the argument lists $\bar{b}$ and $\bar{c}$. Then

$$\{P_{\bar{a}, \bar{b}}^{\bar{x}, \bar{y}} \wedge I\} \quad p(\bar{a}, \bar{b}, \bar{c}) \quad \{Q_{\bar{b}, \bar{c}}^{\bar{y}, \bar{z}} \wedge I\} \quad \square$$

Predicate I of the theorem captures the notion of *invariance*: predicates that do not refer to the result arguments[1] remain unchanged throughout the call of the procedure.

This theorem is simpler than theorem 12.2.1, and should be used whenever only identifiers are used as arguments. Examples of its use are left to the exercises.

12.3 Using Var Parameters

A value-result parameter y with corresponding argument c is handled during a call as follows. The value of c is stored in y; the procedure body is executed; the value of y is stored in c. If y is an array, this implementation can take much time and space.

Another method of argument-parameter correspondence is *call by reference*. Here, before execution of the body, the *address* of c is stored in y. During execution of the body, every reference to y is then treated as an indirect reference to c. For example, the assignment $y := e$ within the body has the immediate effect of the assignment $c := e$. In other words, y and c are considered to be different names for the same location.

Call by value-result requires space equal to the size of the argument, while call by reference requires constant space. Call by value-result requires time at least proportional to the size of the argument to prepare and conclude the call, while call by reference requires constant time for this. But call by reference does require more time for each reference to the parameter during execution of the procedure body.

Especially for arguments that are arrays, call by reference is preferred.

A call by reference parameter is denoted by the attribute **var**, which is short for "variable". The procedure declaration given in (12.1.1) and corresponding call of (12.1.2) are extended as follows:

(12.3.1) **proc** p (**value** $\bar{x}$; **value result** $\bar{y}$; **result** $\bar{z}$; **var** $\bar{r}$);
        $\{P\}$ B $\{Q\}$

(12.3.2) $p(\bar{a}, \bar{b}, \bar{c}, \bar{d})$

How do we extend theorems 12.2.1 and 12.2.12 to allow for call by reference? Call by reference can be viewed as an efficient form of call by value-result; execution is the same, except that the initial assignments to $\bar{r}$ and the final assignments to $\bar{d}$ are not needed. But the proof of the procedure body, $\{P\}\,B\,\{Q\}$, is consistent with our notion of execution for value-result parameters only if value-result parameters occupy separate locations —assignment to one parameter must not affect the value of any other parameter. When using call by reference, then, we must be sure that this condition is still upheld.

Let us introduce the notation $disj(\bar{d})$ to mean that no sharing of memory occurs among the d_i. For example, $disj(d1,d2)$ holds for different identifiers $d1$ and $d2$. Also, $disj(b[i],b[i+1])$ holds, while $disj(b[i],b[j])$ is equivalent to $i \neq j$.

Further, we say that two vectors $\bar{x}$ and $\bar{y}$ are *pairwise disjoint*, written $pdisj(\bar{x};\bar{y})$, if each x_i is disjoint from each y_j —i.e. $disj(x_i, y_j)$ holds. Theorems 12.2.1 and 12.2.12 can then be modified to the following:

(12.3.3)   **Theorem.** Suppose $disj(\bar{d})$ and $pdisj(d;\bar{b},\bar{c})$ hold. Then we have

$$\{P^{\bar{x},\bar{y},\bar{r}}_{\bar{a},\bar{b},\bar{d}} \;\wedge\; (A\,\bar{u},\bar{v},\bar{w}: Q^{\bar{y},\bar{z},\bar{r}}_{\bar{u},\bar{v},\bar{w}} \Rightarrow R^{\bar{b},\bar{c},\bar{d}}_{\bar{u},\bar{v},\bar{w}})\}$$

$$p(\bar{a}, \bar{b}, \bar{c}, \bar{d})$$

$$\{R\} \quad \square$$

(12.3.4)   **Theorem.** Suppose $(\bar{b},\bar{c},\bar{d})$ is a list of distinct identifiers. Let $ref(I)$ denote the list of free identifiers in predicate I. Finally, suppose that

$$pdisj(\bar{b},\bar{c},\bar{d}; ref(I))$$

holds. Then

$$\{P^{\bar{x},\bar{y},\bar{r}}_{\bar{a},\bar{b},\bar{d}} \wedge I\}\;\; p(\bar{a}, \bar{b}, \bar{c}, \bar{d})\;\; \{Q^{\bar{y},\bar{z},\bar{r}}_{\bar{b},\bar{c},\bar{d}} \wedge I\} \quad \square$$

As a simplification, if we restrict attention to call by value and call by reference, theorem 12.3.4 simplifies to

(12.3.5)   **Theorem**. Suppose procedure p is defined and called using

$$\textbf{proc } p\,(\textbf{value } \bar{x};\ \textbf{var } \bar{r});\ \{P\}\ B\ \{Q\}$$

and $p\,(\bar{a},\,\bar{d})$

where $\bar{d}$ is a list of distinct identifiers. Suppose no free identifier of I occurs in d. Then

$$\{P^{\bar{x},\,\bar{r}}_{\bar{a},\,\bar{d}} \wedge I\}\ p\,(\bar{a},\,\bar{d})\ \{Q^{\bar{r}}_{\bar{d}} \wedge I\}\quad\square$$

Examples of the use of these theorems are left to the exercises.

12.4 Allowing Value Parameters in the Postcondition

In procedure declaration 12.1.1, the postcondition Q of the body may not contain the value parameters $\bar{x}$. There is a good reason for this. Value parameters are considered to be local variables of the procedure body. Therefore, they have no meaning once execution of the procedure body has terminated. In general, one can not meaningfully use local variables of a command in the postcondition of a command.

But this restriction irritates, because it (almost) always requires the use of an extra identifier to denote the initial value of a value parameter. Perhaps there is a way of allowing the value parameters to occur in Q, which would eliminate this problem.

Consider theorem 12.2.1:

$$\{PR\colon\ P^{\bar{x},\,\bar{y}}_{\bar{a},\,\bar{b}} \wedge (A\ \bar{u},\bar{v}\colon\ Q^{\bar{y},\,\bar{z}}_{\bar{u},\,\bar{v}} \Rightarrow R^{\bar{b},\,\bar{c}}_{\bar{u},\,\bar{v}})\}$$
$$p\,(\bar{a},\,\bar{b},\,\bar{c})$$
$$\{R\}$$

It would not make sense with respect to the model of execution if $\bar{x}$ occurred in $Q^{\bar{y},\,\bar{z}}_{\bar{u},\,\bar{v}}$, because $\bar{x}$ cannot be referred to before the call (it is a list of parameters of the procedure). What is meant by $\bar{x}$ in this context? Well, it really refers to the value arguments $\bar{a}$, so let us try to textually replace $\bar{x}$ by $\bar{a}$ in Q. But this replacement makes sense with respect to the model of execution only if, upon termination of B, the value parameters still have the initial values of the value arguments. This we can ensure by requiring that no assignments to value parameters occur within Q and the value arguments are not affected by assignments to the other parameters. We then get the following counterparts of theorems 12.2.1, in which $\bar{x}$ can be referred to in Q. The counterparts of theorems 12.2.12, 12.3.3 and 12.3.5 are similar.

(12.4.1) **Theorem.** Suppose procedure p is defined as in (12.1.1), but Q may contain the value parameters $\bar{x}$, no assignments occur to value parameters, and the value arguments are not affected by assignments to the other parameters during execution of the procedure call. Then

$$\{PR: P_{\bar{a},\,\bar{b}}^{\bar{x},\,\bar{y}} \wedge (A\,\bar{u},\bar{v}: Q_{\bar{a},\,\bar{u},\,\bar{v}}^{\bar{x},\,\bar{y},\,\bar{z}} \Rightarrow R_{\bar{u},\,\bar{v}}^{\bar{b},\,\bar{c}})\}$$
$$p(\bar{a},\,\bar{b},\,\bar{c})$$
$$\{R\}$$

holds. In other words, $PR \Rightarrow wp(p(\bar{a},\bar{b},\bar{c}),R)$. □

Examples of the use of these theorems are left to the exercises.

Exercises for Chapter 12

1. Consider the three predicates

$$\{Q(u)\}\ S\ \{R\}$$
$$\{(A\,u: Q(u))\}\ S\ \{R\}$$
$$\{(E\,u: Q(u))\}\ S\ \{R\}$$

where identifier u is not free in command S or predicate R. Suppose the first has been proven to be true —i.e. it is a tautology. Is it equivalent to the second or the third? Hint: use the fact that $\{Q(u)\}\ S\ \{R\}$ is equivalent to $Q(u) \Rightarrow wp(S,R)$. Also, it is equivalent to itself but with identifier u universally quantified, the scope of u being the complete predicate.

2. Use the results of exercise 1 to reason why the quantifier A cannot be omitted in theorem 12.2.1.

3. Find a counterexample to the conjecture that theorem 12.2.12 holds even if the arguments are not identifiers. Hint: there must be arguments that are disjoint but still interact in some fashion.

4. Section 12.2 contained four examples of the use of theorem 12.2.1. Which of the procedure calls in the examples can be proved correct using theorem 12.2.12 instead? Prove them correct.

5. The following procedure inserts x in array $b[0:k-1]$ if it is not present, thus increasing k, and stores in p the position of x in $b[0:k-1]$. It assumed that the element $b[k]$ can be used by the procedure for its own purposes.

$\{Pre: 0 \leqslant k \wedge x = X \wedge b = B\}$
$\{Post: 0 \leqslant p \leqslant k \wedge b[p] = X\}$
proc s (**value** x : *integer* ;
     value result b : **array of** *integer* ;
     value result k , p : *integer*);
   p , $b[k] := 0, x$;
   $\{inv: 0 \leqslant p \leqslant k \wedge x \notin b[0{:}p-1]\}$
   $\{bound: k-p\}$
   do $x \neq b[p] \rightarrow p := p+1$ **od**

Is the procedure fully specified —i.e. has anything omitted from the specification that can be proved of the procedure body? Which of the following calls can be proved correct using theorem 12.2.1. Prove them correct.

(a) $\{d = 0\}$ $s(5, c, d, j)$ $\{c[j] = 5\}$

(b) $\{0 \leqslant m\}$ $s(f, c, m, j)$ $\{c[j] = f\}$

(c) $\{0 < m\}$ $s(b[0], c, m, j)$ $\{c[j] = c[0]\}$

(d) $\{0 < m\}$ $s(5, c, m, m)$ $\{c[m] = 5\}$

6. Which of the calls given in exercise 5 can be proved correct using theorem 12.2.12? Prove them correct.

7. Suppose parameters k and p of exercise 5 have attribute **var** instead of **value result**. Can call (d) of exercise 5 be proved correct using theorem 12.3.3? If so, do so. Can it be proved correct using theorem 12.3.4?. 12.3.5? If so, do so.

Part III
The Development of Programs
Chapter 13   Introduction

Part III discusses a radical methodology for the development of programs, which is based on the notion of weakest precondition and exploits our definition of a programming notation in terms of it. To the reader, the methodology will probably be different from anything seen before. The purpose of this introduction is to prepare the reader for the approach —to give reasons for it, to explain a few points, and to indicate what to expect.

What is a proof?

The word *radical*, used above, is appropriate, for the methodology proposed strikes at the root of the current problems in programming and provides basic principles to overcome them. One problem is that programmers have had little knowledge of what it means for a program to be correct and of how to *prove* a program correct. The word *proof* has unpleasant connotations for many, and it will be helpful to explain what it means.

A proof, according to *Webster's Third New International Dictionary*, is "the cogency of evidence that compels belief by the mind of a truth or fact". It is an argument that convinces the reader of the truth of something.

The definition of proof does not imply the need for formalism or mathematics. Indeed, programmers try to prove their programs correct in this sense of proof, for they certainly try to present evidence that compels their own belief. Unfortunately, most programmers are not adept at this, as can be seen by looking at how much time is spent debugging. The programmer must indeed feel frustrated at the lack of mastery of the subject!

Part of the problem has been that only inadequate tools for understanding have been available. Reasoning has been based solely on how programs are executed, and arguments about correctness have been based on a number of test cases that have been run or hand-simulated. The intuition and mental tools have simply been inadequate.

Also, it has not always been clear what it means for a program to be "correct", partly because specifications of programs have been so imprecise. Part II has clarified this for us; we call a program S correct —with respect to a given precondition Q and postcondition R— if $\{Q\}\ S\ \{R\}$ holds. And we have formal means for proving correctness.

Thus, our development method will center around the concept of a formal proof, involving weakest preconditions and the theorems for the alternative, iterative and procedure call constructs discussed in Part II. In this connection, the following principle is important:

(13.1) •**Principle**: A program and its proof should be developed hand-in-hand, with the *proof* usually leading the way.

It is just too difficult to prove an already existing program correct, and it is far better to use the proof-of-correctness ideas throughout the programming process for insight.

The balance between formality and common sense

Our approach to programming is based on proofs of correctness of programs. But be assured that complete attention to formalism is neither necessary nor desirable. Formality alone is inadequate, because it leads to incomprehensible detail; common sense and intuition alone —the programmer's main tools till now— are inadequate, because they allow too many errors and bad designs.

What is needed is a fine balance between the two. Obvious facts should be left implicit, important points should be stressed, and detail should be presented to allow the reader to understand a program as easily as possible. A notation must be found that allows less formalism to be used. Where suitable, definitions in English are okay, but when the going gets rough, more formalism is required. This takes intelligence, taste, knowledge and practice. It is not easy.

Actually, every mathematician strives for this fine balance. Large gaps will be left in a proof if it is felt that an educated reader will understand how to fill them. The most important and difficult points will receive the most attention. A proof will be organized as a series of lemmas to ease understanding.

This balance between formality and common sense is even more important for the programmer. Programming requires so much more detail, which must be *absolutely* correct without relying on the goodwill of the reader. In addition, some programs are so large that they cannot be comprehended fully by one person at one time. Thus, there is a continual need to strive for balance, conciseness, and even elegance.

The approach we take, then, can be summarized in the following

(13.2)   •**Principle**: Use theory to provide insight; use common sense and intuition where it is suitable, but fall back on the formal theory for support when difficulties and complexities arise.

However, a balance cannot be achieved unless one has *both* common sense and a facility with theory. The first has been most used by programmers; to overcome the current imbalance it is necessary to lean to the formal side for awhile. Thus, the subsequent discussions and the exercises may be more formal than is required in practice.

Proof versus test-case analysis

It was mentioned above that part of the problem has been reliance on test cases, during both program development and debugging. "Development by test case" works as follows. Based on a few examples of what the program is to do, a program is developed. More test cases are then exhibited —and perhaps run— and the program is modified to take the results into account. This process continues, with program modification at each step, until it is believed that enough test cases have been checked.

The approach described in this Part is based instead on developing a proof of correctness and a program hand-in-hand. It is different from the usual operational approach. Experience with the new approach can actually change the way one deals with problems outside the domain of programming, too. Two examples illustrate how effective the approach can be.

The Coffee Can Problem. A coffee can contains some black beans and white beans. The following process is to be repeated as long as possible.

> Randomly select two beans from the can. If they have the same color, throw them out, but put another black bean in. (Enough extra black beans are available to do this.) If they are different colors, place the white one back into the can and throw the black one away.

Execution of this process reduces the number of beans in the can by one. Repetition of the process must terminate with exactly one bean in the can, for then two beans cannot be selected. The question is: what, if anything, can be said about the color of the final bean based on the number of

white beans and the number of black beans initially in the can? Spend
ten minutes on the problem, which is more than it should require, before
reading further.

It doesn't help much to try test cases! It doesn't help to see what happens
when there are initially 1 black bean and 1 white bean, and then to see
what happens when there are initially 2 black beans and one white bean,
etc. I have seen people waste 30 minutes with this approach.

Instead, proceed as follows. Perhaps there is *a simple property of the
beans in the can that remains true as beans are removed* and that,
together with the fact that only one bean remains, can give the answer.
Since the property will always be true, we will call it an *invariant*. Well,
suppose upon termination there is one black bean and no white beans.
What property is true upon termination, which could generalize, perhaps,
to be our invariant? One is an odd number, so perhaps the oddness of the
number of black beans remains true. No, this is not the case, in fact the
number of black beans changes from even to odd or odd to even with
each move. But, there are also zero white beans upon termination
—perhaps the evenness of the number of white beans remains true. And,
indeed, yes, each possible move either takes out two white beans or leaves
the number of white beans the same. Thus, the last bean is black if initially there is an even number of white beans; otherwise it is white.

Closing the curve. This second problem is solved in essentially the same
manner. Consider a grid of dots, of any size:

.   .   .   .   .   .

.   .   .   .   .   .

.   .   .   .   .   .

Two players, *A* and *B*, play the following game. The players alternate
moves, with *A* moving first. *A* moves by drawing | or __ between two
adjacent dots; *B* moves by drawing a dotted line between two adjacent
dots. For example, after three full moves the grid might be as to the left
below. A player may not write over the other player's move.

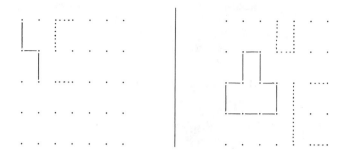

A wins the game if he can get a completely closed curve, as shown to the right above. B, because he goes second, has an easier task: he wins if he can stop A from getting a closed curve. Here is the question: is there a strategy that guarantees a win for either A or B, no matter how big the board is? If so, what is it? Spend some time thinking about the problem before reading further.

Looking at one trivial case, a grid with one dot, indicates that A cannot win all the time —four dots are needed for a closed curve. Hence, we look for a strategy for B to win. Playing the game and looking at test cases will not find the answer! Instead, investigate properties of closed curves, for if one of these properties can be barred from the board, A cannot win. The corresponding invariant is that the board is never in a configuration in which A can establish that property.

What properties does a closed curve have? It has parallel lines, but B cannot prevent parallel lines. It has an even number of parallel lines, but B cannot prevent this. It has four angles $\llcorner$, $\lrcorner$, $\ulcorner$ and $\urcorner$, but B cannot prevent A from drawing angles. It always has at least one angle $\llcorner$, which opens northeast —and B *can* prevent A from drawing such an angle! If A draws a horizontal or vertical line, as shown to the left below, then B simply fills in the corresponding vertical or horizontal line, if it is not yet filled in, as shown to the right below. A simpler strategy couldn't exist!

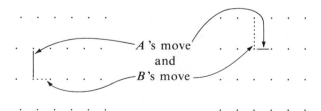

These two problems have extremely simple solutions, but the solutions are extremely difficult to find by simply trying test cases. The problems are easier if one looks for properties that remain true. And, once found, these properties allow one to see in a trivial fashion that a solution has been found.

Besides illustrating the inadequacy of solving by test cases, these problems illustrate the following principle:

(13.3)   •**Principle**: Know the properties of the objects that are to be manipulated by a program.

In fact, we shall see by examples that the more properties you know about the objects, the more chance you have of creating an efficient algorithm. But let us leave further examples of the use of this principle to later chapters.

Programming-in-the-small

For the past ten years, there has been much research in "programming-in-the-small", partially because it seemed to be an area in which scientific headway could be made. More importantly, however, it was felt that the ability to develop small programs is a *necessary* condition for developing large ones —although it may not be sufficient.

This fact is brought home most clearly with the following argument. Suppose a program consists of n small components —i.e. procedures, modules— each with probability p of being correct. Then the probability P that the whole program is correct certainly satisfies $P < p^n$. Since n is large in any good-sized program, to have any hope that the program is correct requires p to be very, very close to 1. For example, a program with 10 components, each of which has 95% chance of being correct, has less than a 60% chance of being correct, while a program with 100 such components has less than a .6% chance of being correct!

Remark: Doug McIlroy (Bell Laboratories) disagrees with this argument, claiming that correct programs *are* made from incorrect parts. Telephone control programs, for example, are more than half audit code, whose business is to recover from unintended states, and the audit code has been known to mask software as well as hardware errors. Also, an incorrect procedure may be called within our own program in a (unknowingly) restricted fashion so that the incorrectness never comes to light. Procedures that blow up for some input work perfectly well in programs that insulate them from these cases. Nevertheless, for most of the situations we face, the argument holds. □

Part III concentrates on the place where many programming errors are made: the development of small program segments. All the program segments in Part III are between 1 and 25 lines long, with the majority being between 1 and 10. It is true, however, that some of the programs are short because of the method of development. Concentrating on principles, with an emphasis on precision, clarity and elegance, can actually result in shorter programs. The most striking example of this is the program The Welfare Crook —see section 16.4.

A disclaimer

The methods described in Part III can certainly benefit almost any programmer. At the same time, it should be made clear that there *are* other ways to develop programs. A difficult task like programming requires many different tools and techniques. Many algorithms require the use of an idea that simply does not arise from the principles given in this Part, so this method alone cannot be used to solve them effectively. Some important ideas, like program transformation and "abstract data types" are not discussed at all, while others are just touched upon. And, of course, experience and knowledge can make all the difference in the world.

Secondly, even though the emphasis is on proofs of correctness, errors will occur. The wise programmer develops a program with the attitude that a correct program can and will be developed, provided enough care and concentration is used, and then tests it thoroughly with the attitude that it must have a mistake in it. The frequency of errors in mathematical theorems, proofs, and applications of theorems is well-recognized and documented, and the area of program-proving will not be an exception. We must simply learn to live with human fallibility and simplify to reduce it to a minimum.

Nevertheless, the study of Part III will provide an education in rigorous thinking, which is essential for good programming. Conscious application of the principles and strategies discussed will certainly be of benefit.

The organization of Part III

In order to convey principles and strategies as clearly as possible, most of the sections are organized as follows. A small example is used to illustrate one or two new points. The points are discussed. One or two examples are then developed in a manner calculated to involve the reader in the use of the points. A question is asked about the development, and the question is followed by blank space, a horizontal line and the answer (as done above). The reader is encouraged to attempt to answer the question first before proceeding! Finally, the reader should do several of the exercises at the end of the section.

Simply reading and listening to lectures on program development can only teach *about* the method; in order to learn how to use it, direct involvement is necessary. In this connection, the following meta-principle is of extreme importance:

(13.4) ●**Principle**: Never dismiss as obvious any fundamental principle, for it is only through *conscious application* of such principles that success will be achieved.

Ideas may be simple and easy to understand, but their application may require effort. Recognizing a principle and applying it are two different things.

Which typewriter do you choose?

Back in 1867, the typewriter was introduced into the United States. By 1873, the current arrangement of the keys on the typewriter, called the QWERTY keyboard (after the first six letters of the upper key row), was implemented, never to be changed again. At that time typing speed was not important —most people used two fingers anyway. Moreover, the typewriters often jammed, and the most-used letters were arbitrarily distributed in order to reduce speed so jamming wouldn't occur so easily.

Today, millions of excellent, speedy touch-typists use the inefficient QWERTY keyboard, because that is the only one made. Every so often, a new arrangement is designed and tested. The tests show that a good typist can learn the new arrangement in a month or so, and thereafter will type much faster with much less energy and strain. Yet the new keyboard never catches on. Why? Too much is invested in hardware and training. Because of the high cost of changeover, because of inertia, QWERTY remains supreme.

Let's face it: the average programmer is a QWERTY programmer. He is stuck with old notations, like FORTRAN and COBOL. More importantly he has been thinking with two fingers, using the same mental tools that were used at the beginnings of computer science, in the 1940s and 1950s. True, "structured programming" has helped, but even that, by itself, is not enough. To put it simply, the mental tools available to programmers have been inadequate.

The work on developing proof and program hand-in-hand is beginning to show fruit, and it may lead to a more efficient arrangement of the programmer's keyboard. Luckily, the hardware need not change. Mental tools and attitudes are far more important in programming than the notation in which the final program is expressed. For example, one can use the principles and strategies espoused in this book even if the final program has to be in FORTRAN: one programs *into* a language, not *in* it. To be sure, considerably more than one month of education and training will be necessary to wean yourself away from QWERTY programming, for old habits are changed very slowly. Nevertheless, I think it is worthwhile.

Let us now turn to the elucidation of principles and strategies that may help give the QWERTY programmer a new keyboard.

Chapter 14
Programming as a Goal-Oriented Activity

A simple example of program development

Consider the following problem. Write a program that, given fixed integers x and y, sets z to the maximum of x and y. (Throughout, we use the convention that variables called "fixed" should not be changed by execution of the program. See section 6.3.) Thus, a command S is desired that satisfies

(14.1) $\{T\}\ S\ \{R: z = max(x, y)\}.$

Before the program can be developed, R must be refined by replacing *max* by its definition —after all, without knowing what max means one cannot write the program. Variable z contains the maximum of x and y if it satisfies

(14.2) $R: z \geqslant x \wedge z \geqslant y \wedge (z = x \vee z = y)$

Now, what command could possibly be executed in order to establish (14.2)? Since (14.2) contains $z = x$, the assignment $z := x$ is a possibility. The assignment $z := x + 1$ is also a possibility, but $z := x$ is favored for at least two reasons. First, it is determined from R: to achieve $z = x$ assign x to z. Second, it is simpler.

To determine the conditions under which execution of $z := x$ will actually establish (14.2), simply calculate $wp(\text{``}z := x\text{''}, R)$:

$$wp(\text{``}z := x\text{''}, R) = x \geqslant x \wedge x \geqslant y \wedge (x = x \vee x = y)$$
$$= T \wedge x \geqslant y \wedge (T \vee x = y)$$
$$= x \geqslant y$$

This gives us the conditions under which execution of $z := x$ will establish R, and our first attempt at a program can be

> **if** $x \geqslant y \to z := x$ **fi**

This program performs the desired task *provided* it doesn't abort. Recall from theorem 10.5 for the alternative construct that, to prevent abortion, precondition Q of the construct must imply the disjunction of the guards, i.e. at least one guard must be true in any initial states defined by Q. But Q, which is T, does not imply $x \geqslant y$. Hence, at least one more guarded command is needed.

Another possible way to establish R is to execute $z := y$. From the above discussion it should be obvious that $y \geqslant x$ is the desired guard. Adding this guarded command yields

(14.3)   **if** $x \geqslant y \to z := x$
         [] $y \geqslant x \to z := y$
         fi

Now, at least one guard is always true, so that this is the desired program. Formally, we know that (14.3) is the desired program by theorem 10.5. To apply the theorem, take

$$S_1: z := x \qquad S_2: z := y$$
$$B_1: x \geqslant y \qquad B_2: y \geqslant x$$
$$Q: T \qquad R: z \geqslant x \wedge z \geqslant y \wedge (z = x \vee z = y)$$

Discussion

The above development illustrates the following

(14.4)   **•Principle**: Programming is a *goal-oriented* activity.

By this we mean that the desired result, or goal, R, plays a more important role in the development of a program than the precondition Q. Of course, Q also plays a role, as will be seen later. But, in general, more insight is gained from the postcondition. The goal-oriented nature of programming is one reason why the programming notation has been defined in terms of weakest preconditions (rather than strongest postconditions —see exercise 4 of section 9.1).

To substantiate this hypothesis of the goal-oriented nature of programming, consider the following. Above, the precondition was momentarily put aside and a program was developed that satisfied

$$\{?\}\ S\ \{R: z = max(x, y)\};$$

whenever S was considered complete, the requirement $Q \Rightarrow wp(S, R)$ was checked. Try doing opposite: forget about postcondition R, and try to develop a program S satisfying only

   $\{T\}\ S\ \{?\ \}$

Whenever S is thought to be complete, check whether $T\ \Rightarrow\ wp(S,\ z=max(x,\ y))$, or $T\ \Rightarrow\ wp(S,(14.2))$. How many programs S will you write before a correct one is found?

Another principle used in the above development is:

(14.5) •**Principle**: Before attempting to solve a problem, make absolutely sure you know what the problem is.

In programming, this general principle becomes:

(14.6) •**Principle**: Before developing a program, make precise and refine the pre- and postconditions.

In the example just developed, the postcondition was refined while the precondition, which was simply T, needed no refining.

A problem is sometimes specified in a manner that lends itself to several interpretations. Hence, it is reasonable to spend some time making the specification as clear and unambiguous as possible. Moreover, the form of the specification can influence algorithmic development, so that striving for simplicity and elegance should be helpful. With some problems, the *major* difficulty is making the specification simple and precise, and subsequent development of the program is fairly straightforward.

Often, a specification may be in English or in some conventional notation —like $max(x,\ y)$— that is at too "high a level" for program development, and it may contain abbreviations dealing with the applications area with which the programmer is unfamiliar. The specification is written to convey *what* the program is to do, and abstraction is often used to simplify it. More detail may be required to determine *how* to do it. The example of setting z to the maximum of x and y illustrates this nicely. It is impossible to write the program without knowing what *max* means, while writing a definition provides the insight needed for further development.

The development of (14.3) illustrates one basic technique for developing an alternative construct, which was motivated by theorem 10.5 for the Alternative Construct.

(14.7) •**Strategy for developing an alternative command**: To invent a guarded command, find a command C whose execution will establish postcondition R in at least some cases; find a Boolean B satisfying $B\ \Rightarrow\ wp(C,R)$; and put them together to form $B \rightarrow C$ (see assumption 2 of the theorem). Continue to invent guarded commands until the precondition of the construct implies that at least one guard is true (see assumption 1 of the theorem).

This technique, and a similar one for the iterative construct, is used often.

Let us return to program (14.3) for a moment. It has a pleasing symmetry, which is possible because of the nondeterminism. If there is no reason to choose between $z := x$ and $z := y$ when $x = y$, one should not be forced to choose. Programming requires deep thinking, and we should be spared any unnecessary irritation. Conventional, deterministic notations force the choice, and this is one reason for preferring the guarded command notation.

Nondeterminism is an important feature even if the final program turns out to be deterministic, for it allows us to devise a good programming methodology. One is free to develop many different guarded commands completely independently of each other. Any form of determinism, such as evaluating the guards in order of occurrence (e.g. the PL/I Select statement), drastically affects the way one thinks about developing alternative constructs.

A second example

Write a program that permutes (interchanges) the values of integer variables x and y so that $x \leqslant y$. Use the method of development discussed above.

As a first step, before reading further, write a suitable precondition Q and postcondition R.

The problem is slightly harder than the first one, for it requires the introduction of notation to denote the initial and final values of variables. Precondition Q is $x = X \wedge y = Y$, where identifiers X and Y denote the initial values of variables x and y, respectively. Postcondition R is

(14.8) $R: x \leqslant y \wedge (x = X \wedge y = Y \vee x = Y \wedge y = X)$.

Remark: One could also use the concept of a permutation and write R as $x \leqslant y \wedge perm((x, y), (X, Y))$. $\square$

Now, what simple commands could cause (14.8) to be established, at least under some conditions?

Precondition Q, which is $x = X \wedge y = Y$, appears as part of R, so there is a good chance that the operation $skip$ could establish R under some conditions. (This is a use of the precondition to provide additional information). Another possibility is the swap $x, y := y, x$, because it also would establish the second conjunct of R. How does one determine the guards for each of these commands, and what are the guards?

The guard B_i of a guarded command $B_i \rightarrow S_i$ of an alternative construct must satisfy $Q \wedge B_i \Rightarrow wp(S_i, R)$, according to the Theorem for the Alternative Construct. For the command $skip$, we have $wp(skip, R) = R$. Hence, B of the guarded command $B \rightarrow skip$ must satisfy $Q \wedge B \Rightarrow R$. Since Q implies the second conjunct of R, the first conjunct $x \leqslant y$ of R can be the guard, so that the guarded command is $x \leqslant y \rightarrow skip$.

For the second command we have

$$wp(``x, y := y, x", R)$$
$$= y \leqslant x \wedge (y = X \wedge x = Y \vee y = Y \wedge x = X).$$

Again, the second conjunct of this weakest precondition is implied by Q, so that the first conjunct $y \leqslant x$ can be the guard. This yields the alternative construct

if $x \leqslant y \rightarrow skip$
$\;[\!]\, y \leqslant x \rightarrow x, y := y, x$
fi

Since the disjunction of the guards, $x \leqslant y \vee y \leqslant x$, is always true, the program is correct (with respect to the given Q and R).

Note carefully how the theorem for the Alternative Construct is used to help determine the guards. This should not be too surprising —after all, the theorem simply formalizes the principles used by programmers to understand alternative commands.

Keeping guards of an alternative command strong

Suppose variable j contains the remainder when k is divided by 10 (for $k > 0$). That is, j and k should *always* satisfy

$$j = k \bmod 10$$

Thus, j will only take on the values $0, 1, \cdots, 9$. Let us determine a command to "increase k under the invariance of $j = k \bmod 10$", assuming that function **mod** is not available.

One possible command is $k,j := k+1, j+1$. However, this does the job only if before its execution $j < 9$, and so we have the guarded command $j < 9 \rightarrow k, j := k+1, j+1$. However, initially we have $0 \leqslant j < 10$, so that the case $j = 9$ must be considered also. The obvious command in this case is $k, j := k+1, 0$, and we arrive at the program segment

(14.8)   **if** $j < 9 \rightarrow k, j := k+1, j+1$
        $[] j = 9 \rightarrow k, j := k+1, 0$
        fi

(Note how strategy (14.7) was used, in an informal but careful manner.) The question is: which is to be preferred, (14.8) or segment (14.9) below, which is the same as (14.8) except that its second guard, $j \geqslant 9$, is weaker. At first thought, (14.9) might be preferred because it executes without abortion in more cases. If initially $j = 10$ (say), it nicely sets j to 0. But this is precisely why (14.9) is *not* to be preferred. Clearly, $j = 10$ is an error caused by a hardware malfunction, a software error, or an inadvertant modification of some kind —j is always supposed to satisfy $0 \leqslant j < 10$. Execution of (14.9) proceeds as if nothing were wrong and the error goes undetected. Execution of (14.8), on the other hand, aborts if $j = 10$, and the error is detected.

(14.9)   **if** $j < 9 \rightarrow k, j := k+1, j+1$
        $[] j \geqslant 9 \rightarrow k, j := k+1, 0$
        fi

This analysis leads to the following

(14.10)   •**Principle**: All other things being equal, make the guards
          of an alternative command as strong as possible, so that
          some errors will cause abortion.

The phrase "all other things being equal" is present to make sure that the principle is reasonably applied. For example, at this point I am not even prepared to advocate strengthening the first guard, as follows:

    if $0 \leqslant j \wedge j < 9 \rightarrow k, j := k+1, j+1$
    $[] j = 9 \qquad\quad \rightarrow k, j := k+1, 0$
    fi

As a final note, program (14.8) can be rearranged to

    $k := k+1$; **if** $j < 9 \rightarrow j := j+1 [] j = 9 \rightarrow j := 0$ **fi**

Exercises for Chapter 14

1. Develop programs for the following problems in a fashion similar to the development of the above programs. Remember, satisfactory pre- and postconditions should be developed first.

(a) Set z to $abs(x)$.

(b) Set x to $abs(x)$.

(c) Suppose x contains the number of odd integers in array $b[0:k-1]$, where $k \geqslant 0$. Write a program to add 1 to k, keeping the property of x the same. That is, upon termination k should be one more than it was initially and x should still contain the number of odd integers in $b[0:k-1]$.

(d) Suppose integer variables a and b satisfy $0 < a+1 < b$, so that the set $\{a, a+1, \cdots, b\}$ contains at least 3 values. Suppose also that the following predicate is true:

$$P: a^2 \leqslant n \wedge b^2 > n.$$

Is it possible to halve the interval $a:b$, by setting either a or b to $(a+b) \div 2$, at the same time keeping P true? Answer the question by trying to develop a program to do so.

2. (The Next Higher Permutation). Consider an integer of n decimal digits $(n > 0)$ contained in an array $d[0:n-1]$, with $d[0]$ being the high-order digit. For example, with $n = 6$ the integer 123542 would be contained in d as $d = (1, 2, 3, 5, 4, 2)$. The *next higher permutation* of $d[0:n-1]$ is an array d' that represents the next higher integer composed of *exactly the same digits*. In the example given, the next higher permutation would be $d' = (1, 2, 4, 2, 3, 5)$.

The problem is to define precisely the next higher permutation d' for an integer $d[0:n-1]$. Does your definition give any insight into developing a program to find it?

Chapter 15
Developing Loops from Invariants and Bounds

This chapter discusses two methods for developing a loop when the precondition Q, the postcondition R, the invariant P and the bound function t are given. The first method leads naturally to a loop with a single guarded command, **do** $B \rightarrow S$ **od**. The second takes advantage of the flexibility of the iterative construct and generally results in loops with more than one guarded command.

Checklist 11.9 will be heavily used, and it may be wise to review it before proceeding. As is our practice throughout, the parts of the development that illustrate the principles to be covered are discussed in a formal and detailed manner, while other parts are treated more informally.

15.1 Developing the Guard First

Summing the elements of an array

Consider the following problem. Write a program that, given fixed integer $n \geq 0$ and fixed integer array $b[0{:}n-1]$, stores in variable s the sum of the elements of b. The precondition Q is simply $n \geq 0$; the postcondition R is

$$R: s = (\Sigma j : 0 \leq j < n : b[j])$$

A loop with the following invariant and bound function is desired.

$$P: 0 \leq i \leq n \ \wedge \ s = (\Sigma j : 0 \leq j < i : b[j])$$
$$t: \ n - i$$

Thus, variable i has been introduced. The invariant states that at any point in the computation s contains the sum of the first i values of b.

The assignment $i, s := 0, 0$ obviously establishes P, so it will suffice as the initialization. (Note that $i, s := 1, b[0]$ does not suffice because, if $n = 0$, it cannot be executed. If $n = 0$, execution of the program must set s to the identity of addition, 0.)

The next step is to determine the guard B for the loop **do** $B \to S$ **od**. Checklist 11.9 requires $P \wedge \neg B \Rightarrow R$, so $\neg B$ is chosen to satisfy it. Comparing P and R, we conclude that $i = n$ will do. The desired guard B of the loop is therefore its complement, $i \neq n$. The program looks like

$$i, s := 0, 0; \ \textbf{do} \ i \neq n \ \to \ ? \ \textbf{od}$$

Now for the command. The purpose of the command is to make progress towards termination —i.e. to decrease the bound function t— and an obvious first choice for it is $i := i+1$. But, this would destroy the invariant, and to reestablish it $b[i]$ must simultaneously be added to s. Thus, the program is

(15.1.1) $i, s := 0, 0; \ \textbf{do} \ i \neq n \ \to \ i, s := i+1, s+b[i] \ \textbf{od}$

Remark: For those uneasy with the multiple assignment, the formal proof that P is maintained is as follows. We have

$$wp(\text{``}i, s := i+1, s+b[i]\text{''}, P)$$
$$= \ 0 \leqslant i+1 \leqslant n \ \wedge \ s+b[i] = (\Sigma j: 0 \leqslant j < i+1: b[j])$$

and this is implied by $P \wedge i \neq n$. $\square$

Discussion

First of all, let us discuss the balance between formality and intuition observed here. The pre- and postconditions, the invariant and the bound function were given formally and precisely. The development of the parts of the program was given less formally, but checklist 11.9, which is based on the formal theorem for the Iterative Construct, provided most of the motivation and insight. In order to check the informal development, we relied on the theory (in checking that the loop body maintained the invariant). This is illustrative of the general approach (13.1) mentioned in chapter 13.

An important strategy in the development was finding the guard before the command. And the prime consideration in finding the guard B was that it had to satisfy $P \wedge \neg B \Rightarrow R$. So, $\neg B$ was developed and then complemented to yield B.

Some object at first to finding the guard this way, because Tradition would use the guard $i < n$ instead of $i \neq n$. However, $i \neq n$ is better, because a software or hardware error that made $i > n$ would result in a nonterminating execution. It is better to waste computer time than suffer the consequences of having an error go undetected, which would happen if the guard $i < n$ were used. This analysis leads to the following

(15.1.2)   •**Principle**: All other things being equal, make the
           guards of a loop as *weak* as possible, so that an error
           may cause an infinite loop.

Principle 15.1.2 should be compared to principle 14.10, which concerns the guards of an alternative command.

The method used for developing the guard of a loop is extremely simple and reliable, for it is based on manipulation of static, mathematical expressions. In this connection, I remember my old days of FORTRAN programming —the early 1960's— when it sometimes took three debugging runs to achieve proper loop termination. The first time the loop iterated once too few, the second time once too many and the third time just right. It was a frustrating, trial-and-error process. No longer is this necessary; just develop $\neg B$ to satisfy $P \wedge \neg B \Rightarrow R$ and complement it.

Another important point about the development was the stress on termination. The need to progress towards termination motivated the development of the loop body; reestablishing the invariant was the second consideration. Actually, every loop with one guarded command has the high-level interpretation

(15.1.3) $\{invariant: P\}$
           $\{bound: t\}$
           do $B \rightarrow$ Decrease t, keeping P true **od**
           $\{P \wedge \neg B\}$

This approach to loop development is summarized as follows:

(15.1.4)   •**Strategy for developing a loop**: First develop the
           guard B so that $P \wedge \neg B \Rightarrow R$; then develop the body
           so that it decreases the bound function while reestab-
           lishing the loop invariant.

Searching a two-dimensional array

Consider the following problem. Write an algorithm that, given a fixed array of arrays $b[0:m-1][0:n-1]$, where $0 < m$ and $0 < n$, searches b for a fixed value x. If x occurs in several places in b, it doesn't matter which place is found. For this problem, we will use conventional two-dimensional notation, writing b as $b[0:m-1, 0:n-1]$. Using variables i and j, upon termination either $x = b[i,j]$ or, if this is not possible, $i = m$. To be more precise, execution of the program should establish

(15.1.5) R: $(0 \leqslant i < m \ \wedge\ 0 \leqslant j < n \ \wedge\ x = b[i,j]) \ \vee\ (i = m \ \wedge\ x \notin b)$.

The invariant P, given below using a diagram, states that x is not in the already-searched rows $b[0:i-1]$ and not in the already-searched columns $b[i, 0:j-1]$ of the current row i.

(15.1.6) P: $0 \leqslant i \leqslant m \ \wedge\ 0 \leqslant j < n \ \wedge$

```
          0        j      n-1
       0 ┌──────────────────┐
         │   x not here     │
       i │        ┌─────────┤
         │        │         │
     m-1 └────────┴─────────┘
```

The bound function t is the number of values in the untested section: $(m-i)*n - j$. As a first step in the development, before reading further determine the initialization for the loop.

The obvious choice is $i, j := 0, 0$, for then the section in which "x is not here" is empty. Next, what should be the guard B of the loop?

Expression $\neg B$ must satisfy $P \wedge \neg B \Rightarrow R$. It must be strong enough so that each of the two disjuncts of R can be established. To provide for the first disjunct, choose $i < m$ **cand** $x = b[i,j]$; to provide for the second, choose $i = m$. The operator **cand** is needed to ensure that the expression is well-defined, for $b[i,j]$ may be undefined if $i \geqslant m$. Therefore, choose $\neg B$ to be

$\neg B$: $i = m \ \vee\ (i < m \ \textbf{cand}\ x = b[i,j])$

Using De Morgan's laws, we find its complement B:

B: $i \neq m \ \wedge\ (i \geqslant m \ \textbf{cor}\ x \neq b[i,j])$

Since the guard B is to be evaluated only when the invariant P is true, which means that $i \leq m$ is true, it can be simplified to

$$B: i \neq m \wedge (i = m \textbf{ cor } x \neq b[i,j])$$

and finally to

$$B: i \neq m \textbf{ cand } x \neq b[i,j].$$

The final line is therefore the guard of the loop. The next step is to determine the loop body. Do it, before reading further.

The purpose of the loop body is to decrease the bound function t, which is the number of elements in the untested section: $(m-i)*n -j$. $P \wedge B$, the condition under which the body is executed, implies that $i < m$, $j < n$ and $x \neq b[i,j]$, so that element $b[i,j]$, which is in the untested section, can be moved into the tested section. A possible command to do this is $j := j+1$, but it maintains the invariant P only if $j < n-1$. So we have the guarded command

$$j < n-1 \rightarrow j := j+1$$

What do we do if $j \geq n-1$? In this case, because invariant P is true, we have $j = n-1$. Hence, we must determine what to do if $j = n-1$, i.e. if $b[i,j]$ is the rightmost element of its row. To move $b[i,j]$ into the tested section requires moving to the beginning of the next row, i.e. executing $i, j := i+1, 0$.

The loop body is therefore

$$\textbf{if } j < n-1 \rightarrow j := j+1 \ [] \ j = n-1 \rightarrow i, j := i+1, 0 \textbf{ fi}$$

The program is therefore

(15.1.7) $i, j := 0, 0$;
$\qquad$ **do** $i \neq m$ **cand** $x \neq b[i,j] \rightarrow$
$\qquad\qquad$ **if** $j < n-1 \rightarrow j := j+1 \ [] \ j = n-1 \rightarrow i, j := i+1, 0$ **fi**
$\qquad$ **od**

If desired, the body of the loop can be rearranged to yield

$i, j := 0, 0;$
do $i \neq m$ **cand** $x \neq b[i,j] \rightarrow$
    $j := j+1;$
    if $j < n \rightarrow skip$ [] $j = n \rightarrow i, j := i+1, 0$ **fi**
od

Discussion

Note that operation **cand** (instead of $\wedge$) is really necessary.

Note that the method for developing an alternative command was used when developing the body of the loop, albeit informally. First, the command $j := j+1$ was chosen, and it was seen that it performed as desired only if $j < n-1$. Formally, one must prove

$$(P \wedge B \wedge j < n-1) \Rightarrow wp(\text{``}j := j+1\text{''}, P)$$

but this case is simple enough to handle informally —if care is used. Second, the command $i, j := i+1, 0$ was chosen to handle the remaining case, $j = n$.

Note that the alternative command has the guards $j < n-1$ and $j = n-1$, and *not* $j < n-1$ and $j \geq n-1$. The guards of the alternative command have been made as strong as possible, in keeping with principle 14.10, in order to catch errors.

We will develop another solution to this problem in section 15.2.

Exercises for Section 15.1

1. Develop a second program for the first example of this section. This time use the invariant and bound function

$$P: 0 \leq i \leq n \wedge s = (\Sigma j : i \leq j < n : b[j])$$
$$t: i$$

2. The invariant of the loop of the second example was given in terms of a diagram (see (15.1.6)). Replace the diagram by an equivalent statement in the predicate calculus.

3. Write a program that, given a fixed integer array $b[0:n-1]$, where $n > 0$, sets x to the smallest value of b. The program should be nondeterministic if the smallest value occurs more than once in b. The precondition Q, postcondition R, loop invariant P and bound function t are

$$Q: 0 < n$$
$$R: x \leq b[0:n-1] \wedge (E j : 0 \leq j < n : x = b[j])$$
$$P: 1 \leq i \leq n \wedge x \leq b[0:i-1] \wedge (E j : 0 \leq j < i : x = b[j])$$
$$t: n-i$$

4. Write a program for the problem of exercise 3, but use the invariant and bound function

$$P: 0 \leqslant i < n \land x \leqslant b[i:n-1] \land (Ej: i \leqslant j < n: x = b[j])$$
$$t: i$$

5. Write a program that, given a fixed integer $n > 0$, sets variable i to the highest power of 2 that is at most n. The precondition Q, postcondition R, loop invariant P and bound function t are

$$Q: 0 < n$$
$$R: 0 < i \leqslant n < 2*i \land (Ep: i = 2^p)$$
$$P: 0 < i \leqslant n \land (Ep: i = 2^p)$$
$$t: n-i$$

6. Translate program (15.1.7) into the language of your choice —PL/I, Pascal, FORTRAN, etc.— remembering the need for the operation **cand**. Compare your answer with (15.1.7).

15.2 Making Progress Towards Termination

Four-tuple Sort

Consider the following problem. Write a program that sorts the four integer variables $q0$, $q1$, $q2$, $q3$. That is, upon termination the following should be true: $q0 \leqslant q1 \leqslant q2 \leqslant q3$.

Implicit is the fact that the values of the variables should be permuted —for example, the assignment $q0, q1, q2, q3 := 0, 0, 0, 0$ is not a solution, even though it establishes $q0 \leqslant q1 \leqslant q2 \leqslant q3$. To convey this information explicitly, we use Qi to denote the initial value of qi, and write the formal specification

$$Q: q0 = Q0 \land q1 = Q1 \land q2 = Q2 \land q3 = Q3$$
$$R: q0 \leqslant q1 \leqslant q2 \leqslant q3 \land perm((q0, q1, q2, q3), (Q0, Q1, Q2, Q3))$$

where the second conjunct $perm(\cdots, \cdots)$ of R means that the four variables $q0, q1, q2, q3$ contain a permutation of their original values.

A loop will be written. Its invariant expresses the fact that the four variables must always contain a permutation of their initial values:

$$P: perm((q0, q1, q2, q3), (Q0, Q1, Q2, Q3))$$

The bound function is the number of *inversions* in the sequence ($q0$, $q1$, $q2$, $q3$). For a sequence ($q_0, \cdots, q_{n-1}$), the number of inversions is the number of pairs (q_i, q_j), $i < j$, that are out of order —i.e. $q_i > q_j$.

Note that this includes *all* pairs, and not just adjacent ones. For example, the number of inversions in $(1, 3, 2, 0)$ is 4. So the bound function is

$$t: (N\,i,j: 0 \leqslant i < j < 4: qi > qj).$$

The invariant indicates that the four variables must always contain a permutation of their initial values. This is obviously true initially, so no initialization is needed.

In the last section, at this point of the development the guard of the loop was determined. Instead, here we will look for a number of guarded commands, each of which makes progress towards termination. The invariant indicates that the only possible commands are those that swap (permute) the values of two or more of the variables. To keep things simple, consider only swaps of two variables. There are six possibilities: $q0, q1 := q1, q0$ and $q1, q2 := q2, q1$, etc.

Now, execution of a command must make progress towards termination. Consider one possible command, $q0, q1 := q1, q0$. It decreases the number of inversions in $(q0, q1, q2, q3)$ *iff* $q0 > q1$. Hence, the guarded command $q0 > q1 \rightarrow q0, q1 := q1, q0$ will do. Each of the other 5 possibilities are similar, and together they yield the program

$$
\begin{aligned}
&\textbf{do } q0 > q1 \rightarrow q0, q1 := q1, q0 \\
&[]\ q1 > q2 \rightarrow q1, q2 := q2, q1 \\
&[]\ q2 > q3 \rightarrow q2, q3 := q3, q2 \\
&[]\ q0 > q2 \rightarrow q0, q2 := q2, q0 \\
&[]\ q0 > q3 \rightarrow q0, q3 := q3, q0 \\
&[]\ q1 > q3 \rightarrow q1, q3 := q3, q1 \\
&\textbf{od}
\end{aligned}
$$

It still remains to prove that upon termination the result R is established —this is point 3 of checklist 11.9, $P \wedge \neg BB \Rightarrow R$. Suppose all the guards are false. Then $q0 \leqslant q1$ (because the first guard is false), $q1 \leqslant q2$ (because the second is false) and $q2 \leqslant q3$ (because the third is false); therefore

$$q0 \leqslant q1 \leqslant q2 \leqslant q3.$$

Together with invariant P, this implies the desired result. But note that only the first three guards were needed to establish the desired result. Therefore, the last three guarded commands can be deleted, yielding the program

> **do** $q0 > q1 \rightarrow q0, q1 := q1, q0$
> $[] \ q1 > q2 \rightarrow q1, q2 := q2, q1$
> $[] \ q2 > q3 \rightarrow q2, q3 := q3, q2$
> **od**

Discussion

The approach used here can be summarized as follows.

(15.2.1)   •**Strategy for developing a loop**: Develop guarded commands, creating each command so that it makes progress towards termination and creating the corresponding guard to ensure that the invariant is maintained. The process of developing guarded commands is finished when enough of them have been developed to prove $P \wedge \neg BB \Rightarrow R$.

Developing the commands as indicated ensures that points 2, 4 and 5 of checklist 11.9 are true. The last sentence of the strategy indicates that the loop is completed when point 3 of the checklist is true. Of course, initialization to make the invariant true initially (point 1 of the checklist) may need to be written.

The emphasis in the strategy is on points 2 and 4 of checklist 11.9, which concern progress towards termination and maintenance of invariance. In the approach used in section 15.1, the emphasis was first on proving point 3, that upon termination the result R is true.

Let us discuss the seemingly magical step of deleting three guarded commands from the loop. Once a correct loop has been developed, a shorter and perhaps more efficient one can sometimes be derived from it. Each guarded command already satisfies points 2 and 4 of checklist 11.9. Strengthening the guards cannot destroy the fact that points 2 and 4 are satisfied, so that the guards can be changed at will, as long as they are strengthened. The only problem is to ensure that upon termination the result still holds —i.e. $P \wedge \neg BB \Rightarrow R$ is still true.

If it is possible to strengthen a guard to F (false) without violating $P \wedge \neg BB \Rightarrow R$, then the corresponding command can never be executed, so that the guarded command can be deleted. This is what happened in this example. Only the first three guards were needed to prove $P \wedge \neg BB \Rightarrow R$, so that the last three could be strengthened to F and then deleted.

We will return to this point in chapter 19 on efficiency.

This little program is nondeterministic in execution, because two, and even three, guards can be true at the same time. But, for any initial state

there is exactly one final state, so that in terms of the result the program
is deterministic.

The number of iterations of the loop is equal to the number of inversions, which is at most 6.

Searching a two-dimensional array

Consider again a problem discussed in section 15.1: writing a program
to search a two-dimensional array. The only difference in the problem is
that here the array may be empty (i.e. it may have 0 rows or 0 columns).
The fixed array is $b[0:m-1, 0:n-1]$, where $0 \leqslant m$ and $0 \leqslant n$, and it is to
be searched for a fixed integer x. Using variables i and j, upon termination either $x = b[i,j]$ or, if this is not possible, $i = m$. To be more precise, R should be established:

(15.2.2) $R: (0 \leqslant i < m \wedge 0 \leqslant j < n \wedge x = b[i, j]) \vee (i = m \wedge x \notin b)$.

The invariant P, given below in a diagram, states that x is not in the
already-searched rows $b[0:i-1]$ and not in the already-searched columns
$b[i,0:j-1]$ of the current row i.

(15.2.3) $P: 0 \leqslant i \leqslant m \wedge 0 \leqslant j \leqslant n \wedge$

The bound function is the sum of number of values in the untested section
and the number of rows in the untested section: $t = (m-i)*n - j + m - i$.
The additional value $m-i$ is needed because possibly $j = n$. As a first
step in the development, determine the initialization for the loop.

The obvious choice is $i, j := 0, 0$, for then the section in which "x is not
here" is empty. Note carefully how the invariant includes $j \leqslant n$, instead
of $j < n$. This is necessary because the number of columns, n, could be
0.

Next, guarded commands for the loop must be developed. What is the
simplest command possible, and what is a suitable guard for it?

The obvious command to try is $j := j+1$, because it decreases t. (Another possibility, to be investigated subsequently, is $i := i+1$). A suitable guard must ensure that P remains true. Formally or informally, we can see that $i \neq m \wedge j \neq n$ **cand** $x \neq b[i,j]$ can be used, so that the guarded command is

$$i \neq m \wedge j \neq n \textbf{ cand } x \neq b[i,j] \rightarrow j := j+1$$

Note that this guard has been made as weak as possible. Now, does a loop with this single guarded command solve the problem? Why or why not? If not, what other guarded command can be used?

A loop with only this guarded command could terminate with $i < m \wedge j = n$, and this, together with the invariant, is not enough to prove R. Indeed, if the first row of b does not contain x, the loop will terminate after searching through only the first row! Some guarded command must deal with increasing i.

The command $i := i+1$ may only be executed if $i < m$. Moreover, it has a chance of keeping P true only if row i does not contain x, so consider executing it only under the additional condition $j = n$. But this means that j should be set to 0 also, so that the condition on the current row i is maintained. This leads to the program

$$
\begin{aligned}
(15.2.4) \quad & i, j := 0, 0; \\
& \textbf{do } i \neq m \wedge j \neq n \textbf{ cand } x \neq b[i,j] \rightarrow j := j+1 \\
& [] \; i \neq m \wedge j = n \qquad\qquad\quad \rightarrow i, j := i+1, 0 \\
& \textbf{od}
\end{aligned}
$$

It still remains to show that upon termination R is true —i.e. $P \wedge \neg BB \Rightarrow R$. Suppose the guards are false. Two cases arise. First, $i = m$ could hold. Secondly, if $i \neq m$, then the falsity of the second guard implies $j \neq n$; therefore the falsity of the first guard implies $x = b[i,j]$. Thus, if the guards are false the following must be true:

$$i = m \textbf{ cor } (i \neq m \wedge j \neq n \wedge x = b[i,j]),$$

and this together with P implies the result R. Hence, the program is correct. Note that in the case $i = m$ the invariant implies that x is not in rows 0 through $m-1$ of b, which means that $x \notin b$.

Discussion

This loop was developed by continuing to develop simple guarded commands that made progress towards termination until $P \wedge \neg BB \Rightarrow R$. This led to a loop with a form radically different from what most programmers are used to developing (partly because they don't usually know about guarded commands). It does take time to get used to (15.2.4) as a loop for searching a two-dimensional array.

This problem is often used to argue for the inclusion of **goto**s or loop "exits" in a conventional language, because, unless one uses an extra variable commonly called a "flag", the conventional solution to the problem needs two nested loops and an "exit" from the inner one:

(15.2.5) $i, j := 0, 0;$
         while $i \neq m$ **do**
           begin while $j \neq n$ **do**
                 if $x = b[i, j]$ **then goto** *loopexit*
                         else $j := j+1;$
              $i, j := i+1, 0$
         end;
       loopexit:

We see, then, that the guarded command notation and the method of development together lead to a simpler, easier-to-understand, solution to the problem —provided one understands the methodology.

How could program (15.2.4) be executed effectively? An optimizing compiler could analyze the guards and commands and determine the paths of execution given in diagram (15.2.6) —in the diagram, an arrow with F (T) on it represents the path to be taken when the term from which it emanates is false (true). But (15.2.6) is essentially a flowchart for program (15.2.5)! At least in this case, therefore, the "high level" program (15.2.4) can be *simulated* using the "lower-level" constructs of Pascal, FORTRAN and PL/I.

Program (15.2.4) is developed from sound principles. Program (15.2.5) is typically developed in an *ad hoc* fashion, using development by test cases, the result being that doubt is raised whether all cases have been covered.

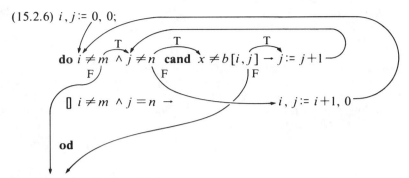

(15.2.6) $i,j := 0, 0;$

$$\textbf{do } i \neq m \wedge j \neq n \textbf{ cand } x \neq b[i,j] \rightarrow j := j+1$$

$$[\!]\ i \neq m \wedge j = n \rightarrow \qquad \qquad i, j := i+1, 0$$

$$\textbf{od}$$

Exercises for Section 15.2

1. Write a program for the following problem. Given is a fixed three-dimensional array $c[0:m-1, 0:n-1, 0:p-1]$, where $m,n,p \geqslant 0$. Given is a fixed variable x. Using three variables i, j and k, find a value $c[i,j,k]$ with value x; if $\neg x \in c$, set i to m.

2. Write a program that, given fixed integers X and Y, $X>0$, $Y>0$, finds the greatest common divisor $gcd(X, Y)$. The greatest common divisor of X and Y that are not both 0 is the greatest integer that divides both of them. For example, $gcd(1,1)=1$, $gcd(2,5)=1$ and $gcd(10,25)=5$. The following properties hold for $x \neq 0$, $y \neq 0$:

$$gcd(x, y) = gcd(x, y-x) = gcd(x-y, y)$$
$$gcd(x, y) = gcd(x, x+y) = gcd(x+y, y)$$
$$gcd(x, x) = x$$
$$gcd(x, y) = gcd(y, x)$$
$$gcd(x, 0) = gcd(0, x) = x$$

The first two lines hold because any divisor of x and y is also a divisor of $x+y$ and $x-y$ —since $x/d \pm y/d = (x \pm y)/d$ for any divisor d of x and y.

Your program has the result assertion

$$R: x = y = gcd(X, Y)$$

The program should not use multiplication or division. It should be a loop (with initialization) with invariant

$$P: 0 < x \wedge 0 < y \wedge gcd(x, y) = gcd(X, Y)$$

and bound function $t: x+y$. Use the properties given above to determine possible guarded commands for the loop.

3. Redo the program of exercise 2 to determine the greatest common divisor of three numbers X, Y and Z that are >0.

4. Write an algorithm to determine $gcd(X, Y)$ for X, $Y \geqslant 0$ using multiplication and division (see exercise 2). For example, it is possible to subtract a multiple of x from y. The result assertion, invariant and bound function are

$$R: x = 0 \wedge y = gcd(X, Y)$$
$$P: 0 \leqslant x \wedge 0 \leqslant y \wedge (0,0) \neq (x,y) \wedge gcd(x, y) = gcd(X, Y)$$
$$t: 2*x + y$$

5. This problem concerns that part of a scanner of a compiler —or any program that processes text— that builds the next word or sequence of nonblank symbols. Characters $b[j:79]$ of character array $b[0:79]$ are used to hold the part of the input read in but "not yet processed", and another line of input can be read into b by executing $read(b)$. Input lines are 80 characters long.

It is known that $b[j:79]$ catenated with the remaining input lines is a sequence

$$W \mid '-' \mid REST$$

where "$\mid$" denotes catenation, "$-$" denotes a blank space, W is a nonempty sequence of nonblank characters, and $REST$ is a string of characters. The purpose of the program to be written is to "process" the input word W, deleting it from the input and putting it in a character array s. W is guaranteed to be short enough to fit in s. For example, the top part of the diagram below shows sample initial conditions with 10-character lines. The bottom diagram gives corresponding final conditions.

W: $'WORD'$

$REST$: $'NEXT-ONE-IS-IT--'$

$b[j:79]$: $'WO'$ input: | $E-IS-IT---$ |
                                                           | $RD-NEXT-ON$ |

Initial Conditions

$b[j:79]$: $'-NEXT-ON'$ input: | $E-IS-IT---$ | $s[0:v-1]$: $'WORD'$

Final Conditions

A loop with initialization is desired. The precondition Q, postcondition R, invariant P and bound function t are:

$$Q: 0 \leqslant j < 80 \wedge b[j:79] \mid \text{"the input lines"} = W \mid '-' \mid REST$$
$$R: 0 \leqslant j < 80 \wedge s[0:length(W)-1] = W \wedge$$
$$(b[j:79] \mid \text{the input lines}) = '-' \mid REST$$
$$P: 0 \leqslant j \leqslant 80 \wedge 0 \leqslant v \leqslant length(W) \wedge$$
$$(s[0:v-1] \mid b[j:79]) = (W \mid '-' \mid REST)$$
$$t: 2*length(W) - 2*v + j$$

Chapter 16
Developing Invariants

Assume we want to develop a program S to satisfy $\{Q\}\ S\ \{R\}$ for given Q and R, and that we have decided to use a loop (possibly with some initialization). How do we find a suitable invariant and bound function for the loop —*before* writing the loop? This chapter explores this question.

Section 16.1 shows how a loop invariant can be seen as a weakening of the result assertion R and outlines various ways of performing this weakening. This illustrates again that programming is a goal-oriented activity. Each of the sections 16.2-16.5 discusses in detail one way of weakening the result assertion and illustrates the technique with several examples.

16.1 The Balloon Theory

This section provides some understanding of the nature of an invariant P of a loop $\{Q\}$ **do** $B \rightarrow S$ **od** $\{R\}$. Fig. 16.1.1(a) represents the set of all states, with those represented by postcondition R encircled. Also encircled is the set of possible initial states IS, which could be established by some simple assignments. (Actually, IS and R could overlap, but this is not shown in the Figure.) Now, an invariant, P, of the loop is a predicate that is true before and after each iteration.

(a)   (b)

Figure 16.1.1 Blowing up the balloon

Hence, the set of states represented by P must contain both the set of possible initial states represented by IS and the set of final states represented by R, as shown in Fig. 16.1.1(b).

Consider R to be the deflated state of a balloon, which is blown up to its complete inflated state, P, just before execution of the loop. Each iteration of the loop will then let some air out of the balloon, until the last iteration reduces the balloon back to its deflated state R. This is illustrated in Fig. 16.1.2, where $P_0 = P$ is the balloon before the first iteration, P_1 the balloon after the first iteration and P_2 the balloon after the second iteration.

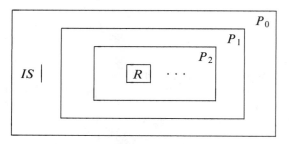

Figure 16.1.2 Letting the air out

Remark: The balloon and its various states of deflation is defined more precisely as follows. P is the completely inflated balloon. Consider the bound function t. Let t_0 be the initial value of t, which is determined by the initialization, t_1 the value of t after the first iteration, t_2 the value of t after the second iteration, etc. Then the predicate

$$P \wedge 0 \leqslant t \leqslant t_i$$

denotes the set of states in the balloon after the ith iteration. Thus, initialization deflates the balloon to include only states in $P \wedge 0 \leqslant t \leqslant t_0$, the first iteration deflates it more to $P \wedge 0 \leqslant t \leqslant t_1$, etc. □

The problem, of course, is to know how to blow up the balloon, so execution of the loop can deflate it. That is, how does one find P and the bound function t? What information is available? Clearly, only the result assertion R and the set of initial states IS. Since the balloon begins as R and is blown up to encompass the initial state but is then deflated, it seems that R would the more important of the two. This becomes more plausible when we consider that the initial conditions may not even be known until P is known. Subsequently, methods will be investigated to blow up a balloon —actually to weaken a relation— until it encompasses a set of states IS that can be easily established.

Weakening a predicate

Here are four ways of weakening a predicate R:

1. **Delete a conjunct**. For example, predicate $A \wedge B \wedge C$ can be weakened to $A \wedge C$.

2. **Replace a constant by a variable**. For example, predicate $x \leqslant b[1{:}10]$, where x is a simple variable, can be weakened to $x \leqslant b[1{:}i] \wedge 1 \leqslant i \leqslant 10$, where i is a fresh variable. Since a new variable has been introduced, its possible set of values must be precisely stated. Of course, the range must include the value of the replaced constant.

3. **Enlarge the range of a variable**. For example, predicate $5 \leqslant i < 10$ can be weakened to $0 \leqslant i < 10$.

4. **Add a disjunct**. For example, predicate A can be weakened to $A \vee B$, for some other predicate B.

The first three methods are quite useful. In each, insight for weakening R comes directly from the form and content of R itself, and the number of possibilities to try is generally small. The methods may therefore provide the kind of directed, disciplined development we are looking for.

The fourth method of weakening a predicate is rarely useful in programming, in all its generality. There is no reason to try to add one disjunct rather than another, and hence adding a disjunct would be a random task with an infinite number of possibilities. We shall not analyze this method further.

16.2 Deleting a Conjunct

In this section, the development of an invariant of a loop by deleting a conjunct of the desired result assertion is illustrated and discussed.

Approximating the square root of a number

Write a program that, given a fixed integer $n \geqslant 0$, establishes the truth of

(16.2.1) $R: 0 \leqslant a^2 \leqslant n < (a+1)^2$

Taking the square root of all terms in R, we find that R is equivalent to $0 \leqslant a \leqslant \sqrt{n} < a+1$. Hence, a is the largest integer that is at most $\sqrt{n}$.

The first step is to rewrite R as a set of conjuncts:

$$R: 0 \leqslant a^2 \wedge a^2 \leqslant n \wedge n < (a+1)^2$$

Deleting the third conjunct of R yields a possible invariant:

$$P: 0 \leqslant a^2 \leqslant n.$$

Because $n \geqslant 0$, P can be established by the assignment $a := 0$. For the guard of the loop, use the *complement* of the deleted conjunct, so that when the loop terminates because the guard is false, the deleted conjunct is true. This yields the almost-completed program

$$a := 0; \ \mathbf{do} \ (a+1)^2 \leqslant n \rightarrow ? \ \mathbf{od}$$

The purpose of the command of the loop is to progress towards termination. Clearly, if the guard of the loop is true then a is too small, so that progress can be made by increasing a. Since a is bounded above by $\sqrt{n}$, a possible bound function is $t = ceil(\sqrt{n}) - a$. Using the easiest way to increase a, incrementing by 1, yields the program

(16.2.2) $a := 0; \ \mathbf{do} \ (a+1)^2 \leqslant n \rightarrow a := a+1 \ \mathbf{od}$

We show that P is indeed an invariant of the loop:

$$\begin{aligned} P \wedge B &= 0 \leqslant a^2 \leqslant n \wedge (a+1)^2 \leqslant n \\ &= 0 \leqslant (a+1)^2 \leqslant n \\ &= wp \ (\text{``}a := a+1\text{''}, P) \end{aligned}$$

Discussion

Here, strategy 15.1.4 was used to develop the loop —first the guard was created and then the loop body. The guard was created in such a simple and useful manner that it deserves being called a strategy itself.

(16.2.3)   •**Strategy**: When deleting a conjunct from R to produce an invariant P, try using the complement of the deleted conjunct for the guard B of the loop.

Choosing B in this manner will ensure that the necessary condition $P \wedge \neg B \Rightarrow R$ (point 3 of checklist 11.9) is automatically satisfied.

Exercise 1 is to develop a program by deleting the second conjunct instead of the third.

The execution time of the program is proportional to $\sqrt{n}$. A faster program to approximate the square root of a number will be developed in section 16.3.

Linear search

As a second example of deleting a conjunct, consider the following problem. Given is a fixed array $b[0:m-1]$ where $0 < m$. It is known that a fixed value x is in $b[0:m-1]$. Write a program to determine the first occurrence of x in b —i.e. to store in a variable i the least integer such that $x = b[i]$.

The first task is to specify the program more formally. This is easy to do; we have the following precondition Q and postcondition R:

$$Q: 0 < m \,\wedge\, x \in b[0:m-1]$$
$$R: 0 \leqslant i < m \,\wedge\, x \notin b[0:i-1] \,\wedge\, x = b[i]$$

R can be written in more detail as follows:

$$R: 0 \leqslant i < m \,\wedge\, (A\,j: 0 \leqslant j < i: x \neq b[j]) \,\wedge\, x = b[i]$$

Now, R contains three conjuncts —which should be deleted to obtain an invariant?

A good invariant should be easy to establish. The first two conjuncts are established by the assignment $i := 0$, while most of the difficulty of the program lies in establishing the third. Hence, it makes sense to delete the third conjunct, yielding the following invariant:

(16.2.4) $P: 0 \leqslant i < m \,\wedge\, (A\,j: 0 \leqslant j < i: x \neq b[j])$

What should be the guard of the loop?

Use the complement of the deleted conjunct. Thus far, the program is

$$i := 0; \quad \textbf{do } x \neq b[i] \rightarrow ? \textbf{ od}$$

Choose the command for the loop, explaining how it was found.

The task of the command is to make progress towards termination. A possible bound function is $t: m-i$, which is always >0 (see the invariant), and the obvious way to decrease it is to increment i by 1. It is fairly easy to see that execution of $i := i+1$ under the condition $x \neq b[i]$ leaves P true. This leaves us with the program well-known as *Linear Search*:

(16.2.5) $\{Q\}\; i := 0; \quad \textbf{do } x \neq b[i] \rightarrow i := i+1 \textbf{ od } \{R\}$

Discussion

The program is certainly correct, but let us try formally to prove it using checklist 11.9. First, show that invariant (16.2.4) is initially true:

$$wp(\text{"}i := 0\text{"}, (16.2.4)) \ = \ 0 \leqslant 0 < m \ \wedge \ x \notin b[0:-1]$$

which is certainly implied by Q. Next, prove that (16.2.4) is indeed an invariant of the loop. This requires showing that

$$(16.2.4) \ \wedge \ x \neq b[i] \ \Rightarrow \ wp(\text{"}i := i+1\text{"}, (16.2.4))$$
$$\text{or} \ \ 0 \leqslant i < m \ \wedge \ x \notin b[0:i] \ \Rightarrow \ 0 \leqslant i+1 < m \ \wedge \ x \notin b[0:i]$$

Is this true? Certainly not —the antecedent is not enough to prove that $i+1 < m$! The problem is that we have neglected to include in the invariant the fact that $x \in b[0:m-1]$. Formally, the invariant should be

$$(16.2.6) \quad P: 0 \leqslant i < m \ \wedge \ x \notin b[0:i-1] \ \wedge \ x \in b[0:m-1]$$

With this slight change, one *can* formally prove that the program is correct (see exercise 5).

In omitting the conjunct $x \in b[0:m-1]$ we were simply using our mathematician's license to omit the obvious. Note that all the free identifiers of $x \in b[0:m-1]$ are fixed throughout Linear Search: x, b and m are not changed. Hence, facts concerning only these identifiers do not change. It can be assumed that the reader of the algorithm and its surrounding text will remember these facts, so that they don't have to be repeated over and over again.

Later on, such obvious detail will be omitted from the picture when it doesn't hamper understanding. For now, however, your task is to gain experience with the formalism and its use in programming, and for this purpose it is better to be as precise and careful as possible. It is also to be remembered that text surrounding a program in a book such as this one rarely surrounds that same program when it appears in a program listing, as it should. Be extremely careful in your program listings to present the program as clearly and fully as possible.

The program illustrates an important —but often forgotten— principle:

(16.2.7) **The Linear Search Principle**: to find a minimum value (at least equal to some lower bound) with a property, investigate values starting at that lower bound in *increasing* order. Similarly, when looking for a maximum value investigate values in decreasing order.

Exercises for Section 16.2

1. A program was developed to find an approximation to the square root of n by deleting the conjunct $n < (a+1)^2$ of result assertion (16.2.1). Develop a different program by deleting the conjunct $a^2 \leq n$ instead. Compare the running times of the two programs (see Appendix 4).

2. Write a program that, given a fixed integer $n > 0$, finds the largest integer that is (1) a power of 2, and (2) at most n. (First write down a formal specification and then derive the invariant by deleting a conjunct.)

3. Write a program that, given two fixed integers x and y satisfying $x \geq 0$ and $y > 0$, finds the quotient q and remainder r when dividing x by y. That is, it establishes $0 \leq r \wedge r < y \wedge q*y+r = x$. The program may not use multiplication or division. Develop the invariant of the loop by deleting a conjunct.

4. Write a program that, given a fixed array $b[0:m-1, 0:n-1]$ and a fixed value x in b, determines the "first" position of x in b. By "first" is meant that x is not in a previous row or in a previous column of the current row. That is, using two variables i and j, the program should establish the predicate

$$R = 0 \leq i < m \wedge 0 \leq j < n \wedge x = b[i, j] \wedge \\ x \notin b[0:i-1, 0:n-1] \wedge x \notin b[i, 0:j-1]$$

5. Prove with the help of checklist 11.9 that program (16.2.5) is correct, using loop invariant (16.2.6) and bound function $t: m-i$.

16.3 Replacing a Constant By a Variable

Summing the elements of an array

A second method for weakening a predicate, replacing a constant by a variable, is illustrated with the following problem. Write a program that, given a fixed integer $n \geq 0$ and fixed integer array $b[0:n-1]$, stores in variable s the sum of the elements of b. The result assertion R can be expressed as

(16.3.1) $R: s = (\Sigma j: 0 \leq j < n: b[j])$

The fact that each array element is involved in the sum suggests that a loop of some form should be developed, so R should be weakened to yield a suitable invariant P. R contains the constant n (i.e. n may not be changed). R can therefore be weakened by replacing n by a fresh variable i, yielding

$$s = (\Sigma j: 0 \leq j < i: b[j])$$

At the same time, however, reasonable bounds should be placed on i. Motivating the choice of bounds is the need to establish the invariant initially and the probable final value of i, which is n. The above predicate can be established by $i, s := 0, 0$, so a possible lower bound for i is 0. Therefore, the range $0:n$ is chosen, yielding the invariant

$$P: 0 \leqslant i \leqslant n \wedge s = (\Sigma j: 0 \leqslant j < i: b[j])$$

Program (15.1.1) for this problem was developed using this loop invariant and the bound function $t = n - i$:

$$i, s := 0, 0; \textbf{ do } i \neq n \rightarrow i, s := i+1, s+b[i] \textbf{ od}$$

Discussion

Two other constants of R could be replaced to yield an invariant. Replacing the constant 0 yields the invariant

$$0 \leqslant i \leqslant n \wedge s = (\Sigma j: i \leqslant j < n: b[j])$$

Using this as an invariant, one can develop a loop that adds the elements $b[j]$ to s in decreasing order of subscript value j (see exercise 1 of section 15.1).

If result assertion R is written as

$$s = (\Sigma j: 0 \leqslant j \leqslant n-1: b[j])$$

the constant expression $n-1$ can be replaced to yield the invariant

$$-1 \leqslant i \leqslant n-1 \wedge s = (\Sigma j: 0 \leqslant j \leqslant i: b[j])$$

Note carefully the lower bound on i this time. Because n can be zero, the array can be empty. Therefore the assignment $i, s := 0, b[0]$, a favorite of many for initializing such a loop, cannot be used here. The initialization must be $i, s := -1, 0$. (See exercise 1).

This example illustrates that there may be several constants to choose from when replacing a constant by a variable. In general, the constant is chosen so that the resulting invariant can be easily established, so that the guard(s) of the loop are simple and, of course, so that the command(s) of the loop can be easily written. This is a trial-and-error process, but one gets better at it with practice.

Too often, variables are introduced into a program without the programmer really knowing why, or whether they are even needed. In general, the following is a good principle to follow.

(16.3.2) •**Principle**: Introduce a variable only when there is a good reason for doing so.

We now have at least one good reason for introducing a variable: the need to weaken a result assertion to produce an invariant. It goes without saying that each variable introduced will be defined in some manner. Part of this definition, which is often forgotten, is the range of the variable. We emphasize the need for this range with the following

(16.3.3) •**Principle**: Put suitable bounds on each variable introduced.

Approximating the square root of a number

As a second example of replacing a constant by a variable, consider the following problem. Write a program that, given a fixed integer $n \geqslant 0$, establishes the truth of

(16.3.4) $R: a^2 \leqslant n <(a+1)^2$

A program for this problem was developed in section 16.2 by deleting the conjunct $n <(a+1)^2$; the program took time proportional to $\sqrt{n}$. Here we use the method of replacing a constant by a variable.

First try replacing the expression $a+1$ by a fresh variable b to yield

$$a^2 \leqslant n <b^2$$

Clearly, b must be greater than a if this predicate is to be true. Moreover, the predicate can be established by executing $a, b := 0, n+1$. Hence, b is bounded by $a+1$ and $n+1$, and the invariant is

$$P: a <b \leqslant n+1 \wedge a^2 \leqslant n <b^2$$

The guard B for the loop, obtained by investigating $P \wedge \neg B \Rightarrow R$, is $a+1 \neq b$. Thus far, the program is

$$a, b := 0, n+1;$$
$$\mathbf{do}\ a+1 \neq b \rightarrow ?\ \mathbf{od}$$

Since P indicates that $a+1 \leqslant b$ and the loop should terminate with $a+1=b$, the task of each iteration is to bring a and b closer together, i.e. to decrease the value of $b-a$. Execution should continue until $b-a =1$. Hence, a possible bound function t is $b-a-1$.

The size of the interval (a,b) could be decreased by one at each iteration, but perhaps a faster technique exists. Perhaps the interval could be halved, by setting either a or b to the midpoint $(a+b)\div 2$. If so, the command of the loop could have the form

(16.3.5)   **if** $? \rightarrow a := (a+b) \div 2$ [] $? \rightarrow b := (a+b) \div 2$ **fi**

Each command must maintain the invariant P. To find a suitable guard for the first command, first calculate

(16.3.6) $wp(\text{``}a := (a+b) \div 2\text{''}, P)$
$= (a+b) \div 2 < b \leqslant n+1 \wedge ((a+b) \div 2)^2 \leqslant n \wedge b^2 > n$.

The precondition of (16.3.5) will be the invariant together with the guard of the loop:

$P \wedge a+1 \neq b$.

The extra condition needed to imply (16.3.6) is $((a+b) \div 2)^2 \leqslant n$, so we take it as the guard for the first command. In a similar fashion, the guard for the second command is found to be $((a+b) \div 2)^2 > n$. Introducing a fresh variable d to save local calculations, we arrive at the program

(16.3.7) $a, b := 0, n+1;$
$\{invariant\ P: a < b \leqslant n+1 \wedge a^2 \leqslant n < b^2\}$
$\{bound\ t: b-a+1\}$
do $a+1 \neq b \rightarrow d := (a+b) \div 2;$
$\qquad$ **if** $d*d \leqslant n \rightarrow a := d$ [] $d*d > n \rightarrow b := d$ **fi**
od

Discussion

It may seem that the technique of halving the interval was pulled out of a hat. It is simply one of the useful techniques that programmers must know about, for its use often speeds up programs considerably. The execution time of this program is proportional to $\log n$, while the execution time of the program developed in section 16.2 is proportional to $\sqrt{n}$.

Program (16.3.7) illustrates another reason to introduce a variable: d has been introduced to make a local optimization. The introduction of d not only reduces the number of times the expression $(a+b) \div 2$ is evaluated, it also makes the program more readable.

Note that no definition is given for d. Variable d is essentially a constant of the loop body. It is assigned a value upon entrance to the loop body, and this value is used throughout the body. It carries no value from iteration to iteration. Moreover, d is used only in two adjacent lines, and its use is obvious from these two lines. A definition of d would belabor the obvious and is therefore omitted.

A similar program can be developed by replacing the second occurrence of a in (16.3.4) by a variable —see exercise 3.

The Plateau problem

Given is a fixed, ordered (by $\leqslant$) array $b[0:n-1]$, where $n>0$. A *plateau* of the array is a sequence of equal values. Write a program to store in variable p a value to establish

(16.3.8) $R: p$ is the length of the longest plateau of $b[0:n-1]$.

It may be possible to develop a satisfactory program without defining the length of the longest plateau in more detail. Nevertheless, as a first step, rewrite (16.3.8) in the predicate calculus.

The value p is the length of the longest plateau if there is a sequence of p equal values and no sequence of $p+1$ equal values. That is,

$b[0:n-1]$ contains a plateau of length p $\wedge$
$b[0:n-1]$ does not contain a plateau of length $p+1$

Because the array is sorted, a subsection $b[k:j]$ is a plateau if and only if its end elements $b[k]$ and $b[j]$ are equal. This allows us to write R in the predicate calculus as follows:

(16.3.9) $R: (\mathbf{E}k: 0\leqslant k \leqslant n-p: b[k]=b[k+p-1]) \wedge$
$(\mathbf{A}k: 0\leqslant k \leqslant n-p-1: b[k]\neq b[k+p])$

The only difficulty in writing (16.3.9) might have been in getting k's bounds correct. Subsequently, we will work with R as written in (16.3.8), but we will turn to the more formal definition (16.3.9) when insight is needed.

Clearly, iteration is needed for this program. Remembering the point of this section, what loop invariant would you choose?

The length of the plateau of an array of length 1 is obviously 1. Therefore, the following invariant, found by replacing the constant n of R by a fresh variable i, can be easily established:

(16.3.10) $P: 1\leqslant i \leqslant n \wedge p$ is the length of the longest plateau of $b[0:i-1]$

What should be the bound function, the initialization and the guard of the loop?

The bound function is $t=n-i$. The loop initialization is $i,p:=1,1$. The guard of the loop is $i\neq n$. What should be the command of the loop?

Each iteration must increase i, and it seems reasonable to increase i by 1 (but see exercise 10). But this may call for a change in p in order to reestablish the invariant. Thus, we consider the two commands $i := i+1$ and $i, p := i+1, p+1$. We determine the conditions under which execution of the first maintains P:

$$wp(``i := i+1", P) \;=\; 1 < i+1 \leqslant n \;\wedge\; p \text{ is the length of the}$$
$$\text{longest plateau of } b[0:i]$$

The first conjunct is implied by the guard of the loop. What extra condition is needed to imply the second conjunct?

It is already known, from P, that p is the length of the longest plateau of $b[0:i-1]$. Therefore, p is the length of the longest plateau of $b[0:i]$ *iff* $b[i-p:i]$ is not a plateau. Looking carefully at definition (16.3.9) of the longest plateau, we determine that this holds *iff* $b[i-p] \neq b[i]$. This leads directly to the guards for both of the commands $i := i+1$ and $i, p := i+1, p+1$, and the loop body is

$$\textbf{if } b[i] \neq b[i-p] \rightarrow i := i+1$$
$$[] \; b[i] = b[i-p] \rightarrow i, p := i+1, p+1$$
$$\textbf{fi}$$

The final program is given in (16.3.11).

(16.3.11) $i, p := 1, 1;$
   $\{invariant\ P\colon 1 \leqslant i \leqslant n\ \wedge$
       p is the length of the longest plateau of $b[0:i-1]\}$
   $\{bound\ t\colon n-i\}$
   $\textbf{do } i \neq n \rightarrow \textbf{if } b[i] \neq b[i-p] \rightarrow i := i+1$
          $[] \; b[i] = b[i-p] \rightarrow i, p := i+1, p+1$
         $\textbf{fi}$
  $\textbf{od}$

Discussion

A common mistake in developing this program is to introduce, too early in the game, a variable v that contains the value of the latest, longest plateau, so that the test would be $b[i] = v$ instead of $b[i] = b[i-p]$. I made this mistake the first time I developed the program. But it only complicates the program. Principle (16.3.2) —introduce a variable only when there is good reason to do so— should be followed.

Carefully writing definition (16.3.9) of the length of a longest plateau did help subsequently in determining the body of the loop. Without (16.3.9), it is too easy to overlook the simple test $b[i]=b[i-p]$. This once again illustrates the usefulness of writing simple, clear definitions.

This program finds the length of the longest plateau for any array, even if not sorted, as long as all equal values are adjacent. It is possible to speed up the program by increasing i by more than 1 —example, by p— but the program becomes more complicated.

Exercises for Section 16.3

1. Write a program to sum array elements $b[0:n-1]$. The result assertion is

$$R: s = (\Sigma j: 0 \leqslant j \leqslant n-1: b[j])$$

The invariant is to be found from the result assertion by replacing the constant $n-1$ by a variable.

2. Prove formally that the body of the loop of program (16.3.7) actually decreases the bound function (point 5 of Checklist 11.9). The important point here is that, when the body of the loop is executed, $a+1<b$.

3. Develop a program for approximating the square root of n by replacing the second occurrence of a in (16.3.4) by b, yielding the invariant

$$a^2 \leqslant n <(b+1)^2$$

Don't forget to choose suitable bounds for b. Compare the resulting program, and the effort needed to derive it, with the development presented earlier.

4. (Binary Search). Write a program that, given fixed x and fixed, ordered (by $\leqslant$) array $b[1:n]$ satisfying $b[1] \leqslant x <b[n]$, finds where x belongs in the array. That is, for a fresh variable i the program establishes

$$R: 1 \leqslant i <n \wedge b[i] \leqslant x <b[i+1]$$

The execution time of the program should be proportional to $\log n$.

After writing the program, incorporate it in a program for a more general search problem: with no restriction on the value x, determine i to satisfy

$$(i =0 \wedge x <b[1]) \vee$$
$$(1 \leqslant i <n \wedge b[i] \leqslant x <b[i+1]) \vee$$
$$(i =n \wedge b[n] \leqslant x)$$

5. Write a program that, given fixed, ordered array $b[0:n-1]$ where $n>0$, finds the number of plateaus in $b[0:n-1]$.

6. Write a program that, given fixed array $b[0:n-1]$ where $n>0$, finds the position of a maximum value in b —i.e. establish

$R: 0 \leqslant k < n \land b[k] \geqslant b[0:n-1]$.

The program should be nondeterministic if the maximum value occurs more than once in b.

7. Write a program that, given fixed array $b[0:n-1]$ where $n \geqslant 0$, stores in d the number of odd values in $b[0:n-1]$.

8. Given are two fixed, ordered arrays $f[0:m-1]$ and $g[0:n-1]$, where $m,n \geqslant 0$. It is known that no two elements of f are equal and that no two elements of g are equal. Write a program to determine the number of values that occur both in f and g. That is, establish

$$k = (\mathbf{N} i,j: 0 \leqslant i < m \land 0 \leqslant j < n: f[i]=g[j])$$

9. Write a program that, given fixed array $b[0:n-1]$, where $n \geqslant 0$, determines whether b is zero: using a fresh Boolean variable s, the program establishes

$$R: s = (\mathbf{A} j: 0 \leqslant j < n: b[j]=0)$$

10. Write another program to find the length of the longest plateau of $b[0:n-1]$. This algorithm uses the idea that the loop body should investigate one plateau at each iteration. The loop invariant is therefore

$0 \leqslant i \leqslant n \land p$ = length of longest plateau of $b[0:i-1] \land$
$(i=0$ **cor** $i=n$ **cor** $b[i-1] \neq b[i])$

You may use the fact that the length of the longest plateau of an empty array is zero. This exercise is illustrative of the fact that not all loop invariants will arise directly from considering the strategies for developing invariants discussed in this chapter. Here, we actually added a conjunct, thus strengthening the invariant, to produce another program.

16.4 Enlarging the Range of a Variable

Another look at Linear Search

The next method for weakening the result assertion is illustrated by an example that was already discussed, Linear Search. Write a program that, given a fixed integer $n > 0$ and an array $b[0:n-1]$ that is known to contain a value x, finds the first occurrence of x in b.

Denote by iv the least value i satisfying $0 \leqslant i \land x = b[i]$. iv is guaranteed to exist, by the definition of the problem. Then, using a variable i, the result assertion for this program can be written as

$$R: i = iv$$

The Linear Search Principle indicates that a search for a value i satisfying R should be in order of increasing value, beginning with the lowest.

The Linear Search Principle indicates that a search for a value i satisfying R should be in order of increasing value, beginning with the lowest. Thus, the invariant for the loop will be

$$P: 0 \leqslant i \leqslant iv$$

The loop is then written as

$$i := 0; \ \textbf{do} \ x \neq b[i] \rightarrow i := i + 1 \ \textbf{od} \ \{i = iv\}$$

Discussion

The method used to develop the invariant was *to enlarge the range of a variable*. In R, variable i could have only one value: iv. This range of values is enlarged to the set $\{0, 1, \cdots, iv\}$. In this case, the enlarging came from weakening the relation $i = iv$ to $i \leqslant iv$ and then putting a lower bound on i. This method is similar to the last one, *introducing a variable and supplying its range* —it just happens that the variable is already present in R.

The example illustrates another important principle:

(16.4.1)   •**Principle**: Introduce a name to denote a value that is to be determined.

Sometimes, introduction of such a name allows us to be more informal —but not less precise. It may be quite easy to describe a relation in English but less easy to put it in the predicate calculus and, moreover, the English description may be enough to give the desired insight. But don't use this technique as a license to avoid the predicate calculus completely, for the calculus enables us to reason more effectively about the programs we are creating.

The Welfare Crook

We now proceed to a second example where enlarging the range of a variable is useful. Suppose we have three long magnetic tapes, each containing a list of names in alphabetical order. The first list contains the names of people working at IBM Yorktown, the second the names of students at Columbia University and the third the names of people on welfare in New York City. Practically speaking, all three lists are endless, so no upper bounds are given. It is known that at least one person is on all three lists. Write a program to locate the first such person (the one with the alphabetically smallest name).

To get at the essence of the problem, consider searching three ordered arrays (with no upper bounds) $f[0:?]$, $g[0:?]$ and $h[0:?]$ for the least value that is on all three of them; this least value is known to exist.

This program is often written in 10 to 30 lines of code in FORTRAN, PL/I or ALGOL 68 by those unexposed to the methods given in this book. The reader might wish to develop the program completely before studying the subsequent development.

What is the first step in writing the program? Do it.

The first step is to write pre- and postconditions Q and R. Since the lists f, g and h are fixed, we will use the fact that they are alphabetically ordered without mentioning it in Q or R. So Q is simply T. Using iv, jv and kv to denote the least values satisfying $f[iv] = g[jv] = h[kv]$, and using three simple variables i, j and k, the postcondition R can be written as

$$R: i = iv \land j = jv \land k = kv$$

Notice how the problem of defining the values iv, jv and kv in detail has been finessed. We know what *least* means, and hope to proceed without a formal definition. Now, why should a loop be used? Develop the invariant and bound function for the loop.

The program must search through a variable number of entries in the lists, and this suggests using iteration. The Linear Search Principle, (16.2.7), suggests that one search from the beginning of the lists. Enlarging the range of the three variables i, j and k yields the invariant

$$P: 0 \leqslant i \leqslant iv \land 0 \leqslant j \leqslant jv \land 0 \leqslant k \leqslant kv$$

The bound function is $t = iv - i + jv - j + kv - k$.

Now, what is the initialization, and what commands would one first think of in order to make progress towards termination?

The initialization is $i, j, k := 0, 0, 0$. The simplest ways to decrease the bound function are: $i := i + 1$, $j := j + 1$ and $k := k + 1$. Generally speaking, it will be necessary to increment all three variables, so a loop of the following form is suggested.

(16.4.2) $i, j, k := 0, 0, 0;$
$\quad$ **do** $? \;\rightarrow\; i := i+1$
$\quad$ **[]** $? \;\rightarrow\; j := j+1$
$\quad$ **[]** $? \;\rightarrow\; k := k+1$
$\quad$ **od**

Now, develop a suitable guard for the command $i := i+1$.

We have:

$$wp(\text{``} i := i+1 \text{''}, P) = 0 \leqslant i+1 \leqslant iv \,\wedge\, 0 \leqslant j \leqslant jv \,\wedge\, 0 \leqslant k \leqslant kv$$

The last two conjuncts, and also $0 \leqslant i+1$, are implied by the invariant, so only $i+1 \leqslant iv$ must be implied by the guard. The guard cannot be $i+1 \leqslant iv$, because the program may not use iv. But, the relation $i+1 \leqslant iv$, together with P, means that $f(i)$ is not the crook, and this is true if $f[i] < g[j]$. Thus, the guard can be $f[i] < g[j]$. In words, since the crook does not come alphabetically before $g[j]$, if $f[i]$ comes alphabetically before $g[j]$, then $f[i]$ cannot be the crook.

But the guard could also be $f[i] < h[k]$ and, for the moment, we choose the disjunction of the two for the guard:

$$f[i] < g[j] \vee f[i] < h[k]$$

The other guards are written in a similar fashion to yield the program

(16.4.3) $i, j, k := 0, 0, 0;$
$\quad$ **do** $f[i] < g[j] \vee f[i] < h[k] \;\rightarrow\; i := i+1$
$\quad$ **[]** $g[j] < h[k] \vee g[j] < f[i] \;\rightarrow\; j := j+1$
$\quad$ **[]** $h[k] < f[i] \vee h[k] < g[j] \;\rightarrow\; k := k+1$
$\quad$ **od**

This program terminates, and, upon termination, P is true. But we have not yet proved that upon termination the desired result holds. Do so.

Point 3 of checklist 11.9 is proved done by showing that

(16.4.4) $P \wedge \neg \text{BB} \Rightarrow R$

holds, where P is the invariant, BB is the disjunction of the guards and R is the result assertion.

So suppose the guards are false. Looking at the first disjunct of each guard, and assuming it is false, we have:

$$f[i] \geqslant g[j] \geqslant h[k] \geqslant f[i]$$

Hence, upon termination we have $f[i] = g[j] = h[k]$ and R holds.

Can any further simple change be made to make the program more efficient?

Note that only the first disjunct of each guard is needed to prove (16.4.4). Hence, the second disjuncts can be eliminated to yield the program

(16.4.5) $i, j, k := 0, 0, 0;$
$\quad$ **do** $f[i] < g[j] \rightarrow i := i+1$
$\quad$ [] $g[j] < h[k] \rightarrow j := j+1$
$\quad$ [] $h[k] < f[i] \rightarrow k := k+1$
$\quad$ **od**

Discussion

In developing this program, for the first guard, at first $f[i] < g[j]$ is developed, and then weakened to $f[i] < g[j] \lor f[i] < h[k]$. Why is it weakened?

Well, the first concern is to obtain a correct program; the second concern is to obtain an efficient one. In proving correctness, one task is to prove that, upon termination, (16.4.4) holds. The *stronger* ¬BB is, the more chance we have of proving (16.4.4). Since BB is the complement of ¬BB, this means that the *weaker* BB is, the more chance we have of proving (16.4.4). Thus, we have the following principle:

(16.4.6) ●**Principle**: The more guarded commands and the weaker their guards, the easier it may be to develop a correct program.

Of course, this principle does not provide a license to develop hundreds of cases; simplicity and minimum case analysis must still be maintained.

The concern for efficiency caused us to simplify the guards to yield program (16.4.5). This will be discussed in some detail in section 19.1.

16.5 Combining Pre- and Postconditions

Sometimes the use of just *one* of the three methods described thus far for weakening an assertion will not yield a suitable loop invariant. This may happen, for example, when the input variables are themselves to be modified to form part of the result of execution. Thus, one may have to use a combination of methods.

In many cases, it is useful to remember from our balloon theory (section 16.1) that both the pre- and postcondition of a loop imply the invariant and, therefore, to consider both of them when developing the invariant. Can both the pre- and postcondition be put in the same form, so that the invariant is seen as a simple generalization of both? Can the invariant be considered as a sort of union of both?

In this section, we illustrate this approach with two problems.

Inserting Blanks

Consider the following problem. Write a program that, given fixed $n \geqslant 0$, fixed $p \geqslant 0$, and array $b[0:n-1]$, adds $p*i$ to each element $b[i]$ of b. Formally, using B_i to represent the initial value of $b[i]$, we have

> Precondition Q: $(A\ i:\ 0 \leqslant i < n:\ b[i] = B_i)$
> Postcondition R: $(A\ i:\ 0 \leqslant i < n:\ b[i] = B_i + p*i)$

This problem arose when writing a program to insert blanks between words of a line in order to right-justify the line. The B_i are the numbers of the columns of the beginning of successive words on a line, and p is the number of blanks to be inserted between each pair of words. After insertion, the first word will begin in column B_0, the second in column $B_1 + p$, the third in $B_2 + 2*p$, and so forth.

The problem suggests a loop that changes one $b[i]$ at each iteration. To derive an invariant, first replace the constant n of R by a variable j:

> P': $0 \leqslant j \leqslant n\ \wedge\ (A\ i:\ 0 \leqslant i < j:\ b[i] = B_i + p*i)$

P' states that the first j elements of b have their final values. But the fact that the other $n-j$ elements have their initial values should also be included, and the full invariant is

> P: $0 \leqslant j \leqslant n\ \wedge\ (A\ i:\ 0 \leqslant i < j:\ b[i] = B_i + p*i)\ \wedge$
> $(A\ i:\ j \leqslant i < n:\ b[i] = B_i)$

This leads to the program

(16.5.1) $j := 0;$
           do $j \neq n \rightarrow j, b[j] := j+1,\ b[j] + p*j$ **od**

The development of the invariant was a two-step process; a constant was replaced by a variable and the resulting predicate was modified to take into account initial conditions. (See section 20.1 for further work with this example.)

Swapping Equal-Length Sections

The next problem is as follows. Write a program that, given an array $b[0:m-1]$ with two non-overlapping sections $b[i:i+n-1]$ and $b[j:j+n-1]$, both of length $n \geqslant 0$, swaps the two sections. For example, if the two sections have the values given in Q below, then upon termination they have the values displayed in R below. In the diagrams, X and Y denote the initial values of $b[i:i+n-1]$ and $b[j:j+n-1]$, respectively.

For the rest of the development, a less formal approach will be used, which uses the insight gained thus far without requiring all the formal details. We take for granted that only the sections mentioned should be changed and that they do not overlap, and use the following diagrams for the pre- and postconditions —"unswapped" ("swapped") means that the values in the indicated section have their initial (final) values:

Since each element of the two sections must be swapped, a loop is suggested that will swap one element of each at a time. The first step in finding the invariant is to replace the constant n of R by a variable k:

$$P': 0 \leqslant k \leqslant n \ \wedge \ b \ \begin{array}{|c|} \hline \overset{i \qquad \qquad i+k-1}{\text{swapped}} \\ \hline \end{array} \ \wedge \ b \ \begin{array}{|c|} \hline \overset{j \qquad \qquad j+k-1}{\text{swapped}} \\ \hline \end{array}$$

But P' does not indicate the state of array elements with indices in $i+k$: $i+n-1$ and $j+k:j+n-1$. Adjusting P' suitably yields invariant P as the predicate $0 \leqslant k \leqslant n$ together with

$$(16.5.2) \quad b \ \begin{array}{|c|c|} \hline \overset{i \quad i+k-1}{\text{swapped}} & \overset{i+k \quad i+n-1}{\text{unswapped}} \\ \hline \end{array} \ \wedge \ b \ \begin{array}{|c|c|} \hline \overset{j \quad j+k-1}{\text{swapped}} & \overset{j+k \quad j+n-1}{\text{unswapped}} \\ \hline \end{array}$$

The obvious bound function is $n-k$, and the program is

$k := 0;$
$\textbf{do } k \neq n \ \rightarrow \ k, b[i+k], b[j+k] := k+1, \ b[j+k], b[i+k] \ \textbf{od}$

For later purposes (section 18.1), we write this as a procedure in (16.5.3). Review chapter 12 for parameter-argument correspondence conventions, if necessary.

(16.5.3)   {Swap non-overlapping sections $b[i:i+n-1]$ and $b[j:j+n-1]$}
$\quad$ **proc** *swapequals*(**var** b: **array of** *integer*,
$\qquad\qquad\qquad\qquad$ **value** i, j, n: *integer*);
$\quad$ **begin var** k: *integer*;
$\quad$ $k := 0;$
$\quad$ {*invariant*: see above, *bound*: $n-k$}
$\quad$ **do** $k \neq n \ \rightarrow \ k, b[i+k], b[j+k] := k+1, \ b[j+k], b[i+k]$ **od**
$\quad$ **end**

Discussion

Again, the invariant was developed by replacing a constant of R by a variable and then adding a conjunct in order to reflect the initial conditions. We used diagrams in order to avoid some formalism and messy detail. For some, pictures are easier to understand. But be especially careful when using them, for they can lead to trouble. It is too easy to forget about special cases, for example that an array section may be empty, and this can lead to either an incorrect or less efficient program. To avoid such cases, always define the ranges of new variables carefully and be sure each picture is drawn in such a way that you *know* it can be translated easily into a statement of the predicate calculus.

The development of the invariant was a two-step process. The invariant can also be developed as follows. Both Q (or a slightly perturbed version of it due to initialization) and R must imply the invariant. That is, Q and R must be *instances* of the more general predicate P. Q states that the sections are unswapped; hence, the invariant must include, for each section, an unswapped subsection, which could be the complete section. On the other hand, R states that the sections are swapped; hence, the invariant must include, for each section, a swapped subsection, which could be the complete section. One is led to draw diagram (16.5.2), using a variable k to indicate the boundary between the unswapped and swapped subsections.

Exercises for Section 16.5

1. Formally define the pre- and postconditions for the program to swap two non-overlapping array sections of equal size (without using pictures or diagrams).

2. (Array Reversal). Write a program that reverses an array section $b[i:j]$. That is, if initially $b[i:j] = (B_i, B_{i+1}, \cdots, B_j)$, then upon termination $b[i:j] = (B_j, \cdots, B_{i+1}, B_i)$. Assume that i and j are within the array bounds and that $i \leqslant j+1$. (If $i = j+1$ the array section is empty; this is permitted.)

3. Write a program that, given fixed x, fixed m and n, $m < n$, and array section $b[m:n-1]$, permutes the values of b and sets an integer variable p to achieve

$$R: m \leqslant p \leqslant n \wedge b \begin{array}{|c|c|} \hline \overset{m \qquad\quad p-1}{\leqslant x} & \overset{p \qquad\quad n-1}{>x} \\ \hline \end{array}$$

More formally, if initially $b[m:n-1] = B[m:n-1]$, then the program establishes

$$R: m \leqslant p \leqslant n \wedge b[m:p-1] \leqslant x < b[p:n-1] \wedge perm(b, B).$$

4. (Partition). Write a procedure $Partition(b, m, n, p)$ that, given fixed m and n, $m < n$, and array $b[m:n-1]$ with initial value $B[m:n-1]$, permutes the values of b and sets p to achieve

$$R: m \leqslant p < n \wedge perm(b, B) \wedge b \begin{array}{|c|c|c|} \hline \overset{m}{\leqslant B[m]} & \overset{p}{B[m]} & \overset{n-1}{>B[m]} \\ \hline \end{array}$$

Procedure *Partition* is a slight modification of the answer to exercise 3.

5. (The Dutch National Flag). Given is an array $b[0:n-1]$ for fixed $n \geqslant 0$, each element of which is colored either red, white or blue. Write a program to permute the elements so that all the red elements are first and all the blue ones last. That is, the program is to establish

$$b \begin{array}{|c|c|c|} \hline \text{red elements} & \text{white elements} & \text{blue elements} \\ \hline \end{array}$$

The color of an element may be tested with Boolean expressions $red(b[i])$, $white(b[i])$ and $blue(b[i])$, which return the obvious values. The number of such tests should be kept to a minimum. The only way to permute array elements is to swap two of them; the program should make at most n swaps.

6. (Link Reversal). A simple variable p and two arrays $v[0:?]$ and $s[0:?]$ are used to contain a sequence of values $V_0, V_1, \cdots, V_{n-1}$ as a *linked list*:

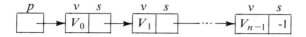

That is,

> (1) $v[p]$ contains the first value V_0;
>
> (2) for $0 \leq i < n-1$, if $v[k]$ contains the value V_i, then $v[s[k]]$ contains the value V_{i+1};
>
> (3) if $v[k]$ contains the last value V_{n-1}, then $s[k] = -1$.

No ordering of values in array elements is implied. For example, the fact that V_0 is followed by V_1 in the linked list does not mean that $v[p+1]$ contains V_1. Write a program that reverses the links —the arrows implemented by array s. Array v should not be altered, and upon termination the linked list should be

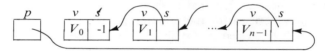

7. Write formal pre- and postconditions for problem 6.

8. (Saddleback Search). It is known that a fixed integer x occurs in fixed, two-dimensional array $b[0:m-1, 0:n-1]$. Further, it is known that each row and each column of b is ordered (by $\leq$). Write a program to find the position of x in b —i.e. using variables i and j, the program should establish $x = b[i,j]$. If x occurs in several places in b, it does not matter which place if found. Try to minimize the number of comparisons in the worst case. This kind of problem arises in multiplying sparse polynomials, each given by an ordered list of coefficient-exponent pairs.

9. (Decimal to Binary). Given is an integer variable $x = X$, where $X > 0$. Write a program to calculate an integer k and array $v[0:k-1]$ that gives the binary representation of X, where $v[i]$ is the ith bit of the representation and the high order bit, $v[k-1]$, is nonzero. The value in x may be destroyed.

10. (Decimal to Base B). Given is an integer variable $x = X$, where $X > 0$, and an integer $B > 1$. Write a program to calculate an integer k and array $v[0:k-1]$ that gives the base B representation of X, where $v[k-1]$, the high order digit of the representation, is nonzero. The value in x may be destroyed.

Chapter 17
Notes on Bound Functions

A bound function serves two purposes. First, it is used to show that a loop terminates. Secondly, it gives an upper bound on how many iterations can be executed before termination occurs, and thus can be used to approximate the time required to execute the program. Different bound functions may be used for the same program, depending on whether the programmer is interested in just showing termination or in showing that a program is almost optimal or faster than another one. For example, consider program (16.3.7), which approximates the square root of a positive integer:

$$\{n \geqslant 0\}$$
$$a, b := 0, n+1;$$
$$\{inv: a < b \leqslant n+1 \land a^2 \leqslant n < b^2\}$$
$$\textbf{do } a+1 \neq b \rightarrow d := (a+b) \div 2;$$
$$\qquad \textbf{if } d*d \leqslant n \rightarrow a := d \; [\!] \; d*d > n \rightarrow b := d \textbf{ fi}$$
$$\textbf{od } \{a^2 \leqslant n < (a+1)^2\}$$

The bound function $b-a+1$ was used to prove termination. But the smaller bound function $ceil(log(b-a))$ shows that this program is indeed much faster than program ((16.2.3)), which performs approximately $b-a$ iterations:

$$a := 0; \; \textbf{do } (a+1)^2 \leqslant n \rightarrow a := a+1 \textbf{ od}$$

Comparison of speeds of execution is treated briefly in Appendix 4.

Usually, the invariant of a prospective loop will suggest a bound function. This was the case in most of the programs developed in earlier chapters —e.g. summing the elements of an array (15.1.1), Linear Search (16.2.2), the Plateau Problem (16.3.11) and the Welfare Crook (16.4.2). However, we give two pointers here to help in finding bound functions.

Using the notation of the problem and its solution

Consider a problem from section 16.3, searching a non-empty, two-dimensional array $b[0:n-1, 0:m-1]$ for a value x. The invariant for this algorithm was:

$$P: 0 \leqslant i \leqslant m \wedge 0 \leqslant j < n \wedge$$

Since x has to be in the untested section, a possible bound function is

the number of elements in the untested section

which is $(m-i)*n - j$. It can be formally proven that this is indeed a bound function for the loop.

The general idea is the following:

(17.1)   ●**Strategy**: Express the bound function, in words, as a simple property of the invariant and the problem, and then formalize it (if necessary) as a mathematical expression.

A second example of the use of this strategy is the problem Four-tuple Sort of section 15.2. Four variables $q0, q1, q2, q3$ were to be permuted to achieve $q0 \leqslant q1 \leqslant q2 \leqslant q3$. The bound function was chosen to be the number of inversions in the sequence $(q0, q1, q2, q3)$. (Of course, not knowing what an inversion is might present some initial difficulties.)

Using lexicographic ordering

Consider pairs of integers (i, j). We say that one pair (i, j) *is less than* another pair (h, k), written $(i, j) < (h, k)$, if either

$$i < h \quad \text{or} \quad i = h \wedge j < k$$

For example, $(-1, 5) < (5, 1) < (5, 2)$. This is called the *lexicographic ordering* of integer pairs. It is extended in the natural way to the operators $\leqslant, >$ and $\geqslant$. It is also extended to triples, 4-tuples, etc. For example,

$$(3, 5, 5) < (4, 5, 5) < (4, 6, 0) < (4, 6, 1).$$

Now consider program (17.2), whose only purpose is to illustrate using lexicographically ordered tuples to prove termination.

(17.2) $\{0 < m \ \wedge \ 0 < n\}$
        $i, j := m-1, n-1;$
        do $j \ne 0$ $\qquad\quad \rightarrow j := j-1$
        [] $i \ne 0 \wedge j = 0 \rightarrow i, j := i-1, n-1$
        od

Execution is guaranteed to terminate, because

   (1) Variable i satisfies $0 \le i < m$ and j satisfies $0 \le j < n$.

   (2) Each iteration transforms the pair (i,j) into a smaller pair (lexicographically speaking). By (1), this, can only happen a finite number of times.

   But what bound function should be used to prove termination? Presumably, it should include a term i and a term j, since both variables are decremented. However, in the second guarded command the decrease of 1 in i is accompanied by an increase of $n-1$ in j. In order to have an effective decrease, the term i should be weighted: $i*n$. Therefore the bound function is

   $t: i*n + j.$

Each iteration decreases t by exactly 1, so that t indicates exactly how many more iterations are to be performed.

   We state the general idea in the following theorem, which is given without formal proof since it is obvious from the previous discussion.

(17.3) **Theorem.** Consider a pair (i, j), where i and j are expressions containing variables used in a loop. Suppose each iteration of the loop decreases (i, j) (lexicographically speaking). Suppose further that i satisfies $mini \le i \le maxi$ and j satisfies $minj \le j \le maxj$, for constants $mini$, $maxi$, $minj$ and $maxj$. Then execution of the loop must terminate, and a suitable bound function is

   $(i-mini)*(1+maxj-minj)+j-minj$

   A similar statement can be made concerning a triple (i, j, k), 4-tuple (i, j, k, l), etc., instead of pair (i, j). $\square$

   If one can exhibit a pair (triple, etc.) that satisfies theorem 17.3, there is no need to actually produce the bound function, unless it makes things clearer or is needed for other reasons. We give three examples.

   In section 15.2 the following program (15.2.4) was written for searching a (possibly empty) two-dimensional array.

$\{0 \leqslant m \ \wedge \ 0 \leqslant n\}$

$i, j := 0, 0;$

do $i \neq m \ \wedge \ j \neq n$ **cand** $x \neq b[i, j] \rightarrow j := j+1$

$\qquad$ [] $i \neq m \ \wedge \ j = n$ $\qquad\qquad\qquad\qquad \rightarrow i, j := i+1, 0$

od

$\{(0 \leqslant i < m \ \wedge \ 0 \leqslant j < n \ \wedge \ x = b[i, j]) \vee (i = m \ \wedge \ x \notin b)\}$

The pair (i, j) is initially $(0, 0)$ and each iteration *increases* it. Therefore, the pair $(m-i, n-j)$ is decreased at each iteration. Further, we have $0 \leqslant m-i \leqslant m$ and $0 \leqslant n-j \leqslant n$. Hence, theorem 17.3 can be applied and the loop terminates. The bound function that arises from the use of the theorem is $(m-i)*(n+1)+n-j$.

As a second example, consider program Four-tuple Sort from section 15.2, which permutes variables $q0$, $q1$, $q2$ and $q3$ to achieve $q0 \leqslant q1 \leqslant q2 \leqslant q3$:

do $q0 > q1 \rightarrow q0, q1 := q1, q0$

$\qquad$ [] $q1 > q2 \rightarrow q1, q2 := q2, q1$

$\qquad$ [] $q2 > q3 \rightarrow q2, q3 := q3, q2$

od

The tuple $(q0, q1, q2, q3)$ is decreased (lexicographically speaking) by each iteration. It is bounded below by the tuple whose values are $min(q0, q1, q2, q3)$ and is bounded above by the 4-tuple whose values are $max(q0, q1, q2, q3)$. Hence, the loop terminates.

As a final example, consider the Railroad Shunting Yard problem. A shunting yard contains a number of trains, each with one or more cars. An algorithm is to remove all cars from the yard, but under the condition that only one car be removed at a time. This means that trains must be split into smaller trains, and the following algorithm is proposed.

do shunting yard is not empty $\rightarrow$

$\qquad$ Select a train *train*;

$\qquad$ **if** *train* has exactly one car $\quad \rightarrow$ Remove *train* from yard

$\qquad$ [] *train* has more than one car $\rightarrow$ Split *train* into two trains

$\qquad$ **fi**

od

Removing *train* from the yard reduces the number of trains and reduces the total number of cars in the yard. On the other hand, splitting a train leaves the total number of cars the same but increases the number of trains by 1. So we choose the pair (number of cars in the yard, $-$(number of trains in the yard))

Each execution of the loop reduces (lexicographically speaking) the pair. Further, we have

$$0 \leqslant number\ of\ cars \leqslant initial\ number\ of\ cars$$
$$-(initial\ number\ of\ cars) \leqslant -(number\ of\ trains) \leqslant 0$$

By theorem 17.3, the loop terminates.

Exercises for Chapter 17

1. Find the bound function of theorem 17.3 for the Four-tuple Sort program whose termination is proved using the 4-tuple $(q0, q1, q2, q3)$.

Chapter 18
Using Iteration Instead of Recursion

A procedure or function is *recursive* if during its execution it may be called again. Recursive procedures often arise from recursive definitions in mathematics. The usual example given is the factorial function, $n!$, which for nonnegative integers is defined

$$0! = 1$$
$$n! = n * (n-1)! \quad \text{for } n > 0.$$

Note how $n!$ is defined in terms of $(n-1)!$; it is recursively defined.

This definition can be translated easily into a recursive procedure to compute $n!$:

```
{Given n ≥ 0, store n! in answer}
proc fac(value n: integer ;result answer: integer);
    if n = 0 → answer := 1
    [] n > 0 → fac(n-1, answer); answer := n*answer
    fi
```

Recursion is useful, and it definitely belongs in the programmer's tool kit. For example, top-down parsing using recursive procedures (sometimes called recursive descent) has been a favorite of mine in compiler construction courses for over ten years.

At the same time, in theory at least, any recursive program can be written iteratively (and vice versa), and in practice it may make sense to do so. Perhaps the available programming notations force the use of iteration, perhaps problems of efficiency of space and time force the use of iteration, or perhaps an algorithm just seems easier expressed iteratively.

Through a series of examples, we provide some tools and techniques for writing programs iteratively that could have been written recursively. One trick in doing so will be to think iteratively right from the beginning. That is, if the program will be written using iteration, then the invariant for the loop will have to be developed *before* writing the loop (as much as possible).

The topic will allow us to bring up two important strategies and discuss the relation between them, for recursive procedures often evolve from their use. These strategies are: —solving problems in terms of simpler ones, and divide and conquer. While not on the same level of detail and precision as some of the strategies presented earlier, these two old methods can still be useful when practised consciously.

At the end of section 18.3, some comments are made concerning the choice of data structures in programming and the use of program transformations.

18.1 Solving Simpler Problems First

Sometimes, we simply don't know how to begin solving a problem, and the methods analyzed thus far don't seem to help. In such situations, the following may help.

(18.1.1)   •**Strategy**: Try to solve a problem in terms of simpler ones.

"Simpler" may mean different things at different times. A problem may be simpler because some restrictions have been omitted (this is generalization). It may be simpler because restrictions have been added. Whatever the change in the problem, if it leads to a solution of the simpler problem it may be possible to solve the original problem in terms of it.

In order to illustrate the technique, let us develop a program for the problem Swapping Sections. Given are fixed integer variables m, n and p satisfying $m < n < p$. Given is (part of) an array, $b[m:p-1]$, considered as two sections:

$$Q: \quad b \; \boxed{\; B[m:n-1] \; | \; B[n:p-1] \;}$$

where B denotes the initial value of array b. The program should swap the two array sections, using only a constant amount of extra space (independent of m, n and p), thus establishing the predicate

$$(18.1.2) \quad R: \quad b \; \begin{array}{|c|c|} \hline \overset{m}{B[n:p-1]} & \overset{p-1}{B[m:n-1]} \\ \hline \end{array}$$

How should one begin? Well, a procedure *swapequals*, (16.5.3), has already been written to swap non-overlapping sections *of equal size*. Perhaps the current problem, which involves sections of unequal size, can be solved in terms of this simpler one.

So suppose for the moment that section $b[m:n-1]$ is bigger than $b[n:p-1]$. Consider $b[m:n-1]$ to consist of two sections, the first of which is the same size as $b[n:p-1]$ (diagram (a) below). Then the equal-sized sections containing $\bar{x}_1$ and $\bar{y}$ can be swapped to yield diagram (b) below; further, the original problem can then be solved by swapping the two sections containing $\bar{x}_2$ and $\bar{x}_1$. These two sections may be of unequal sizes, but at least one of them is smaller than in the original problem, so that progress has been made.

(a) b $\begin{array}{|c|c|c|} \hline \overset{m}{\bar{x}_1} & \overset{m+p-n}{\bar{x}_2} & \overset{n \quad p-1}{\bar{y}} \\ \hline \end{array}$ (c) b $\begin{array}{|c|c|c|} \hline \overset{m}{\bar{y}} & \overset{n}{\bar{x}_1} & \overset{m+p-n \quad p-1}{\bar{x}_2} \\ \hline \end{array}$

(b) b $\begin{array}{|c|c|c|} \hline \overset{m}{\bar{y}} & \overset{m+p-n}{\bar{x}_2} & \overset{n \quad p-1}{\bar{x}_1} \\ \hline \end{array}$ (d) b $\begin{array}{|c|c|c|} \hline \overset{m}{\bar{x}_2} & \overset{n}{\bar{x}_1} & \overset{m+p-n \quad p-1}{\bar{y}} \\ \hline \end{array}$

Now suppose that the second section, $b[n:p-1]$, is larger. Then the case is as given in diagram (c), and procedure *swapequals* can be used to transform it into diagram (d).

Now let's try to work this idea into a program. Diagrams (b) and (d) indicate that, after execution of *swapequals*, n is always the left boundary of the rightmost section to be swapped. But this is also true initially. Therefore, an invariant can be obtained by replacing constants m and p by variables and taking into account initial conditions:

$$b \; \begin{array}{|c|c|c|c|} \hline \text{already} & \overset{h}{\text{swap with}} & \overset{n}{\text{swap with}} & \overset{k \quad p-1}{\text{already}} \\ \text{swapped} & b[n:k-1] & b[h:n-1] & \text{swapped} \\ \hline \end{array}$$

However, note that the algorithm requires comparison of the lengths of $b[n:k-1]$ and $b[h:n-1]$. Also, procedure *swapequals* requires the lengths of sections. Therefore it may be better to represent the lengths of the sections rather than their endpoints. The invariant P becomes the predicate $0 < i \leqslant n-m \; \wedge \; 0 < j \leqslant p-n$ together with the following:

	m	$n-i$	n	$n+j$ $p-1$
b	already swapped	swap with $b[n:n+j-1]$	swap with $b[n-i:n-1]$	already swapped

Using the bound function $t = max(i, j)$, the program is written as

$i, j := n-m, p-n;$ $\{P\}$
do $i > j \rightarrow$ *swapequals*$(b, n-i, n, j)$; $i := i-j$
 $[]$ $i < j \rightarrow$ *swapequals*$(b, n-i, n+j-i, i)$; $j := j-i$
od;
$\{P \wedge i = j\}$
swapequals$(b, n-i, n, i)$

Discussion

This program could also have been written in recursive fashion as

$\{$Swap sections $b[m:n-1]$ and $b[n:p-1]$, where $m < n < p\}$
proc *swap_sections*(**var** b: **array of** *integer*;
                      value m, n, p: *integer*);
     if $n-m = p-n \rightarrow$ *swapequals*$(b, m, n, p-n)$
     $[]$ $n-m > p-n \rightarrow$ *swapequals*$(b, m, n, p-n)$;
                      swap_sections$(b, m+p-n, n, p)$
     $[]$ $n-m < p-n \rightarrow$ *swapequals*$(b, m, p+m-n, n-m)$;
                      swap_sections$(b, m, n, m+p-n)$
     fi

In this case, I like the iterative version better. It was not difficult to discover the invariant, and it is, to me, easier to understand (this is not always the case). The iterative version does require two extra variables i and j, which are not needed in the recursive version.

The iterative version has the neat property that deleting all the calls of *swapequals* results in program (18.1.3) to compute the greatest common divisor, $gcd(n-m, p-n)$, of the initial array-section sizes. To see this old, elegant program emerge from a useful, practical programming problem was a delightful experience!

(18.1.3) $\{m < n < p\}$
       $i, j := n-m, p-n;$
       $\{inv: 0 < i \wedge 0 < j \wedge gcd(n-m, p-n) = gcd(i, j)\}$
       do $i > j \rightarrow i := i-j$
        $[]$ $i < j \rightarrow j := j-i$
       od
       $\{i = j = gcd(n-m, p-n)\}$

The program *could* have been developed by first replacing n and p by variables h and k, and then determining how to reduce the size of the unswapped portion. There are often many ways to arrive at the same program, and one cannot really say that one is better than the other. Redoing a problem once done, using the principles and asking why they weren't used the first time, can increase programming skill and lead to better programs. The following confession concerns this point.

Confession: When I first developed this program, my old habits got in the way and I failed to follow the principles of introducing variables only when needed and finding the invariant by replacing constants by variables. I immediately introduced *four* variables, which indicated the beginning of the two sections to be swapped and their lengths. A student recognized that one variable wasn't needed because the beginning of the rightmost section was always n. This caused me to stop and redo the development as shown above, this time adhering to principle 16.3.2 and introducing variables only when there is a good reason to do so. This led to the recognition that the *gcd* algorithm was embedded in the solution.

Exercises for Section 18.1

1. Consider a procedure *reverse*(b, i, j), which reverses the list of values in $b[i:j]$ —see exercise 2 of section 16.5. Use this procedure, which solves a simpler problem, to write a program to swap adjacent sections.

This exercise illustrates that the simpler problems used to solve a given problem may be difficult to find. It is difficult to give a methodology to develop *any* program. Some programs arise just out of new ideas, and without those ideas the solutions won't be found.

2. The Fibonacci numbers f_n are defined as follows:

$$f_0 = 0$$
$$f_1 = 1$$
$$f_n = f_{n-1} + f_{n-2} \quad \text{for } n > 1$$

The first eight Fibonacci numbers are 0, 1, 1, 2, 3, 5, 8, 13.

The definition of f_n for $n > 1$ can be written in matrix notation as follows:

$$\begin{matrix} f_n \\ f_{n-1} \end{matrix} = \begin{matrix} 1 & 1 \\ 1 & 0 \end{matrix} \quad \begin{matrix} f_{n-1} \\ f_{n-2} \end{matrix}$$

It is fairly easy to write a program that takes time proportional to n to calculate f_n. However, in a subsequent section, 19.1, a program is given to perform exponentiation i^n for positive integers n in time proportional to $\log n$, where i could be a matrix. Write a program to calculate f_n in logarithmic time using the simpler(?) problem of exponentiation.

18.2 Divide and Conquer

In the preceding section, we discussed solving a problem in terms of a known, simpler problem. In this section, we discuss a related strategy, which has been around for some time:

(18.2.1)   •**Strategy**: Divide and Conquer

In programming, this strategy is often used in the following sense. One tries to divide a problem into two or more smaller, similar problems. If the division can be done, then the same process can be performed on the smaller problems. If the division can be done without too much effort (during execution), then an effective, efficient algorithm may have been developed.

This strategy usually leads to dividing something *in half* and then processing each part in the same manner, until the parts are small enough to process directly. This often leads to a logarithmic factor in the formula describing the speed of execution.

The difference between strategy 18.1.1, solving a problem in terms of simpler ones, and strategy 18.2.1, divide and conquer, may be slight. For some problems, it may be more a matter of what question motivates the development than anything else. In strategy 18.1.1, one first recognizes a simpler problem and then asks how it can be used effectively. This was the case in the development of program Swapping Sections. In strategy 18.2.1, on the other hand, one first asks what it would mean to divide the problem into smaller pieces, and then looks for ways to solve the original problem in terms of the pieces.

In strategy 18.1.1, the simpler problem motivates the development. In strategy 18.2.1, the idea of division leads the way, although it may lead to using a simpler problem.

We illustrate the approach by developing the program Quicksort, one of the faster sorting algorithms. Given is a fixed integer $n \geq 0$ and an array $b[0:n-1]$. The array is to be sorted.

If the array is small enough, say $n \leq 2$, then any simple algorithm may be used to sort it —for example

> Sort $b[0:n-1]$ directly, assuming $n \leq 2$:
> **if** $n \neq 2$ **cor** $b[0] \leq b[1]$ → *skip*
> [] $n = 2$ **cand** $b[0] > b[1]$→ $b[0], b[1] := b[1], b[0]$
> **fi**

However, if $n > 2$ then a more general method must be used. The divide and conquer strategy invites us to perform the sort by sorting two (or more) sections of the array separately. Suppose the array is partitioned as follows.

```
      0       k     n-1
b  [    ?     |    ?    ]
```

What condition must be placed on the two sections so that sorting them separately yields an ordered array?

___

Every value in the first section should be $\leq$ every value in the second section:

$$\text{(18.2.2)} \quad b \; \boxed{\leq b[k:n-1] \;\Big|\; \geq b[0:k-1]}$$

with labels $0 \quad k \quad n-1$ above.

This means that if the values of b can be permuted to establish the above predicate, then to sort the array it remains only to sort the partitions $b[0:k-1]$ and $b[k:n-1]$.

Actually, a procedure similar to one that establishes (18.2.2) has already been written —see exercise 4 of section 16.5— so we will make use of it. Procedure *Partition* splits a non-empty array section $b[m:n-1]$ into three partitions, where the value x in the middle one is the initial value in $b[m]$:

$$\text{(18.2.3)} \quad R: \; m \leq p < n \;\wedge\; b \; \boxed{\leq x \;\Big|\; x \;\Big|\; > x}$$

with labels $m \quad p \quad n-1$ above.

After partitioning the array as above, it remains to sort the two partitions $b[m:p-1]$ and $b[p+1:n-1]$. If they are small enough, they can be sorted directly; otherwise, they can be sorted by partitioning again and sorting the smaller sub-partitions. While one sub-partition is being sorted, the bounds of the other must be stored somewhere. But sorting one will generate two more smaller partitions to sort, and *their* bounds must be stored somewhere also. And so forth.

To keep track of the partitions still to be sorted, use a set variable s to contain their boundaries. That is, s is a set of pairs of integers and, if (i,j) is in s, then $b[i:j]$ remains to be sorted. We write the invariant

(18.2.4) P: s is a set of pairs (i,j) representing disjoint array
sections $b[i:j]$ of b. Further, $b[0:n-1]$ is ordered
iff all the disjoint partitions given by set s are.

Note how English is used to eliminate the need for formally introducing an identifier to denote the initial value of array b.

Thus, we arrive at the following program:

(18.2.5) $s := \{(0, n-1)\}$;
             $\{Invariant: (18.2.4)\}$
             do $s \neq \{\}$ → $Choose((i, j), s)$; $s := s - \{(i, j)\}$;
                        if $j - i < 2$ → Sort $b[i:j]$ directly
                        $[]\ j - i \geqslant 2$ → $Partition(b, i, j, p)$;
                                    $s := s \cup \{(i, p-1)\} \cup \{(p+1, j)\}$
                        fi
             od

Operation $Choose((i, j), s)$ stores in i and j the value of a pair (i, j) that is in s, without changing s. This is a nondeterministic action, since any member of s may be chosen. See Appendix 2.

Discussion

Program (18.2.5) describes the basic idea behind *Quicksort*. Proof of termination is left to exercise 1. The execution time of Quicksort is $O(n \log n)$ on the average and $O(n^2)$ in the worst case. The space needed in the worst case is $O(n)$, which is more than it need be; exercise 2 shows how to reduce the space.

In the development of this program, the guiding motivation was the desire to divide and conquer. The simpler problem needed to effect the divide and conquer was procedure Partition. Had we first noticed that procedure Partition was available and asked how it could have been used, we would have been using strategy 18.1.1, solve the problem in terms of simpler ones.

Exercises for Section 18.2

1. Prove termination using the method developed in chapter 17 (theorem 17.3). Be careful: a partition $b[i:j]$ can be empty.

2. How big can set s of program (18.2.5) get? The maximum size of s can be reduced tremendously by maintaining a sequence (see Appendix 2) instead of a set and, after partitioning, putting the two pairs $(i, p-1)$ and $(p+1:j)$ in the sequence in a certain order. Revise algorithm (18.2.5) to do this and recalculate the maximum size the sequence.

18.3 Traversing binary trees

Definitions and notations

An *ordered binary tree* is a finite set of *nodes*, or values, that either is empty or consists of one node, called the *root* of the tree, and two disjoint ordered binary trees, called the *left subtree* and *right subtree*, respectively.

An ordered binary tree is represented in Fig. 18.3.1. Its root is A; its left and right subtrees consist of the nodes $\{B, E, I, J\}$ and $\{C, F, G, K, L\}$, respectively. The roots of A's left and right subtrees are B and C.

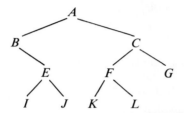

Figure 18.3.1   Example of a Binary Tree

The adjective "ordered" is used to indicate that an ordering on subtrees is involved: the left subtree is always listed first (or to the left). The adjective "binary" is used to indicate that there are at most two subtrees. From now on, we use the shorter term "tree" for "ordered binary tree".

The tree whose root is B in Fig. 18.3.1 has an empty left subtree. Nodes with two empty subtrees are called *leaves*. In Fig. 18.3.1, G, I, J, K and L are leaves.

If p is a tree, then *empty*(p) has the value of the sentence "tree p has no nodes." Further, if $\neg$ *empty*(p), then *left*$[p]$ and *right*$[p]$ are used to denote the left and right subtrees, respectively. Finally, if tree p is not empty, *root*$[p]$ denotes the value of the root node of p.

Trees, graphs and related mathematical structures play an important role in computer science. They make some ideas easier to understand, their properties allow the understanding of efficiency of many algorithms, and they are fundamental parts of many algorithms. The (ordered binary) tree, for example, is an important concept in several sorting algorithms, in some storage allocation algorithms, and in compilers. Thus, it is important to understand the basic algorithms that manipulate these structures.

Above, the term *tree* is defined in the easiest possible manner: recursively. For that reason, many algorithms that manipulate trees are given recursively also. Here, we wish to describe a few basic algorithms dealing with trees, but using iteration. With a firm grasp of this material, it should not be difficult to develop other algorithms that deal with trees, graphs and other structures.

Implementing a tree

We describe *one* typical implementation of a tree, which is motivated by the need in many algorithms to insert nodes into and delete nodes from a tree. The implementation uses a simple variable p and three arrays: $root[0:?]$, $left[0:?]$ and $right[0:?]$.

Variable p contains an integer satisfying $-1 \leqslant p$. It describes, or represents, the tree.

If integer k describes a tree or subtree, then the following holds:

1. $empty(k)$ is equivalent to $k = -1$.

2. $\neg empty(k)$ is equivalent to $0 \leqslant k$. If $\neg empty(k)$ holds, the value of the root is in $root[k]$, the left subtree of the root is given by $left[k]$ and the right subtree by $right[k]$.

For example, the tree of Fig. 18.3.1 could appear as given in (18.3.1).

	0	1	2	3	4	5	6	7	8	9	10
root	B	A		C	E	F	I	J	K	L	G
left	−1	0		5	6	8	−1	−1	−1	−1	−1
right	4	3		10	7	9	−1	−1	−1	−1	−1

(18.3.1) $p = 1$

Some comments are in order. First, p need not equal 0; the root node need *not* be described by the first elements of the arrays, $root[0]$, $left[0]$ and $right[0]$. In fact, several trees could be maintained in the same three arrays, using $p1$, $p2$ and $p3$ (say) to "point to their roots". This, of course, implies that the nodes of the trees in the arrays need not be in any particular order. In (18.3.1), the elements with index 2 of the three arrays are not used in the representation of tree p at all. Moreover, the root of the left subtree of A precedes A in the array, while the root of its right subtree follows it. This means that one can *not* process the tree by processing the elements of *root* (and *left* and *right*) in sequential order.

In the rest of this section, we will deal with a tree p using the original notations $empty(p)$, $root[p]$, $left[p]$ and $right[p]$. Note, however, that this notation is quite close to what one would use in a program dealing with a tree implemented as just shown.

Counting the nodes of a tree

As a first example, we write a program, Node Count, to calculate the number of nodes in a tree p. As an abbreviation, let

$$\#p$$

denote the number of nodes in tree p. Thus, using a simple variable c to contain the number of nodes, the program should establish

(18.3.2) $R: \#p = c$

The first step, of course, is to give a definition of $\#p$, in the hope that it will yield insight into the program. Write a definition of $\#p$ —it may help to use recursion since tree is defined recursively.

(18.3.3) $\#p = \begin{cases} empty(p) & \to 0 \\ \neg empty(p) & \to 1 + \#left[p] + \#right[p] \end{cases}$

This definition gives us the germ of an idea for the algorithm: if $empty(p)$, use the result 0; otherwise evaluate $1 + \#left[p] + \#right[p]$. This evaluation requires calculating the number of nodes in $left[p]$ and calculating the number of nodes in $right[p]$. But $\#left[p]$ is defined recursively by (18.3.3) also, and therefore calculating it can be expected to force us to calculate the number of nodes in its subtrees in the same manner. Thus, we see the need for counting the number of nodes in several subtrees of p, and it seems wise to consider using a set variable s (say) to maintain the set of trees whose nodes must be counted. And this hints at iteration.

We develop a loop invariant by extending the range of variable c in result assertion R and taking into account the fact that s contains trees still to be counted:

(18.3.4) $P: \#p = c + (\Sigma r : r \in s : \#r)$

where each member r of s is some subtree of p. That is, the number of nodes in tree p is c plus the number of nodes in the trees given in set s.

The invariant is easily established by $c, s := 0, \{p\}$. Each iteration of a loop should lead closer to termination, and this means that it should process a subtree of s in some manner. Using definition (18.3.3), the program is easily written as

(18.3.5) $c, s := 0, \{p\}$;
           {*inv*: (18.3.4)}
           {*bound*: $2*(\#p - c) + |s|$}
           do $s \neq \{\} \rightarrow Choose(q, s);\ s := s - \{q\}$;
                   if $empty(q)\ \rightarrow skip$
                   [] $\neg empty(q) \rightarrow c, s := c+1, s \cup \{right[q]\} \cup \{left[q]\}$
                   fi
           od $\{c = \#p\}$

The bound function was discovered by noting that the pair $(\#p - c, |s|)$ is decreased (lexicographically speaking) by each iteration —see Chapter 17.

Note that it does not matter in which order the subtrees in set s are processed. This is because the number of nodes in each subtree will be added to c and addition is a commutative operation. In this case, the use of the nondeterministic operation $Choose(q, s)$, which stores an arbitrary value in s into q, nicely frees us from having to make an unnecessary choice.

Preorder traversal

The *preorder* list of the nodes of a tree p, written *preorder*(p), is defined as follows. If the tree is empty, it is the empty sequence (); otherwise, it is the sequence consisting of

    1. The root, followed by

    2. The nodes of the left subtree, in preorder, followed by

    3. The nodes of the right subtree, in preorder.

For example, for the subtree e of Fig. 18.3.1 with root E we have

    $preorder(e) = (E, I, J)$

For the whole tree a of Fig. 18.3.1 we have

    $preorder(a) = (A, B, E, I, J, C, F, K, L, G)$

Using $|$ to denote catenation of sequences, *preorder*(p) can be written as

$$(18.3.6)\quad preorder(p) = \begin{cases} empty(p) & \rightarrow () \\ \neg empty(p) & \rightarrow (root(p)) \mid preorder(left[p]) \mid \\ & \quad preorder(right[p]) \end{cases}$$

Note that *preorder*(p) is defined recursively. This notation and the definition of preorder in terms of catenation has been designed to allow us to state and analyze various properties and algorithms in a simple, crisp manner; it is illustrative of the use of notation to help promote under-standing.

A *preorder traversal* of a tree consists of "walking" through the tree in the order given by its preorder list, "visiting" each node in turn in order to perform some operation on it. We now consider developing a program that performs a preorder traversal, storing the values of the nodes in an array. More precisely, for a tree p, execution of the program should es-tablish

(18.3.7) $R: c = \#p \wedge preorder(p) = b[0:c-1]$

Note the similarity between definitions (18.3.3) and (18.3.6). They have the same form, but the first uses the commutative operator $+$ while the second uses the non-commutative operator $|$. Perhaps the program to calculate the preorder list may be developed by transforming program Node Count so that it processes the trees of set s in a definite order. First, let's rewrite Node Count in (18.3.8) to store the node values into array b, instead of simply counting nodes. The invariant is

$$0 \leqslant c \leqslant \#p \wedge$$
$$\text{set of nodes of } p = b[0:c-1] \cup \{\text{nodes of trees in } s\}$$

(18.3.8) $c, s := 0, \{p\};$
      $\{bound: 2*(\#p-c) + |s|\}$
      do $s \neq \{\} \rightarrow Choose(q, s);\ s := s - \{q\};$
            if $empty(q) \rightarrow skip$
            $[]\ \neg empty(q) \rightarrow c, b[c] := c+1, root[q];$
                              $s := s \cup \{right[q]\} \cup \{left[q]\}$
            fi
      od $\{c = \#p \wedge b[0:c-1] \text{ contains the nodes of } p\}$

Now transform (18.3.8) as follows. Instead of a set s use a sequence r. The key is to insert trees into r and take them out in a manner that allows us to conclude that b contains the preorder list of p. This is easily done by observing the definition of preorder, and we have the invariant

(18.3.9) $P: 0 \leqslant c \leqslant \#p \wedge$
      $preorder(p) = b[0:c-1]\ |\ preorder(r_0)\ |\ \cdots\ |$
         $preorder(r_{|r|-1})$

Each iteration of a loop will then process tree r_0. If it is empty, it is deleted from the sequence of trees to be visited; if not, its preorder is given by (18.3.6), and the preorder list b and the sequence of trees r are changed accordingly:

(18.3.10) $c, r := 0, (p)$;
$\qquad \{bound: 2*(\#p - c) + |r|\}$
$\qquad$ **do** $r \neq () \rightarrow q, r := r[0], r[1..]$;
$\qquad\qquad$ **if** $empty(q) \quad \rightarrow skip$
$\qquad\qquad$ [] $\neg\, empty(q) \rightarrow c, b[c] := c + 1, root[q]$;
$\qquad\qquad\qquad\qquad\qquad\qquad r := left[q] \,|\, right[q] \,|\, r$
$\qquad\qquad$ **fi**
$\qquad$ **od** $\{c = \#p\}$

Discussion

In (18.3.5), the order in which the left and right subtrees are stored in set s is immaterial, because addition, which is being performed on the number of nodes in each, is commutative. In (18.3.10), however, the order in which nodes are stored in sequence r is important because operation $|$ is not commutative.

My first development of this program, done over 5 years ago, was not performed like this. It was an *ad hoc* process, with little direction, because I was new at the game and had to struggle to learn and perfect techniques.

Without the sequence notation (see Appendix 2), including the notation for catenation, one tries to work with English phrases, for example, writing the invariant as

$\qquad$ $t[1:i]$ is a sequence of pointers to subtrees that have not been visited, and $preorder(p)$ is equal to $b[0:c-1]$, followed by the preorder list of these trees.

The use of English is worthwhile in some contexts, for example it was used heavily in section 18.1 to discuss swapping sections. In this section, the concepts of "traversing a tree" and "visiting nodes" are useful in general discussions. But their use in developing this algorithm can be confusing, for it is not at all easy to see from the algorithm what has and has not been visited. Far better is to make the result assertion and invariant more formal, as has been done, because it leads to a crisp, precise, clear explanation.

The ability to easily write such iterative traversal algorithms is necessary in many applications. Study of these two algorithms and mastery of the few execises is essential.

A note on data refinement

In developing Quicksort in section 18.2 and Node Counting in this section, we used objects (and operations on them) that suited the problem —sets of pairs of integers and sets of trees— and operations on them. Only after this did we consider using other data structures to make the program more efficient with respect to space or time (e.g. exercise 2 of section 18.2, where sequences are used instead of sets). And we never did really consider how to rewrite the program in terms of arrays, for that is almost a trivial step compared to the development preceding it. Further, it would have been slightly more difficult to work in terms of arrays instead of sets right from the beginning. This illustrates the important principle

(18.3.11) •**Principle**: Program *into* a programming language, not *in* it.

In general, this principle deals with data and its representation, as well as with commands. We should use data structures that suit the problem, and, once a correct program has been developed, deal with the problem of changing the data structures to make their use more efficient and implementing them in the programing language. This latter task, often called "data refinement", has not received the attention that "program refinement" has.

In a "modern" programming notation allowing "data encapsulation", data refinement may just mean appending a program segment that describes how the objects are to be represented and the operations are to be implemented. In other programming notations, it may mean transforming the program so that it operates on allowable objects of the language.

A note on program transformation

Program transformation is a hot topic these days; many advocate using an interactive system to transform a problem description into an efficient program through a series of such transformations. In this section, we used program transformation to transform program Node Count into a program to derive a preorder list of a tree.

This is not the place to give a detailed account of program transformation systems, but one comment should be made. When making a transformation, as we did, always make sure the result can be understood by itself, without having to study the transformation. Thus, the result should have its own proof of correctness in terms of loop invariants and so forth. It is extremely difficult to understand a program by studying a long sequence of transformations; one quickly becomes lost in details or bored with the process.

Exercises for Section 18.3

1. Write a program to count the number of leaves of tree p.

2. Write a program to store in array b the *inorder list* of nodes of tree p. The inorder list is defined as follows. If p is empty the inorder list is the empty sequence (). If p is not empty, the inorder list is:

> 1. The nodes of $left[p]$, in inorder, followed by
> 2. The root, followed by
> 3. The nodes of $right[p]$, in inorder.

3. Write a program to store in array b the *postorder list* of nodes of tree p. The postorder list is defined as follows. If p is empty the postorder list is the empty sequence (). If p is not empty, the postorder list is

> 1. The nodes of $left[p]$, in postorder, followed by
> 2. The nodes of $right[p]$, in postorder, followed by
> 3. The root.

4. The root of a tree is defined to have depth 0, the roots of its subtrees have depth 1, the roots of their subtrees have depth 2, and so on. The depth of the tree itself is the maximum depth of its nodes. The depth of an empty tree is -1. For example, in tree (18.3.1), A has depth 0, F has depth 2, and the tree itself has depth 3. Write a program to calculate the depth of a tree.

Chapter 19
Efficiency Considerations

The programmer has two main concerns: correctness and efficiency. Thus far, this book has dealt mainly with the issue of correctness. This does not mean that efficiency is unimportant. When faced with any large task, it is usually best to put aside some of its aspects for a moment and to concentrate on the others, and that is what we have been doing. This important principle is called *Separation of Concerns*.

The two main concerns of the programmer can be handled by different mechanisms. The correctness concern is handled using a theory of correctness, such as the one developed in Part II. The formal definition of correctness is given not in terms of how a program is executed, but, instead, in terms of how theorems of the form $\{Q\}\ S\ \{R\}$ are to be proved. It is mathematical in nature, relying heavily on the predicate calculus.

On the other hand, at this time, efficient use of time and space can best be discussed in terms of some model of execution. Knowledge is required of the space needed by integer variables, arrays, etc., and one must understand how the commands of the programming notation are executed on a computer.

Actually, we have been dealing with both concerns to some extent all along. For example, in the Four-tuple Problem (section 15.2) three guarded commands were deleted in order to make the program shorter and perhaps more efficient. We also developed two programs for approximating the square root of an integer (sections 16.2 and 16.3) and discussed their relative speeds. However, as it should be, our first concern has been correctness. An efficient program is useless if it does not do what it is supposed to do.

In this chapter, we turn our attention to a few general techniques for improving the efficiency of programs.

19.1 Restricting Nondeterminism

Nondeterminism arises when two or more guards of an alternative construct or a loop can be true at the same time. It also arises when commands like $Choose(q, s)$ are used (see Appendix 2). Sometimes, a program can be made more efficient by restricting or deleting the nondeterminism.

Recall from section 15.2 that, in a correct loop, the guards can be strengthened without disturbing correctness as long as point 3 of checklist 11.9, $P \wedge \neg BB \Rightarrow R$, remains true ($P$ is the invariant, R the result assertion and BB the disjunction of the guards). Thus, one may restrict the nondeterminism by strengthening the guards. And, if a guard is strengthened to the everywhere-false predicate F, then the corresponding guarded command may be deleted because the command will never be executed.

Nondeterminism can be eliminated without fear of destroying point 3 of checklist 11.9 using the following simple theorem.

(19.1.1)   **Theorem.** Suppose a loop has (at least) two guarded commands, with guards $B1$ and $B2$. Then strengthening $B2$ to $B2 \wedge \neg B1$ leaves BB, and hence $P \wedge \neg BB \Rightarrow R$, unchanged.

Proof. BB contains the disjunct $B1 \vee B2$. Strengthening $B2$ as indicated changes this disjunct (and *only* this part of BB) to $B1 \vee (B2 \wedge \neg B1)$. Using De Morgan's law and simplifying, we see this is equivalent to the original disjunct $B1 \vee B2$. Hence, BB remains unchanged.   □

Use of theorem 19.1.1 eliminates nondeterminism because then the two guards cannot both be true in the same state.

A few examples of strengthening guards and using theorem 19.1.1 may provide a better understanding.

Revisiting the Welfare Crook

In section 16.4 and exercise 1 of section 16.4, a program for the Welfare Crook was developed. We re-analyze it here. Given are three alphabetically ordered lists of names, stored in fixed, ordered, arrays $f[0:?]$, $g[0:?]$ and $h[0:?]$. Some names appear on all three lists; the problem is to find the first such name. Let iv, jv and kv be the smallest integers satisfying $f[iv] = g[jv] = h[kv]$. Then, using variables i, j and k, the following should be established:

$$R: i = iv \wedge j = jv \wedge k = kv$$

The invariant for a loop is found by using the Linear Search Principle, (16.2.7), and enlarging the range of variables in R:

$$P: 0 \leqslant i \leqslant iv \wedge 0 \leqslant j \leqslant jv \wedge 0 \leqslant k \leqslant kv$$

The obvious bound function is $t: iv - i + jv - j + kv - k$ and the first program developed ((16.4.3)) is

(19.1.2) $i, j, k := 0, 0, 0;$
```
        do f[i] <g[j] ∨ f[i] <h[k] → i := i+1
        [] g[j] <h[k] ∨ g[j] <f[i] → j := j+1
        [] h[k]<f[i] ∨ h[k]<g[j] → k := k+1
        od
```

Now comes the concern for efficiency. Point 3 of checklist 11.9, $P \wedge \neg BB \Rightarrow R$ (where P is the invariant, BB the disjunction of the guards and R the result assertion) can be proved using only the first disjunct of each guard. Therefore, the guards can be strengthened by deleting their second conjuncts without violating point 3. This yields the shorter and more efficient program

```
        i, j, k := 0, 0, 0;
        do f[i] <g[j] → i := i+1
        [] g[j] <h[k] → j := j+1
        [] h[k]<f[i] → k := k+1
        od
```

Note that theorem 19.1.1 could now be used to strengthen two of the guards, but it is better not to. There is no reason for preferring one of the commands over the others, and strengthening the guards using the theorem will only complicate them and make the program less efficient. In this case, the nondeterminism aids in producing the simplest solution.

Revisiting Four-tuple Sort

In the Four-tuple Sort problem of section 15.2, three guards could be strengthened to F, the everywhere-false predicate, and therefore the corresponding guarded commands could be deleted. This eliminated some of the nondeterminism, but not all of it.

Exponentiation

Consider writing a program that, given two fixed integers X and Y, $X \geqslant 0$ and $Y \geqslant 0$, establishes

$R: z = X^Y.$

(Define $0^0 = 1$.) The program is to consist of a loop with the following invariant and bound function:

$P: 0 \leqslant y \wedge z * x^y = X^Y.$
$t: y$

P is easily established using $x, y, z := X, Y, 1$, and (at least) two simple commands can be used to reduce the bound function: $y := y - 1$ and $y := y \div 2$. Finding the weakest preconditions of these commands with respect to the invariant leads directly to the program

$\{0 \leqslant X \wedge 0 \leqslant Y\}$
$x, y, z := X, Y, 1;$
do $0 < y \wedge even(y) \rightarrow y, x := y \div 2, x * x$
$[] \ 0 < y \qquad\qquad \rightarrow y, z := y - 1, z * x$
od $\{z = X^Y\}$

Now consider the efficiency of the program. Dividing by 2 generally reduces y more than subtracting 1; hence, division is preferred. However, if y is > 0 and even, then both guards are true, and an implementation is free to choose to execute either command. Using theorem 19.1.1, replace the guard $0 < y$ by

$0 < y \wedge \neg(0 < y \wedge even(y))$

and simplify it to yield

$\{0 \leqslant X \wedge 0 \leqslant Y\}$
$x, y, z := X, Y, 1;$
do $0 < y \wedge even(y) \rightarrow y, x := y \div 2, x * x$
$[] \ 0 < y \wedge odd(y) \rightarrow y, z := y - 1, z * x$
od $\{z = X^Y\}$

With the preliminary, nondeterministic version the loop could iterate up to Y times; in the final, deterministic version, the number of iterations is at most $1 + 2 * ceil(log \ Y)$. The algorithm can be rewritten once more as

$x, y, z := X, Y, 1;$
do $0 < y \rightarrow$ **do** $even(y) \rightarrow y, x := y \div 2, x * x$ **od**;
$\qquad\qquad y, z := y - 1, z * x$
od

19.2 Taking an Assertion Out of a Loop

Consider the following program segment, where dots $\cdots$ represent arbitrary pieces of code that do not assign to i:

$$
\begin{aligned}
&\textbf{do } i < n \; \rightarrow \; \cdots; \; k := 5 * i; \\
&\qquad\qquad \cdots; \; i := i + 2; \; \cdots \\
&\textbf{od}
\end{aligned}
$$

This program can be transformed to use the faster arithmetic operation addition instead of multiplication as follows. First, introduce a fresh variable z to contain the value $5*i$ and transform the program as follows:

$$
\begin{aligned}
&\textbf{do } i < n \; \rightarrow \; \cdots; \; z := 5 * i; \; k := z; \\
&\qquad\qquad \cdots; \; i := i + 2; \; \cdots \\
&\textbf{od}
\end{aligned}
$$

Next, make $z = 5*i$ part of the invariant of the loop. This means that the assignment $z := 5*i$ within the loop becomes unnecessary, but whenever i is increased z must be altered accordingly:

$$
\begin{aligned}
&z := i * 5; \\
&\{\text{Part of invariant: } z = 5*i\} \\
&\textbf{do } i < n \; \rightarrow \; \cdots; \; k := z; \\
&\qquad\qquad \cdots; \; i, z := i + 2, z + 10; \; \cdots \\
&\textbf{od}
\end{aligned}
$$

Compiler writers call this transformation *strength reduction*. It has been used as early as the late 1950's and early 1960's, in both FORTRAN and ALGOL compilers, to make references to two-dimensional arrays more efficient. For example, suppose an array $b[0:99, 0:50]$ is stored in row-major order. The calculation of the address of an element $b[i, j]$ is performed as

$$
address(b[0,0]) + i * 51 + j
$$

Then, within a loop that increments i with each iteration, all calculations of the address of $b[i, j]$ can be transformed as above to make them more efficient. This optimization is also effective because it allows the detection and elimination of certain kinds of common arithmetic expressions.

In general, this transformation is called *taking an assertion out of a loop* (and making it part of the loop invariant). In this case, the assertion $z = 5*i$ was taken out of the loop to become part of the invariant. The technique can be used wherever the value of some variable like z can be calculated by adjusting its current value, instead of calculating it afresh each time.

In the above example, taking the relation out of the loop can reduce execution time by only a constant factor, but examples exist that show that the technique can actually reduce the order of execution time of an algorithm.

Horner's rule

Consider evaluating a polynomial $a_0 + a_1 * x^1 + \cdots + a_{n-1} * x^{n-1}$ for $n \geq 1$ and for a value x and given constants a_i. The result assertion is

$$R: y = a_0 * x^0 + \cdots + a_{n-1} * x^{n-1}$$

An invariant can be produced by replacing the constant n by a variable i, and the following program can be developed:

$i, y := 1, a_0;$
$\{invariant: 1 \leq i \leq n \wedge y = a_0 * x^0 + \cdots + a_{i-1} * x^{i-1}\}$
$\{bound: n - i\}$
do $i \neq n \rightarrow i, y := i+1, y + a_i * x^i$ **od**

But note that calculating x^i each iteration is costly, requiring, in general, time proportional to $\log i$. Noting that $x^i = x * x^{i-1}$, we see that introducing a fresh variable z and making

$$z = x^i$$

part of the invariant of the loop allows us to transform the program into

$i, y, z := 1, a_0, x;$
$\{invariant: 1 \leq i \leq n \wedge z = x^i \wedge y = a_0 * x^0 + \cdots + a_{i-1} * x^{i-1}\}$
$\{bound: n - i\}$
do $i \neq n \rightarrow i, y, z := i+1, y + a_i * z, z * x$ **od**

This transformation can also be called strength reduction; the operation exponentiation has been replaced by the faster operation multiplication. Its use here reduces the order of execution time of the program from $O(n \log n)$ to $O(n)$.

Remark: One can rewrite the polynomial as

$$((\cdots (a_{n-1} * x + a_{n-2}) * x + \cdots) * x + a_0$$

This form leads directly to the slightly simpler program

$$y, i := a_{n-1},\ n-1;$$
$$\{invariant:\ 0 \leqslant i < n\ \wedge$$
$$y = ((\ \cdots\ (a_{n-1}*x + a_{n-2})*x + \cdots\ )*x + a_i\}$$
$$\{bound:\ i\}$$
$$\textbf{do}\ i \neq 0 \rightarrow i := i-1;\ y := y*x + a_i\ \textbf{od}$$

This method of computing a polynomial is named after W.G. Horner, who gave it in connection with another famous problem in 1819, but it was, in fact, proposed over 100 years earlier by Isaac Newton. This illustrates that first analyzing the specification of a program and transforming it into a slightly different form can be of more help than looking for efficient programs for the original specification.   □

An exercise attributed to Hamming

Consider the sequence $q = 1, 2, 3, 4, 5, 6, 8, 9, 10, 12,\ \cdots$ of all numbers divisible by no primes other than 2, 3 and 5. We shall call this sequence *Seq*. Another way to describe *Seq* is to give axioms that indicate which values are in it:

> Axiom 1. 1 is in *Seq*.
> Axiom 2. If x is in *Seq*, so are $2*x$, $3*x$ and $5*x$.
> Axiom 3. The only values in *Seq* are given by Axioms 1 and 2.

The problem is to write a program that stores the first 1000 values of *Seq*, in order, in an array $q[0:999]$, i.e. that establishes

R: $q[0:999]$ contains the first 1000 values of *Seq*, in order

A loop of some form is needed. What is a possible loop invariant?

Since Axiom 2 specifies that a value is in *Seq* if a smaller one is, it may make sense to generate the values in order. A possibility, then, is to replace the constant 1000 of R by a variable i, yielding the invariant

$P = 1 \leqslant i \leqslant 1000\ \wedge\ q[0:i-1]$ contains the first i values of *Seq*.

With this invariant, the obvious program structure is

$$i, q[0] := 1, 1;\ \{P\}$$
$$\{invariant:\ P;\ bound:\ 1000-i\}$$
$$\textbf{do}\ i \neq 1000 \rightarrow \text{Calculate } xnext, \text{ the } i^{th} \text{ value in } Seq;$$
$$i, q[i] := i+1,\ xnext$$
$$\textbf{od}$$

It remains to determine how to calculate *xnext*, the next value of *Seq* to be generated. Since the values of *Seq* are generated in order, *xnext* must be $>q[i-1]$. Secondly, since 1 is already in $q[0:i-1]$, *xnext* must satisfy Axiom 2 above. This means that *xnext* must have the form $2*x$, $3*x$ or $5*x$ for some value x already in $q[0:i-1]$. Therefore,

> *xnext* is the minimum value $>q[i-1]$ of the form $2*x$, $3*x$ or $5*x$ for x in $q[0:i-1]$.

So, we introduce three variables *x2*, *x3* and *x5* with meaning as expressed in the following assertion:

> *P1*: *x2* is the minimum value $>q[i-1]$ with form
> $2*x$ for x in $q[0:i-1]$,
> *x3* is the minimum value $>q[i-1]$ with form
> $3*x$ for x in $q[0:i-1]$,
> *x5* is the minimum value $>q[i-1]$ with form
> $5*x$ for x in $q[0:i-1]$.

Value *xnext* is the minimum of *x2*, *x3* and *x5*. We see, then, that variable *xnext* is not really needed, and we modify the program structure to

> $i, q[0]:= 1, 1; \{P\}$
> $\{invariant: P; bound: 1000-i\}$
> **do** $i \neq 1000 \rightarrow$ Calculate $x2, x3, x5$ to satisfy *P1*;
> $\qquad\qquad i, q[i]:= i+1, min(x2, x3, x5)$
> **od**

We now illustrate taking an assertion out of a loop. Calculating *x2*, *x3* and *x5* to establish *P1* at each iteration can be time-consuming. However, they change quite slowly as i is increased (and P is kept invariant), and it may be possible to speed up the algorithm by taking *P1* out of the loop and making it part of the loop invariant. The fact that $q[0:i-1]$ is ordered gives additional hope. Thus, we investigate the program structure

> $i, q[0]:= 1, 1; \{P\}$
> Establish *P1* for $i = 1$;
> $\{invariant: P \wedge P1; bound: 1000-i\}$
> **do** $i \neq 1000 \rightarrow i, q[i]:= i+1, min(x2, x3, x5);$
> $\qquad\qquad$ Reestablish *P1*
> **od**

Now, how is *P1* to be reestablished? Consider *x2*. For some j, $x2 = 2*q[j]$. Further, *x2* can only be increased, and not decreased, to $2*q[j+1]$ or $2*q[j+2]$, etc. This suggests maintaining the position j. A similar statement holds for *x3* and *x5*. We therefore introduce three variables $j2$, $j3$ and $j5$ and modify PI as follows:

PI: $x2 = 2*q[j2]$ is the minimum value $> q[i-1]$ with form
$2*x$ for x in $q[0:i-1]$,
$x3 = 3*q[j3]$ is the minimum value $> q[i-1]$ with form
$3*x$ for x in $q[0:i-1]$ and
$x5 = 5*q[j5]$ is the minimum value $> q[i-1]$ with form
$5*x$ for x in $q[0:i-1]$

We are now able to develop the final program:

$i, q[0]:= 1, 1;$ $\{P\}$
Establish PI: $x2, x3, x5, j2, j3, j5:= 2, 3, 5, 0, 0, 0;$
$\{invariant: P \wedge PI;\ bound: 1000-i\}$
do $i \neq 1000 \rightarrow i, q[i]:= i+1, min(x2, x3, x5);$
Reestablish PI:
do $x2 \leqslant q[i-1] \rightarrow j2:= j2+1;\ x2:= 2*q[j2]$ **od**;
do $x3 \leqslant q[i-1] \rightarrow j3:= j3+1;\ x3:= 3*q[j3]$ **od**;
do $x5 \leqslant q[i-1] \rightarrow j5:= j5+1;\ x5:= 5*q[j5]$ **od**
od

Exercises for Section 19.2

1. *Writing a Value as the Sum of Squares.* Write a program that, given a fixed integer $r \geqslant 0$, generates all different ways in which r can be written as the sum of two squares —i.e. that generates all pairs (x, y) satisfying

(19.2.1) $x^2 + y^2 = r \wedge 0 \leqslant y \leqslant x$

To help in writing it (and to arrange to use the strategy of taking a relation out of a loop), assume the following. Two arrays xv and yv will hold the values of the pairs (x, y) satisfying (19.2.1). Furthermore, the pairs are to be generated in increasing order of their x-values, and a variable x is used to indicate that all pairs with x-value less than x have been generated. Thus, the first approximation to the invariant of the main loop of the program will be

PI: $0 \leqslant i \wedge ordered(xv[0:i-1]) \wedge$
the pairs $(xv[j], yv[j]), 0 \leqslant j < i$, are all the pairs
with x-value $< x$ that satisfy (19.2.1).

19.3 Changing a Representation

It is sometimes useful to transform a program into one that uses a different representation of the data. As simple examples of different representations for some value, we use both rectangular coordinates and polar coordinates for points on a plane. The day of the year, which may be kept in the form (month, day) or in the form (day number within the year), is another example.

The motivation for changing representation often comes from the desire to apply one of the following two strategies, in the hope that they will yield a simpler or more efficient program:

•**Strategy:** Replace an expensive operation by a cheaper one.

•**Strategy:** Defer an expensive operation, so that it won't be executed as often.

Other reasons will probably suggest themselves once familiarity with the technique is acquired. We illustrate with three examples.

Approximating the Square Root

In section 16.3 the following program was developed to approximate the square root of a fixed integer $n \geq 0$:

(19.3.1) $a, b := 0, n+1$;
$\quad$ {*invariant* P: $a < b \leq n+1 \wedge a^2 \leq n < b^2$}
$\quad$ {*bound* t: $b-a+1$}
$\quad$ **do** $a+1 \neq b \rightarrow d := (a+b) \div 2$;
$\qquad\qquad\qquad$ **if** $d*d \leq n \rightarrow a := d$ [] $d*d > n \rightarrow b := d$ **fi**
$\quad$ **od** {$a^2 \leq n < (a+1)^2$}

We present a minor transformation of this program to illustrate changing a representation. A less trivial one is required in exercise 2.

Let us assume we want to replace operator $\div$ in the program by division $/$. This can be done easily if $a+b$ is always even, since then the two will yield the same result. Keeping $a+b$ even may not be so easy, but if the difference $b-a$ is always even, then d can be calculated using

$$d := a + (b-a)/2$$

Therefore, let us attempt to deal with the difference c (say) between b and a and to keep this difference even. This will be easiest if c is always a power of 2. Thus we have:

$$b = a + c$$
$$d = a + c / 2$$
$$(\mathbf{E}p: 1 \leqslant p: c = 2^p) \quad \text{(therefore } c \text{ is even)}$$

Because b and d are defined in terms of a and c, we may be able to write the program using only a and c. Thus, we try the loop invariant and bound function

$$P: a^2 \leqslant n < (a+c)^2 \wedge (\mathbf{E}p: 1 \leqslant p: c = 2^p)$$
$$t: c + 1$$

The initialization will require a loop to establish P, since c must be a power of 2. The rest of the program is derived from program (19.3.1) essentially by deleting the assignments to b and d and transforming the other commands into commands involving c:

(19.3.2) $a, c := 0, 1;$ **do** $c^2 \leqslant n \rightarrow c := 2*c$ **od**; $\{P\}$
          do $c \neq 1 \rightarrow c := c / 2;$
                    if $(a+c)^2 \leqslant n \rightarrow a := a+c$ [] $(a+c)^2 > n \rightarrow skip$ **fi**
          od $\{a^2 \leqslant n < (a+1)^2\}$

Controlled Density Sorting

In solving this problem, we attempt to convey the idea of the development without presenting all the formal details. The complete details are left as an exercise.

A table of (not necessarily different) numbers, which is initially empty, must be maintained. At any time, one of the following three operations may be performed.

(1) *Insert*(V_i): insert a new value V_i into the table.

(2) *Search*(x, p): Return in p the position in the table of a value x ("position" must be further specified later on).

(3) *Print*: Print the list of values in the table, in ascending order.

Operation (3) should be performed in time proportional to the number of values in the table. Furthermore, the total time spent in inserting and searching should be "small".

The requirement for operation (3) suggests that the table of values be kept in (ascending) order. In fact, one is led to think of algorithm *Insertion Sort*. Using an array $v[0:n-1]$ to contain the values and a simple variable i, the table of values $V_0, \cdots, V_{i-1}$ that have already been inserted will satisfy

(19.3.3) $P: 0 \leqslant i \;\wedge\; ordered(v[0:i-1]) \;\wedge\; perm(v[0:i-1], \{V_0, \;\cdots, V_{i-1}\})$

Printing can be done in linear time and searching can be done in time proportional to the logarithm of the current size of v, using Binary Search.

But what about inserting a new value x? Inserting will require finding the position j where x belongs —i.e. finding the value j such that $v[j-1] \leqslant x < v[j]$— then shifting $v[j:i-1]$ up one position to $v[j+1:i]$, and finally placing x in $v[j]$. Shifting $v[j:i-1]$ may take time proportional to i, which means that each insertion may take time proportional to i, and therefore, in the worst case the total time spent inserting n items may be on the order of n^2. This is expensive, and a modification is in order.

Shifting is the expensive operation, so we try to change the data representation to make it less expensive. How can this be done, perhaps to eliminate the need for shifting altogether?

A simple way to make shifting less expensive is to spread the values out, so that an empty array element, or "gap", appears between each pair of values. Thus, an array $v[0:2n-1]$ of twice the size is defined by

(19.3.4) $P: 0 \leqslant i \;\wedge\; ordered(v[0:2i-1]) \;\wedge\; \{V_0, \;\cdots, V_{i-1}\} \in v[0:2i-1] \;\wedge\;$
           $v[0:2i-1] = (\text{gap, value, gap, value, ..., gap, value})$

Gaps can be implemented by using a second array $gap[0:2n-1]$ of bits, where $gap[j]$ has the value "$v[j]$ is a gap". It is advantageous to let a gap $v[j]$ contain the non-gap value occurring in $v[j+1]$, so that Binary Search can still be used for searching.

Remark: If all values are known to be positive, then the sign bit of $v[j]$ can be used to distinguish values from gaps.   □

Now, shifting and inserting takes no time at all, because the new value can be placed in a gap. But shifting and inserting destroys the fact that a gap separates each pair of values, and after inserting it necessary to *reconfigure* the array to reestablish (19.3.4). Reconfiguring can be costly, so we must find a way to avoid it as much as possible.

We can *defer* reconfiguring the array simply by *weakening the invariant* to allow several values to be adjacent to each other. However, there are never adjacent gaps; the odd positions of v always contain values. We introduce a fresh variable k to indicate the number of array elements being used, and use the invariant

(19.3.5) $P: 0 \leqslant i \; \wedge \; ordered(v[0:k-1]) \; \wedge \; \{V_0, \cdots, V_{i-1}\} \in v[0:k-1] \; \wedge$
$(A \, j: 0 \leqslant j < k \; \wedge \; odd(j): v[j] \text{ is not a gap}) \; \wedge$
$v[0:k-1] \text{ contains } k-i \text{ gaps} \; \wedge$
$(A \, j: 0 \leqslant j < k: v[j] \text{ a gap} \Rightarrow v[j] = v[j+1])$

Note, now, that when inserting the first value no shifting is required, since it can fill a gap. The second value is likely to fill a gap also, but it *may* cause a shift. The third value inserted may fill a gap also, but the probability is greater that it will cause some shifting because there are fewer gaps. At some time, so many values will have been inserted that shifting again becomes too expensive. At this point, it is wise to reconfigure the array so that there is again one gap between each pair of values.

To summarize, the table is defined by (19.3.5), with (19.3.4) also being true initially. That is, values are separated by gaps. The table is initially set to empty using

$i, k := 0, 0$
{(19.3.4) and (19.3.5) are true}

Inserting a value V_i is done by

(19.3.6)   {(19.3.5)}
if shifting too expensive $\rightarrow$ Reconfigure to reestablish (19.3.4)
[] shifting is not too expensive $\rightarrow$ *skip*
fi;
Find the position j where V_i belongs;
Shift $v[j:...]$ up one position to make room for V_i;
$i, v[j] := i+1, V_i$

When does shifting become so expensive that reconfiguring should again be considered? Analysis has shown that reconfiguring is best performed either when a previous shift requires at least $\sqrt{i}$ values to be moved *or* when $i/2$ values have been inserted since the last reconfiguration. This makes the total time spent shifting roughly equal to the total time spent reconfiguring, so that neither one overshadows the other. Under these circumstances, the worst-case total time spent shifting or reconfiguring is proportional to $n\sqrt{n}$, while the average-case total time is proportional to $n \log n$.

The development of a complete algorithm is left to the reader (exercise 1).

Discussion

The first idea in developing this algorithm was to find a way to make *shifting* less expensive; the method used was to put a gap between each pair of values. The second idea was to *defer* reconfiguration, because it was too expensive. The first idea made shifting cheap, but introduced the expensive reconfiguration operation; the second idea deferred reconfiguration often enough so that the total costs of shifting and reconfiguration were roughly the same.

The algorithm is a competitor to balanced tree schemes in situations where a table of values is to be maintained in memory.

Efficient Queues in LISP

The programming notation LISP allows functions on lists $v = (v_0, \cdots, v_{n-1})$ of n values, where $n \geqslant 0$. The five functions with which we will be concerned are

(1) $v = ()$ yields the value of the assertion "list v is empty";

(2) $head(v)$ yields the value v_0 (undefined if v is empty);

(3) $tail(v)$ yields the value $(v_1, \cdots, v_n)$ —the list without its first element— (undefined if v is empty);

(4) $construct(w, v)$, where w is a value and $v = (v_0, \cdots, v_n)$ a list, yields the list $(w, v_0, \cdots, v_n)$;

(5) $append(v, w)$, where w is a value and $v = (v_0, \cdots, v_n)$ a list, yields the list $(v_0, \cdots, v_n, w)$.

The first four functions are executed in constant time. Function *append*, however, takes time proportional to the length of the list v to which w is being appended.

This is all we will need to know about LISP.

Consider implementing a queue using LISP lists and the five functions just given. A queue is a list v on which three operations may be performed: the first is to reference the first element on the list, the second is to delete the first element and the third is to insert a value w at the end of the queue. Thus, the operations on queue v can be implemented as

(1) Reference the first element: $head(v)$,

(2) Delete the first element: $v := tail(v)$,

(3) Insert value w at the end: $v := append(v, w)$.

Now, suppose n values $v_0, \cdots, v_{n-1}$ are to be inserted in a queue and, between insertions, values may be taken off the queue or the first value on

the queue can be examined. In the worst case, the time needed to perform the insertions is on the order of n^2. Why?

To insert a value takes time proportional to the length of the queue. To
insert n values into an empty queue can take time proportional to
$0+1+\cdots+n-1 = O(n^2)$. Clearly, insertion, performed in terms of
the LISP *append*, is the expensive operation, and a different data representation must be used to make it less expensive. What different representation would allow insertion to be done in constant time?

Insertion can be done easily if the queue is kept in reverse order. But
this would make deletion expensive. Thus, we compromise: implement
queue $v =(v_0, \cdots, v_{i-1})$ using *two* lists vh and vt, where the second is
reversed:

(19.3.7) $vh =(v_0, \cdots, v_{k-1})$,   for some k, and
$\qquad\quad vt =(v_{i-1}, v_{i-2}, \cdots, v_k)$ where $vh =()$ only if $vt =()$

Now let us look at the implementations of the queue operations again.
Referencing the first element is still implemented as $head(vh)$ —the restriction that vh is empty only if vt is allows us to implement it so simply.

Next, operation Delete must delete the first element from vh, but if vh
becomes empty, keeping (19.3.7) true requires that vt be reversed and
moved to vh. Thus, Delete —i.e. $v := tail(v)$— is implemented as

> $vh := tail(vh)$;
> **if** $vh =() \wedge vt \neq () \rightarrow$
> $\qquad$ {*inv*: queue is $(reverse(vt) \mid vh)$}
> $\qquad$ {*bound*: $\mid vt \mid$}
> $\qquad$ **do** $vt \neq () \rightarrow vh, vt := construct(head(vt), vh), tail(vt)$ **od**
> $\qquad$ {(19.3.7) $\wedge$ $vt =()$}
> [] $vh \neq () \vee vt =() \rightarrow skip$
> **fi**

Finally, Insert can be implemented as $vt := construct(w, vt)$.

Now, Insert is performed in constant time, while the loop in Delete
will take time proportional to the length of list vt. But, the *total* time
spent executing this loop is proportional to the total number of values n
inserted in the queue.

Exercises for Section 19.3

1. Write a reconfiguration procedure

> **procedure** $config$ (**value** i, k: $integer$;
>   **var** v: **array of** $integer$;
>   **var** $isgap$: **array of** $Boolean$);

that, given fixed $i > 0$, fixed integer k, array v and array $isgap$ satisfying (19.3.5), spreads the array values out to establish (19.3.4).

2. Change the representation of variables in program (19.3.2) so that no squaring operations are used.

3. Develop a program that, given fixed integers X, $Y > 0$, establishes $z = X^Y$. Develop it using the idea that z should be calculated through a series of multiplications, so that it may make sense to initialize z to the identity of $*$, 1, trying to create the invariant of a loop first, and changing a representation to make it all possible.

Chapter 20
Two Larger Examples of Program Development

Two programs are developed to show the use of the methodology on slightly larger and more complicated problems. Each has a few further lessons to offer on the subject of program development. An attempt will be made to guide the reader to produce the solutions, as has been done in previous chapters. The developments will proceed at a faster rate than before at the places that involve only principles and strategies illustrated earlier.

The exercises contain a series of longer and more difficult problems on which to try the techniques and strategies discussed in this book.

20.1 Justifying Lines of Text

Consider the following problem. Write a procedure that justifies lines of text by inserting extra spaces between words so that the last word on each line ends in the last column. For example, using "#" to denote a blank, the three lines

(20.1.1)   justifying#lines#by#########
            inserting#extra#blanks#is##
            one#task#of#a#text#editor.#

might appear justified as

(20.1.2)   justifying#####lines#####by
            inserting#extra##blanks##is
            one##task#of#a#text#editor.

Several restrictions are placed on how blanks are to be inserted between words, in order to lessen the visual impact of justification. The number of

blanks between different pairs of adjacent words on a line should differ by
no more than one. Secondly, so that long gaping holes don't appear on
one side of the paper, an alternating technique should be used: for even
(odd) lines, more blanks should be inserted on the right (left) side of the
line if necessary. For example, line 2 of (20.1.1) is changed to line 2 of
(20.1.2) by inserting the 2 extra blanks just before the ultimate and the
penultimate word on the line; on line 3, the only extra blank is inserted
after the first word.

We will write a procedure to calculate the column numbers of the
beginning of the words in the justified line, given their column numbers in
the unjustified line. For line 1 above, the list $(1, 12, 18)$ of column
numbers where the words begin will be changed to the list $(1, 16, 26)$ of
column numbers where the words begin in the justified line 1 of (20.1.2).
For line 2, the input list $(1, 11, 17, 24)$ will be changed to $(1, 11, 18, 26)$.

The following procedure heading is suggested:

> **proc** *justify* (**value** n, z, s: *integer*;
>   **var** b: **array of** *integer*);
> Line z has n words on it. They begin in columns $b[1]$, ...,
> $b[n]$. Exactly one blank separates each adjacent pair of words.
> Parameter s is the total number of extra blanks that must be
> inserted between words in order to justify a line. The procedure
> determines new column numbers $b[1:n]$ so that the line is justi-
> fied in the manner described above.

Beginning the development

Given the task of writing procedure *justify*, how would you proceed?

The first step is to write pre- and postconditions for the procedure body.
We begin with the precondition. The words themselves are not part of
the specification, since only column numbers are given. So the precondition won't be written in terms of words. But it may help to give an
intepretation of the precondition in terms of words. Initially, the input
line has the form

$$W1 \; [1] \; W2 \; [1] \; ... \; [1] \; Wn \; [s]$$

where W1 is the first word, W2 the second, ..., Wn the last, s is the
number of extra blanks, and the number of blanks at each place has been
shown within brackets. The precondition Q itself must give restrictions
on the input —e.g. that there cannot be a negative number of words or of
extra blanks. In addition, because array b will be modified, it is

20.2 The Longest Upsequence

Consider a sequence of values $(v_0, \cdots, v_{n-1})$. If one deletes i (not necessarily adjacent) values from the list, one has a subsequence of length $n-i$. This subsequence is called an *upseqence* if its values are in non-decreasing order. For example, the list $(1,3,4,6,2,4)$ has a subsequence $(1,3,2)$, which is not an upsequence, and another subsequence $(1,3,6)$, which is an upsequence.

We want to write a program that, given a sequence in $b[0{:}n-1]$, where $n > 0$, calculates the length of the longest upsequence of $b[0{:}n-1]$. As an abbreviation, use the notation $lup(s)$ to mean:

$lup(s) = $ the length of the longest upsequence of sequence s

Thus, using a variable k to contain the answer, the program has the pre- and postconditions:

$Q{:}\ n > 0$
$R{:}\ k = lup(b[0{:}n-1])$

Note that a change in any one value of a sequence could change its longest upsequence, and this means that possibly every value of a sequence s must be interrogated to determine $lup(s)$. This suggests a loop. Begin by writing a possible invariant and an outline of the loop.

The loop will interrogate the values of $b[0{:}n-1]$ in some order. Since $lup(b[0{:}0])$ is 1, a possible invariant can be derived by replacing the constant n of R by a variable:

$P{:}\ 1 \leq i \leq n \ \wedge \ k = lup(b[0{:}i-1])$

The loop itself will have the form

$i, k := 1, 1;$
do $i \neq n \rightarrow$ increase i, maintaining P **od**

Increasing i extends the sequence $b[0{:}i-1]$ for which k is the length of a longest upsequence, and hence may call for an increase in k. Whether k is to be increased depends on whether $b[i]$ is at least as large as a value that ends a longest upsequence of $b[0{:}i-1]$ (there may be more than one longest upsequence). It makes sense to maintain information in other variables so that such a test can be efficiently made. What is the minimum information needed to ascertain whether k should be increased?

The *smallest* value m (say) that ends an upsequence of length k of $b[0: i-1]$ must be known, for then $b[0:i]$ has an upsequence of length $k+1$ *iff* $b[i] \geqslant m$. Therefore, we revise invariant P to include m:

$$P: \ 1 \leqslant i \leqslant n \ \wedge \ k = lup(b[0:i-1]) \ \wedge$$
$$m \text{ is the smallest value in } b[0:i-1] \text{ that ends an}$$
$$\text{upsequence of length } k$$

In the case $b[i] \geqslant m$, k can be increased and m set to $b[i]$, so that the program thus far looks like

$$i, k, m := 1, 1, b[0]; \ \{P\}$$
$$\textbf{do } i \neq n \ \rightarrow \ \textbf{if } b[i] \geqslant m \ \rightarrow \ k, m := k+1, b[i]$$
$$\qquad\qquad\qquad [] \ b[i] < m \ \rightarrow \ ?$$
$$\qquad\qquad \textbf{fi};$$
$$\qquad\qquad i := i+1$$
$$\textbf{od}$$

The question now becomes what to do if $b[i] < m$. Variable k should not be changed, but what about m? Under what condition must m be changed?

If $b[0:i-1]$ contains an upsequence of length $k-1$ that ends in a value $\leqslant b[i]$, then $b[i]$ ends an upsequence of length k of $b[0:i]$. If, in addition, $b[i] < m$, then m must be changed. In order to check this condition, consider maintaining the minimum value $m1$ that ends an upsequence of length $k-1$ of $b[0:i-1]$.

This means that two values are needed: the minimum value m that ends an upsequence of length k and the minimum value $m1$ that ends an upsequence of length $k-1$. Judging by the development thus far, can you generalize this?

Maintaining m caused us to introduce $m1$; maintaining $m1$ will cause us to introduce $m2$ to contain the minimum value that ends an upsequence of length $k-2$. And so on. Therefore, an array of values is needed. We modify the invariant once more:

(20.2.1) $P: \ 1 \leqslant i \leqslant n \ \wedge \ k = lup(b[0:i-1]) \ \wedge$
$$(A j: \ 1 \leqslant j \leqslant k: \ m[j] \text{ is the smallest value that ends}$$
$$\text{an upsequence of length } j \text{ of } b[0:i-1])$$

And the program is changed to

```
i, k, m[1]:= 1, 1, b[0];  {P}
do i ≠ n → if b[i] ⩾ m[k] → k:= k+1;  m[k]:= b[i]
           [] b[i] < m[k] → ?
           fi;
           i:= i+1
od
```

Before proceeding further, it makes sense to investigate array m; does it have any properties that might be useful?

Array m is ordered, because the minimum value that ends an upsequence of length j (say) must be at most the minimum value that ends an upsequence of length $j+1$.

We are now faced with determining which values of $m[1:k]$ must be changed in case $b[i] < m[k]$. Solve this problem.

The case $b[i] < m[1]$ is the easiest to handle. Since $m[1]$ is the smallest value that ends an upsequence of length 1 of $b[0:i-1]$, if $b[i] < m[1]$, then $b[i]$ is the smallest value in $b[0:i]$ and it should become the new $m[1]$. No other value of m need be changed, since all upsequences of $b[0:i-1]$ end in a value larger than $b[i]$.

Finally, consider the case $m[1] ⩽ b[i] < m[k]$. Which values of m should be changed? Clearly, only those greater than $b[i]$ can be changed, since they represent minimum values. So suppose we find the j satisfying

$$m[j-1] ⩽ b[i] < m[j]$$

Then $m[1:j-1]$ should not be changed. Next, since $m[j-1]$ ends an upsequence of length $j-1$ of $b[0:i-1]$, $b[i]$ ends an upsequence of length j of $b[0:i]$. Hence, $m[j]$ should be changed to $b[i]$. Finally, $m[j+1:k]$ should not be changed (why?).

Binary search (exercise 4 of section 16.3) can be used to locate j. The final program is given in (20.2.2).

The execution time of program (20.2.2) is proportional to $(n \log n)$ in the worst case and to n in the best. It requires space proportional to n in the worst case, for array m. It uses a technique called "dynamic programming", although it was developed without conscious knowledge of that technique.

(20.2.2) $i, k, m[1] := 1, 1, b[0]; \{P\}$
$\{inv: (20.2.1); bound: n-i\}$
do $i \neq n \rightarrow$ **if** $b[i] \geq m[k]$ $\rightarrow k := k+1; m[k] := b[i]$
         $[\!]\ b[i] < m[1]$ $\rightarrow m[1] := b[i]$
         $[\!]\ m[1] \leq b[i] < m[k] \rightarrow$
              Establish $m[j-1] \leq b[i] < m[j]$:
              $h, j := 1, k;$
              $\{inv: 1 \leq h < j \leq k \wedge m[h] \leq b[i] < m[j]\}$
              $\{bound: j-h-1\}$
              do $h \neq j-1 \rightarrow e := (h+j) \div 2;$
                        if $m[e] \leq b[i] \rightarrow h := e$
                        $[\!]\ m[e] > b[i] \rightarrow j := e$
                        fi
         od;
         $m[j] := b[i]$
    fi;
    $i := i+1$
od

Exercises for Chapter 20

1. (Unique 5-bit Sequences). Consider sequences of 36 bits. Each such sequence has 32 5-bit sequences consisting of *adjacent* bits. For example, the sequence 1101011... contains the 5-bit sequences 11010, 10101, 01011, ... Write a program that prints all 36-bit sequences with the two properties

  (1) The first 5 bits of the sequence are 00000.
  (2) No two 5-bit subsequences are the same.

2. (The Next Higher Permutation). Suppose array $b[0:n-1]$ contains a sequence of (not necessarily different) digits, e.g. $n = 6$ and $b[0:5] = (2, 4, 3, 6, 2, 1)$. Consider this sequence as the integer 243621. For any such sequence (except for the one whose digits are in decreasing order) there exists a permutation of the digits that yields the next higher integer (using the same digits). For the example, it is $(2, 4, 6, 1, 2, 3)$, which represents the integer 246123.

Write a program that, given an array $b[0:n-1]$ that has a next higher permutation, changes b into that next higher permutation.

3. (Different Adjacent Subsequences). Consider sequences of 1's, 2's and 3's. Call a sequence *good* if no two adjacent non-empty subsequences of it are the same. For example, the following sequences are *good*:

    2
    32
    32123
    1232123

The following sequences are bad (not *good*):

        33
        32121323
        123123213

It is known that a good sequence exists, of any length. Consider the "alphabetical ordering" of sequences, where sequence $s1$.<. sequence $s2$ if, when considered as decimal fractions, $s1$ is less than $s2$. For example, 123 .<. 1231 because .123 < .1231 and 12 .<. 13. Note that if we allow 0's in a sequence, then $s1 \mid 0$.=. $s1$. For example, 110 .=. 11, because .110 = .11.

   Write a program that, given a fixed integer $n \geqslant 0$, stores in array $b[0{:}n-1]$ the smallest *good* sequence of length n.

4. (The Line Generator). Given is some text stored one character to an array element in array $b[0{:}n-1]$. The possible characters are the letter A, ..., Z, a blank and a new line character (NL). The text is considered to be a sequence of words separated by blanks and new line characters. Desired is a program that breaks the text into lines in a two-dimensional array $line[0{:}nolines-1, 0{:}maxpos-1]$, with $line[0, 0{:}maxpos-1]$ being the first line, $line[1, 0{:}maxpos-1]$ being the second line, etc. The lines must satisfy the following properties:

   1. No word is split onto two lines.

   2. Each line contains no more than *maxpos* characters.

   3. A line contains as many words as possible, with one blank between each pair of words. Lines are padded on the end with blanks to *maxpos* characters.

   4. A new line character denotes the end of a line, but will not appear in array *line*.

5. (Perm_to_Code). Let N be an integer, $N > 0$, and let $X[0{:}N-1]$ be an array that contains a permutation of the integers $0, 1, \cdots, N-1$:

$$perm(X[0{:}N-1], (0, 1, \cdots, N-1))$$

For X, we can define a second array $X'[0{:}N-1]$ as follows. For each i, element $X'[i]$ is the number of values in $X[0{:}i-1]$ that are less than $X[i]$. For example, we show one possible array X and the corresponding array X', for $N = 6$.

$$X = (2, 0, 3, 1, 5, 4)$$
$$X' = (0, 0, 2, 1, 4, 4)$$

Formally, array X' satisfies

$$(A\ i{:}\ 0 \leqslant i < N{:}\ X'[i] = (N\ j{:}\ 0 \leqslant j < i{:}\ X[j] < X[i]))$$

Write a program that, given an array x that contains a permutation X of $\{0, \cdots, N-1\}$, changes x so that it contains the corresponding values X'. The program may use other simple variables, but no arrays besides x.

6. (Code_to_Perm). Read exercise 5. Write a program that, given an array $x = X'$, where X' is the code for permutation X, stores X in x. No other arrays should be used.

7. (The Non-Crooks). Array $f[0:F-1]$ contains the names of people who work at Cornell, in alphabetical order. Array $g[0:G-1]$ contains the names of people on welfare in Ithaca, in alphabetical order. Thus, neither array contains duplicates and both arrays are monotonically increasing:

$$f[0]<f[1]<f[2]< \cdots <f[F-1]$$
$$g[0]<g[1]<g[2]< \cdots <g[G-1]$$

Count the number of people who are presumably not crooks: those that appear in at least one array but not in both.

8. Read exercise 7. Suppose the arrays may contain duplicates, but the arrays are still ordered. Write a program that counts the number of distinct names that are not on both lists —i.e. don't count duplicates.

9. (Period of a Decimal Expansion). For $n > 1$, the decimal expansion of $1/n$ is periodic. That is, it consists of an initial sequence of digits $d_1 \cdots d_i$ followed by a sequence $d_{i+1} \cdots d_{i+j}$ that is repeated over and over. For example, $1/4 = .2500000...$, so the sequence 0 is repeated over and over ($i = 2$ and $j = 1$), while $1/7 = .142857142857142857...$, so the sequence 142857 is repeated over and over ($i = 0$ and $j = 6$, although one can take i to be any positive integer also). Write a program to find the length j of the repeating part. Use only simple variables —no arrays.

10. (Due to W.H.J. Feijen) Given is an array $g[0:N-1]$, $N \geqslant 2$, satisfying $0 \leqslant g[0] \leqslant \cdots < g[N-1]$. Define

$$h_1 = g[0]+g[1]$$
$$h_k = h_{k-1}+g[k] \text{ for } 1<k \leqslant N-1$$

Write a program to construct an array $X[0:2*N-2]$ containing the values

$$g[0], \cdots ,g[N-1],h_1, \cdots ,h_{N-1}$$

in increasing order. The execution speed of the program should be linear in N.

11. (Exponentiation). Write a program that, given two integers $x \geqslant 0$ and $y > 0$, calculates the value $z = x^y$. The binary representation $b_{k-1} \cdots b_1 b_0$ of y is also given, and the program can refer to bit i using the notation b_i. Further, the value k is given. The program is to begin with $z = 1$ and reference each bit of the binary representation once, in the order $b_{k-1}, b_{k-2}, \cdots$.

Chapter 21
Inverting Programs

Wouldn't it be nice to be able to run a program backwards or, better yet, to derive from one program P a second program P^{-1} that computes the inverse of P? That means that running P followed by P^{-1} would be the same as not running any program at all! Also, if we had the result of executing P, but had lost the input, we could execute P^{-1} to determine that input. This chapter is devoted to having fun inverting programs.

Some Simple Program Inversions

Some simple commands are easily inverted. The inverse of $x := x+1$, written $(x := x+1)^{-1}$, is $x := x-1$. But some commands are not invertible. For example, computing the inverse of $x := 1$ requires knowledge of the value of x before the assignment. Such a command may be invertible with respect to a precondition, though. For example, the inverse of

$$\{x = 3\} \ x := 1$$

is

$$\{x = 1\} \ x := 3$$

Thus, execution of the first begins with $x = 3$ and ends with $x = 1$, while execution of the second does the opposite. (Note carefully how one gets an inverse by reading backwards —except that the assertion becomes the command and the command becomes the assertion. This itself is a sort of inversion.) This example shows that we may have to compute inverses of programs *together with* their pre- and/or postconditions.

The command $x := x*x$ has no inverse, because two different initial values $x = 2$ and $x = -2$ yield the same result $x = 4$. To have an inverse, a program must yield a different result for each different input.

Swapping two variables

What is the inverse of $x, y := y, x$? By reading the symbols of the command in reverse, or inverse, order, we get $x, y := y, x$. And sure enough, the command $x, y := y, x$ is its own inverse!

The idea of copying a program in reverse order to get its inverse is appealing, so let us push it further. Let's compute the inverse of

(21.1) $x := x + y; \quad y := x - y; \quad x := x - y$

Executing backwards to undo the effects of execution of this sequence would mean first undoing —or executing the inverse of— the third command $x := x - y$, then undoing the second one, $y := x - y$, and finally undoing the first one, $x := x + y$. We write this as follows, where again the superscript -1 denotes inversion:

(21.2) $(x := x - y)^{-1}; \; (y := x - y)^{-1}; \; (x := x + y)^{-1}$

The inverse of $x := x - y$ is $x := x + y$, and vice versa. Let's calculate the inverse of $y := x - y$. This is equivalent to $y := -(y - x)$, which is equivalent to $y := y - x; \; y := -y$. The inverse of this sequence is $y := -y$; $y := y + x$, which is equivalent to $y := -y + x$, which is equivalent to $y := x - y$. Hence, $y := x - y$ is its own inverse, and (21.2) is equivalent to

$$x := x + y; \quad y := x - y; \quad x := x - y$$

But then (21.1) is its own inverse! We leave to exercise 1 the proof that (21.1) swaps the values of the integer variables x and y.

Inversion of general commands

With this introduction to the idea of inversion, we now investigate some inversions that will be needed later. In doing so, keep in mind the general method of reading backwards.

The inverse of skip. The inverse of *skip* would be *piks*, so we will have to introduce *piks* as a synonym for *skip*.

The inverse of S1; S2; $\cdots$; Sn. According to what we did previously, the inverse of a sequence of commands is the reverse of the sequence of inverses of the individual commands.

$$(S1; \; S2; \; \cdots; \; Sn)^{-1} \; = \; Sn^{-1}; \; \cdots; \; S2^{-1}; \; S1^{-1}$$

The inverse of $x := c1$; S $\{x = c2\}$, where c1 and c2 are constants. This is a kind of a "block". A new variable x is initialized to a value $c1$, S is executed, and upon termination x has a final value $c2$. The inverse assigns $c2$ to x, executes the inverse of S, and terminates with $x = c1$:

$$(x := c1; \ S \ \{x = c2\})^{-1} \ = \ x := c2; \ S^{-1} \ \{x = c1\}$$

Note how, in performing the inversion, the assertion becomes an assignment and the assignment becomes an assertion.

The inverse of an alternative command. Consider the command

(21.3) $\{B1 \lor B2\}$ **if**
$$B1 \ \rightarrow \ S1 \ \{R1\}$$
$$\square$$
$$B2 \ \rightarrow \ S2 \ \{R2\}$$
$$\textbf{fi} \ \{R1 \lor R2\}$$

Execution must begin with at least one guard true, so the disjunction of the guards has been placed before the command. Execution terminates with either $R1$ or $R2$ true, depending on which command is executed, so $R1 \lor R2$ is the postcondition.

To perform the inverse of (21.3), we must know whether to perform the inverse of $S2$ or to perform the inverse of $S1$, since only one of them is executed when (21.3) is executed. To determine this requires knowing which of $R2$ and $R1$ is true, which means they cannot both be true at the same time. We therefore require that $R1 \land R2 = F$. For symmetry, we also require $B1 \land B2 = F$.

Now let's develop the inverse of (21.3). Begin at the end of (21.3) and read backwards. The last line of (21.3) gives us the first line of the inverse: $\{R2 \lor R1\}$ **if**. This makes sense; since (21.3) must end in a state satisfying $R1 \lor R2$, its inverse must begin in a state satisfying $R2 \lor R1$.

Reading the fourth line backwards gives us the first guarded command:

$$R2 \ \rightarrow \ S2^{-1} \ \{B2\}$$

This is understood as follows. Execution of (21.3) beginning with $B2$ true executes $S2$ and establishes $R2$. Execution of its inverse beginning with $R2$ true undoes what $S2$ has done, thus establishing $B2$.

Note carefully how, when inverting a guarded command with a postcondition, the guard and postcondition switch places.

Continuing to read backwards yields the following inverse of (21.3) (provided $R1 \land R2 = F$):

(21.4) $\{R2 \lor R1\}$ **if**
$$R2 \to S2^{-1} \{B2\}$$
$$[\!]$$
$$R1 \to S1^{-1} \{B1\}$$
fi $\{B2 \lor B1\}$

The inverse of an iterative command. Consider the command

(21.5)   **do** $B1 \to S1$ **od** $\{\neg B1\}$

Loop (21.5) contains the barest information —it is annotated only with the fact that $B1$ is false upon termination. It turns out that a loop invariant is not needed to invert a loop.

From previous experience in inverting an alternative command, we know that a guarded command to be inverted requires a postcondition. Further, we can expect $\neg B1$ to become the precondition of the loop (because we read backwards) and therefore the loop must have a precondition that will become the postcondition. The two occurrences of $B1$ in (21.5), lead us to insert another predicate $C1$ as follows:

(21.6) $\{\neg C1\}$ **do** $B1 \to S1$ $\{C1\}$ **od** $\{\neg B1\}$

Now it's easy to invert: simply read backwards, inverting the delimiters **do** and **od** and inverting a guarded command as done earlier in the case of the alternative command. The inverse of (21.6) is

(21.7) $\{\neg B1\}$ **do** $C1 \to S1^{-1} \{B1\}$ **od** $\{\neg C1\}$

Inverting swap_equals

In section 16.5 a program was developed to swap two non-overlapping sections $b[i:i+n-1]$ and $b[j:j+n-1]$ of equal size n, where $n \geq 0$. The invariant for the loop of the program is $0 \leq k \leq n$ together with

	i	$i+k-1$	$i+k$	$i+n-1$			j	$j+k-1$	$j+k$	$j+n-1$
b	swapped		unswapped		$\land$	b	swapped		unswapped	

The bound function is $n-k$ and the program is

$$k := 0;$$
$$\textbf{do } k \neq n \to b[i+k], b[j+k] := b[j+k], b[i+k]; \ k := k+1 \textbf{ od}$$

This program looks like a "block", in that a new variable k is initialized. To use the inversion technique described earlier for a block it must have a postcondition that describes the value of k. This postcondition is $k = n$, the complement of the guard of the loop. Also, to invert the loop we will need a precondition for it and a postcondition for its body; these can be $k = 0$ and $k \neq 0$, respectively. Thus, we rewrite the program as

(21.8) $k := 0;$
  $loop: \{k = 0\}$
    do $k \neq n \rightarrow$
      $b[i+k], b[j+k] := b[j+k], b[i+k]; k := k+1 \{k \neq 0\}$
    od
    $\{k = n\}$
  $\{k = n\}$

where *loop* labels the five indented lines: the loop and its pre- and post-conditions. Using the rule for inverting a block, we find the inverse of this program to be

  $k := n; \ loop^{-1} \{k = 0\}$

Using the rule for inverting the loop, we find $loop^{-1}$ to be

  pool:
   $\{k = n\}$
   do $k \neq 0 \rightarrow$
    $(b[i+k], b[j+k] := b[j+k], b[i+k]; k := k+1)^{-1} \{k \neq n\}$ **od**
   $\{k = 0\}$

Further, the body of the loop —the inverse of the multiple assignment in the original loop— is

  $k := k-1; \ b[i+k], b[j+k] := b[j+k], b[i+k]$

Putting this together yields the inverse of program 21.2.1:

  $k := n;$
  $pool: \{k = n\}$
    do $k \neq 0 \rightarrow$
      $k := k-1; \ b[i+k], b[j+k] := b[j+k], b[i+k] \{k \neq n\}$ **od**
    $\{k = 0\}$
  $\{k = 0\}$

Note how the original program swaps values beginning with the first elements of the sections, while its inverse begins with the last elements and works its way backward. Note also that (21.8) is its own inverse, so (21.8) has at least two inverses.

Inverting Perm_to_Code

Exercise 5 of chapter 20 was to write a program for the following problem. Let N be an integer, $N > 0$, and let $X[0:N-1]$ be an array that contains a permutation of the integers $0, 1, \cdots, N-1$. Formally,

(21.9) $perm(X[0:N-1], \{0, 1, \cdots, N-1\})$

For X, we define a second array $X'[0:N-1]$ as follows. Element $X'[i]$ is the number of values in $X[0:i-1]$ that are $< X[i]$. As an example, we show one possible array X and the corresponding array X', for $N = 6$:

(21.10) $X = (2, 0, 3, 1, 5, 4)$
$\quad\quad\;\; X' = (0, 0, 2, 1, 4, 4)$

X' is called the *code* for X. Formally, array X' satisfies

(21.11) $(A\,i: 0 \leqslant i < N: X'[i] = (N\,j: 0 \leqslant j < i: X[j] < X[i]))$

Write a program that, given an array x containing a permutation X of $\{0, \cdots, N-1\}$, changes x so that it contains the code X' for X instead. The program may use other simple variables, but no arrays besides x.

We now develop the program and then invert it; this constructively proves that for each permutation X there exists exactly one code X', and vice versa.

The program is to convert an array x containing an initial value X into its code X'. A possible specification is therefore

$\quad\quad \{(A\,i: 0 \leqslant i < N: x[i] = X[i])\}$
$\quad\quad S$
$\quad\quad \{(A\,i: 0 \leqslant i < N: x[i] = X'[i])\}$

Each element of array x must be changed, so it probably requires iteration. What is a possible loop invariant?

We try to write a loop that changes one value of array x from its initial to its final value at each iteration. The usual strategy in such cases is to replace a constant of the result assertion by a variable. Here, we can replace 0 or N, which leads to calculating the array values in descending or ascending order of subscript value, respectively. Which should we do?

In example (21.10), the values $X[N-1]$ and $X'[N-1]$ are the same. If the last values of X and X' were always the same, working in descending order of subscript values might make more sense. So let's try to prove that they are always the same.

$X[N-1]$ is the last value of X. Since the array values are 0, ..., $N-1$, there are exactly $X[N-1]$ values less than $X[N-1]$ in $X[0:N-2]$. But $X'[N-1]$ is *defined* to be the number of values in $X[0:N-2]$ less than $X[N-1]$. Hence, $X[N-1]$ and $X'[N-1]$ are the same.

Replacing the constant 0 of the postcondition by a variable k yields the first attempt at an invariant:

$$0 \leqslant k \leqslant N \wedge (A\ i: k \leqslant i < N: x[i] = X'[i])$$

But the invariant must also indicate that the lower part of x still contains its initial value, so we rewrite the invariant as

$$0 \leqslant k \leqslant N \wedge (A\ i: k \leqslant i < N: x[i] = X'[i]) \wedge$$
$$(A\ i: 0 \leqslant i < k: x[i] = X[i])$$

The obvious bound function is k, and the loop invariant can be established using $k := N$.

There is still a big problem with using this as the loop invariant. We began developing the invariant by noticing that $X[N-1] = X'[N-1]$, so that the final value of $x[N-1]$ was the same as its initial value. To generalize this situation, at each iteration we would like $x[k-1]$ to contain its final value, but the invariant developed thus far doesn't indicate this.

The generalization would work if at each iteration $x[0:k-1]$ contained a permutation of the integers $\{0, \cdots, k-1\}$ and if the code for this permutation was equal to $X'[0:k-1]$. But this is not the case: the invariant does not even indicate that $x[0:k-1]$ is a permutation of the integers $\{0, \cdots, k-1\}$.

Perhaps x can be modified during each iteration so that this is the case. Let us rewrite the invariant as

$$P: 0 \leqslant k \leqslant N \wedge (A\ i: k \leqslant i < N: x[i] = X'[i]) \wedge$$
$$perm(x[0:k-1], \{0, \cdots, k-1\}) \wedge x[0:k-1]' = X'[0:k-1]$$

The program will therefore have the form

```
k := N;
do k ≠ 0 → k := k-1;
            Reestablish P
od
```

The question is how to reestablish P. Note that, after executing $k := k-1$, $x[0:k-1]$ contains the set $\{0, \cdots, k\}$ minus the value $x[k]$. If we subtract 1 from every value in $x[0:k-1]$ that is $> x[k]$, $x[0:k-1]$ will contain a permutation of $\{0, \cdots, k-1\}$. For example, if we begin with

$$x = (2, 5, 4, 1, 0, 3) \quad \text{and} \quad k = 6$$

the first iteration will reduce k to yield

$$x = (2, 5, 4, 1, 0, 3) \quad \text{and} \quad k = 5$$

and then change x to yield

$$x = (2, 4, 3, 1, 0, 3) \quad \text{and} \quad k = 5$$

It is easily seen that the permutation $(2, 4, 3, 1, 0)$ is consistent with the original one, in the sense that the code for $(2, 4, 3, 1, 0)$ is the same as the first 5 integers of the code for the original array $(2, 5, 4, 1, 0, 3)$. And, in general, the code $x[0:k-1]'$ for $x[0:k-1]$ will be the same as $X'[0:k-1]$, because the values in $x[0:k-1]$ will be in the same relative order as the values in $X[0:k-1]$.

These considerations lead directly to program 21.12; the invariant of the inner loop is simple enough to leave to the reader.

```
(21.12) k := N;
        do k ≠ 0 →
           k := k −1;
           Subtract 1 from every member of x[0:k−1] that is > x[k]:
           j := 0;
           do j ≠ k → {x[j] ≠ x[k]}
                      if x[j] > x[k] → x[j]:= x[j]−1
                      [] x[j] < x[k] → skip
                      fi;
                      j := j+1
           od
        od
```

We want to invert program 21.12. The first step is to insert assertions so that the inversions given earlier can be applied. We have left out the pre- and postconditions of the alternative command, since they are just the disjunctions of the guards and postconditions of the commands, respectively.

$$k := N;$$
$$loopa: \{k = N\}$$

        do $k \neq 0 \rightarrow$

          $k := k - 1;$

          $j := 0;$

          $loopb: \{j = 0\}$

                do $j \neq k \rightarrow$

                    if $x[j] > x[k] \rightarrow x[j] := x[j] - 1 \; \{x[j] \geqslant x[k]\}$

                    [] $x[j] < x[k] \rightarrow skip \; \{x[j] < x[k]\}$

                    fi;

                    $j := j + 1$

                  $\{j \neq 0\}$

                od

                $\{j = k\}$

          $\{j = k\}$

          $\{k \neq N\}$

        od

        $\{k = 0\}$

$\{k = 0\}$

Now invert the program, step by step, applying the inversion rules given earlier. First, invert the block $k := N;$ *loopa* $\{k = 0\}$ to yield $k := 0;$ *loopa*$^{-1}$ $\{k = N\}$. Next, *loopa*$^{-1}$ is

$$apool: \{k = 0\}$$

        do $k \neq N \rightarrow (k := k - 1; \; j := 0; \; loopb \; \{j = k\})^{-1} \; \{k \neq 0\}$ **od**

        $\{k = N\}$

Continuing in this fashion yields the following inverse of (21.11).

```
    k := 0;
    apool: {k =0}
            do k ≠ N →
              j:= k;
              bpool: {j =k}
                      do j ≠0 →
                        j:= j−1;
                        if x[k]>x[j] → piks {x[k]>x[j]}
                        [] x[k]≤x[j] → x[j]:= x[j]+1 {x[k]<x[j]}
                        fi
                        {j ≠k}
                      od;
                        {j =0}
              {j =0}
              k := k +1
              {k ≠0}
            od
            {k = N}
    {k = N}
```

or, without the assertions,

```
    k := 0;
    do k ≠ N →
      j:= k;
      do j ≠0 →
        j:= j−1;
        if x[k]>x[j] → piks
        [] x[k]≤x[j] → x[j]:= x[j]+1
        fi
      od;
      k := k +1
    od
```

Exercises for Chapter 21

1. Prove that $wp((21.1), x = X \land y = Y) = (x = Y \land y = X)$

2. Is $x := x/2$ invertible in theory? in practice? Is $x := x \div 2$ invertible?

3. Invert program Array Reversal (exercise 2 of 16.5).

4. Invert program Link Reversal (exercise 6 of 16.5). What is the problem with it?

5. Invert the program of exercise 1, section 18.1.

6. Discover and invert some interesting programs of your own.

Chapter 22
Notes on Documentation

Almost all programs in this book have been written in the guarded command notation, with the addition of multiple assignment, procedure call and procedure declaration. To execute the programs on a computer usually requires translation into Pascal, PL/I, FORTRAN or another implemented language. Nevertheless, it still makes sense to use the guarded command notation because the method of program development is so intertwined with it. Remember Principle 18.3.11: program *into* a programming language, not *in* it.

In this chapter, we discuss the problems of writing programs in other languages as well as in the guarded command notation. We give general rules for indenting and formatting, describe problems with definitions and declarations of variables, and show by example how the guarded command notation might be translated into other languages.

22.1 Indentation

In the early days, programs were written in FORTRAN and assembly languages with no indentation whatsoever, and they were hard to understand because of it. The crutch that provided some measure of relief was the flaw chart, since it gave a two-dimensional representation that exhibited the program structure or "flow of control" more clearly.

Maintaining *two* different forms of the program —the text itself and the flaw chart— has always been prone to error because of the difficulty in keeping them consistent. Further, most programmers have never liked drawing flaw charts, and have often produced them only after programs were finished, and only because they were told to provide them as documentation. Therefore the relief expected from the use of flaw charts was missing when most needed —during program development.

Following some simple rules, indentation of a program provides a two-dimensional representation that shows its structure in simple manner. Further, indentation is something that a programmer can do as a matter of course, as a habit, *during* the programming process. Therefore, only *one* document is needed, the indented program. All the problems of consistency over two forms dissappear.

Good indentation obviates the need for a flaw chart.

We shall give some simple rules for indentation, which can be used with most available programming languages. There may be slight differences from language to language, but, in general, the rules are the same.

Sequential composition

Many programming conventions force the programmer to write each command on a separate line. This tends to spread a program out, making it difficult to keep the program on one page. Then, indentation becomes hard to follow. The rule to use is the following:

(22.1.1) •**Rule**: Successive commands can be written on the same line provided that, logically, they belong together.

Here is an example. In program 20.2.2, the following command is used to establish loop invariant $P: i,k,m[1] := 1, 1, b[0]$. In PL/I, which has no multiple assignment command, this can be written on one line as

$$i = 1; \quad k = 1; \quad m(1) = b(0); \quad /* P */$$

Together, the three assignments perform the single function of establishing P. There is no reason to force the programmer to write them as

$$i = 1;$$
$$k = 1;$$
$$m(1) = b(0);$$

(As an aside, note how the PL/I assignment is written with no blank to the left of $=$ and one blank to the right. Since PL/I uses the same symbol for equality and assignment, it behooves the programmer to find a way to make them appear different.)

Don't use rule 22.1.1 as a license to cram programs into as little space as possible; use the rule with care and reason.

The rule concerning indentation of sequences of commands is obvious:

(22.1.2)   **•Rule**: Commands of a sequence that appear on successive lines should begin in the same column.

Thus, don't write

$$i = 1;$$
$$k = 1;$$
$$m(1) = b(0);$$

Indenting subcommands

The rule concerning subcommands of a command is:

(22.1.3)   **•Rule**: Indent subcommands of a command 3 or 4 spaces from the column where the command begins (or more, if it seems appropriate).

For example, write

> **do** $a + 1 \neq b \;\rightarrow\; d := (a+b) \div 2;$
> $\quad\quad\quad\quad$ **if** $d*d \leq n \;\rightarrow\; a := d$
> $\quad\quad\quad\quad$ $[\!] \; d*d > n \;\rightarrow\; b := d$
> $\quad\quad\quad\quad$ **fi**
> **od**

or, in PL/I,

> DO WHILE $(a + 1 \,\neg= b);$
> $\quad d =$ FLOOR$((a+b)/2);$
> $\quad$ IF $d*d \leq n$
> $\quad\quad$ THEN $a = d;$
> $\quad\quad$ ELSE $b = d;$
> $\quad$ END;

Note that the body of the loop is indented. Further, the body is a sequence of two commands, which, following rule 22.1.2, begin in the same column. Also, the subcommands of the PL/I conditional statement are indented with respect to its beginning.

The PL/I conditional statement could also have been written as

> IF $d*d \leq n$ THEN $a = d;$
> $\quad\quad\quad$ ELSE $b = d;$

or even, since it is short and simple, on one line as

IF $d*d \leqslant n$ THEN $a = d$; ELSE $b = d$;

With respect to exact placement of THEN and ELSE, it doesn't matter what conventions you follow as long as (1) you are consistent and (2) rule 22.1.3 is followed, so that the structure of the program is easily seen. Consistency is important, so the reader knows what to expect.

Indentation can, and should, be used with FORTRAN. The loop given above could have been written in FORTRAN 77 as

```
C      DO WHILE (a+1 .NE. b); · · ·
05     IF (a+1 .NE. b) GOTO 25
10       d = FLOOR((a+b)/2)
         IF (d*d − n) 12, 12, 14
12         a = d
           GOTO 20
14         b = d
20       GOTO 05
25     CONTINUE
```

Assertions

As mentioned as early as chapter 6, it helps to put assertions in programs. Include enough so that the programmer can understand the program, but not so many that he is overwhelmed with detail. The most important assertion, of course, is the invariant of a loop. Actually, if the program is annotated with the precondition, the postcondition, an invariant for each loop, and a bound function for each loop, then the rest of the pre- and postconditions can, in principle, be generated automatically.

Assertions, of course, must appear as comments in languages that don't allow them as a construct. (Early versions of Ada included an "assert" statement; mature Ada does not.) Two rules govern the indentation of assertions:

(22.1.4) •**Rule**: The pre- and postcondition of a command should begin in the same column as the command.

(22.1.5) •**Rule**: A loop should be preceded by an invariant and a bound function; these should begin in the same column as the beginning of the loop.

We have used these rules throughout the book, so they should appear natural by now (naturalness must be learned). For two examples of the use of rule 22.1.5, see program 20.2.2.

Indentation of delimiters

There are three conventions for indenting a final delimiter (e.g. **od**, **fi** and the END; of PL/I). The first convention puts the delimiter on a separate line, beginning in the same column as the beginning of the command.

The second convention is to indent the delimiter the same distance as the subcommands of the command —as in the PL/I loop

> DO WHILE (*expression*);
>   . . .
>
>   . . .
>
> END;

This convention has the advantage that it is easy to determine which command sequentially follows this one: simply search down in the column in which the DO WHILE begins until a non-blank is found.

The third convention is to hide the delimiter completely on the last line of the command. For example,

> DO WHILE (*expression*);
>   . . .
>
>   . . . END;

or

> **do** *guard* → . . .
>   . . .
>
>   . . . **od**

This convention recognizes that the indenting rules make the end delimiters redundant. That is, if a compiler used the indentation to determine the program structure, the end delimiters wouldn't be necessary. The delimiters are still written, because they provide a useful redundancy that can be checked by the compiler, but they are hidden from view.

Which of the three conventions you use is not important; the important point is to be consistent, so that the reader is not surprised:

(22.1.6)   •**Rule**: Whatever convention you use for indenting end delimiters, use it consistently.

The command-comment

Some of the programs presented in this book, like program 20.2.2, have used an English sentence as a label (followed by a colon) or a comment. The English sentence was really a command to do something, and the program text that performed the command was indented underneath it. Here is an example.

Set z to the maximum of x and y:
 if $x \geqslant y \rightarrow z := x$
 $\boxed{} y \geqslant x \rightarrow z := y$
 fi

In Pascal, the English sentence would be a comment, and since comments are delimited by (* and *), this would appear as

(*Set z to the maximum of x and y*)
 if $x \geqslant y$ **then** $z := x$
  else $z := y$

In reading a program containing such a command-comment, the command-comment is considered to be a command in the program, just as any other. The program text *indented underneath it* is considered to be its refinement —it is a program segment that shows how to perform the command-comment.

When reading a program containing a command-comment, one need read the refinement only to understand *how* its refinement works; otherwise, one need only read the command-comment itself, which explains *what* is to be done. Command-comments can be used to break a program into pieces to reduce the amount of text the reader must look at in order to find something. Just as binary search allows one to find a value in a sorted list in logarithmic time, so judicious use of the command-comment allows one to wend one's way through a program to find something in a shorter time.

The use of command-comments during programming can be an invaluable aid, for it forces the programmer to be precise and also forces him to be careful about structuring the program. To be most helpful, and to be in keeping with the methodology presented in this book, the command-comment should be written *before* its refinement.

The command-comment must be precise: it must state exactly what its refinement does, in terms of its input and output variables. For example, the command-comment

Add elements of the array b together

is not precise enough, for it forces the reader to read the refinement in order to determine where the sum of the array elements is placed. Far better is the command-comment

> Store the sum of elements of $b[0:n-1]$ into x

or

> Given fixed $n \geq 0$ and fixed array b,
>   establish $x = (\Sigma j : 0 \leq j < n : b[j])$

As you can see from the last example, the command-comment can be in the form we have been using throughout the book for specifying a program (segment).

Here is the indentation rule for command-comments.

(22.1.7)   ●**Rule**: The command-comment itself has the level of indentation that any other command in its place would have. Its refinement, which follows it, is *indented* 3 or 4 spaces.

Some people use the convention that a command-commment and its refinement appear at the same level of indentation, e.g.

> (∗Set z to the maximum of x and y ∗)
> **if** $x \geq y$ **then** $z := x$
>   **else** $z := y$;
> $k := 20$

The reason for not using this convention should be clear from the example: one cannot tell where the refinement ends. Much better is to use rule 22.1.7:

> (∗Set z to the maximum of x and y ∗)
>   **if** $x \geq y$ **then** $z := x$
>   **else** $z := y$;
> $k := 20$

Judicious use of spacing (skipping lines) may help, but no simple rule for spacing after refinements can cover all cases if refinements are not indented. So follow rule 22.1.7.

One more point concerning indentation of comments. Don't insert them in such a manner that the structure of the program becomes hidden. For example, if a sequence of program commands begin in column 10, no comment between them should begin in columns to the left of column 10.

Keeping program segments small

One way to keep programs intellectually manageable is to keep program segments to a reasonable size, for the amount of detail that can be understood at any one time is limited. The rule usually used is to keep the procedural part (not counting specification and declarations) of a program segment to one page. This is not much of a restriction if procedures and macros are used reasonably to present the right level of abstraction and structure. In fact, it is often hard to make program segments that long.

The restriction to one page also helps to keep the indentation reasonable; without the restriction, the indentation can get ridiculously far to the right.

Procedure headings

As mentioned in chapter 12, the purpose of a procedure is to provide a level of abstraction: the user of a procedure need only know *what* the procedure does and how to call it, and not *how* the procedure works. To emphasize this, the procedure declaration should be indented as follows.

(22.1.8) •**Rule**: The procedure heading, which includes a list of the parameters, a specification of the parameters and a description of what the procedure does, appears at the same level of indenting as any command would be indented in that context. The procedure body is indented 3 or 4 columns with respect to the procedure heading.

It may be reasonable to have a blank line before and after the procedure declaration in order to set it off from the surrounding text.

As an example, here is a Pascal-like procedure declaration:

$(*Pre: n = N \wedge x = X \wedge b = B \wedge X \in B[0:N-1]*)$
$(*Post: 0 \leqslant i < N \wedge B[i] = X*)$
proc *search*(**value** n, x: *integer*;
                    value b: **array of** *integer*;
                    result i: *integer*);
        body of procedure

It may be worthwhile to give the pre- and post-conditions less formally (but not less precisely), as shown below. This is often more understandable than the pure predicate calculus approach.

(* Given fixed n, x and $b[0:N-1]$ satisfying $x \in b$, *)
(* store a value in i to establish $x = b[i]$ *)
proc *search*(**value** n, x: *integer*;
                        value b: **array of** *integer*;
                        result i: *integer*);
            body of procedure

As an aside, let us illustrate a special problem with PL/I. In PL/I, parameter specifications are treated in the same way as, and may appear along with, declarations of local variables. For example, one can write

/* Given fixed n, x and $b(0:n-1)$ satisfying $x \in b$,*/
/* Store a value in i to establish $x = b(i)$ */
search: PROC (n, x, b, i);
DCL $(n, x, b(*), k, i)$ FIXED;
            body of procedure
            END;

Writing a call on *search* requires knowledge of the types of the parameters, and in reading these types one is confronted with the declaration of the local variable k. To avoid this problem and to give the reader only what is necessary to write a call, the specification of the parameters should be separated from the declaration of the local variables:

/* Given fixed n, x and $b(0:n-1)$ satisfying $x \in b$, */
/* Store a value in i to establish $x = b(i)$ */
search: **proc** (n, x, b, i);
DCL $(n, x, b(*), i)$ FIXED;
      DCL k FIXED;
      body of procedure
      END;

22.2 Definitions and Declarations of Variables

The Definition of variables

Here is one of the simplest and most important strategies:

(22.2.1)   •**Strategy**: Define your variables before you use them, and then be sure to adhere to the definitions.

This strategy lies behind much of what has been presented in this book. A definition of a set of variables is simply an assertion about their logical relationship, which must be true at key places of the program. In the same vein, a loop invariant is only a definition of a set of variables that holds before and after each loop iteration. The balloon theory of section 16.1 simply gives heuristics for developing definitions of variables (in some cases) from the specification of the program.

Rule 22.2.1 seems so obvious; yet apparently it is difficult to learn and practice. Time and again I have found errors in a program —when its owner was unable to do so or thought it correct— by asking the critical question "what do these variables mean" and, after spending ten minutes with the owner determining what the definitions should have been, pointing out places in the program that destroyed the definitions.

The critical point is to precisely define variables before writing code that uses them and to adhere rigourously to these definitions.

Just as definitions of variables are important during program development, so they are important when reading a program. The reader should first be presented with these definitions, along with text to help understand them. Once the definitions are understood, the program itself is often obvious. On the other hand, it is grossly unprofessional and unfair to present a program without precise variable definitions.

Placement of definitions of variables

The proper place to put definitions of (most) variables is at the head of the program, along with their declarations. This has certain advantages:

> 1. It forces the grouping of variables by logical relationship (instead of by type or in haphazard order). The declarations for each logically related group of variables, together with their definition, should be set off as a group, perhaps with blank lines before and after it.

> 2. If written early enough and precisely enough, the definitions give the programmer an added checklist. Whenever he writes program text to change one variable of a group, he can refer to the definition of the group to see what others must be changed to maintain the definition. Note that the programming method defined in Part III is oriented towards defining variables before using them; the program specification, the loop invariant, etc., all come before the corresponding program text.

> 3. The reader knows where to look to understand a use of a variable: its declaration is accompanied by its definition and the definition of logically related variables.

4. Comments within the program text, for example command-comments, can refer to the definitions, thus shortening the program. For example, instead of writing the command-comment

> Add 1 to n, and then set $b[n]$ to ... and c to ... and $d[n]$ to the maximum of ... and then, if e is ... add to j ...

one can simply write

> Add 1 to n and reestablish its definition.

It is then up to the reader to read the definition and see what assertion must be reestablished.

Examples of declarations and definitions

We present a simple example in Pascal to illustrate proper placement of declarations and definitions; the reader should be able to extend this to more complicated and longer sequences of declarations.

The variables are used in a program that maintains a list of employees, their phone numbers, and the division in the company for which they work. Within the program, at times it will be necessary to build and process a list of people and their phone numbers in a particular division. Both lists will be maintained in alphabetical order. The following type declaration will be used

```
type String24 = packed array [1..24] of char;
     String8  = packed array [1..8] of char;
     Emprec  = record    (*Employee record *)
         name: String24;   (*Employee name: last name, first name *)
         phone: integer;    (*phone number (7 digits) *)
         division: String8  (*Division *)
       end;
     Phonerec= record
         name: String24;   (*Employee name: last name, first name *)
         phone: integer    (*phone number (7 digits) *)
       end
```

Note that the format of a name is given. Next is shown an example of how *not* to write the declarations; the reason will be explained below.

```
var staff: array [0..10000] of Emprec;
    phones: array [0..1000] of Phonerec;
    staffsize, divsize, i, j: integer;
    div: char;
    q: Phonerec;
```

These declarations suffer for several reasons. First, the variables have not been grouped by their logical relationship. From the name *staffsize*, one might deduce that this variable is logically related to array *staff*, but it need not be so. Also, there is no way to understand the purpose or need for *divsize*. Further, the definitions of globally important variables are mixed up with the definitions of local variables, which are used in only a few, adjacent places (*i* and *j*, for example).

Then there is no definition of the variables. For example, how do we know just *where* in array *staff* the employees can be found. Are they inserted at the beginning of the array, or the end, or in the middle? It has also not been indicated that the lists are sorted.

Here is a better version of these declarations.

> **var** *staff*: **array** [0..10000]   (**staff*[0:*staffsize*−1] are *)
>   **of** *Emprec*;   (*the employee records, *)
>   *staffsize*: *integer*;   (*in alphabetical order *)
>
>   *phones*: **array** [0..1000]   (**phones*[0:*divsize*−1] are *)
>   **of** *Phonerec*;   (*the employees in division *)
>   *divsize*: *integer*;   (**whichdiv*, in *)
>   *whichdiv*: *String* 8;   (*alphabetical order *)
>
>   *i*, *j*: *integer*;   *q*: *Phonerec*;

Now the variables are grouped according to their logical relationship, and definitions are given that describe the relationship. These definitions are actually invariants (but not loop invariants), which hold at (almost) all places of the program.

Variables *i*, *j* and *q* are presumably used only in a few, localized places, and hence need no definition at this point.

Note carefully the format of the declarations. The variables themselves begin in the same column, which makes it easy to find a particular variable when necessary. Further, the comments describing each group appear to the right of the variables, again all beginning in the same column. Spending a few minutes arranging the declarations in this format is worthwhile, for it aids the programmer as well as the reader.

One more point. Nothing is worse than a comment like "*i* is an index into array *b*". When defining variables, refrain from buzzwords like "pointer", "counter" and "index", for they serve only to point out the laziness and lack of precision of your thought. Of course, at times such comments may be worthwhile, but in general try to be more precise.

22.3 Writing Programs in Other Languages

Until the multiple assignment and guarded command notations find
their way into implemented programming notations, it will be necessary to
translate programs into Pascal, FORTRAN, PL/I or some other notation
in order to be able to execute them on a computer. The multiple assignment, alternative and iterative commands must be simulated using the
commands of the language into which a program is being translated.

Sometimes the translation is easy. For example, an iterative command
with one guarded command can be written using the Pascal or PL/I *while*
loop, and an alternative command can be written deterministically using
the case or SELECT statement. However, an iterative command with
more than one guarded command has no simple counterpart in these
other languages and must be simulated.

For example, consider program (16.4.5) for the Welfare Crook, which
finds the first value $f[iv]=g[jv]=k[hv]$ (which is guaranteed to exist)
that occurs in three ordered arrays $f[0:?]$, $g[0:?]$ and $h[0:?]$:

$$i, j, k := 0, 0, 0;$$
$$\{inv: 0 \leqslant i \leqslant iv \wedge 0 \leqslant j \leqslant jv \wedge 0 \leqslant k \leqslant kv\}$$
$$\{bound: i-iv+j-jv+k-kv\}$$
do $f[i]<g[j] \rightarrow i:=i+1$
$[]\ g[j]<h[k] \rightarrow j:=j+1$
$[]\ h[k]<f[i] \rightarrow k:=k+1$
od
$$\{i=iv \wedge j=jv \wedge k=kv\}$$

This program can be written in PL/I as

```
i= 0; j= 0; k= 0;
/*Simulate 3-guarded-command loop:*/
/*inv: 0≤i≤iv ∧ 0≤j≤jv ∧ 0≤k≤kv*/
/*bound: i−iv+j−jv+k−kv*/
LOOP:
    IF f(i)<g(j) THEN DO; i=i+1; GOTO LOOP; END;
    IF g(j)<h(k) THEN DO; j=j+1; GOTO LOOP; END;
    IF h(k)<f(i) THEN DO; k=k+1;GOTO LOOP; END;
/*i=iv ∧ j=jv ∧ k=kv*/
```

The convention used here is the following. The simulation of a guarded
command loop contains a comment indicating the simulation, a label
(*LOOP*) to jump to for the next iteration, and an IF-statement for each
of the guarded commands of the loop. Note that exactly one of the commands of the guarded commands will be executed at each iteration.

The same thing can be done in FORTRAN, although the language hampers succinctness of expression even more, as illustrated below. In the case of FORTRAN, a CONTINUE statement is used at the end of each simulated guarded command loop to indicate where to jump to upon termination of the loop. *Don't* label the following statement and jump to that labeled statement instead, for then the simulated loop is no longer independent of the rest of the program. It should be possible to take *any* command that performs a particular task and put it in another program, without modification, and this is not possible if the command contains a jump out of itself.

```
C     Simulate 3-guarded-command loop -labels 20-26
C       inv: 0 ≤ i ≤ iv ∧ 0 ≤ j ≤ jv ∧ 0 ≤ k ≤ kv
C       bound: i − iv + j − jv + k − kv
20        IF (f(i) .GE. g(j)) GOTO 22
            i = i + 1
          GOTO 20
22        IF (g(j) .GE. h(k)) GOTO 24
            j = j + 1
          GOTO 20
24        IF (h(k) .GE. f(i)) GOTO 26
            k = k + 1
          GOTO 20
26  CONTINUE
C       {i = iv ∧ j = jv ∧ k = kv}
```

These examples indicate how guarded commands can be simulated reasonably in other languages. Be sure to use the same conventions for simulating the iterative commands for *every* iterative command. Unless efficiency of the program is extremely important, don't try to use knowledge of the program to make the simulation more efficient or shorter. For the benefit of yourself and the reader, use the same convention for all similar constructs.

At this point, we give a program in four different notations: the notation of this book, Pascal, PL/I and FORTRAN. Each is fully documented, under the assumption that no other text will accompany it.

Program in the Notation of this Book

{The n words, $n \geqslant 0$, on line number z begin in columns $b[1]$, ..., $b[n]$. Exactly one blank separates each adjacent pair of words. s, $s \geqslant 0$, is the total number of blanks to insert between words to justify the line. Determine new column numbers $b[1{:}n]$ to represent the justified line. Result assertion R, below, specifies that the numbers of blanks inserted between different pairs of words differ by no more than one, and that extra blanks are inserted to the left or right, depending on the line number. Unless $0 \leqslant n \leqslant 1$, the justified line has the following format, where Wi is word i:

W1 $[p+1$ blanks$]$ ... $[p+1]$ Wt $[q+1]$ ... $[q+1]$ Wn

where p, q, t satisfy

$Q1$: $1 \leqslant t \leqslant n \wedge 0 \leqslant p \wedge 0 \leqslant q \wedge p*(t-1)+q*(n-t)=s \wedge$
$\quad (odd(z) \wedge q = p+1 \vee even(z) \wedge p = q+1)$

Using B to represent the initial value of array b, result assertion R is

R: $(0 \leqslant n \leqslant 1 \wedge b = B) \vee ((A\ i: 1 \leqslant i \leqslant t: b[i] = B[i]+p*(i-1)) \wedge$
$\quad (A\ i: t < i \leqslant n: b[i] = B[i]+p*(t-1)+q*(i-t)))\}$

```
proc justify (value n, z, s: integer;
                  var b: array of integer);
  var p, q, t, e, k: integer;
  if n ≤ 1 → skip
  [] 1 < n →
     Determine p, q and t:
        if even(z) → q := s ÷ (n−1); t := 1+(s mod (n−1)); p := q+1
        [] odd(z)  → p := s ÷ (n−1); t := n−(s mod (n−1)); q := p+1
        fi;
     Calculate new column numbers b[1:n]:
        k, e := n, s;
        {inv: t ≤ k ≤ n ∧ e = p*(t−1)+q*(k−t) ∧
              b[1:k] = B[1:k] ∧ b[k+1:n] has its final values}
        do k ≠ t → b[k] := b[k]+e; k, e := k−1, e−q od;
        {inv: 1 ≤ k ≤ t ∧ e = p*(t−1) ∧
              b[1:k] = B[1:k] ∧ b[k+1:n] has its final values}
        do e ≠ 0 → b[k] := b[k]+e; k, e := k−1, e−p od
  fi
```

Program in Pascal

(*The n words, $n \geq 0$, on line number z begin in columns $b(1)$, ..., $b(n)$. Exactly one blank separates each adjacent pair of words. s, $s \geq 0$, is the total number of blanks to insert between words to justify the line. Determine new column numbers $b(1:n)$ to represent the justified line. Result assertion R, below, specifies that the numbers of blanks inserted between different pairs of words differ by no more than one, and that extra blanks are inserted to the left or right, depending on the line number. Unless $0 \leq n \leq 1$, the justified line has the following format, where Wi represents word i:

W1 $[p+1$ blanks$]$ ... $[p+1]$ Wt $[q+1]$ ... $[q+1]$ Wn

where p, q, t satisfy

$Q1$: $1 \leq t \leq n \wedge 0 \leq p \wedge 0 \leq q \wedge p*(t-1)+q*(n-t)=s \wedge$
    $(odd(z) \wedge q=p+1 \vee even(z) \wedge p=q+1)$

Using B to represent the initial value of array b, result assertion R is

R: $(0 \leq n \leq 1 \wedge b=B) \vee ((A\ i\colon 1 \leq i \leq t\colon b(i)=B(i)+p*(i-1)) \wedge$
    $(A\ i\colon t < i \leq n\colon b(i)=B(i)+p*(t-1)+q*(i-t)))*)$

procedure *justify*$(n, z, s\colon$ *integer*; **var** b: **array of** *integer*);

var $p, q, t, e, k\colon$ *integer*;
begin if $n > 1$ **then**
  begin
  (*Determine p, q and t:*)
    if z **mod** $2 = 0$
      then begin $q := s$ **div** $(n-1)$; $t := 1+(s$ **mod** $(n-1))$; $p := q+1$ **end**
      else begin $p := s$ **div** $(n-1)$; $t := n-(s$ **mod** $(n-1))$; $q := p+1$ **end**;
  (*Calculate new column numbers $b(1:n)$:*)
    $k := n$; $e := s$;
    (*inv: $t \leq k \leq n \wedge e = p*(t-1)+q*(k-t) \wedge$
        $b(1:k)=B(1:k) \wedge b(k+1:n)$ has its final values*)
    while $k <> t$ **do begin** $b(k) := b(k)+e$; $k := k-1$; $e := e-q$ **end**;
    (*inv: $1 \leq k \leq t \wedge e = p*(t-1) \wedge$
        $b(1:k)=B(1:k) \wedge b(k+1:n)$ has its final values*)
    while $e <> 0$ **do begin** $b(k) := b(k)+e$; $k := k-1$; $e := e-p$ **end**
end
end

Program in PL/I

/ *The n words, $n \geq 0$, on line number z begin in columns $b(1)$, ..., $b(n)$.
Exactly one blank separates each adjacent pair of words. s, $s \geq 0$,
is the total number of blanks to insert between words to justify the
line. Determine new column numbers $b(1:n)$ to represent the justified
line. Result assertion R, below, specifies that the numbers of blanks
inserted between different pairs of words differ by no more than one,
and that extra blanks are inserted to the left or right, depending on
the line number. Unless $0 \leq n \leq 1$, the justified line has the format

W1 $[p+1$ blanks] ... $[p+1]$ Wt $[q+1]$ ... $[q+1]$ Wn

where p, q, t satisfy

Q1: $1 \leq t \leq n \wedge 0 \leq p \wedge 0 \leq q \wedge p*(t-1)+q*(n-t)=s \wedge$
$\quad (odd(z) \wedge q = p+1 \vee even(z) \wedge p = q+1)$

Using B to represent the initial value of array b, result assertion R is

R: $(0 \leq n \leq 1 \wedge b = B) \vee ((A \, i: 1 \leq i \leq t: b(i)=B(i)+p*(i-1)) \wedge$
$\quad (A \, i: t < i \leq n: b(i)=B(i)+p*(t-1)+q*(i-t)))*/$

```
justify: PROC(n, z, s, b);
        DECLARE (n, z, s, b(*)) FIXED;
  DECLARE (q, p, t, e, k) FIXED;
  IF n > 1 THEN
    DO; / *Determine p, q and t:*/
        IF MOD(z, 2)=0
            THEN DO; q = s /(n-1);
                    t = 1+MOD(s, (n-1)); p = q+1; END;
            ELSE DO; p = s /(n-1);
                    t = n-MOD(s, (n-1)); q = p+1; END;
        / *Calculate new column numbers b(1:n):*/
        k = n; e = s;
        / *inv: t ≤ k ≤ n ∧ e = p*(t-1)+q*(k-t) ∧
            b(1:k) = B(1:k) ∧ b(k+1:n) has its final values*/
        DO WHILE(k ¬=t); b(k)= b(k)+e;
                    k = k-1; e = e-q; END;

        / *inv: 1 ≤ k ≤ t ∧ e = p*(t-1) ∧
            b[1:k] = B(1:k) ∧ b(k+1:n) has its final values*/
        DO WHILE(e ¬=0); b(k)= b(k)+e;
                    k = k-1; e = e-p; END;
  END; END justify;
```

Program in FORTRAN

In the FORTRAN example given below, note how each guarded command loop is implemented using an IF-statement that jumps to a labeled CONTINUE statement. These CONTINUE statements are included only to keep each loop as a separate entity, independent of the preceding and following statements.

```
C    The n words, n ≥0, on line number z begin in cols b(1), ..., b(n).
C    Exactly one blank separates each adjacent pair of words. s, s ≥0, is
C    the number of blanks to insert between words to right-justify the
C    line. Determine new col numbers b(1:n) to represent the justified
C    line. Result assertion R, below, specifies that the numbers of blanks
C    inserted between different pairs of words differ by no more than one.
C    Also, extra blanks are inserted to the left or right, depending on
C    the line number. Unless 0 ≤n ≤1, the justified line has the format
C
C    W1 [p +1 blanks]...[p +1] Wt [q +1] ... [q +1] Wn
C    where p,q,t satisfy
C
C    Q1: 1≤t ≤n ∧ 0≤p ∧ 0≤q ∧ p*(t−1)+q*(n−t)=s ∧
C        (odd(z) ∧ q =p +1 ∨ even(z) ∧ p =q +1)
C
C    Using B to represent the initial value of array b, result assertion R is
C
C    R: (0≤n ≤1 ∧ b = B) ∨ ((A i: 1≤i ≤t: b(i)= B(i)+p*(i−1)) ∧
C        (A i: t <i ≤n: b(i)= B(i)+p*(t−1)+q*(i−t)))
C
     SUBROUTINE justify (n, z, s, b)
              INTEGER n, z, s, b(n)
C
     INTEGER q,p,t,e,k
     IF (n .LE. 1) GOTO 100
C        Determine p, q and t:
         e = z/2
         IF (z .NE. 2*e) GOTO 20
             q= s / (n−1)
             t= 1 +s − q*(n−1)
             p= q +1
             GOTO 30
20           p= s / (n−1)
             t= n − s +p*(n−1)
             q= p +1
30           CONTINUE
```

```
C        Calculate new column numbers b[1:n]:
         k = n
         e = s
C        Guarded command loop.
C        inv: t ≤ k ≤ n ∧ e = p*(t−1) + q*(k−t) ∧
C              b(1:k) = B(1:k) ∧ b(k+1:n) has its final values
40       IF (k .EQ. t) GOTO 50
           b(k)= b(k)+e
           k = k −1
           e = e −q
           GOTO 40
50       CONTINUE

C        Guarded command loop.
C        inv: 1 ≤ k ≤ t ∧ e = p*(t−1) ∧
C              b(1:k) = B(1:k) ∧ b(k+1:n) has its final values
60       IF (e .EQ. 0) GOTO 70
           b(k)= b(k)+e
           k = k −1
           e = e −p
           GOTO 60
70       CONTINUE
100  CONTINUE
     END
```

Chapter 23
Historical Notes

This chapter contains a brief history of research on programming and a short account of the programming problems presented in this book. It is a personal view of the field, in that only events that influenced my research concerning the method of programming are described. For example, it covers only programming methodology as it relates to sequential, rather than concurrent, programs. Furthermore, an enormous amount of research on the theory of correctness of programs goes completely unmentioned, simply because it did not influence my own ideas and opinions on the method of programming presented here.

23.1 A Brief History of Programming Methodology

Pre-1960

FORTRAN and FAP, the IBM 7090 assembly language, were my first programming languages, and I loved them. I could code with the best of them, and my flaw charts were always neat and clean. In 1962, as a research assistant on a project to write the ALCOR-ILLINOIS 7090 Algol 60 Compiler, I first came in contact with Algol 60 [39]. Like many, I was confused on this first encounter. The syntax description using BNF (see Appendix 1) seemed foreign and difficult. Dynamic arrays, which were allocated on entrance to and deallocated on exit from a block, seemed wasteful. The use of ":=" as the assignment symbol seemed unnecessary. The need to declare all variables seemed stupid. Many other things disturbed me.

I'm glad that I stuck with the project, for after becoming familiar with Algol 60 I began to see its attractions. BNF became a useful tool. I began to appreciate the taste and style of Algol 60 and of the Algol 60 report itself. And I now agree with Tony Hoare that

> Algol 60 was indeed a great achievement, in that it was a significant advance over most of its successors.

Algol 60 has outlived its usefulness as a language, for it is inadequate in many ways (as is FORTRAN). But the lessons learned on that project, in the need for simplicity, taste, precision, and mathematical integrity —in the description of the language as well as the language itself— have had a profound influence on the field.

The 1960s

The 1960s was the decade of syntax and compiling. One sees this in the wealth of papers on context-free languages, parsing, compilers, compiler-compilers and so on. The linguists also got into the parsing game, and people received Ph.D.s for writing compilers.

Algol was a focal point of much of the research, perhaps because of the strong influence of IFIP Working Group 2.1 on Algol, which met once or twice a year (mostly in Europe). (*IFIP* stands for International Federation for Information Processing). Among other tasks, WG2.1 published the Algol Bulletin in the 1960s, an informal publication with fairly wide distribution, which kept people up to date on the work being done in Algol and Algol-like languages.

Few people were involved deeply in understanding programming *per se* at that time (although one does find a few early papers on the subject) and, at least in the early 1960s, people seemed to be satisfied with programming as it was being performed. If efforts were made to develop formal definitions of programming languages, they were made largely to understand languages and compilers, rather than programming. Concepts from automata theory and formal languages played a large role in these developments, as is evidenced by the proceedings [42] of one important conference that was held under IFIP's auspices.

A few isolated papers and discussions did give some early indications that much remained to be done in the field of programming. One of the first references to the idea of proving programs correct was in a stimulating paper [35] presented in 1961 and again at the 1962 IFIP Congress by John McCarthy (then at M.I.T., now at Stanford University). In that paper, McCarthy stated that "instead of trying out computer programs on test cases until they are debugged, one should prove that they have the desired properties." And, at the same Congress, Edsger W. Dijkstra (Technological University Eindhoven, the Netherlands, and later also with Burroughs) gave a talk titled *Some meditations on advanced program-*

ming [11]. At the 1965 IFIP Congress, Stanley Gill, of England, remarked that "another practical problem, which is now beginning to loom very large indeed and offers little prospect of a satisfactory solution, is that of checking the correctness of a large program."

But, in the main, the correctness problem was attacked by the more theoretically inclined researchers only in terms of the problem of formally proving the equivalence of two different programs; this approach has not yet been that useful from a practical standpoint.

As the 1960s progressed, it was slowly realized that there really were immense problems in the software field. The complexity and size of projects increased tremendously in the 1960s, without commensurate increases in the tools and abilities of the programmers; the result was missed deadlines, cost overruns and unreliable software. In 1968, a NATO Conference on Software Engineering was held in Garmisch, Germany, [6] in order to discuss the critical situation. Having received my degree (Dr. rer. nat) two years earlier in Munich under F.L. Bauer, one of the major organizers of the conference, I was invited to attend and help organize. Thus, I was able to listen to the leading figures from academia and industry discuss together the problems of programming from their two, quite different, viewpoints. People spoke openly about their failures in software, and not only about their successes, in order to get to the root of the problem. For the first time, a consensus emerged that there really was a software crisis, that programming was not very well understood.

In response to the growing awareness, in 1969 IFIP approved the formation of Working Group 2.3 on *programming methodology*, with Michael Woodger (National Physics Laboratory, England) as chairman. Some of its members —including Dijkstra, Brian Randell (University of Newcastle upon Tyne), Doug Ross (Softech), Gerhard Seegmueller (Technical University Munich), Wlad M. Turski (University of Warsaw) and Niklaus Wirth (Eidgenossische Technische Hochschule, Zurich)— had resigned from WG2.1 earlier when Algol 68 was adopted by WG2.1 as the "next Algol". Their growing awareness of the problems of programming had convinced them that Algol 68 was a step in the wrong direction, that a smaller, simpler programming language and description was necessary.

Thus, just around 1970, programming had become a recognized, respectable —in fact, critical— area of research. Dijkstra's article on the harmfulness of the **goto** in 1968 [12] had stirred up a hornets' nest. And his monograph *On Structured Programming* [14] (in which the term was introduced in the title but never used in the text), together with Wirth's article [44] on stepwise refinement, set the tone for many years to come.

The early work on program correctness

Although proving programs correct had been mentioned many times, few people worked in that area until the late 1960s. However, three important articles written in the 1960s had a profound impact on the field. The first article on proving programs correct was by Peter Naur (University of Copenhagen) in 1966 [40]. In the paper, Naur emphasized the importance of program proofs and provided an informal technique for specifying them.

A seminal piece of work was presented by Robert Floyd at a meeting of the American Mathematical Society in 1967 [19]. In his talk, Floyd discussed attaching assertions to the edges of a flaw chart, with the meaning that each assertion would be true during execution of the corresponding program whenever execution reached that edge. For a loop —i.e. a cycle of the flaw chart— Floyd placed an assertion P on an arbitrary (but fixed, of course) edge of the cycle, called a *cut point*. He would then prove that if execution of the cycle beginning at the cut point with P true reached the cut point again, P would still be true at that point. Thus was born the idea of a loop invariant. Floyd also suggested that a specification of proof techniques could provide an adequate definition of a programming language.

Tony Hoare (then at the University of Belfast; now at Oxford) took Floyd's suggestion to heart in his article [27] and defined a small programming language in terms of a logical system of axioms and inference rules for proving partial correctness of programs —an extension to the predicate calculus. For example, the assignment statement was defined by the axiom (schema):

$$P_e^x \{ x := e \} P$$

and the while loop was defined by an inference rule:

$$\frac{P \wedge B \{ S \} P}{P \{ \text{ while } B \text{ do } S \} P \wedge \neg B}$$

This inference rule means: if $P \wedge B \{ S \} P$ has been proved, one may infer that $P \{ \text{ while } B \text{ do } S \} P \wedge \neg B$ holds also.

Hoare's article attempts to deal directly with the programming problem. It restricts the programming language to "manageable" control structures, (instead of dealing with flaw charts). It attempts to convey the need for such restrictions. It shows how defining the language in terms of how to prove a program correct, instead of how to execute it, might lead to a simpler design. The *tone* of the article, together with its comprehensive evaluation of the possible benefits to be gained by adopting the axiomatic approach to language definition, both for programming and for formal language definition, are what made the article so unique.

I must confess that I was not turned on by Hoare's paper in 1969. I did not understand its implications —perhaps I was not ready to think deeply about the problems of programming because I was too involved in the field of compiler construction at that time. This involvement illustrates one reason why, today, teaching of programming has lagged so far behind the research; by and large, people are too busy performing their own research to spend time thinking about and learning about programming. This is a pity, for teaching programming well is an important part of our task as computer scientists and educators.

Two years later, I did become more interested and began to understand the implications of Hoare's work. In fact, I was so impressed that in 1972 I made the subject of loop invariants part of the content of the second programming course at Cornell University and included it in the text [9].

Research on axiomatic definitions in the 1970s

Tony Hoare's article [27] founded a whole school of research on the axiomatic definition of programming languages. Today, there are literally hundreds of papers dealing with the axiomatic treatment of various constructs, from the assignment command to various forms of loops to procedure calls to coroutines. Even the *goto* has been axiomatized, and, indeed, very simply.

The research was fraught with lack of understanding and frustration. One reason for this was that computer scientists in the field, as a whole, did not know enough formal logic. Some papers were written simply because the authors didn't understand earlier work; others contained errors that wouldn't have happened had the authors been educated in logic.

It is difficult to do a good job developing an axiomatic system when the only place you have seen such a system is in Hoare's 1969 paper [27], and yet, I and others operated under just those circumstances. We spent a good deal of time thrashing, just treading water, instead of swimming, because of our ignorance. With hindsight, I can say that the best thing for me to have done 10 years ago would have been to take a course in logic. I persuaded many students to do so, but I never did so myself.

Let me list a number of achievements in the field of axiomatization during the 1970's. Some have been independently achieved and published by others also; these are the papers that influenced me. Also, the work was usually done a year or two before the date of publication.

In 1971, proof rules for restricted procedure calls were developed [28]. Several later papers, which built on the results of [28], contained mistakes that [28] didn't have.

In 1972, article [29] on the proof of correctness of data representations did much to spur on research in "abstract data types". The algebraic specification of data types [25] came later, based on initial work in 1974 in [33].

In 1973, proof rules were written for most of the programming language Pascal [30]. This work included the first proof rule for assignment to array elements, viewing an array as a function as in chapter 9. The work was actually hampered by the language in a number of places; it is easier to build a language with axiomatization in mind than to axiomatize as an afterthought.

In 1975, an automatic verification system for (much of) Pascal, based on axioms and inference rules, was developed [32].

In 1975, a model of execution of a program was used to prove the "relative completeness" of a set of axioms and inference rules for an Algol fragment [8]. Thus, it was shown that if a program could not be proved correct within the axiomatic system, then the fault could be attributed to something other than the axiomatic definition of the language, for example, on the fact that any axiomatization of the integers is incomplete.

In 1979, the programming language Euclid was defined with the idea of axiomatization imposed on the project from the beginning [34].

In 1980, a general multiple assignment statement, including assignment to array elements, was defined and used to describe axioms for procedure calls [23]. This paper clarified some of the problems concerning initial and final values of variables.

Research in developing proof and program hand-in-hand

In the early 1970's one often heard the cry: the disadvantage of Hoare's stuff is that it forces you to find an invariant of each loop! Others shouted back, including myself: the *advantage* of Hoare's stuff is that it forces you to find an invariant of each loop!

To some extent, the first cry was on the mark at that time. When the theory was first presented, it seemed terribly difficult to prove an existing program correct, and it was soon admitted that the only way to prove a program correct was to develop the proof and program hand-in-hand —with the former leading the way.

And yet, we didn't really know how to do this. For example, we *knew* that the loop invariant should come before the loop, but we had no good methods for doing so and certainly could not teach others to do it. The arguments went back and forth for some time, with those in favor of loop invariants becoming more adept at producing them and coming up with more and more examples to back up their case.

The issue was blurred by the varying notions of the word *proof*. Some felt that the only way to prove a program correct formally was to use a theorem prover or verifier. Some argued that mechanical proofs were and would continue to be useless, because of the complexity and detail that arose. Others argued that mechanical proofs were useless because no one could read them. Article [10] contains a synthesis of arguments made against proofs of correctness of programs, and it is suggested reading. In this book, a middle view has been used: one *should* develop a proof and program hand-in-hand, but the proof should be a mixture of formality and common sense.

Several forums existed throughout the 1970's for discussing technical work on programming. Besides the usual conferences and exchanges, two other forums deserve mention. First, IFIP Working group 2.3 on programming methodology, and later WG2.1, WG2.2 and WG2.4, were used quite heavily to present and discuss problems related to programming. Since its formation, WG2.3 has met once or twice a year for five days to discuss various aspects of programming. No formal proceedings have ever emerged from the group; rather the plan has been to provide a forum for discussion and cross-fertilization of ideas, with the results of the interaction appearing in the normal scientific publications of its members. The group has produced an anthology of already-published articles by its members [22], which illustrates well the influence of WG2.3 on the field of programming during the 1970s. It is recommended reading for those interested in programming methodology.

Secondly, several two-week courses were organized throughout the 1970's by the Technical University Munich. These courses were taught by the leaders in the field and attended by advanced graduate students, young Ph.D.s, scientists new to the field and people from industry from Europe, the U.S. and Canada; they were not just organized to teach a subject but to establish a forum for discussion of ongoing research in a very well-organized fashion. Many of the ones dealing with programming itself (some were on compiling, operating systems, etc.) were sponsored by NATO. These schools are unusual in that 50 to 100 researchers were together for two weeks to discuss one topic. The lectures of many of the schools have been published —see for example [2], [4] and [3].

Back to the development of programs. In 1975, Edsger W. Dijkstra published a paper [15], which was a forerunner to his book [16]. The book introduced weakest preconditions for a small language and then showed, through many examples, how they could be used as a "calculus for the derivation of programs".

For the first time, it began to become clear how one could develop a loop invariant (before the loop). It became clear that emphasis on theory and formalism, but tempered with common sense, could actually lead to the development of programs in a more reliable manner. The concepts and principles on which a science of programming could be founded began to emerge.

The text you are now reading is my attempt to convey these concepts and principles, to show how programming can be practised as a science.

23.2 The Problems Used in the Book

The following list gives the history of problems, as far as I know them, in the order in which they appear in this book.

The Coffee Can Problem (Chapter 13). Dijkstra mentioned the problem in a letter in Fall 1979; he learned of it from his colleague, Carel Scholten. It took five minutes to solve.

Closing the Curve (Chapter 13). John Williams (then at Cornell, now at IBM, San Jose) asked me to solve this problem in 1973. I was not able to do so, and Williams had to give me the answer.

The Maximum Problem (Chapter 14). [16], pp. 52-53.

The Next Higher Permutation Problem (exercise 2 of chapter 14 and exercise 2 of Chapter 20). The problem has been around for a long time; the development is from [16], pp. 107-110.

Searching a Two-dimensional Array (sections 15.1, 15.2). My solution.

Four-tuple Sort (section 15.2). [16], p. 61.

gcd(x, y) (exercise 2 of section 15.2). This, of course, goes back to Euclid. The versions presented here are largely from [16].

Approximating the Square Root (sections 16.2, 16.3 and 19.3). [16], pp. 61-65.

Linear Search and the Linear Search Principle (section 16.2). The development is from [16], pp. 105-106.

The Plateau Problem (section 16.3). I used this problem to illustrate loop invariants at a conference in Munich, Germany, in 1974. Because of lack of experience, my program used too many variables (see the discussion at the end of section 16.3). Michael Griffiths (University of Nancy) wrote a recursive definition of the plateau of an array and then changed the definition into an iterative program; the result was a program similar to (16.3.11). The idealized development given in section

16.3 came much later.

Binary Search (exercise 4 of section 16.3). The development given in the answers to the exercise is due to Dijkstra, in 1978.

The Welfare Crook (section 16.4). Due to a colleague of Dijkstra's, Wim Feijen, this problem was used as an exercise at the International Summer School in Marktoberdorf, Germany, in 1975 [2]. Blame the particular setting on me.

Swapping Equal-Length Sections (section 16.5). Part of the folklore.

Array Reversal (exercise 2 of section 16.5). Part of the folklore.

Partition (exercise 4 of section 16.5). This is used in a sorting algorithm developed by Tony Hoare (Oxford) in 1962 [26]. The solution is mine.

Dutch National Flag (exercise 5 of section 16.5). [16], pp. 111-116.

Link Reversal (exercise 6 of section 16.5). This has been a favorite exercise and test question in the second programming course at Cornell for years.

Saddleback Search (exercise 8 of section 16.5). A prospective graduate student from Berkeley gave me this problem in Spring 1980 during a discussion on programming; Gary Levin (then a Cornell graduate student, now at the University of Arizona) solved the problem essentially as given in the answer to the exercise.

Decimal to Binary (exercise 9 of section 16.5). Part of the folklore.

Decimal to Base B (exercise 10 of section 16.5). A simple generalization of Decimal to Binary.

Swapping Sections (section 18.1). The problem was given to Harlan Mills (IBM, Maryland) and me at the 1980 IFIP Congress in Japan, by Ed Nelson, who had difficulty solving it. This is one of two solutions we came up with while traveling [24]). The history of a third solution in terms of reversing array sections —the answer to exercise 1 of section 18.1 is $Reverse(b, m, n-1)$; $Reverse(b, n, p-1)$; $Reverse(b, m, p-1)$— is lost in the sands of time. Shown to me by Alan Demers (Cornell), the third solution is used in the UNIX editor and in the Terak screen editor on which I have typed and edited most of this book.

Quicksort (section 18.2). This is due to Hoare [26].

Counting the Nodes of a Tree (section 18.3). In 1972, this problem was used to illustrate how difficult it was to find loop invariants [5]! Now, the problem seems almost trivial.

Preorder, Inorder, Postorder Traversal (section 18.3). The names were invented by Donald Knuth (Stanford University); the program derivations are mine.

An Exercise Attributed to Hamming (section 19.2). Dijkstra derives this program in [16], pp. 129-134; he attributes the problem to R.W. Hamming (Bell Laboratories).

Finding Sums of Squares (exercise 1 of section 19.2). [16], pp. 140-142.

Exponentiation (section 19.1 and exercise 15 of chapter 20).   The development as done in section 19.1 appears in [16], pp. 65-67.   The program of exercise 11, which processes the binary representation in a different order, was shown to me by John Williams.   I once listened to two computer scientists discuss exponentiation talk right past each other; each thought he was talking about *the* exponentiation routine, not knowing that the other existed.

Controlled Density Sorting (section 19.3).   Robert Melville derived this algorithm as part of his Ph.D. thesis at Cornell [36]; it appeared in [37].

Efficient Queues in LISP (section 19.3).   Robert Melville derived this algorithm as part of his Ph.D. thesis at Cornell [36].

Justifying Lines of Text (section 20.1).   The derivation first appeared in [21].

The Longest Upsequence (section 20.2).   Dijkstra gave this as an exercise a day before he derived it at the 1978 Marktoberdorf Course on Program Construction [4].   Four or five people present, who were experienced in the method of programming, had no difficulty with it; the rest of the audience did.   Jay Misra (University of Texas, Austin) had presented a similar solution earlier in a paper on program development [38], and a generalization of it is used in the UNIX program DIFF [31].

Unique 5-bit Subsequences (exercise 1, chapter 20).   In [13].

Different Adjacent Subsequences (exercise 2, chapter 20).   In [13].

Perm-to-Code (exercise 5 of chapter 20).   This problem was solved by Dijkstra and his colleague, Willem H.J. Feijen, in connection with inverting programs (see chapter 21) in [17].   The concept of inverting programs and most of the inversions presented in chapter 21 are due to them.

Code-to-Perm (exercise 6 of chapter 20).   See Perm-to-Code.

Appendix 1
Backus-Naur Form

BNF, or Backus-Naur form, is a notation for describing (part of) the syntax of "sentences" of a language. It was proposed in about 1959 for describing the syntax of Algol 60 by John Backus, one of the thirteen people on the Algol 60 committee. (John Backus, of IBM, was also one of the major figures responsible for FORTRAN.) Because of his modifications and extensive use of BNF as editor of the Algol 60 report, Peter Naur (University of Copenhagen) is also associated with it. The ideas were independently discovered earlier by Noam Chomsky, a linguist, in 1956. BNF and its extensions have become standard tools for describing the syntax of programming notations, and in many cases parts of compilers are generated automatically from a BNF description.

We will introduce BNF by using it to describe digits, integer constants, and simplified arithmetic expressions.

In BNF, the fact that 1 is a digit is expressed by

(A1.1)   <digit> ::= 1

The term <digit> is delimited by angular brackets to help indicate that it cannot appear in "sentences" of the language being described, but is used only to help *describe* sentences. It is a "syntactic entity", much like "verb" or "noun phrase" in English. It is usually called a *nonterminal*, or *nonterminal symbol*. The symbol 1, on the other hand, can appear in sentences of the language being described, and is called a *terminal*.

(A1.1) is called a *production*, or (rewriting) *rule*. Its left part (the symbol to the left of ::=) is a nonterminal; its right part (to the right of ::=) is a nonempty, finite sequence of nonterminals and terminals. The symbol ::= is to be read as "may be composed of", so that (A1.1) can be read as

A <digit> may be composed of the sequence of symbols: 1

Two rules can be used to indicate a <digit> may be a 0 or a 1:

    <digit> ::= 0   (a <digit> may be composed of 0)
    <digit> ::= 1   (a <digit> may be composed of 1)

These two rules, which express different forms for the same nonterminal, can be abbreviated using the symbol |, read as "or", as

    <digit> ::= 0 | 1   (A <digit> may be composed of 0 or 1)

This abbreviation can be used in specifying all the digits:

    <digit> ::= 0 | 1 | 2 | 3 | 4 | 5 | 6 | 7 | 8 | 9

An integer constant is a (finite) sequence of one or more digits. Using the nonterminal <constant> to represent the class of integer constants, integer constants are defined recursively as follows:

(A1.2)   <constant> ::= <digit>
         <constant> ::= <constant> <digit>
         <digit>   ::= 0 | 1 | 2 | 3 | 4 | 5 | 6 | 7 | 8 | 9

The first rule of (A1.2) is read as follows: a <constant> may be composed of a <digit>. The second rule is read as follows: a <constant> may be composed of another <constant> followed by a <digit>.

The rules listed in (A1.2) form a *grammar* for the language of <constant>s; the *sentences* of the language are the sequences of terminals that can be *derived* from the nonterminal <constant>, where sequences are derived as follows. Begin with the sequence of symbols consisting only of the nonterminal <constant>, and successively rewrite one of the nonterminals in the sequence by a corresponding right part of a rule, until the sequence contains only terminals.

Indicating the rewriting action by =>, the sentence 325 is derived:

(A1.3) <constant> => <constant> <digit>   (rewrite using second rule)
                  => <constant> 5   (rewrite <digit> as 5)
                  => <constant> <digit> 5   (rewrite using second rule)
                  => <constant> 2 5   (rewrite <digit> as 2)
                  => <digit> 2 5   (rewrite using first rule)
                  => 3 2 5   (rewrite <digit> as 3)

The derivation of one sequence of symbols from another can be defined schematically as follows. Suppose $U ::= u$ is a rule of the grammar, where U is a nonterminal and u a sequence of symbols. Then, for any (possibly empty) sequences x and y define

$$x \: U \: y \: \Rightarrow \: x \: u \: y$$

The symbol $\Rightarrow$ denotes a single derivation —one rewriting action. The symbol $\Rightarrow$* denotes a sequence of zero or more single derivations. Thus,

$$<\text{constant}> 1 \: \Rightarrow^* \: <\text{constant}> 1$$

since $<\text{constant}> 1$ can be derived from itself in zero derivations. Also

$$<\text{constant}> 1 \: \Rightarrow^* \: <\text{constant}> <\text{digit}> 1$$

because of the second rule of grammar (A1.2). Finally,

$$<\text{constant}> 1 \: \Rightarrow^* \: 3 \: 2 \: 5 \: 1$$

since (A1.3) showed that $<\text{constant}> \Rightarrow^* 3 \: 2 \: 5$.

A grammar for (simplified) arithmetic expressions

Now consider writing a grammar for arithmetic expressions that use addition, binary subtraction, multiplication, parenthesized expressions, and integer constants as operands. This is fairly easy to do:

```
<expr> ::=  <expr> + <expr>
<expr> ::=  <expr> - <expr>
<expr> ::=  <expr> * <expr>
<expr> ::=  ( <expr> )
<expr> ::=  <constant>
```

where $<\text{constant}>$ is as described above in (A1.2). Here is a derivation of the expression (1+3)*4 according this grammar:

(A1.4)
```
<expr> =>  <expr> * <expr>
       => ( <expr> ) * <expr>
       => ( <expr> + <expr> ) * <expr>
       => ( <constant> + <expr> ) * <expr>
       => ( <constant> + <constant> ) * <expr>
       => ( <constant> + <constant> ) * <constant>
       => ( <digit> + <constant> ) * <constant>
       => ( <digit> + <digit> ) * <constant>
       => ( <digit> + <digit> ) * <digit>
       => ( 1 + <digit> ) * <digit>
       => ( 1 + 3 ) * <digit>
       => ( 1 + 3 ) * 4
```

Hence, <expr> =>* (1 + 3) + 4.

Syntax trees and ambiguity

A sequence of derivations can be described by a *syntax tree*. As an example, the syntax tree for derivation (A1.4) is

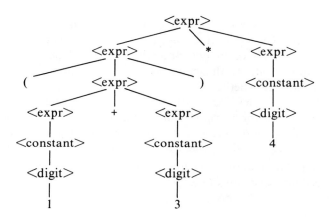

In the syntax tree, a single derivation using the rule $U ::= u$ is expressed by a node U with lines emanating down to the symbols of the sequence u. Thus, for every single derivation in the sequence of derivations there is a nonterminal in the tree, with the symbols that replace it underneath. For example, the first derivation is <expr> => <expr> * <expr>, so at the top of the diagram above is the node <expr> and this node has lines emanating downward from it to <expr>, * and <expr>. Also, there is a derivation using the rule <digit> ::= 1, so there is a corresponding branch from <digit> to 1 in the tree.

The main difference between a derivation and its syntax tree is that the syntax tree does not specify the order in which some of the derivations were made. For example, in the tree given above it cannot be determined whether the rule <digit> ::= 1 was used before or after the rule <digit> ::= 3. To every derivation there corresponds a syntax tree, but more than one derivation can correspond to the same tree. These derivations are considered to be equivalent.

Now consider the set of derivations expressed by <expr> =>* <expr> + <expr> * <expr>. There are actually two different derivation trees for the two derivations of <expr> + <expr> * <expr>:

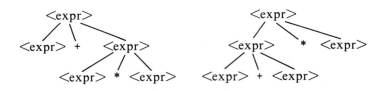

A grammar that allows more than one syntax tree for some sentence is called *ambiguous*. This is because the existence of two syntax trees allows us to "parse" the sentence in two different ways, and hence to perhaps give two meanings to it. In this case, the ambiguity shows that the grammar does not indicate whether + should be performed before or after *. The syntax tree to the left (above) indicates that * should be performed first, because the <expr> from which it is derived is in a sense an operand of the addition operator +. On the other hand, the syntax tree to the right indicates that + should be performed first.

One can write an unambiguous grammar that indicates that multiplication has precedence over plus (except when parentheses are used to override the precedence). To do this requires introducing new nonterminal symbols, <term> and <factor>:

$$
\begin{aligned}
\text{<expr>} \quad &::= \quad \text{<term>} \mid \text{<expr>} + \text{<term>} \\
&\mid \quad \text{<expr>} - \text{<term>} \\
\text{<term>} \quad &::= \quad \text{<factor>} \mid \text{<term>} * \text{<factor>} \\
\text{<factor>} \quad &::= \quad \text{<constant>} \mid (\ \text{<expr>}\ ) \\
\text{<constant>} &::= \quad \text{<digit>} \\
\text{<constant>} &::= \quad \text{<constant>} \text{<digit>} \\
\text{<digit>} \quad &::= \quad 0 \mid 1 \mid 2 \mid 3 \mid 4 \mid 5 \mid 6 \mid 7 \mid 8 \mid 9
\end{aligned}
$$

In this gramar, each sentence has one syntax tree, so there is no ambiguity. For example, the sentence 1+3*4 has one syntax tree:

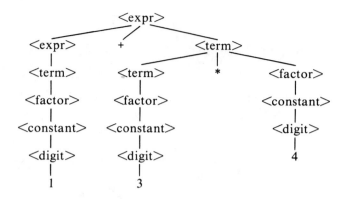

This syntax tree indicates that multiplication should be performed first, and, in general, in this grammar * has precedence over + except when the precedence is overridden by the use of parentheses.

Extensions to BNF

A few extension to BNF are used to make it easier to read and understand. One of the most important is the use of braces to indicate repetition: {x} denotes zero or more occurrences of the sequence of symbols x. Using this extension, we can describe <constant> using one rule as

<constant> ::= <digit> {<digit>}

In fact, the grammar for arithmetic expressions can be rewritten as

```
<expr>      ::=  <term> {+ <term>  |  − <term>}
<term>      ::=  <factor> {* <factor>}
<factor>    ::=  <constant>  |  ( <expr> )
<constant>  ::=  <digit> {<digit>}
<digit>     ::=  0 | 1 | 2 | 3 | 4 | 5 | 6 | 7 | 8 | 9
```

References

The theory of syntax has been studied extensively. An excellent text on the material is *Introduction to Automata Theory, Languages and Computation* (Hopcroft, J.E. and J.D. Ullman; Addison-Wesley, 1979). The practical use of the theory in compiler construction is discussed in the texts *Compiler Construction for Digital Computers* (Gries, D.; John Wiley, 1971) and *Principles of Compiler Design* (Aho, A.V., and J. Ullman; Addison Wesley, 1977).

Appendix 2
Sets, Sequences, Integers, and Real Numbers

This appendix briefly defines the important types of variables used throughout the book. Sets will be described in more detail than the others, so that the reader can learn important material he might have missed earlier in his education.

Sets and operations on them

A set is a collection of distinct objects, or elements, as they are usually called. Because the word *collection* is just as vague as *set*, we give some examples to make the idea more concrete.

> The set $\{3,5\}$ consists of the integers 3 and 5.
>
> The set $\{5,3\}$ consists of the integers 3 and 5.
>
> The set $\{3,3,5\}$ consists of the integers 3 and 5.
>
> The set $\{3\}$ consists of the integer 3.
>
> The set $\{\}$ is called the *empty set*; it contains no elements. The Greek character ϕ is sometimes used to denote the empty set.

These examples illustrate one way of describing a set: write its elements as a list within braces { and }, with commas joining adjacent elements. The first two examples illustrate that the order of the elements in the list does not matter. The third example illustrates that an element listed more than once is considered to be in the set only once; elements of a set must be distinct. The final example illustrates that a set may contain zero elements, in which case it is called the empty set.

It is not possible to list all elements of an infinite set (a set with an infinite number of elements). In this case, one often uses dots to indicate that the reader should use his imagination, but in a conservative fashion, in extending the list of elements actually given. For example,

$\{0, 1, 2, \cdots \}$ is the set of natural numbers

$\{\cdots, -2, -1, 0, 1, 2, \cdots \}$ is the set of all integers

$\{1, 2, 4, 8, 16, 32, \cdots \}$ is the set of powers of 2.

We can be more explicit using a different notation:

$\{i \mid$ *there is a natural number j satisfying* $i = 2^j\}$

In this notation, between $\{$ and $\mid$ is an identifier i; between $\mid$ and $\}$ is a true-false statement —a predicate. The set consists of all elements i that satisfy the true-false statement. In this case, the set consists of the powers of 2. The following describes the set of all even integers.

$\{k \mid$ *even*$(k)\}$

The notation can be extended somewhat:

$\{(i,j) \mid i = j+1\}$

Assuming i and j are integer-valued, this describes the set of pairs

$\{\cdots, (-1, -2), (0, -1), (1, 0), (2, 1), (3, 2), \cdots)$

The *cardinality* or size of a set is the number of elements in it. The notations $|a|$ and *card*(a) are often used to denote the cardinality of set a. Thus, $|\{\}| = 0$, $|\{1,5\}| = 2$, and *card*$(\{3,3,3\}) = 1$.

The following three operations are used build new sets: set union $\cup$, set intersection $\cap$ and set difference $-$.

$a \cup b$	is the set consisting of elements that are in at least one of the sets a and b
$a \cap b$	is the set consisting of elements that are in both a and b
$a - b$	is the set consisting of elements that are in a but not in b

For example, if $a = \{A, B, C\}$ and $b = \{B, C, D\}$, then $a \cup b = \{A, B, C, D\}$, $a \cap b = \{B, C\}$ and $a - b = \{A\}$.

Besides tests for set equality or inequality (e.g. $a = b$, $a \neq \{2, 3, 5\}$), the following three operations yield a Boolean value T or F (true or false):

$x \in a$ has the value of "x is a member of set a"

$x \notin a$ is equivalent to $\neg(x \in a)$

$a \subset b$ has the value of "set a is a subset of set b"

            —i.e. each element of a is in b

Thus, $1 \in \{2, 3, 5, 7\}$ is false, $1 \notin \{2, 3, 5, 7\}$ is true, $\{1, 3, 5\} \subset \{1, 3, 5\}$ is true, $\{3, 1, 5\} \subset \{1, 3, 5, 0\}$ is true, and $\{3, 1, 5, 2\} \subset \{1, 3, 5, 0\}$ is false.

It is advantageous from time to time to speak of the minimum and maximum values in a set (if an ordering is defined on its elements): $min(a)$ denotes the minimum value in set a and $max(a)$ the maximum value.

Finally, we describe a command that is useful when programming using sets. Let a be a nonempty set and x be a variable that can contain values of the type of the set elements. Execution of the command

$Choose(a, x)$

stores in x one element of set a. Set a remains unchanged. This command is nondeterministic (see chapter 7), because it is not known before its execution which element of a will be stored in x. The command is assumed to be used only with finite sets. Its use with infinite sets causes problems, which are beyond the scope of this book (see [16] for a discussion of unbounded and bounded nondeterminism). Further, in our programs the sets we deal with are finite.

$Choose(a, x)$ is defined in terms of weakest preconditions as follows (see chapter 7):

$$wp(Choose(a, x), R) = a \neq \{\} \wedge (\mathbf{A}\, i: i \in a: R_i^x)$$

Sequences

A *sequence* is a list of elements (joined by commas and delimited by parentheses). For example, the sequence $(1, 3, 5, 3)$ consists of the four elements $1, 3, 5, 3$, in that order, and $()$ denotes the empty sequence. As opposed to sets, the ordering of the elements in a sequence is important.

The length of a sequence s, written $|s|$, is the number of elements in it.

Catenation of sequences with sequences and/or values is denoted by $|$. Thus,

$$(1, 3, 5) \,|\, (2, 8) = (1, 3, 5, 2, 8)$$
$$(1, 3, 5) \,|\, 8 \,|\, 2 = (1, 3, 5, 8, 2)$$
$$(1, 3, 5) \,|\, () = (1, 3, 5)$$

In programming, the following notation is used to refer to elements of a sequence. Let variable s be a sequence with n elements. Then

$$s = (s[0], s[1], s[2], \cdots, s[n-1])$$

That is, s[0] refers to the first element, $s[1]$ to the second, and so forth. Further, the notation $s[k..]$, where $0 \leqslant k \leqslant n$, denotes the sequence

$$s[k..] = (s[k], s[k+1], \cdots, s[n-1])$$

That is, $s[k..]$ denotes a new sequence that is the same as s but with the first k elements removed. For example, if s is not empty, the assignment

$$s := s[1..]$$

deletes the first element of s. Executing the assignment when $s = ()$ causes abortion, because the expression $s[1..]$ is not defined in that case.

One can implement a last-in-first-out stack using a sequence s by limiting the operations on s to

$s[0]$	reference the top element of the stack
$s := ()$	empty the stack
$x, s := s[0], s[1..]$	Pop an element into variable x
$s := v \mid s$	Push value v onto the stack

One can implement a (first-in-first-out) queue using a sequence s by limiting the operations on s to

$s[0]$	Reference the front element of the queue
$s := ()$	empty the queue
$x, s := s[0], s[1..]$	Delete the front element and store it in x
$s := s \mid v$	Insert value v at the rear

Using the sequence notation, rather than the usual pop and push of stacks and insert into and delete from queues, may lead to more understandable programs. The notion of assignment is already well understood —see chapter 9— and is easy to use in this context.

Operations on integers and real numbers

We typically use the following sets:

The set of integers: $\{ \cdots, -2, -1, 0, 1, 2, \cdots \}$
The set of natural numbers: $\{0, 1, 2, \cdots \}$

We also use the set of real numbers, although on any machine this set and operations on it are approximated by some form of floating point numbers and operations. Nevertheless, we assume that real arithmetic is performed, so that problems with floating point are eliminated.

The following operations take as operands either integers or real numbers:

$+, -, *$ addition, subtraction, multiplication

$/$ division x / y; yields a real number

$<, \leq, =, \geq, >, \neq$ the relational operators:

                               $x < y$ is read "x is less than y"

                               $x \leq y$ is read "x is at most y"

                               $x = y$ is read "x equals y"

                               $x \geq y$ is read "x is at least y"

                               $x > y$ is read "x exceeds y"

                               $x \neq y$ is read "x differs from y"

$abs(x)$ or $|x|$ absolute value of x: if $x < 0$ then $-x$ else x

$floor(x)$ greatest integer not more than x

$ceil(x)$ smallest integer not less than x

$min(x, y, \cdots)$ The minimum of $x, y, \cdots$. The minimum of an empty set is ∞ (infinity)

$max(x, y, \cdots)$ The maximum of $x, y, \cdots$. The maximum of an empty set is $-\infty$ (infinity)

$log(x)$ base 2 logarithm of x: $y = log(x)$ iff $x = 2^y$

The following operations take only integers as operands.

$\div$ $x \div y$ is the greatest integer at most x / y

$x \bmod y$ the remainder when x is divided by y (for $x \geq 0, y > 0$)

$even(x)$ "x is an even integer", or $x \bmod 2 = 0$

$odd(x)$ "x is an odd integer", or $x \bmod 2 = 1$

Appendix 3
Relations and Functions

Relations

Let A and B be two sets. The *Cartesian product* of A and B, written $A \times B$, is the set of ordered pairs (a,b) where a is in A and b is in B:

$$A \times B = \{(a,b) \mid a \in A \land b \in B\}$$

The Cartesian product is named after the father of analytic geometry, Rene Descartes, a 17th century mathematician and philosopher. The number of elements in $A \times B$ is $|A| * |B|$; hence the name Cartesian *product*.

A *binary relation* over the sets A and B is a subset of $A \times B$. Since we will be dealing mainly with binary relations, we drop the adjective *binary* and call them simply *relations*. A few words will be said about other relations at the end of this Appendix.

Let P be the set of people. One relation over $P \times P$ is the relation *parent*:

$$parent = \{(a, b) \mid b \text{ is } a\text{'s } parent\}$$

Let N be the set of integers. One relation over $N \times N$ is the *successor* relation:

$$succ = \{(i, i+1) \mid i \in N\}$$

The following relation associates with each person the year in which he left his body:

$$died\_in = \{(p, i) \mid person \; p \; died \; in \; year \; i\}$$

The *identity relation* over $A \times A$, denoted by I, is the relation

$$I = \{(a, a) \mid a \in A\}$$

When dealing with binary relations, we often use the name of a relation as a binary operator and use infix notation to indicate that a pair belongs in the relation. For example, we have

> c *parent* d *iff* $(d, c) \in \{(a, b) \mid b$ *is* $a's$ *parent*$\}$
> i *succ* j *iff* $i+1 = j$
> q *died_in* j *iff* $(q, j) \in \{(p, i) \mid$ *person* p *died in year* $i\}$

From the three relations given thus far, we can conclude several things. For any value a there may be different pairs (a, b) in a relation. Such a relation is called a *one-to-many* relation. Relation *parent* is one-to-many, because most people have more than one parent.

For any value b there may be different pairs (a, b) in a relation. Such a relation is called a *many-to-one* relation. Many people may have died in any year, so that for each integer i there may be many pairs (p, i) in relation *died_in*. But for any person p there is at most one pair (p, i) in *died_in*. Relation *died_in* is an example of a *many-to-one* relation.

In relation *succ*, no two pairs have the same first value and no two pairs have the same second value. Relation *succ* is an example of a *one-to-one* relation.

A relation on $A \times B$ may contain no pair (a, b) for some a in A. Such a relation is called a *partial* relation. On the other hand, a relation on $A \times B$ is *total* if for each $a \in A$ there exists a pair (a, b) in the relation. Relation *died_in* is partial, since not all people have died yet. Relation *succ* is total (on $N \times N$).

If relation R on $A \times B$ contains a pair (a, b) for each b in B, we say that R is *onto* B. Relation *parent* is onto, since each child has a parent (assuming there was no beginning).

Let R and S be two relations. Then the *composition* $R \circ S$ of R and S is the relation defined by

> a $R \circ S$ c *iff* $(E b: a R b \wedge b S c)$

For example, the relation *parent* $\circ$ *parent* is the relation *grandparent*. Rrelation *died_in* $\circ$ *succ* associates with each person the year after the one in which the person died.

Composition is *associative*. This means the following. Let R, S and T be three relations. Then $(R \circ S) \circ T = R \circ (S \circ T)$. This fact is easily deduced from the definitions of relation and composition. Because composition is associative, we usually omit the parentheses and write simply $R \circ S \circ T$.

The composition of a relation with itself is denoted with a superscript 2:

> $parent^2$ is equivalent to $parent \circ parent$
> $succ^2$ is equivalent to $succ \circ succ$

Similarly, for any relation R and natural number i one defines R^i as

> $R^0 = I,$ the identity relation
> $R^i = R \circ R^{i-1}$,   for $i > 0$

For example,

> $parent^0 = I$
> $parent^1 = parent$
> $parent^2 = grandparent$
> $parent^3 = great\text{-}grandparent$

and

> $(i \; succ^k \; j)$ iff $i+k = j$

Looking upon relations as sets and using the superscript notation, we can define the *closure* R^+ and *transitive closure* R^* of a relation R as follows.

> $R^+ = R^1 \cup R^2 \cup R^3 \cup \cdots$
> $R^* = R^0 \cup R^1 \cup R^2 \cup \cdots$

In other words, a pair (a, b) is in R^+ if and only if it is in R^i for some $i > 0$. Here are some examples.

> $parent^+$ is the relation *ancestor*
> $i \; succ^+ \; j$ iff $i+k = j$ for some $k > 0$, i.e. $i < j$
> $i \; succ^* \; j$ iff $i \leqslant j$

Finally, we can define the inverse R^{-1} of a relation R:

> $b \; R^{-1} \; a$ iff $a \; R \; b$

That is, (b, a) is in the inverse R^{-1} of R if and only if (a, b) is in R. The inverse of *parent* is *child*, the inverse of $<$ is $>$, the inverse of $\leqslant$ is $\geqslant$, and the inverse of the identity relation I is I itself.

Functions

Let A and B be sets. A function f from A to B, denoted by

$$f: A \rightarrow B$$

is a relation that for each element a of A contains at most one pair (a, b) —i.e. is a relation that is not one-to-many. The relation *parent* is not a function, because a child can have more than one parent —for each person p there may be more than one pair (p, q) in the set *parent*. The relations *succ* and *died_in* are functions.

We write each pair in a function f as $(a, f(a))$. The second value, $f(a)$, is called the value of function f at the argument a. For example, for the function *succ* we have

$$succ(i) = i + 1, \text{ for all natural numbers } i,$$

because *succ* is the set of pairs

$$\{..., (-2, -1), (-1, 0), (0, 1), (1, 2), ...\}$$

Note carefully the three ways in which a function name f is used. First, f denotes a set of pairs such that for any value a there is at most one pair (a, b). Second, $a \, f \, b$ holds if (a, b) is in f. Third, $f(a)$ is the value associated with a, that is, $(a, f(a))$ is in the function (relation) f.

The beauty of defining a function as a restricted form of relation is that the terminology and theory for relations carries over to functions. Thus, we know what a one-to-one function is. We know that composition of (binary) functions is associative. We know, for any function, what f^0, f^1, f^2, f^+ and f^* mean. We know what the inverse f^{-1} of f is. We know that f^{-1} is a function *iff* f is not many-to-one.

Functions from expressions to expressions

Consider an expression, for example $x*y$. We can consider $x*y$ as a function of one (or more) of its identifiers, say y:

$$f(y) = x*y$$

In this case, we can consider f to be a function from expressions to expressions. For example,

$$f(2) = x*2$$
$$f(x+2) = x * (x+2)$$
$$f(x*2) = x * x*2$$

Thus, to apply the function to an argument means to replace *textually* the identifier y everywhere within the expression by the argument. In making the replacement, one should insert parentheses around the argument to maintain the precedence of operators in the expression (as in the second example), but we often leave them out where it doesn't matter. This textual substitution is discussed in more detail in section 4.4. The reason for including it here is that the concept is used earlier in the book, and the reader should be familiar with it.

n-ary relations and functions

Thus far, we have dealt only with binary relations. Suppose we have sets A_0, ..., A_n for $n > 0$. Then one can define a relation on $A_0 \times A_2 \times \cdots \times A_n$ to be a set of ordered tuples

$$(a_0, a_2, \cdots, a_n)$$

where each a_i is a member of set A_i.

Suppose g is such a relation. Suppose, further, that for each distinct $n-1$ tuple $(a_0, \cdots, a_{n-1})$ there is at most one n-tuple $(a_0, ..., a_{n-1}, a_n)$ in g. Then g is an n-ary function —a function of n arguments— where the value a_n in each tuple is the value of the function when applied to the arguments consisting of the first $n-1$ values:

$$(a_0, a_2, \cdots, a_{n-1}, g(a_0, \cdots, a_{n-1})) \quad \text{and}$$
$$g(a_0, \cdots, a_{n-1}) = a_n$$

The terminology used for binary relations and functions extends easily to n-ary relations and functions.

Appendix 4

Asymptotic Execution Time Properties

Execution time measures of algorithms that hold for any implementation of the algorithms and for any computer, especially for large input values (e.g. large arrays), are useful. The rest of this section is devoted to describing a suitable method for measuring execution times in this sense. The purpose is not to give an extensive discussion, but only to outline the important ideas for those not already familiar with them.

First, assign units of execution time to each command of a program as follows. The assignment command and *skip* are each counted as 1 unit of time, since their executions take essentially the same time whenever they are executed. An alternative command is counted as the maximum number of units of its alternatives (this may be made finer in some instances). An iterative command is counted as the sum of the units for each of its iterations, or as the number of iterations times the maximum number of units required by each iteration.

One can understand the importance of bound functions for loops in estimating execution time as follows. If a program has no loops, then its execution time is bounded no matter what the input data is. Only if it has a loop can the time depend on the input values, and then the number of loop iterations, for which the bound function gives an upper bound, can be used to give an estimate on the time units used.

Consider the three following loops, $n \geqslant 0$:

$$i := n; \ \textbf{do} \ i > 1 \rightarrow i := i - 1 \ \textbf{od}$$
$$i := n; \ j := 0; \ \textbf{do} \ i > 1 \rightarrow i := i - 1; \ j := 0 \ \textbf{od}$$
$$i := n; \ \textbf{do} \ i > 1 \rightarrow i := i \div 2 \ \textbf{od}$$

The first requires n units of time; the second $2n$. The units of time required by the third program is more difficult to determine. Suppose n

is a power of 2, so that

$$i = 2^k$$

holds for some k. Then dividing i by 2 is equivalent to subtracting 1 from k: $(2^k) \div 2 = 2^{k-1}$. Therefore, each iteration decreases k by 1. Upon termination, $i = 1 = 2^0$, so that $k = 0$. Hence, a suitable bound function is $t = k$, and, in fact, the loop iterates *exactly* k times. The third program makes exactly $ceil(log\,n)$ iterations, for any $n > 0$.

Whenever an algorithm iteratively divides a variable by 2, you can be sure that a log factor is creeping into its execution time. We see this in Binary Search (exercise 4 of section 16.3) and in Quicksort (18.2). This log factor is important, because $log\,n$ is ever so much smaller than n, as n grows large.

The execution time of the first and second programs given above can be considered roughly the same, while that of the third is much lower. This is illustrated in the following table, which gives values of n, $2n$ and $log\,n$ for various values of n. Thus, for $n = 32768$ the first program requires 32769 basic units of time, the second twice as many, and the third only 15!

	1	2	64	128	32768
n:	1	2	64	128	32768
$2n$:	2	4	128	256	65536
$log\,n$:	0	1	6	7	15

We need a measure that allows us to say that the third program is by far the fastest and that the other two are essentially the same. To do this, we define the *order of execution time*.

(A4.1) **Definition**. Let $f(n)$ and $g(n)$ be two functions. We say that $f(n)$ is (no more than) order $g(n)$, written $O(g(n))$, if a constant $c > 0$ exists such that, for all (except a possibly finite number) positive values of n,

$$f(n) \leqslant c*g(n).$$

Further, $f(n)$ *is proportional to* $g(n)$ if $f(n)$ is $O(g(n))$ and $g(n)$ is $O(f(n))$. We also say that $f(n)$ and $g(n)$ are *of the same order*. □

Example 1. Let $f(n) = n + 5$ and $g(n) = n$. Choose $c = 5$. Then, for $1 < n$, $f(n) = n + 5 \leqslant 5n = 5*g(n)$. Hence, $f(n)$ is $O(g(n))$. Choosing $c = 1$ indicates that $g(n)$ is $O(f(n))$. Hence $n + 5$ is proportional to n. □

Example 2. Let $f(n)=n$ and $g(n)=2n$. With $c=1$ we see that $f(n)$ is $O(g(n))$. With $c=1/2$, we see that $g(n)$ is $O(f(n))$. Hence n is proportional to $2n$. For any constants $K1\neq 0$ and $K2$, $K1*n+K2$ is proportional to n. □

Since the first and second programs given above are executed in n and $2n$ units, respectively, their execution times are of the same order. Secondly, one can prove that $\log n$ is $O(n)$, but *not* vice versa. Hence the order of execution time of the third is less than that of the first two programs.

We give below a table of typical execution time orders that arise frequently in programming, from smallest to largest, along with frequent terms used for them. They are given in terms of a single input parameter n. In addition, the (rounded) values of the orders are given for $n=100$ and $n=1000$, so that the difference between them can be seen.

Order	$n=100$	$n=1000$	Term Used
1	1	1	Constant-time algorithm
$\log n$	7	10	logarithmic algorithm
$\sqrt{n}$	10	32	
n	100	1000	linear algorithm
$n \log n$	700	10000	
$n \sqrt{n}$	1000	31623	
n^2	10000	1000000	quadratic (or simply n^2) algorithm
n^3	1000000	10^9	cubic algorithm
2^n	$1.26*10^{30}$	$\sim 10^{300}$	exponential algorithm

For algorithms that have several input values the calculation of the order of execution time becomes more difficult, but the technique remains the same. When comparing two algorithms, one should first compare their execution time orders, and, if they are the same, then proceed to look for finer detail such as the number of times units required, number of array comparisons made, etc.

An algorithm may require different times depending on the configuration of the input values. For example, one array $b[1:n]$ may be sorted in n steps, another array $b'[1:n]$ in n^2 steps by the same algorithm. In this case there are two methods of comparing the algorithms: average- or expected-case time analysis and worst-case time analysis. The former is quite difficult to do; the latter usually much simpler.

As an example, Linear Search, (16.2.5), requires n time units in the worst case and $n/2$ time units in the average case, if one assumes the value being looked for can be in any position with equal probability.

Answers to Exercises

Answers for Chapter 1

1. We show the evaluation of the expressions for state $s1$.

(a) $\lnot(m \lor n) = \lnot(T \lor F) = \lnot T = F$

(b) $\lnot m \lor n = \lnot T \lor F = F \lor F = F$

(c) $\lnot(m \land n) = \lnot(T \land F) = \lnot F = T$

(d) $\lnot m \land n = \lnot T \land F = F \land F = F$

(e) $(m \lor n) \Rightarrow p = (T \lor F) \Rightarrow T = T \Rightarrow T = T$

(f) $m \lor (n \Rightarrow p) = T \lor (F \Rightarrow T) = T \lor T = T$

(g) $(m = n) \land (p = q) = (F = F) \land (T = F) = T \land F = F$

(h) $m = (n \land (p = q)) = F = (F \land (T = F))$
$$= F = (F \land F) = F = F = T$$

(i) $m = (n \land p = q) = F = (F \land T = F) = F = (F = F) = F = T = F$

(j) $(m = n) \land (p \Rightarrow q) = (F = T) \land (F \Rightarrow T) = F \land T = F$

(k) $(m = n \land p) \Rightarrow q = (F = T \land F) \Rightarrow T = (F = F) \Rightarrow T = T \Rightarrow T = T$

(l) $(m \Rightarrow n) \Rightarrow (p \Rightarrow q) = (F \Rightarrow F) \Rightarrow (F \Rightarrow F) = T \Rightarrow T = T$

(m) $(m \Rightarrow (n \Rightarrow p)) \Rightarrow q = (F \Rightarrow (F \Rightarrow F)) \Rightarrow F$
$$= (F \Rightarrow T) \Rightarrow F = T \Rightarrow F = F$$

2. a,b

b c d	$b \lor c$	$b \lor c \lor d$	$b \land c$	$b \land c \land d$
T T T	T	T	T	T
T T F	T	T	T	F
T F T	T	T	F	F
T F F	T	T	F	F
F T T	T	T	F	F
F T F	T	T	F	F
F F T	F	T	F	F
F F F	F	F	F	F

3. Let the Boolean identifiers and their meanings be:

$xlessy$: $x < y$ $xequaly$: $x = y$ $xgreatery$: $x > y$ $xatleasty$: $x \geq y$

$ylessz$: $y < z$ $yequalz$: $y = z$ $ygreaterz$: $y > z$

$vequalw$: $v = w$

$beginxlessy$: Execution of program P begins with $x < y$

$beginxless0$: Execution of program P begins with $x < 0$

$endyequal2powerx$: Execution of P terminates with $y = 2^x$

$noend$: Execution of program P does not terminate

We give one possible proposition; there are others.

(a) $xlessy \lor xequaly$

(d) $xlessy \land ylessz \land vequalw$

(k) $beginxless0 \Rightarrow noend$

Answers for Chapter 2

1. Truth table for the first Commutative law (only) and the law of Negation:

b c	$b \land c$	$c \land b$	$(b \land c) = (c \land b)$	$\neg b$	$\neg \neg b$	$\neg \neg b = b$
T T	T	T	T	F	T	T
T F	F	F	T			
F T	F	F	T	T	F	T
F F	F	F	T			

Truth table for the first Distributive law (only) (since the last two columns are the same, the two expressions heading the columns are equivalent and the law holds):

b c d	$c \land d$	$b \lor c$	$b \lor d$	$b \lor (c \land d)$	$(b \lor c) \land (b \lor d)$
T T T	T	T	T	T	T
T T F	F	T	T	T	T
T F T	F	T	T	T	T
T F F	F	T	T	T	T
F T T	T	T	T	T	T
F T F	F	T	F	F	F
F F T	F	F	T	F	F
F F F	F	F	F	F	F

3. $\neg T = \neg (T \lor \neg T)$ (Excluded Middle)

$= \neg T \land \neg \neg T$ (De Morgan)

$= \neg T \land T$ (Negation)

$= T \land \neg T$ (Commutativity)

$= F$ (Contradiction)

5. Column 1: (b) Contradiction, (c) **or**-simpl., (d) **or**-simpl., (e) **and**-simpl., (f) Identity, (g) Contradiction, (h) Associativity, (i) Distributivity, (j) Distributivity, (k) Commutativity (twice), (l) Negation, (m) De Morgan.

6. (a) $x \lor (y \lor x) \lor \lnot y$
$= x \lor (x \lor y) \lor \lnot y$ (Commut.)
$= (x \lor x) \lor (y \lor \lnot y)$ (Ass.)
$= x \lor T$ (**or**-simpl., Excl. Middle)
$= T$ (**or**-simpl.)

(b) $(x \lor y) \land (x \lor \lnot y)$
$= x \lor (y \land \lnot y)$ (Dist.)
$= x \lor F$ (Contradiction)
$= x$ (**or**-simpl.)

(g) $\lnot x \Rightarrow (x \land y)$
$= x \lor (x \land y)$ (Imp., Neg.)
$= x$ (**or**-simpl.)

(h) $T \Rightarrow (\lnot x \Rightarrow x)$
$= \lnot T \lor (x \lor x)$ (Imp., Neg.)
$= F \lor (x \lor x)$ (exercise 3)
$= x$ (**or**-simpl., twice)

7. Proposition e is transformed using the equivalence laws in 6 major steps:

1. Use the law of Equality to eliminate all occurrences of $=$.

2. Use the law of Implication to eliminate all occurrences of $\Rightarrow$.

3. Use De Morgan's laws and the law of Negation to "move **not** in" so that it is applied only to identifiers and constants. For example, transform $\lnot (a \lor (F \land \lnot c))$ as follows:

$$\lnot (a \lor (F \land \lnot c))$$
$$= \lnot a \land \lnot (F \land \lnot c)$$
$$= \lnot a \land (\lnot F \lor \lnot \lnot c)$$
$$= \lnot a \land (\lnot F \lor c)$$

4. Use $\lnot F = T$ and $\lnot T = F$ to eliminate all occurrences of $\lnot F$ and $\lnot T$ (see exercises 3 and 4).

5. The proposition now has the form $e_0 \lor \cdots \lor e_n$ for some $n \geq 0$, where each of the e_i has the form $(g_0 \land \cdots \land g_m)$. Perform the following until all g_j in all e_i have one of the forms id, $\lnot id$, T and F:

> Consider some e_i with a g_j that is not in the desired form. Use the law of Commutativity to place it as far right as possible, so that it becomes g_m. Now, g_m must have the form $(h_0 \lor \cdots \lor h_k)$, so that the complete e_i is
>
> $$g_0 \land \cdots \land g_{m-1} \land (h_0 \lor \cdots \lor h_k)$$
>
> Use Distributivity to replace this by

$$(g_0 \wedge \cdots \wedge g_{m-1} \wedge h_0) \vee \cdots \vee (g_0 \wedge \cdots \wedge g_{m-1} \wedge h_k)$$

This adds m propositions e_i at the main level, but reduces the level of nesting of operators in at least one place. Hence, after a number of iterations it must terminate.

6. The proposition now has the form $e_0 \vee \cdots \vee e_n$ for some $n \geqslant 0$, where each of the e_i has the form $(g_0 \wedge \cdots \wedge g_m)$ and the g_j are id, $\neg id$, T or F. Use the laws of Commutativity, Contradiction, Excluded Middle and **or**-simplification to get the proposition in final form. If any of the e_i reduces to T then reduce the complete proposition to T; if any reduces to F use the law of **or**-simplification to eliminate it (unless the whole proposition is F).

9. The laws have already been proved to be tautologies in exercise 1. We now show that use of the rule of Substitution generates a tautology, by induction on the form of proposition $E(p)$, where p is an identifier.

Case 1: $E(p)$ is either T, F or an identifier that is not p. In this case, $E(e1)$ and $E(e2)$ are both E itself. By the law of Identity, $E = E$, so that a tautology is generated.

Case 2: $E(p)$ is p. In this case, $E(e1)$ is $e1$ and $E(e2)$ is $e2$, and by hypothesis $e1 = e2$ is a tautology.

Case 3: $E(p)$ has the form $\neg E1(p)$. By induction, $E1(e1) = E1(e2)$. Hence, $E1(e1)$ and $E1(e2)$ have the same value in every state. The following truth table then establishes the desired result:

$E1(e1)$	$E1(e2)$	$\neg E1(e1)$	$\neg E1(e2)$	$\neg E1(e1) = \neg E1(e2)$
T	T	F	F	T
F	F	T	T	T

Case 4: $E(p)$ has the form $E1(p) \wedge E2(p)$. By induction, we have that $E1(e1) = E1(e2)$ and $E2(e1) = E2(e2)$. Hence, $E1(e1)$ and $E1(e2)$ have the same value in every state, and $E2(e1)$ and $E2(e2)$ have the same value in every state. The following truth table then establishes the desired result:

$E1(e1)$	$E1(e2)$	$E2(e1)$	$E2(e2)$	$E1(e1) \wedge E2(e1)$	$E1(e2) \wedge E2(e2)$
T	T	T	T	T	T
T	T	F	F	F	F
F	F	T	T	F	F
F	F	F	F	F	F

The rest of the cases, $E(p)$ having the forms $E1(p) \vee E2(p)$, $E1(p) \Rightarrow E2(p)$ and $E1(p) = E2(p)$ are similar and are not shown here.

We now show that use of the rule of Transitivity generates only tautologies. Since $e1 = e2$ and $e2 = e3$ are tautologies, we know that $e1$ and $e2$ have the same value in every state and that $e2$ and $e3$ have the same value in every state. The following truth table establishes the desired result:

$e1$	$e2$	$e3$	$e1 = e3$
T	T	T	T
F	F	F	T

10. Reduce e to a proposition $e1$ in conjunctive normal form (see exercise 8). By exercise 9, $e = e1$ is a tautology, and since e is assumed to be a tautology, $e1$ must be a tautology. Hence it is true in all states. Proposition $e1$ is T, is F or has the form $e_0 \wedge \cdots \wedge e_n$, where each of the e_i has the form $g_0 \vee \cdots \vee g_m$ and each g_i is id or $\neg id$ and the g_i are distinct. Proposition $e1$ cannot have the latter form, because it is not a tautology. It cannot be F, since F is not a tautology. Hence, it must be T, and $e = T$ has been proved.

Answers for Section 3.2

3. (a) From $p \wedge q, p \Rightarrow r$ infer r

1	$p \wedge q$	pr 1
2	$p \Rightarrow r$	pr 2
3	p	$\wedge$-E, 1
4	r	$\Rightarrow$-E, 2, 3

or **From $p \wedge q, p \Rightarrow r$ infer p**

1	p	$\wedge$-E, pr 1
2	p	$\Rightarrow$-E, pr 2, 1

3. (b) From $p = q$, q infer p

1	$p = q$	pr 1
2	q	pr 2
3	$q \Rightarrow p$	=-E, 1
4	p	$\Rightarrow$-E, 3, 2

3. (c) From p, $q \Rightarrow r$, $p \Rightarrow r$ infer $p \wedge r$

1	r	$\Rightarrow$-E, pr 3, pr 1
2	$p \wedge r$	$\wedge$-I, pr 1, 1

328 Answers to Exercises

4. Proof of 3(a). Since $p \wedge q$ is true, p must be true. From $p \Rightarrow r$, we then conclude that r must be true.

Proof of 3(b). Since $p = q$ is true, q being true means that p must be true.

Answers for Section 3.3

1. Infer $(p \wedge q \wedge (p \Rightarrow r)) \Rightarrow (r \vee (q \Rightarrow r))$

1	$(p \wedge q \wedge (p \Rightarrow r)) \Rightarrow (r \vee (q \Rightarrow r))$	$\Rightarrow$-I, (3.2.11)

2. Infer $(p \wedge q) \Rightarrow (p \vee q)$

2	**From** $p \wedge q$ **infer** $p \vee q$	
	2.1	p	$\wedge$-E, pr 1
	2.2	$p \vee q$	$\vee$-I, 1
3	$(p \wedge q) \Rightarrow (p \vee q)$	$\Rightarrow$-I, 2

4. Infer $p = p \vee p$

1	**From** p **infer** $p \vee p$	
	1.1	$p \vee p$	$\vee$-I, pr 1
2	$p \Rightarrow p \vee p$	$\Rightarrow$-I, 1
3	**From** $p \vee p$ **infer** p	
	3.1	p	$\vee$-E, pr 1, (3.3.3), (3.3.3)
4	$p \vee p \Rightarrow p$	$\Rightarrow$-I, 3
5	$p = p \vee p$	=-I, 2, 4

8. The reference on line 2.2 to line 2 is invalid.

11. From $\neg q$ **infer** $q \Rightarrow p$

1	$\neg q$	pr 1
2	**From** q **infer** p	
	2.1	q	pr 1
	2.2	**From** $\neg p$ **infer** $q \wedge \neg q$	
		2.2.1	$q \wedge \neg q$	$\wedge$-I, 2.1, 1
	2.3	p	$\neg$-E, 2.2
2	$q \Rightarrow p$	$\Rightarrow$-I, 2

26. From p **infer** p

1	p		pr 1
2	**From** $\neg p$ **infer** $p \wedge \neg p$		
	2.1	$p \wedge \neg p$	$\wedge$-I, 1, pr 1
3	p		$\neg$-E, 2

27. The following "English" proofs are not intended to be particularly noteworthy; they only show how one might attempt to argue in English. Building truth tables or using the equivalence transformation system of chapter 2 is more reasonable.

Many of these proofs rely on the property that a proposition $b \Rightarrow c$ is true in any state in which the consequent c is true, and hence to prove that $b \Rightarrow c$ is a tautology one need only investigate states in which c is false.

27. Proof of 1. The proposition $(p \wedge q \wedge (p \Rightarrow r)) \Rightarrow (r \vee (q \Rightarrow r))$ is true because it was already proven in (3.2.11) that $(r \vee (q \Rightarrow r))$ followed from $(p \wedge q \wedge (p \Rightarrow r))$.

27. Proof of 2. If $p \wedge q$ is true, then p is true. Hence, anything "ored" with p is true, so $p \vee q$ is true.

27. Proof of 3. If q is true, then so is $q \wedge q$.

27. Proof of 5. Suppose p is true. Then $e \Rightarrow p$ is true no matter what e is. Hence $(r \vee s) \Rightarrow p$ is true. Hence, $p \Rightarrow ((r \vee s) \Rightarrow p)$ is true.

Answers for Section 3.4

1. From $p \Rightarrow (q \Rightarrow (p \vee q))$ **infer** $(p \wedge q) \Rightarrow (p \vee q)$

1	$p \Rightarrow (q \Rightarrow (p \vee q))$		pr 1
2	**From** $p \wedge q$ **infer** $p \vee q$		
	2.1	p	$\wedge$-E, pr 1
	2.2	$q \Rightarrow (p \vee q)$	$\Rightarrow$-E, 1, 2.1
	2.3	q	$\wedge$-E, pr 1
	2.4	$p \vee q$	$\Rightarrow$-E, 2.2, 2.3
3	$(p \wedge q) \Rightarrow (p \vee q)$		$\Rightarrow$-I, 2

8.(a) From $b \vee c$ **infer** $\neg b \Rightarrow c$

1	$b \vee c$		pr 1
2	**From** $\neg b$ **infer** c		
	2.1	c	(3.4.6), 1, pr 1
3	$\neg b \Rightarrow c$		$\Rightarrow$-I, 2

8.(b) From $\neg b \Rightarrow c$ infer $b \vee c$

1	$\neg b \Rightarrow c$	pr 1
2	$b \vee \neg b$	(3.4.14)
3	**From b infer $b \vee c$**	
	3.1 $\quad b \vee c$	$\vee$-I, pr 1
4	$b \Rightarrow b \vee c$	$\Rightarrow$-I, 3
5	**From $\neg b$ infer $b \vee c$**	
	5.1 $\quad c$	$\Rightarrow$-E, 1, pr 1
	5.2 $\quad b \vee c$	$\vee$-I, 5.1
6	$\neg b \Rightarrow b \vee c$	$\Rightarrow$-I, 5
7	$b \vee c$	$\vee$-E, 2, 4, 6

8.(c) Infer $b \vee c = (\neg b \Rightarrow c)$

1	$(b \vee c) \Rightarrow (\neg b \Rightarrow c)$	$\Rightarrow$-I, 8(a)
2	$(\neg b \Rightarrow c) \Rightarrow b \vee c$	$\Rightarrow$-I, 8(b)
3	$b \vee c = (\neg b \Rightarrow c)$	=-I, 1, 2

10. We prove the theorem by induction on the structure of expression $E(p)$.

Case 1: E(p) is the single identifier p. In this case, $E(e1)$ is simply $e1$ and $E(e2)$ is $e2$, and we have the proof

From $e1 = e2$, $e1$ infer $e2$

1	$e1 \Rightarrow e2$	=-E, pr 1
2	$e2$	$\Rightarrow$-E, 3, pr 2

Case 2: $E(p)$ is an identifier different from p, say v. In this case $E(e1)$ and $E(e2)$ are both v and the theorem holds trivially.

Case 3: $E(p)$ has the form $\neg G(p)$, for some expression G. By induction, we may assume that a proof of

From $e2 = e1$, $G(e2)$ infer $G(e1)$

exists, and we prove the desired result as follows.

From $el = e2$, $\neg G(el)$ **infer** $\neg G(e2)$

1	$el = e2$	pr 1
2	$\neg G(el)$	pr 2
3	**From** $G(e2)$ **infer** $G(el) \wedge \neg G(el)$	

3.1	$e2 = el$	$\Rightarrow$-E, ex. 25 of 3.3, 1
3.2	$(e2 = el) \wedge G(e2) \Rightarrow G(el)$	$\Rightarrow$-I, assumed proof
3.3	$(e2 = el) \wedge G(e2)$	$\wedge$-I, 3.1, pr 1
3.4	$G(el)$	$\Rightarrow$-E, 3.2, 3.3
3.5	$G(el) \wedge \neg G(el)$	$\wedge$-I, 3.4, 2

4	$\neg G(e2)$	$\neg$-I, 3

Case 4: $E(p)$ has the form $G(p) \wedge H(p)$ for some expressions G and H. In this case, by induction we may assume that the following proofs exist.

From $el = e2$, $G(el)$ **infer** $G(e2)$
From $el = e2$, $H(el)$ **infer** $H(e2)$

We can then give the following proof.

From $el = e2$, $G(el) \wedge H(el)$ **infer** $G(e2) \wedge H(e2)$

1	$G(el)$	$\wedge$-E, pr 2
2	$G(e2)$	Assumed proof, pr 1, 1
3	$H(el)$	$\wedge$-E, pr 2
4	$H(e2)$	Assumed proof, pr 1, 3
5	$G(e2) \wedge H(e2)$	$\wedge$-I, 2, 4

The rest of the cases, where $E(p)$ has one of the forms $G(p) \vee H(p)$, $G(p) \Rightarrow H(p)$ and $G(p) = H(p)$, are left to the reader.

11. From $a = b$, $b = c$ **infer** $a = c$

1	$a \Rightarrow b$	=-E, pr 1
2	$b \Rightarrow c$	=-E, pr 2
3	**From** a **infer** c	

3.1	b	$\Rightarrow$-E, 1, pr 1
3.2	c	$\Rightarrow$-E, 2, 3.1

4	$a \Rightarrow c$	$\Rightarrow$-I, 3
5	$c \Rightarrow a$	proof omitted, similar to 1-4
6	$a = c$	=-I, 4, 5

Answers for Section 3.5

1. Conjecture 4, which can be written as $bl \land \neg gj \Rightarrow \neg tb$, is not valid, as can be seen by considering the state with $tb = T$, $ma = T$, $bl = T$, $gh = F$, $fd = T$ and $gj = F$.

Conjecture 8, which can be written as $gh \land tb \Rightarrow (bl \Rightarrow \neg fd)$, is proved as follows:

From gh, tb infer $bl \Rightarrow \neg fd$

1	$\neg\neg tb$	subs, Negation, pr 2
2	$\neg bl \lor ma$	(3.4.6), Premise 1, 1
3	$\neg\neg gh$	subs, Negation, pr 1
4	$\neg ma \lor \neg fd$	(3.4.6), Premise 2, 3
5	**From bl infer $\neg fd$**	

	5.1	$\neg\neg bl$	subs, Negation, pr 1
	5.2	ma	(3.4.6), 2, 5.1
	5.3	$\neg\neg ma$	subs, Negation, 5.2
	5.4	$\neg fd$	(3.4.6), 4, 5.3
6	$bl \Rightarrow \neg fd$		$\Rightarrow$-I, 5

2. For the proofs of the valid conjectures using the equivalence transformation system of chapter 2, we first write here the disjunctive normal form of the Premises:

Premise 1: $\neg tb \lor \neg bl \lor ma$
Premise 2: $\neg ma \lor \neg fd \lor \neg gh$
Premise 3: $gj \lor (fd \land \neg gh)$

Conjecture 2, which can be written in the form $(ma \land gh) \Rightarrow gj$, is proved as follows. First, use the laws of Implication and De Morgan to put it in disjunctive normal form:

(E.1) $\neg ma \lor \neg gh \lor gj$.

To show (E.1) to be true, it is necessary to show that at least one of the disjuncts is true. Assume, then, that the first two are false: $ma = T$ and $gh = T$. In that case, Premise 2 reduces to $\neg fd$, so we conclude that $fd = F$. But then Premise 3 reduces to gj, and since Premise 3 is true, gj is true, so that (E.1) is true also.

Answers for Section 4.1.

1. (a) T. (b) T. (c) F. (d) T.

2. (a) $\{1, 2, 3, 4, 6\}$. (b) $\{2, 4\}$. (c) F. (d) F.

3. (a) U. (b) T. (c) U. (d) U.

5. We don't build all the truth tables explicitly, but instead analyze the various cases.

Associativity. To prove a **cor** (b **cor** c) and (a **cor** b) **cor** c equivalent, we investigate possible values of a. Suppose $a = T$. Then evaluation using the truth table for **cor** shows that both expressions yield T. Suppose $a = F$. Then evaluation shows that both yield b **cor** c, so that they are the same. Suppose $a = U$. Then evaluation shows that both expressions yield U. The proof of the other associative law is similar.

Answers for Section 4.2

1. The empty string ε —the string containing zero characters— is the identity element, because for all strings x, $x \mid \varepsilon = x$.

4. $(N i: 0 \leqslant i < n: x = b[i]) = (N i: 0 \leqslant i < m: x = c[i])$.

5. $(A k: 0 \leqslant k < n:$
$\quad (N i: 0 \leqslant i < n: b[k] = b[i]) = (N j: 0 \leqslant j < n: b[k] = c[i]))$.

6. (a) $(A i: j \leqslant i < k+1: b[i] = 0)$

(b) $\neg(E i: j \leqslant i < k+1: b[i] = 0)$, or $(A i: j \leqslant i < k+1: b[i] \neq 0)$

(c) Some means at least one: $(E i: j \leqslant i < k+1: b[i] = 0)$, or, better yet, $(N i: j \leqslant i < k+1: b[i] = 0) > 0$

(d) $(0 \leqslant i < n$ **cand** $b[i] = 0) \Rightarrow j \leqslant i \leqslant k$,   or
$(A i: 0 \leqslant i < n: b[i] = 0 \Rightarrow j \leqslant i \leqslant k)$

Answers for Section 4.3

1. (a) $(E k: 0 \leqslant k < n: P \wedge H_k^i(T)) \wedge k > 0$ (invalid)

(b) $(A j: 0 \leqslant j < n: B_j^i \Rightarrow wp(SL_j^i, R))$

Answers for Section 4.4

1. $E_j^i = E$ (i is not free in E)

$E_{n+1}^n = (A i: 0 \leqslant i < n+1: b[i] < b[i+1])$

2. E_j^i is invalid, because it yields two interpretations of j:

$E_j^i = n > j \wedge (N j: 1 \leqslant j < n: n \div j = 0) > 1$

3. $E_j^i = E$ (since i is not free in E)

4. The precondition is $x+1>0$, which can be written as R_{x+i}^x (compare with the assignment statement $x := x+1$).

6. (a) For the expressions T, F and id where id is an identifier that is not i, $E_e^i = E$.

(b) For the expression consisting of identifier i, $E_e^i = e$.

(c) $(E)_e^i = (E_e^i)$

(d) $(\neg E)_e^i = \neg(E_e^i)$

(e) $(E1 \wedge E2)_e^i = E1_e^i \wedge E2_e^i$ (Similarly for $\vee$, $=$ and $\Rightarrow$)

(f) $(A\, i : m \leqslant i \leqslant n : E)_e^i = (A\, i : m \leqslant i \leqslant n : E)$

For identifier j not identifier i,
$(A\, j : m \leqslant j \leqslant n : E)_e^i = (A\, j : m_e^i \leqslant j \leqslant n_e^i : E_e^i)$ (Similarly for E and N.)

Answers for Section 4.5

1. (a) E is commutative, as is A; this can be written as $(E\,t : (E\,p : fool(p, t)))$, or $(E\,p : (E\,t : fool(p, t)))$, or $(E\,p, t : fool(p, t))$.

2. (b) $(A\, a, b, c : integer(a, b, c):$
$sides(a, b, c) = a+b \geqslant c \wedge a+c \geqslant b \wedge b+c \geqslant a)$

Answers for Section 4.6

1. (a) $x = 6$, $y = 6$, $b = T$. (b) $x = 5$, $y = 5$, $b = T$.

Answers for Section 5.1

1. (a) (3, 4, 6, 8). (d) (8, 6, 4, 2).

2. (a) 0. (b) 2. (c) 0.

3. (a) $(i = j \wedge 5 = 5) \vee (i \neq j \wedge 5 = b[j]) = (i = j) \vee b[j] = 5$.
(b) $b[i] = i$.

Answers for Section 5.2

1. (Those exercises without abbreviations are not answered.)
(a) $b[j:k] = 0$.
(b) $b[j:k] \neq 0$.
(c) $0 \in b[j:k]$.
(d) $0 \notin b[0:j-1] \wedge 0 \notin b[k+1:n-1]$.

2. (a) $0 \leqslant p \leqslant q+1 \leqslant n \wedge b$

Answers for Section 6.2

1. (a) *First specification*: $\{n > 0\}$ S $\{x = max(\{y \mid y \in b[0:n-1]\})\}$.

Second specification: Given fixed n and fixed array $b[0:n-1]$, establish

$$R: x = max(\{y \mid y \in b\}).$$

For program development it may be useful to replace *max* by its meaning. The result assertion R would then be

$$R: (E\, i: 0 \leqslant i < n: x = b[i]) \wedge (A\, i: 0 \leqslant i < n: b[i] \leqslant x)$$

(d) *First specification*:

$$\{n > 0\}$$
$$S$$
$$\{0 \leqslant i < n \wedge (A\, j: 0 \leqslant j < n: b[i] \geqslant b[j]) \wedge b[i] > b[0:i-1]\}.$$

Second specification: Given fixed $n > 0$ and fixed array $b[0:n-1]$, set i to establish

$$R: 0 \leqslant i < n \wedge b[0:n-1] \leqslant b[i] \wedge b[i] > b[0:i-1]$$

(k) Define $average(i) = (\Sigma\, j: 0 \leqslant j < 4: grade[i, j])$.

First specification:

$$\{n > 0\}\ S\ \{0 \leqslant i < n \wedge (A\, j: 0 \leqslant j < n: average(i) \geqslant average(j))\}.$$

Answers for Chapter 7

1. (a) $i + 1 > 0$, or $i \geqslant 0$.
(b) $i + 2 + j - 2 = 0$, or $i + j = 0$.

3. Suppose $Q \Rightarrow R$. Then $Q \wedge R = Q$. Therefore

$$
\begin{aligned}
wp(S, Q) &= wp(S, Q \wedge R) && \text{(since } Q \wedge R = R) \\
&= wp(S, Q) \wedge wp(S, R) && \text{(by (7.4))} \\
&\Rightarrow wp(S, R)
\end{aligned}
$$

This proves (7.5).

6. By (7.6), we see that LHS (of (7.7)) $\Rightarrow$ RHS. Hence it remains to show that RHS $\Rightarrow$ LHS. To prove this, we must show that any state s in $wp(S, Q \vee R)$ is either guaranteed to be in $wp(S, Q)$ or guaranteed to be in $wp(S, R)$. Consider a state s in $wp(S, Q \vee R)$. Because S is deterministic, execution of S beginning in s is guaranteed to terminate in a single, unique state s', with s' in $Q \vee R$. This unique state s' must be either in Q, in which case s is in $wp(S, Q)$, or in R, in which case s is in

$wp(S, R)$.

7. This exercise is intended to make the reader more aware of how quantification works in connection with wp, and the need for the rule that each identifier be used in only one way in a predicate. Suppose that $Q \Rightarrow wp(S, R)$ is true in every state. This assumption is equivalent to

(E7.1) $(A\ x\colon Q \Rightarrow wp(S, R))$.

We are asked to analyze predicate (7.8): $\{(A\ x\colon Q)\}\ S\ \{(A\ x\colon R)\}$, which is equivalent to

(E7.2) $(A\ x\colon Q) \Rightarrow wp(S, (A\ x\colon R))$.

Let us analyze this first of all under the rule that no identifier be used in more than one way in a predicate. Hence, rewrite (E7.2) as

(E7.3) $(A\ x\colon Q) \Rightarrow wp(S, (A\ z\colon R_z^x))$.

and assume that x does not appear in S and that z is a fresh identifier. We argue operationally that (E7.3) is true. Suppose the antecedent of (E7.3) is true in some state s, and that execution of S begun in s terminates in state s'. Because S does not contain identifier x, we have $s(x) = s'(x)$.

Because the antecedent of (E7.3) is true in s, we conclude from (E7.1) that $(A\ x\colon wp(S, R))$ is also true in state s. Hence, no matter what the value of x in s, $s'(R)$ is true. But $s(x) = s'(x)$. Thus, no matter what the value of x in s', $s'(R)$ is true. Hence, so is $s'((A\ x\colon R))$, and so is $s'((A\ z\colon R_z^x))$. Thus, the consequent of (E7.3) is true in s, and (E7.3) holds.

We now give a counterexample to show that (E7.2) need not hold if x is assigned in command S and if x appears in R. Take command $S\colon x := 1$. Take $R\colon x = 1$. Take $Q\colon T$. Then (E7.1) is

$(A\ x\colon T \Rightarrow wp(\text{``}x := 1\text{''}, x = 1))$

which is true. But (E7.2) is false in this case: its antecedent $(A\ x\colon T)$ is true but its consequent $wp(\text{``}x := 1\text{''}, (A\ x\colon x = 1))$ is false because predicate $(A\ x\colon x = 1)$ is F.

We conclude that if x occurs both in S and R, then (E7.2) does not in general follow from (E7.1).

Answers for Chapter 8

3. By definition, $wp(make-true, F) = T$, which violates the law of the Excluded Miracle, (7.3).

5. $wp(\text{"}S1; \ S2\text{"}, Q) \vee wp(\text{"}S1; \ S2\text{"}, R)$

$\qquad = wp(S1, wp(S2, Q)) \vee wp(S1, wp(S2, R))$ (by definition)

$\qquad = wp(S1, wp(S2, Q) \vee wp(S2, R))$ (since $S1$ satisfies (7.7))

$\qquad = wp(S1, wp(S2, Q \vee R))$ (since $S2$ satisfies (7.7))

$\qquad = wp(\text{"}S1; \ S2\text{"}, Q \vee R)$ (by definition)

Answers for Section 9.1

1. (a) $(2*y+3) = 13$, or $y = 5$.

(b) $x+y < 2*y$, or $x < y$.

(c) $0 < j+1 \wedge (A \ i: 0 \leqslant i \leqslant j+1: b[i] = 5)$.

(d) $(b[j] = 5) = (A \ i: 0 \leqslant i \leqslant j: b[i] = 5)$

3. Execution of $x := e$ in state s evaluates e to yield the value $s(e)$ and stores this value as the new value of x. This is our conventional model of execution. Hence, for the final state s' we have $s' = (s; x:s(e))$.

We want to show that $s'(R) = s(R_e^x)$. But this is simply lemma 4.6.2. This means that if R is to be true (false) after the assignment (i.e. in state s') then R_e^x must be true (false) before (i.e. in state s). This is exactly what definition (9.1) indicates.

4. Writing both Q and e as functions of x, we have

$$wp(\text{"}x := e(x)\text{"}, sp(Q(x), \text{"}x := e(x)\text{"}))$$

$$= \ wp(\text{"}x := e(x)\text{"}, (E\,v: Q(v) \wedge x = e(v)))$$

$$= \ (E\,v: Q(v) \wedge x = e(v))_{e(x)}^x$$

(E4.1) $\qquad = \ (E\,v: Q(v) \wedge e(x) = e(v))$

The last line follows because neither $Q(v)$ nor $e(v)$ contains a reference to x. Now suppose Q is true in some state s. Let $v = s(x)$, the value of x in state s. For this v, $(Q(v) \wedge e(x) = e(v))$ is true in state s, so that (E4.1) is also true in s. Hence $Q \Rightarrow (E4.1)$, which is what we needed to show.

Answers for Section 9.2

1. We prove only that $x := e1; \ y := e2$ is equivalent to $x, y := e1, e2$. Write any postcondition R as a function of x and y: $R(x,y)$.

$$wp(\text{"}x := e1; \ y := e2\text{"}, R(x, y))$$

$$= \ wp(\text{"}x := e1\text{"}, wp(\text{"}y := e2\text{"}, R(x, y))$$

$$= \ wp(\text{``}x := e1\text{''}, \ R(x, y)^y_{e2})$$
$$= \ wp(\text{``}x := e1\text{''}, \ R(x, e2))$$
$$= \ R(x, e2)^x_{e1}$$
$$= \ R(e1, e2) \qquad\qquad (\text{since } x \text{ is not free in } e2)$$
$$= \ wp(\text{``}x, y := e1, e2\text{''}, \ R(x, y)) \quad (\text{by definition})$$

3. (a) $1*c^d = c^d$, or T

(b) $1 \leqslant 1 < n \ \wedge \ b[0] = (\Sigma j : 0 \leqslant j \leqslant 0 : b[j]$], or $1 < n$

(c) $0^2 < 1 \ \wedge \ (0+1)^2 \geqslant 1$, or T

4. In these, it must be remembered that x is a function of the identifiers involved. Hence, if x occurs in an expression in which a substitution is being made, that substitution may change x also. In the places where this happens, x is written as a function of the variables involved. See especially exercise (b).

(a) $wp(\text{``}a, b := a+1, x\text{''}, b = a+1) = x = a+2$. Hence, take $x = a+2$.

(b) $wp(\text{``}a := a+1; \ b := x(a)\text{''}, b = a+1)$
$$= \ wp(\text{``}a := a+1\text{''}, x(a) = a+1)$$
$$= \ x(a+1) = a+2$$

This is satisfied by taking $x(a) = a+1$. Hence, take $x = a+1$.

(e) $wp(\text{``}i := i+1; \ j := x(i)\text{''}, i = j)$
$$= \ wp(\text{``}i := i+1\text{''}, i = x(i))$$
$$= \ i+1 = x(i+1)$$

Answers for Section 9.3

1. For each part, the weakest precondition, determined by textual substitution, is given and then simplified.

(a) $(b; i:i)[(b; i:i)[i]] = i \ = \ (b; i:i)[i] = i$
$$= \ i = i \ = \ T$$

(b) $(E j : i \leqslant j < n : (b; i:5)[i] \leqslant (b; i:5)[j])$
$$= \ (E j : i \leqslant j < n : 5 \leqslant (b; i:5)[j])$$
$$= \ (E j : i < j < n : 5 \leqslant (b; i:5)[j]) \ \vee \ 5 \leqslant (b; i:5)[i]$$
$$= \ (E j : i < j < n : 5 \leqslant (b; i:5)[j]) \ \vee \ 5 \leqslant 5$$
$$= \ T$$

Answers for Section 9.4

1. (a) $R^{b, \ x}_{(b; \ i:e; \ j:f), \ g}$

2. For each part, the weakest precondition determined by textual substitution is given and then simplified.

(a) $(b; i:3; 2:4)[i] = 3$
$$= (i = 2 \wedge 4 = 3) \vee (i \neq 2 \wedge 3 = 3)$$
$$= i \neq 2$$
(g) $b[p] = (b; p:b[b[p]]; b[p]:p)[(b; p:b[b[p]]; b[p]:p)[b[p]]]$
$$= b[p] = (b; p:b[b[p]]; b[p]:p)[p]$$
$$= (p = b[p] \wedge b[p] = p) \vee (p \neq b[p] \wedge b[p] = b[b[p]])$$
$$= p = b[p] \vee b[p] = b[b[p]] \quad \text{(see (c))}$$

5. The lemma has been proven for the case that $\bar{x}$ consists of distinct identifiers, and we need only consider the case that $\bar{x} = b \circ s_1, ..., b \circ s_n$. To prove this case, we will need to use the obvious fact that

(E5.1) $(b; s:b \circ s) = b$

Remembering that x_i *equiv* $b:s_i$, we have

$$(E_{\bar{u}}^{\bar{x}})_{\bar{x}}^{\bar{u}} = (E_{(b; s_1:u_1; \cdots; s_n:u_n)}^{b})_{\bar{x}}^{\bar{u}}$$
$$= E_{(b; s_1:b \circ s_1; \cdots; s_n:b \circ s_n)}^{b} \quad \text{(substitute } x_i \text{ for each } u_i\text{)}$$
$$= E_b^b \quad (n \text{ applications of (E5.1))}$$
$$= E$$

Answers for Chapter 10

3. Letting $R = q*w + r = x \wedge r \geqslant 0$, we have

$$wp(S3, R) = (w \leqslant r \vee w > r) \wedge$$
$$(w \leqslant r \Rightarrow wp(\text{``}r, q := r - w, q + 1\text{''}, R)) \wedge$$
$$(w > r \Rightarrow wp(skip, R))$$
$$= (w \leqslant r \Rightarrow ((q+1)*w + r - w = x \wedge r - w \geqslant 0)) \wedge (w > r \Rightarrow R)$$
$$= (w \leqslant r \Rightarrow q*w + r = x \wedge r - w \geqslant 0) \wedge (w > r \Rightarrow R)$$

This is implied by R.

6. $wp(S6, R) = (f[i] < g[j] \vee f[i] = g[j] \vee f[i] > g[j]) \wedge$
$$(f[i] < g[j] \Rightarrow R_{i+1}^{i}) \wedge$$
$$(f[i] = g[j] \Rightarrow R) \wedge$$
$$(f[i] > g[j] \Rightarrow R_{j+1}^{j})$$
$$= R \wedge (f[i] < g[j] \Rightarrow f[i+1] \leqslant X) \wedge (f[i] > g[j] \Rightarrow g[j] \geqslant X)$$
$$= R \quad (\text{since } R \text{ implies that } g[j] \leqslant X \text{ and } f[i] \leqslant X)$$

Answers for Chapter 11

2. In the proof of theorem 10.5 it was proven that

$$(A\, i: P \wedge B_i \Rightarrow wp(S_i, P)) = P \wedge (A\, i: B_i \Rightarrow wp(S_i, P)).$$

Therefore, given assumption 1, we have

$$
\begin{aligned}
P \wedge \mathrm{BB} &= P \wedge \mathrm{BB} \wedge T \\
&= P \wedge \mathrm{BB} \wedge (A\,i\colon P \wedge B_i \Rightarrow wp(S_i, P)) \text{ (since 1. is true)} \\
&= P \wedge \mathrm{BB} \wedge P \wedge (A\,i\colon B_i \Rightarrow wp(S_i, P)) \\
&\Rightarrow \mathrm{BB} \wedge (A\,i\colon B_i \Rightarrow wp(S_i, P)) \\
&= wp(\mathrm{IF}, P)
\end{aligned}
$$

3. By a technique similar to that used in exercise 2, we can show that assumption 3 of theorem 11.6 implies

$$(E3.1) \quad P \wedge \mathrm{BB} \Rightarrow wp(``T\!:=\!t;\ \mathrm{IF}", t < T)$$

Thus, we need only show that (E3.1) implies 3' of theorem 11.6. Note that P, IF, and t do not contain $t1$ or $t0$. Since IF does not refer to T and $t0$, we know that $wp(\mathrm{IF}, t1 \leqslant t0+1) = \mathrm{BB} \wedge t1 \leqslant t0+1$. We then have the following:

$$
\begin{aligned}
(E3.1) &= P \wedge \mathrm{BB} \Rightarrow wp(\mathrm{IF}, t < t1)_t^{t1} \\
&\qquad \text{(by definition of :=)} \\
&\Rightarrow P \wedge \mathrm{BB} \wedge t \leqslant t0+1 \Rightarrow wp(\mathrm{IF}, t \leqslant t1-1)_t^{t1} \wedge t \leqslant t0+1 \\
&\qquad \text{(Insert } t \leqslant t0+1 \text{ on both sides of } \Rightarrow) \\
&= P \wedge \mathrm{BB} \wedge t \leqslant t0+1 \Rightarrow wp(\mathrm{IF}, t \leqslant t1-1)_t^{t1} \wedge (t1 \leqslant t0+1)_t^{t1} \\
&= P \wedge \mathrm{BB} \wedge t \leqslant t0+1 \Rightarrow (wp(\mathrm{IF}, t \leqslant t1-1) \wedge t1 \leqslant t0+1)_t^{t1} \\
&\qquad \text{(Distributivity of textual substitution)} \\
&= P \wedge \mathrm{BB} \wedge t \leqslant t0+1 \Rightarrow (wp(\mathrm{IF}, t \leqslant t1-1) \wedge wp(\mathrm{IF}, t1 \leqslant t0+1))_t^{t1} \\
&\qquad \text{(IF does not contain } t1 \text{ nor } t0) \\
&= P \wedge \mathrm{BB} \wedge t \leqslant t0+1 \Rightarrow wp(\mathrm{IF}, t \leqslant t1-1 \wedge t1 \leqslant t0+1)_t^{t1} \\
&\qquad \text{(Distributivity of Conjunction)} \\
&= P \wedge \mathrm{BB} \wedge t \leqslant t0+1 \Rightarrow wp(\mathrm{IF}, t \leqslant t0)_t^{t1} \\
&= P \wedge \mathrm{BB} \wedge t \leqslant t0+1 \Rightarrow wp(``t1\!:=\!t;\ \mathrm{IF}", t \leqslant t0) \\
&= P \wedge \mathrm{BB} \wedge t \leqslant t0+1 \Rightarrow wp(``\mathrm{IF}", t \leqslant t0)
\end{aligned}
$$

Since the derivation holds irrespective of the value $t0$, it holds for all $t0$, and 3' is true.

4. We first show that (11.7) holds for $k = 0$ by showing that it is equivalent to assumption 2:

$$
\begin{aligned}
P \wedge \mathrm{BB} &\Rightarrow t > 0 & \text{(Assumption 2)} \\
&= \neg P \vee \neg \mathrm{BB} \vee t > 0 & \text{(Implication, De Morgan)} \\
&= \neg P \vee \neg(t \leqslant 0) \vee \neg \mathrm{BB} \\
&= P \wedge t \leqslant 0 \Rightarrow \neg \mathrm{BB} & \text{(De Morgan, Implication)} \\
&= P \wedge t \leqslant 0 \Rightarrow P \wedge \neg \mathrm{BB}
\end{aligned}
$$

$$= P \wedge t \leqslant 0 \Rightarrow H_0(P \wedge \neg BB) \quad \text{(Definition of } H_0)$$

Assume (11.7) true for $k = K$ and prove it true for $k = K+1$. We have:

$$P \wedge BB \wedge t \leqslant K+1 \Rightarrow wp(IF, P \wedge t \leqslant K) \quad \text{(this is 3')}$$
$$\Rightarrow wp(IF, H_K(P \wedge \neg BB)) \quad \text{(Induction hyp.)}$$

and
$$P \wedge \neg BB \wedge t \leqslant K+1 \Rightarrow P \wedge \neg BB$$
$$= H_0(P \wedge \neg BB)$$

These two facts yield

$$P \wedge t \leqslant K+1 \Rightarrow H_0(P \wedge \neg BB) \vee wp(IF, P \wedge \neg BB)$$
$$= H_{K+1}(P \wedge \neg BB)$$

which shows that (11.7) holds for $k = K+1$. By induction, (11.7) holds for all k.

6. $H'_0(R) = \neg BB \wedge R$. For $k > 0$, $H'_k(R) = wp(IF, H'_{k-1}(R))$. ($\boldsymbol{E}k$: $0 \leqslant k$: $H'_k(R)$) represents the set of states in which DO will terminate with R true in *exactly* k iterations. On the other hand, $wp(DO, R)$ represents the set of states in which DO will terminate with R true in k *or less* iterations.

10. (1) $wp(\text{"}i := 1\text{"}, P) = 0 < 1 \leqslant n \wedge (\boldsymbol{E}p: 1 = 2^p)$
$$= T \quad \text{(above, take } p = 0).$$

(2) $wp(S_1, P) = wp(\text{"}i := 2*i\text{"}, 0 < i \leqslant n \wedge (\boldsymbol{E}p: i = 2^p))$
$$= 0 < 2*i \leqslant n \wedge (\boldsymbol{E}p: 2*i = 2^p),$$

which is implied by $P \wedge 2*i \leqslant n$.

(3) $P \wedge \neg BB = 0 < i \leqslant n \wedge (\boldsymbol{E}p: i = 2^p) \wedge 2*i > n$,
which is equivalent to R.

(4) $P \wedge BB \Rightarrow 0 < i \leqslant n \wedge 2*i \leqslant n$
$$\Rightarrow n - i > 0, \text{ which is } t > 0.$$

(5) $wp(\text{"}t1 := t; S_1\text{"}, t < t1)$
$$= wp(\text{"}t1 := n-i; i := 2*i\text{"}, n-i < t1)$$
$$= wp(\text{"}t1 := n-i\text{"}, n-2*i < t1)$$
$$= n - 2*i < n - i$$
$$= -i < 0, \text{ which is implied by } P.$$

Answers for Chapter 12

1. We have the following equivalence transformations:
$$\{T(u)\} \, S \, \{R\} = (\boldsymbol{A}u: \{T(u)\} \, S \, \{R\})$$
$$= (\boldsymbol{A}u: T(u) \Rightarrow wp(S, R))$$
$$= (\boldsymbol{A}u: \neg T(u) \vee wp(S, R)) \quad \text{(Implication)}$$

$$= (A\,u:\; \neg\,T(u))\; \vee\; wp(S,R)$$
$$\text{(Since neither } S \text{ nor } R \text{ contains } u)$$
$$= \neg(E\,u:\; T(u))\; \vee\; wp(S,R)$$
$$= (E\,u:\; T(u)) \Rightarrow wp(S,R) \qquad \text{(Implication)}$$

(E1.1) $$= \{(E\,u:\; T(u))\}\; S\; \{\} \qquad \text{(Implication)}$$

The quantifier A in the precondition of (12.7) of theorem 12.6 is necessary; without it, predicate (12.7) has a different meaning. With the quantifier, the predicate can be interpreted as follows: The procedure call can
be executed in a state s to produce the desired result R if all *possible*
assignments $\bar{u}$, $\bar{v}$ to the result parameters and arguments establish the
truth of R. Without the quantifier, the above equivalence indicates that
an existential quantifier is implicitly present. With this implicit existential
quantifier, the predicate can be interpreted as follows: The procedure call
can be executed in a state s to produce the desired result R if there exists
at least one possible assignment of values $\bar{u}$, $\bar{v}$ that establishes the truth
of R. But, since there is no quarantee that this one possible set of values
$\bar{u}$, $\bar{v}$ will actually be assigned to the parameters and arguments, this statement is generally false.

Answers for Chapter 14

1. (b) $Q: x = X$. $R: (X \geq 0 \wedge x = X) \vee (X \leq 0 \wedge x = -X)$.
   if $x \geq 0 \rightarrow skip$ $[\!]$ $x \leq 0 \rightarrow x := -x$ **fi**.

2. Assume the next highest permutation exists (it doesn't for example, for
$d = 543221$). In the following discussion, it may help to keep the example

$$d = (1, 2, 3, 5, 4, 2)$$
$$d' = (1, 2, 4, 3, 2, 5)$$

in mind. There is a least integer i, $0 \leq i < n$, such that $d[0:i-1] =$
$d'[0:i-1]$ and $d[i] < d'[i]$. One can show that i is well-defined by the
fact that $d[i+1:n-1]$ is a non-increasing sequence and that $d[i] <$
$d[i+1]$.

In order for d' to be the next highest permutation, $d'[i]$ must contain
the smallest value of $d[i+1:n-1]$ that is greater than $d[i]$. Let the rightmost element of $d[i+1:n-1]$ with this value be $d[j]$. Consider $d'' =$
$(d; i:d[j]; j:d[i])$. d'' represents the array d but with the values at positions i and j interchanged. In the example above, $d'' = (1, 2, 4, 5, 3, 2)$.
Obviously, d'' is a higher permutation than d, but perhaps not the *next*
highest. Moreover, $d'[0:i] = d''[0:i]$.

It can be proved that $d''[i+1:n-1]$ is a non-increasing sequence.
Hence, reversing $d''[i+1:n-1]$ makes it an increasing sequence and, therefore, as small as possible. This yields the desired next highest permutation d.

To summarize, let i and j satisfy, respectively,

$0 \leqslant i < n-1 \wedge d[i] < d[i+1] \wedge d[i+1:n-1]$ is non-increasing
$i < j < n \wedge d[j] > d[i] \wedge d[j+1:n-1] \leqslant d[i]$

Introducing the notation $reverse(b, f, g)$ to denote the array b but with $b[f:g]$ reversed, we then have that the next highest permutation d' is

$$d' = reverse((d; i:b[j]; j:b[i]), i+1, n-1).$$

The algorithm is then: calculate i; calculate j; swap $b[i]$ and $b[j]$; reverse $b[i+1:n-1]$! Here, formalizing the idea of a next highest permutation leads directly to an algorithm to calculate it!

Answers for Section 15.1

3. $i, x := 1, b[0]$;
   do $i \neq n \to$ **if** $x \geqslant b[i] \to i, x := i+1, b[i]$
                           $[] x \leqslant b[i] \to i := i+1$
                    fi
   od

Answers for Section 15.2

2. The initialization is $x, y := X, Y$. Based on the properties given, the obvious commands to try are $x := x+y$, $x := x-y$, $x := y-x$, etc. Since $Y > 0$, the first one never reduces the bound function $t: x+y$, so it need not be used. The second one reduces it, but maintains the invariant only if $x > y$. Thus we have the guarded command $x > y \to x := x-y$. Symmetry encourages also the use of $y > x \to y := y-x$ and the final program is

      $x, y := X, Y$;
      do $x > y \to x := x-y$
      $[] y > x \to y := y-x$
      od
      $\{0 < x = y \wedge gcd(x, y) = gcd(X, Y)\}$
      $\{x = gcd(X, Y)\}$

5. $t := 0$;
   do $j \neq 80$ **cand** $b[j] \neq '\ ' \to t, s[t+1], j := t+1, b[j], j+1$
   $[] j = 80$ $\to read(b); j := 0$
   od

Answers for Section 16.2

2. Delete the conjunct $n < 2*i$ from R:

$$\{Q: 0 < n\}$$
$$i := 1;$$
$$\{inv: 0 < i \leqslant n \land (E p: 2^p = i)\}$$
$$\{bound: n-i \ (\text{actually, } \log(n-i) \text{ will do})\}$$
$$\textbf{do } 2*i \leqslant n \rightarrow i := 2*i \textbf{ od}$$
$$\{R: 0 \leqslant i \leqslant n < 2*i \land (E p: 2^p = i)\}$$

4. Delete the conjunct $x = b[i,j]$ from R:

$$i, j := 0, 0;$$
$$\{inv: 0 \leqslant i < m \land 0 \leqslant j < n \land x \notin b[0:i-1, 0:n-1] \land$$
$$\qquad x \notin b[i, 0:j-1] \land x \in b\}$$
$$\{bound: (m-i)*n-j\}$$
$$\textbf{do } x \neq b[i,j] \land j \neq n-1 \rightarrow j := j+1$$
$$\text{[]} \ x \neq b[i,j] \land j = n-1 \rightarrow i, j := i+1, 0$$
$$\textbf{od}$$

Answers for Section 16.3

4. (a) $i, j := 1, n;$
$$\{inv: 1 \leqslant i < j \leqslant n \land b[i] \leqslant x < b[j]\}$$
$$\{bound: \log(j-i)\}$$
$$\textbf{do } i+1 \neq j \rightarrow e := (i+j) \div 2;$$
$$\qquad\qquad\qquad \textbf{if } b[e] \leqslant x \rightarrow i := e \ \text{[]} \ b[e] > x \rightarrow j := e \textbf{ fi}$$
$$\textbf{od}$$

The obvious choice for the second part of the problem is to embed the program for the first part in an alternative command:

$$\textbf{if } x < b[1] \qquad\qquad \rightarrow i := 0$$
$$\text{[]} \ b[1] \leqslant x < b[n] \rightarrow \text{The program (a)}$$
$$\text{[]} \ b[n] \leqslant x \qquad\qquad \rightarrow i := n$$
$$\textbf{fi}$$

However, there is a simpler way. Assume the existence of $b[0]$, which contains the value $-\infty$, and $b[n+1]$, which contains the value $+\infty$. As long as the program never references these values, this assumption may be made. Then, with a slight change in initialization, the program for the first part used —it even works when the array is empty, setting j to 1 in that case.

$$i, j := 0, n+1;$$
$$\{inv:\ 0 \leqslant i < j \leqslant n+1 \wedge b[i] \leqslant x < b[j]\}$$
$$\{bound:\ \log(j-i)\}$$
do $i+1 \neq j \ \rightarrow\ e := (i+j) \div 2;$
                 $\{1 \leqslant e \leqslant n\}$
                 if $b[e] \leqslant x \ \rightarrow\ i := e$ [] $b[e] > x \ \rightarrow\ j := e$ **fi**
od

10. $i, p := 0, 0;$
    $\{inv:\ see\ exercise\ 10;\ \ bound:\ n-i\}$
    do $i \neq n \ \rightarrow\ Increase\ i,\ keeping\ invariant\ true:$
                 $j := i+1;$
                 $\{inv:\ b[i:j-1]\ are\ all\ equal;\ \ bound:\ n-j\}$
                 do $j \neq n$ **cand** $b[j] = b[i] \ \rightarrow\ j := j+1$ **od**;
                 $p := max(p, j-i);$
                 $i := j$
    od

Answers for Section 16.5

4. The only differences in this problem and exercise 3 are that the value used to separate the array into two sections is already in the array and that that value must be placed in $b[p]$. The invariant of the loop (except for the fact that $b[1] = B[1]$ and that b is a permutation of B) given in the procedure below is:

$$P:\ m < q \leqslant p+1 \leqslant n \wedge x = B[1] \wedge b$$

proc $Partition$(**value result** b: **array** $[*]$ **of** $integer$;
                     value m, n: $integer$; **result** k: $integer$);
    var x, q, p: $integer$;
    begin
       $x, q, p := b[m], m+1, n-1;$
       $\{inv:\ P;\ bound:\ p-q+1\}$
       do $q \leqslant p \ \rightarrow$ **if** $b[q] \leqslant x$ $\rightarrow q := q+1$
                  [] $b[p] > x$ $\rightarrow p := p-1$
                  [] $b[q] > x \geqslant b[p] \ \rightarrow\ b[q], b[p] := b[p], b[q];$
                                        $q, p := q+1, p-1$
                 fi
       od; $\{p = q-1 \wedge b[m+1:p] \leqslant b[m] \wedge$
               $b[p+1:n-1] > b[m] \wedge b[m] = B[m] = x\}$
       $b[m], b[p] := b[p], b[m]$
    end

6. The precondition states that the linked list is in order; the postcondition that it is reversed. This suggests an algorithm that at each step reverses one link: part of the list is reversed and part of it is in order. Thus, using another variable t to point to the part of the list that is in order, the invariant is

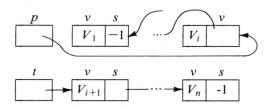

Initially, the reversed part of the list is empty and the unreversed part is the whole list. This leads to the algorithm

p, $t := -1$, p;
do $t \neq -1 \rightarrow p, t, s[t] := t, s[t], p$ **od**

8. The precondition and postconditions are

$Q: x \in b[0:m-1, 0:n-1]$
$R: 0 \leqslant i < m \ \wedge \ 0 \leqslant j < n \ \wedge \ x = b[i,j]$

Actually, Q and R are quite similar, in that both state that x is in a rectangular section of b —in R, the rectangular section just happens to have only one row and column. So perhaps an invariant can be used that indicates that x is in a rectangular section of b:

$$P: 0 \leqslant i \leqslant p < m \ \wedge \ 0 \leqslant q \leqslant j < n \ \wedge \ x \in b[i:p, q:j]$$

To make progress towards termination the rectangle must be made smaller, and there are four simple ways to do this: $i := i+1$, etc. Thus, we try a loop of the form

$i, p, q, j := 0, m-1, 0, n-1$;
do $? \rightarrow i := i+1$
$[] \ ? \rightarrow p := p-1$
$[] \ ? \rightarrow q := q+1$
$[] \ ? \rightarrow j := j-1$
od

What could serve as guards? Consider $i := i+1$. Its execution will maintain the invariant if x is not in row i of b. Since the row is ordered, this can be tested with $b[i, j] < x$, for if $b[i, j] > x$, so are all values in row i. In a similar fashion, we determine the other guards:

$i, p, q, j := 0, m-1, 0, n-1;$
do $b[i,j] < x \quad \rightarrow i := i+1$
$[] \; b[p,q] > x \quad \rightarrow p := p-1$
$[] \; b[p,q] < x \quad \rightarrow q := q+1$
$[] \; b[i,j] \; > x \quad \rightarrow j := j-1$
od

In order to prove that the result is true upon termination, only the first and last guards are needed. So the middle guarded commands can be deleted to yield the program

$i, j := 0, n-1;$
do $b[i,j] < x \quad \rightarrow i := i+1$
$[] \; b[i,j] > x \quad \rightarrow j := j-1$
od $\{x = b[i,j]\}$

This program requires at most $n+m$ comparisons. One cannot do much better than this, for the following reason. Assume the array is square: $m = n$. The off-diagonal elements $b[0:m-1]$, $b[1, m-2]$, ..., $b[m-1:0]$ form an unordered list. Given the additional information that x is on the off-diagonal, in the worst case a minimum of m comparisons is necessary.

Answers for Section 18.2

1. Algorithm (18.2.5) was developed under the general hope that each iteration of the loop would decrease the total number of elements S (say) in the partitions still to be sorted, and so S is a first approximation to the bound function. However, a partition described in set s may be empty, and choosing an empty partition and deleting it from s does not decrease S.

Consider the pair $(S, |s|)$, where $|s|$ is the number of elements in s. Execution of the body with the first alternative of the alternative command being executed decreases the tuple (lexicographically speaking) because it decreases $|s|$. Execution with the second alternative being executed also decreases it —even though $|s|$ is increased by 1, S is decreased by at least one. Hence, a bound function is $2*S + |s|$.

Answers for Section 18.3

3. Define

$$postorder(p) = \begin{cases} empty(p) \rightarrow () \\ \neg empty \quad \rightarrow (postorder(left[p]) \, | \\ \qquad postorder(right[p]) \, | \, (root(p)) \end{cases}$$

An iterative formulation of postorder traversal is slightly more complicated than the corresponding ones of preorder and inorder traversal. It must be remembered whether the right subtree of a tree in s has been visited. Since (pointers to) nodes of trees are represented by nonnegative integers, we make the distinction using the sign bit.

The postcondition of the program is

(E3.1) $R: c = \#p \land postorder(p) = b[0:c-1]$

Before stating the invariant, we indicate the postorder traversal of a signed integer q that represents a tree:

$$post(q) = \begin{cases} q < -1 \rightarrow root(abs(q)-2) \\ q = -1 \rightarrow () \\ q \geqslant 0 \rightarrow postorder(right[q]) \mid root(q) \end{cases}$$

Using a sequence variable s, the invariant is:

(E3.2) $P: 0 \leqslant c \land q \geqslant -1 \land$
$\qquad postorder(p) = b[0:c-1] \mid postorder(q) \mid$
$\qquad\qquad post(s[0]) \mid \cdots \mid post(s[\mid s \mid -1])$

The program is then

$$\begin{aligned}
& c, q, s := 0, p, (); \\
& \{invariant: (\text{E3.2})\} \\
& \textbf{do } q \neq -1 \qquad\qquad \rightarrow q, s := left[q], (q) \mid s \\
& [] \; q = -1 \land s \neq () \rightarrow q, s := s[0], s[1..] \\
& \qquad\qquad\qquad\qquad \textbf{if } q < -1 \rightarrow q, c, b[c] := 0, c+1, root[-q-2] \\
& \qquad\qquad\qquad\qquad [] \; q = -1 \rightarrow skip \\
& \qquad\qquad\qquad\qquad [] \; q > -1 \rightarrow q, s := right[q], (-q-2) \mid s \\
& \qquad\qquad\qquad\qquad \textbf{fi} \\
& \textbf{od } \{R\}
\end{aligned}$$

Answers for Section 19.2

1. PI is easily established using $i, x := 0, 0$. If $(xv[i], yv[i])$ is a solution to (19.2.1), then

$$r = xv[i]^2 + yv[i]^2 \leqslant 2*xv[i]^2$$

Hence, all solutions $(xv[i], yv[i])$ to the problem satisfy $r \leqslant 2*xv[i]^2$. Using the Linear Search Principle, we write an initial loop to determine the smallest x satisfying $r \leqslant 2*x^2$, and the first approximation to the program is

$i, x := 0, 0;$ **do** $r > 2*x^2 \rightarrow x := x+1$ **od**;
$\{inv: P1 \wedge r \leqslant 2*x^2\}$
do $x^2 \leqslant r \rightarrow$ Increase x, keeping invariant true **od**

In order to increase x and keep $P1$ true, it is necessary to determine if a suitable y exists for x and to insert the pair (x, y) in the arrays if it does. To do this requires first finding the value y satisfying

(E1.1) $\quad x^2 + y^2 \leqslant r \;\wedge\; x^2 + (y+1)^2 > r$

Taking the second conjunct,

$P2: x^2 + (y+1)^2 > r$

as the invariant of an inner loop, rewrite the program as

$i, x := 0, 0;$ **do** $r > 2*x^2 \rightarrow x := x+1$ **od**;
$\{inv: P1 \wedge r \leqslant 2*x^2\}$
do $x^2 \leqslant r \rightarrow$
    Increase x, keeping invariant true:
        Determine y to satisfy (E1.1):
            $y := x;$
            $\{inv: P2\}$
            do $x^2 + y^2 > r \rightarrow y := y-1$ **od**;
        if $x^2 + y^2 = r \rightarrow xv[v], yv[v], i, x := x, y, i+1, x+1$
        [] $x^2 + y^2 < r \rightarrow x := x+1$
        fi
od

Now note that execution of the body of the main loop does not destroy $P2$, and therefore $P2$ can be taken out of the loop. Rearrangement then leads to the more efficient program

$i, x := 0, 0;$
do $r > 2*x^2 \rightarrow x := x+1$ **od**;
$y := x;$
$\{inv: P1 \wedge P2\}$
do $x^2 \leqslant r \rightarrow$
    Increase x, keeping invariant true:
        Determine y to satisfy (E1.1):
            do $x^2 + y^2 > r \rightarrow y := y-1$ **od**;
        if $x^2 + y^2 = r \rightarrow xv[v], yv[v], i, x := x, y, i+1, x+1$
        [] $x^2 + y^2 < r \rightarrow x := x+1$
        fi
od

Answers for Section 19.3

2. Program 19.3.2, which determines an approximation to the square root of a nonnegative integer n, is

$$\{n \geqslant 0\}$$
$$a, c := 0, 1; \; \textbf{do } c^2 \leqslant n \; \rightarrow \; c := 2*c \; \textbf{od};$$
$$\{inv: \; a^2 \leqslant n < (a+c)^2 \wedge (\boldsymbol{E}p: 1 \leqslant p: c = 2^p)\}$$
$$\{bound: \; \sqrt{n} - a\}$$
$$\textbf{do } c \neq 1 \; \rightarrow \; c := c/2;$$
$$\qquad\qquad \textbf{if } (a+c)^2 \leqslant n \; \rightarrow \; a := a+c$$
$$\qquad\qquad [\!] \; (a+c)^2 > n \; \rightarrow \; skip$$
$$\qquad\qquad \textbf{fi}$$
$$\textbf{od}$$
$$\{a^2 \leqslant n < (a+1)^2\}$$

We attempt to illustrate how a change of representation to eliminate squaring operations could be discovered.

Variables a and c are to be represented by other variables and eliminated, so that no squaring is necessary. As a first step, note that the squaring operation c^2 must be performed in some other fashion. Perhaps a fresh variable p can be used, which will always satisfy the relation

$$p = c^2$$

Now, which operations involving c can be replaced easily by operations involving p instead?

Command $c := 1$ can be replaced by $p := 1$, expression c^2 by p, $c := 2*c$ by $p := 4*p$, $c \neq 1$ by $p \neq 1$ and $c := c/2$ by $p := p/4$.

The remaining operations to rewrite are $a := 0$ (if necessary), $a := a+c$, $(a+c)^2 \leqslant n$ and $(a+c)^2 > n$. Consider the latter two expressions, which involve squaring. Performing the expansion $(a+c)^2 = (a^2+2*a*c+c^2)$ isolates another instance of c^2 to be replaced by p, so we rewrite the first of these as

(E3.1) $a^2 + 2*a*c + p - n \leqslant 0$

Expression (E3.1) must be rewritten, using new variables, in such a way that the command $a := a+c$ can also be rewritten. What are possible new variables and their meaning?

There are a number of possibilities, for example $q = a^2$, $q = a*c$, $q = a^2 - n$, and so forth. The definition

(E3.2) $q = a*c$

is promising, because it lets us replace almost all the operations involving a. Thus, before the main loop, q will be 0 since a is 0 there. Secondly, to maintain (E3.2) across $c := c \,/\, 2$ we can insert $q := q \,/\, 2$. Thirdly, (E3.2) maintained across execution of the command $a := a + c$ by assigning a new value to q —what is the value?

To determine the value x to assign to q, calculate

$$wp(\text{``}a, q := a + c, x\text{''}, q = a*c) \;=\; x = (a + c)*c$$

The desired assignment is therefore

$$q := (a + c)*c, \qquad \text{which is equivalent to}$$
$$q := a*c + c^2, \qquad \text{which is equivalent to}$$
$$q := q + p$$

With this representation, (E3.1) becomes

(E3.3) $a^2 + 2*q + p - n \leqslant 0$

Now try a third variable r to contain the value $n - a^2$, which will always be $\geqslant 0$. (E3.3) becomes

$$2*q + p - r \leqslant 0$$

And, indeed, the definition of r can also be maintained easily.

To summarize, use three variables p, q and r, which satisfy

$$p = c^2, \quad q = a*c, \quad r = n - a^2$$

and rewrite the program as

$\{n \geqslant 0\}$
$p, q, r := 1, 0, n;$ **do** $p \leqslant n \rightarrow p := 4*p$ **od**;
do $p \neq 1 \rightarrow p := p/4;\ q := q/2;$
$\qquad\qquad$ **if** $2*q + p \leqslant r \rightarrow q, r := q+p,\ ;\ r-2*q-p$
$\qquad\qquad$ [] $2*q + p > r \rightarrow skip$
$\qquad\qquad$ **fi**
od
$\{q^2 \leqslant n < (q+1)^2\}$

Upon termination we have $p = 1$, $c = 1$, and $q = a*c = a$, so that the desired result is in q. Not only have we eliminated squaring, but all multiplications and divisions are by 2 and 4; hence, they could be implemented with shifting on a binary machine. Thus, the approximation to the square root can be performed using only adding, subtracting and shifting.

Answers for Chapter 20

1. Call a sequence (of zeroes and ones) that begins with 0000 (4 zeroes) and satisfies property 2 a *good* sequence. Call a sequence with k bits a k-sequence.

Define an ordering among good sequences as follows. Sequence $s1$ is less than sequence $s2$, written $s1.<.s2$, if, when viewed as decimal numbers with the decimal point to the extreme left, $s1$ is less than $s2$. For example, $101.<.1011$ because $.101 < .1011$. In a similar manner, we write $101.=.101000$, because $.101 = .101000$. Appending a zero to a sequence yields an equal sequence; appending a one yields a larger sequence.

Any *good* sequence s to be printed satisfies $0.<.s.<.00001$, and must begin with 00000.

The program below iteratively generates, in order, all *good* sequences satisfying $0.\leqslant.s.\leqslant.00001$, printing the 36-bit ones as they are generated. The sequence currently under consideration will be called s. There will be no variable s; it is just a name for the sequence currently under consideration. s always contains at least 5 bits. Further, to eliminate problems with equal sequences, we will always be sure that s is the longest *good* sequence equal to itself.

$\qquad$ $P1$: $good(s) \wedge \neg good(s \mid 0) \wedge 5 \leqslant |s| \wedge 0.\leqslant.s.\leqslant.00001 \wedge$
$\qquad\qquad$ All *good* sequences $.<.s$ are printed

Sequence s with n bits could be represented by a bit array. However, it is better to represent s by an integer array $c[4:n-1]$, where $c[i]$ is the decimal representation of the 5-bit subsequence of s ending in bit i. Thus, we will maintain as part of the invariant of the main loop the assertion

$P2$: $5 \leqslant n = |s| \leqslant 36 \; \wedge$
$\qquad c[i] = s[i-4]*2^4 + s[i-3]*2^3 + s[i-2]*2^2 + s[i-1]*2 + s[i]$
$\qquad$ (for $4 \leqslant i < n$)

Further, in order to keep track of which 5-bit subsequences s contains, we use a Boolean array $in[0:31]$:

$P3$: $(Ai: 0 \leqslant i < 32: in[i] = (i \in c[4:n-1]))$

With this introduction, the program should be easy to follow.

```
n, c[4],in[0]:= 5, 0, T;
in[1:31]:= F;     {s =(0,0,0,0,0)}
{inv: P1 ∧ P2 ∧ P3 ∧ ¬good(s | 0)}
do c[4] ≠ 1 →
   if n =36 → Print sequence s
   [] n ≠ 36 → skip
   fi;
   Change s to next higher good sequence:
      do in[(c[n-1]*2+1) mod 32]  {(i.e. ¬good(s | 1)}
         → Delete ending 1's from s:
               do odd(c[n-1]) → n:= n-1; in[c[n]]:= F od;
            Delete ending 0:
               n:= n-1; in[c[n]]:= F
      od;
      Append 1 to s:
         c[n]:= (c[n-1]*2+1) mod 32; in[c[n]]:= T; n:= n+1
od
```

7. The result assertion is

R: $c = (Ni: 0 \leqslant i < F: f[i] \notin g[0:G-1]) +$
$\qquad (Nj: 0 \leqslant j < G: g[j] \notin f[0:F-1])$

We would expect to write a program that sequences up the two arrays together, in some synchronized fashion, performing a count as it goes. Thus, it makes sense to develop an invariant by replacing the two constants F and G of R as follows:

$0 \leqslant h \leqslant F \wedge 0 \leqslant k \leqslant G \; \wedge$
$c = (Ni: 0 \leqslant i < h: f[i] \notin g[0:G-1]) +$
$\qquad (Nj: 0 \leqslant j < k: g[j] \notin f[0:F-1])$

Now, consider execution of $h := h+1$. Under what conditions does its execution leave P true? The guard for this command must obviously imply $f[h] \notin g[0:G-1]$, but we want the guard to be simple. As it stands, this seems out of the question.

Perhaps strengthening the invariant will allow us to find a simple job. One thing we haven't tried to exploit is moving through the arrays in a synchronized fashion —the invariant does not imply this at all. Suppose we add to the invariant the conditions $f[h-1] < g[k]$ and $g[k-1] < g[h]$ —this might provide the synchronized search that we desire. That is, we use the invariant

$$P: 0 \leqslant h \leqslant F \wedge 0 \leqslant k \leqslant G \wedge f[h-1] < g[k] \wedge g[k-1] < f[h]$$
$$c = (N i: 0 \leqslant i < h: f[i] \notin g[0:G-1]) +$$
$$(N j: 0 \leqslant j < k: g[j] \notin f[0:F-1])$$

Then the additional condition $f[h] < g[k]$ yields

$$g[k-1] < f[h] < g[k]$$

so that $f[h]$ does not appear in G, and increasing h will maintain the invariant. Similarly the guard for $k := k+1$ will be $g[k] < f[h]$.

This gives us our program, written below. We assume the existence of virtual values $f[-1] = g[i-1] = -\infty$ and $f[F] = g[G] = +\infty$; this allows us to dispense with worries about boundary conditions in the invariant.

```
h, k, c := 0, 0, 0;
{inv: P; bound: F−p + G−q}
do f ≠ F ∧ g ≠ G →
      if f[h] < g[k] → h, c := h+1, c+1
      [] f[h] = g[k] → h, k := h+1, k+1
      [] f[h] > g[k] → k, c := k+1, c+1
      fi
od;
Add to c the number of unprocessed elements of f and g:
      c := c + F−h + G−k
```

References

[1] Allen, L.E. *WFF'N PROOF: The Game of Modern Logic*. Autotelic Instructional material Publishers, New Haven, 1972.

[2] Bauer, F.L. and K. Samelson (eds.). *Language Hierarchies and Interfaces*. Springer Verlag Lecture Notes in Computer Science 46, 1976.

[3] Bauer, F.L. and M. Broy (eds.). Software Engineering: an Advanced Course. Springer Verlag Lecture Notes in Computer Science 30, 1975.

[4] ___ and ___ (eds.). *Program Construction*. Springer Verlag Lecture Notes in Computer Science 69, 1979.

[5] Burstall, R. Proving programs as hand simulation with a little induction. *Information Processing 74* (Proceedings of IFIP 74), North-Holland, Amsterdam, 1974, 308-312.

[6] Buxton, J.N., P. Naur, and B. Randell. *Software Engineering*, Petrocelli, 1975. (Report on two NATO Conferences held in Garmisch, Germany (Oct 68) and Rome, Italy (Oct 69)).

[7] Constable, R.L. and M. O'Donnell. *A Programing Logic*. Winthrop Publishers, Cambridge, 1978.

[8] Cook, S.A. Axiomatic and interpretative semantics for an Algol fragment. Computer Science Department, University of Toronto, TR 79, 1975.

[9] Conway, R., and D. Gries. *An Introduction to Programming*. Winthrop Publishers, Cambridge, Mass., 1973 (third edition, 1979).

[10] De Millo, R.A., R.J. Lipton and A.J. Perlis. Social processes and proofs of theorems and programs. *Comm. of the ACM* 22 (May 1979), 271-280.

[11] Dijkstra, E.W. Some meditations on advanced programming. *IFIP 1962*, 535-538.

[12] ___. Go to statement considered harmful. *Comm. ACM* 11 (March

1968), 147-148.

[13] ___. A short introduction to the art of programming. EWD316, Technological University Eindhoven, August 1971.

[14] ___. *Notes on Structured Programming*. In Dahl, O.-J., C.A.R. Hoare and E.W. Dijkstra, *Structured Programming*, Academic Press, New York 1972. (Also appeared a few years earlier in the form of a technical report).

[15] ___. Guarded commands, nondeterminacy and the formal derivation of programs. *Comm. of the ACM* 18 (August 1975), 453-457.

[16] ___. *A Discipline of Programming*. Prentice Hall, Englewood Cliffs, 1976.

[17] ___. *Program inversion*. EWD671, Technological University Eindhoven, 1978.

[18] Feijen, W.H.J. A set of programming exercises. WF25, Technological University Eindhoven, July 1979.

[19] Floyd, R. Assigning meaning to programs. In *Mathematical Aspects of Computer Science*, XIX American Mathematical Society (1967), 19-32.

[20] Gentzen, G. Untersuchungen ueber das logische Schliessen. *Math. Zeitschrift* 39 (1935), 176-210, 405-431.

[21] Gries, D. An illustration of current ideas on the derivation of correctness proofs and correct programs. IEEE Trans. Software Eng. 2 (December 1976), 238-244.

[22] ___ (ed.). *Programming Methodology, a Collection of Articles by Members of WG2.3*. Springer Verlag, New York, 1978.

[23] ___ and G. Levin. Assignment and procedure call proof rules. *TOPLAS* 2 (October 1980), 564-579.

[24] ___ and Mills, H. Swapping sections. TR 81-452, Computer Science Dept., Cornell University, January 1981.

[25] Guttag, J.V. and J.J. Horning. The algebraic specification of data types. *Acta Informatica* 10 (1978), 27-52.

[26] Hoare, C.A.R. Quicksort. *Computer Journal* 5 (1962), 10-15.

[27] ___. An axiomatic basis for computer programming. *Comm ACM* 12 (October 1969), 576-580, 583.

[28] ___. Procedures and parameters: an axiomatic approach. In *Symposium on Semantics of Programming Languages*. Springer Verlag, New York, 1971, 102-116.

[29] ___. Proof of correctness of data representations. *Acta Informatica* 1 (1972), 271-281.

[30] ___ and N. Wirth. An axiomatic definition of the programming language Pascal. *Acta Informatica* 2 (1973), 335-355.

[31] Hunt, J.W. and M.D. McIlroy. An algorithm for differential file comparison. Computer Science Technical Report 41, Bell Labs, Murray Hill, New Jersey, June 1976.

[32] Igarashi, S., R.L. London and D.C. Luckham. Automatic program verification: a logical basis and its implementation. *Acta Informatica* 4 (1975), 145-182.

[33] Liskov, B. and S. Zilles. Programming with abstract data types. *Proc. ACM SIGPLAN Conf. on Very High Level Languages*, SIGPLAN Notices 9 (April 1974), 50-60.

[34] London, R.L., J.V. Guttag, J.J. Horning, B.W. Mitchell and G.J. Popek. Proof rules for the programming language Euclid. *Acta Informatica* 10 (1978), 1-79.

[35] McCarthy, J. A basis for a mathematical theory of computation. *Proc. Western Joint Comp. Conf.*, Los Angeles, May 1961, 225-238, and *Proc. IFIP Congress 1962*, North Holland Publ. Co., Amsterdam, 1963.

[36] Melville R. *Asymptotic Complexity of Iterative Computations.* Ph.D. thesis, Computer Science Department, Cornell University, January 1981.

[37] ___ and D. Gries. Controlled density sorting. *IPL* 10 (July 1980), 169-172.

[38] Misra, J. A technique of algorithm construction on sequences. *IEEE Trans. Software Eng.* 4 (January 1978), 65-69.

[39] Naur, P. et al. Report on ALGOL 60. *Comm. of the ACM* 3 (May 1960), 299-314.

[40] Naur, P. Proofs of algorithms by general snapshots. *BIT 6* (1969), 310-316.

[41] Quine, W.V.O. *Methods of Logic.* Holt, Reinhart and Winston, New York, 1961.

[42] Steel, T.B. (ed.). *Formal Language Description Languages for Computer Programming.* Proc. IFIP Working Conference on Formal Language Description Languages, Vienna 1964, North-Holland, Amsterdam, 1971.

[43] Szabo, M.E. *The Collected Works of Gerhard Gentzen.* North Holland, Amsterdam, 1969.

[44] Wirth, N. Program development by stepwise refinement. *Comm ACM 14* (April 1971), 221-227.

Index